X/1999

VOL. 12

MOVEMENT

Shōjo Edition

STORY & ART BY CLAMP

ENGLISH ADAPTATION BY FRED BURKE

Translation/Lillian Olsen
Touch-Up Art & Lettering/Stephen Dutro
Cover Design/Yuki Ameda
Graphic Design/Carolina Ugalde
Supervising Editor/Julie Davis
Editor/P. Duffield

Managing Editor/Annette Roman
Editorial Director/Alvin Lu
Director of Production/Noboru Watanabe
Sr. Director of Licensing & Acquisitions/Rika Inouye
VP of Sales & Marketing/Liza Coppola
Executive Vice President/Hyoe Narita
Publisher/Seiji Horibuchi

X/1999 is rated "T+" for Older Teens. It may contain violence, language,
alcohol or tobacco use, or suggestive situations.

Printed in Canada

Published by VIZ, LLC
P.O. Box 77010 • San Francisco, CA 94107

Shōjo Edition
10 9 8 7 6 5 4 3 2
First printing, November 2003
Second printing, October 2004

www.viz.com   www.animerica-mag.com

X/1999™

Vol. 12
MOVEMENT

Shōjo Edition

Story and Art by
CLAMP

X/1999
THE STORY THUS FAR

The End of the World has been prophesied
…and time is running out. Kamui Shiro is a
young man who was born with a special
power—the power to decide the fate of the
Earth itself.

Kamui had grown up in Tokyo, but had
fled with his mother after the suspicious death
of a family friend. Six years later, his mother
too, dies under suspicious circumstances,
engulfed in flames. Her last words to him are
that he should return to Tokyo…that his destiny
awaits.

Kamui obeys his mother's words, but
almost immediately upon his arrival, he's chal-
lenged to a psychic duel—a first warning that
others know of his power, and of his return.

Kamui is also reunited with his childhood
friends, Fuma and Kotori Monou. Although
Kamui attempts to push his friends away, hop-
ing to protect them, they too are soon drawn
into the web of destiny that surrounds him.

Meanwhile, the two sides to the great con-
flict to come are being drawn. On one side is
the dreamseer Hinoto, a blind princess who
lives beneath Japan's seat of government, the
Diet Building. On the other side is Kanoe,
Hinoto's dark sister with similar powers, but a
different vision of Earth's ultimate future.
Around these two women gather the Dragons of
Heaven and the Dragons of Earth, the forces
that will fight to decide the fate of the planet.
The only variable in the equation is Kamui,
whose fate it will be to choose which side he
will join.

And Kamui finally does make a choice. He
chooses to defend the Earth as it stands now.
But by making this choice, he pays a terrible
price. For fate has chosen his oldest friend to be
his "twin star"—the other "Kamui" who will
fight against him. And in this first battle, the
gentle Kotori is the first casualty.

Now Kamui must face the consequences of
his decision…and try to come to terms with not
only his ultimate fate, but that of the Earth….

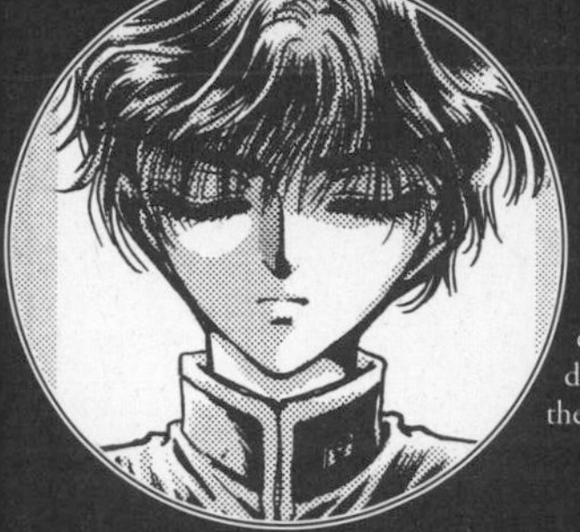

Kamui Shiro
A young man with psychic powers whose choice of destiny will decide the fate of the world.

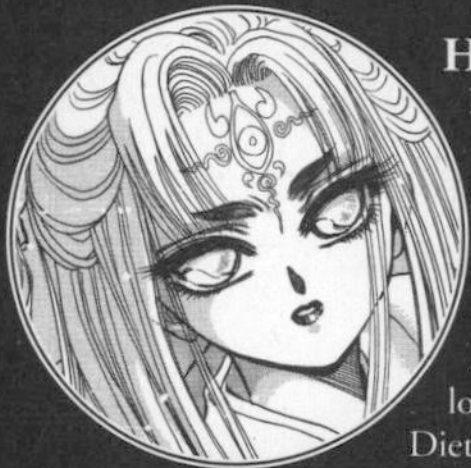

Hinoto
Blind, unable to speak or walk, Hinoto is a powerful prophetess, far older than she looks, who communicates with the power of her mind alone. She lives in a secret shrine located beneath Tokyo's Diet Building.

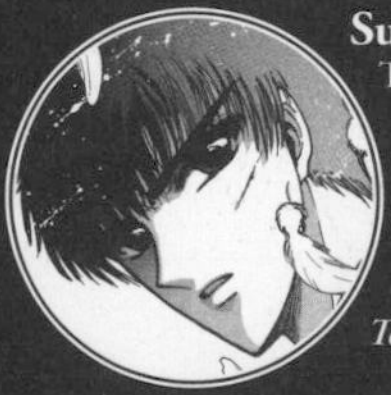

Subaru Sumeragi
The 13th family head of a long line of spiritualists and a powerful medium and exorcist. He is the lead character of another CLAMP manga series, ***Tokyo Babylon***.

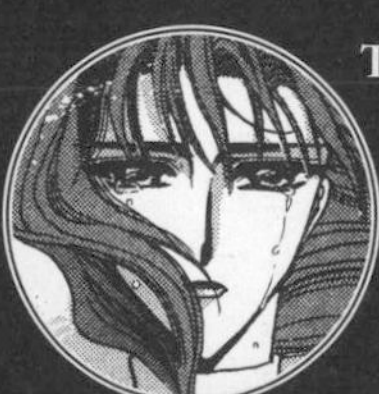

Toru
Kamui's mother was heir to the Magami clan, an ancient family of "Shadow Sacrifices," people who absorb the misfortunes of others.

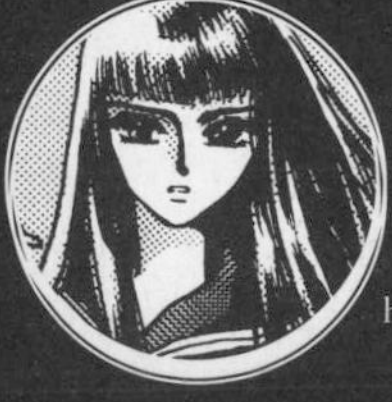

Arashi Kishu
Priestess of the Ise Shrine, Arashi can materialize a sword from the palm of her hand.

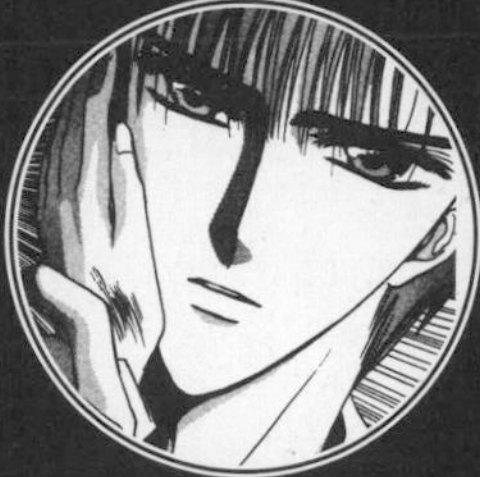

Fuma Monou
Kamui's childhood friend. When Kamui made his choice, Fuma was chosen by fate to become his "Twin Star" — the other "Kamui."

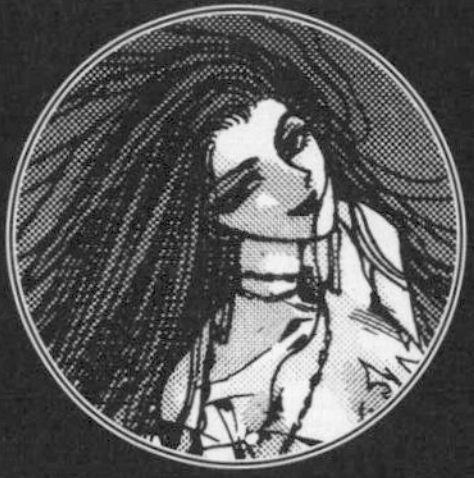

Kanoe
Hinoto's sister shares her ability to see the future… but Kanoe has predicted a different final result.

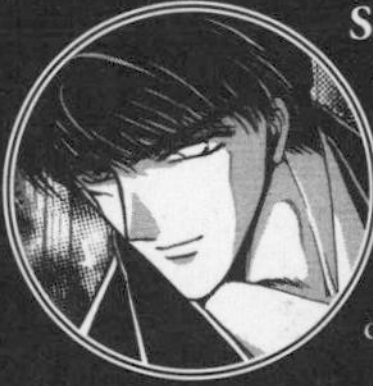

Seishiro Sakurazuka
Also called *Sakurazukamori*, the mysterious Seishiro is a crossover character from ***Tokyo Babylon***. He lost his sight in one eye during that series. He shares a deep rivalry with Subaru.

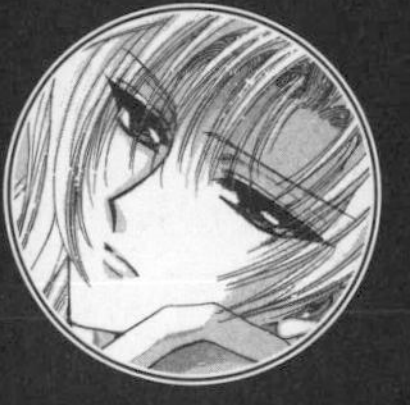

Kakyo Kuzuki
A dreamseer like Hinoto, Kakyo is a hospital-bound invalid kept alive by machines.

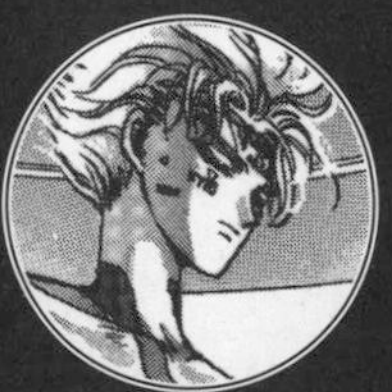

Nataku
A genetically engineered human, Nataku wields a ribbonlike piece of cloth.

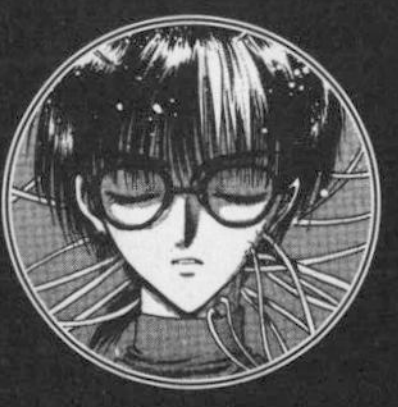

Satsuki Yatoji
A computer expert, Satsuki can interface directly with her personal machine, "The Beast."

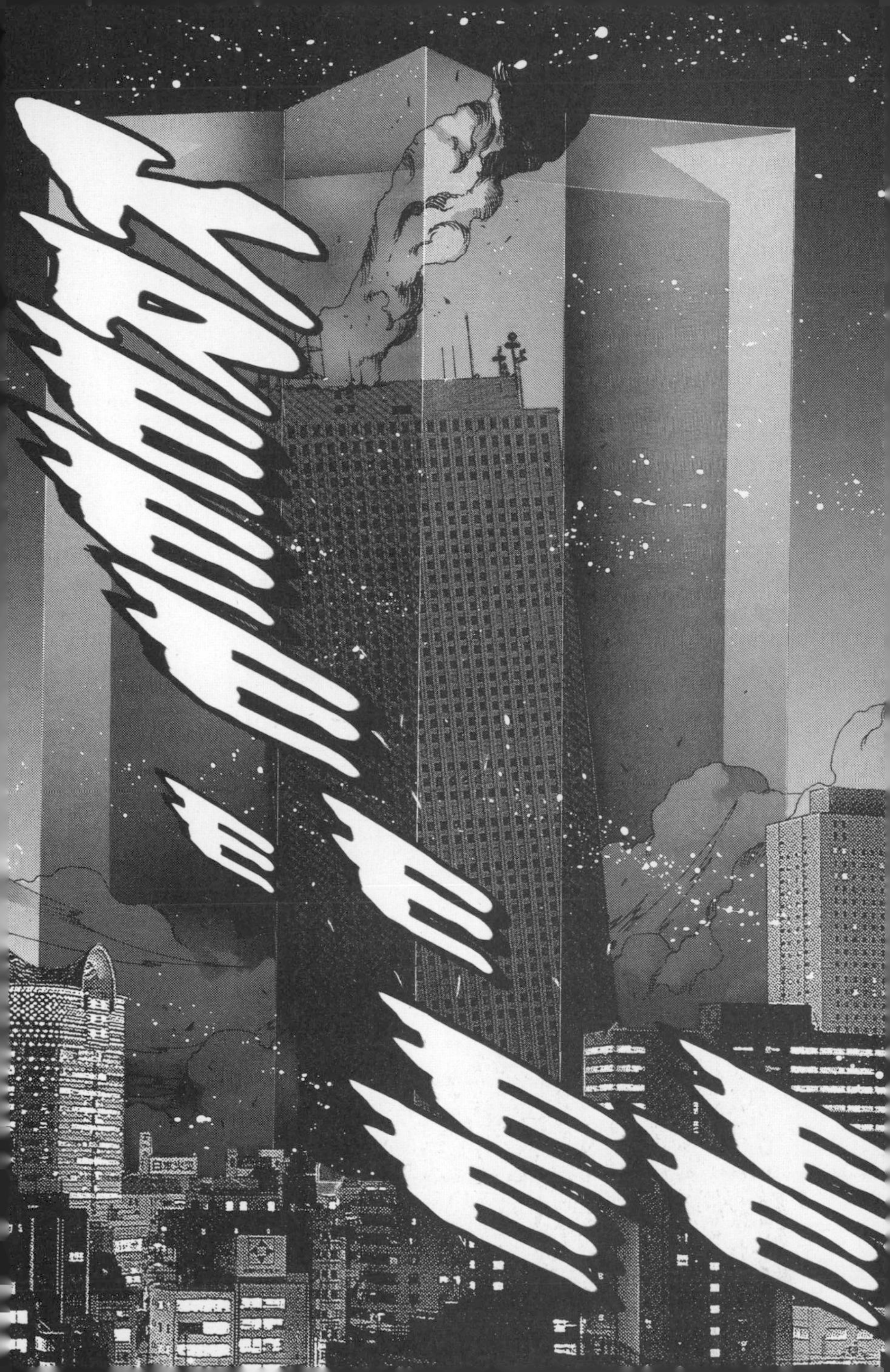

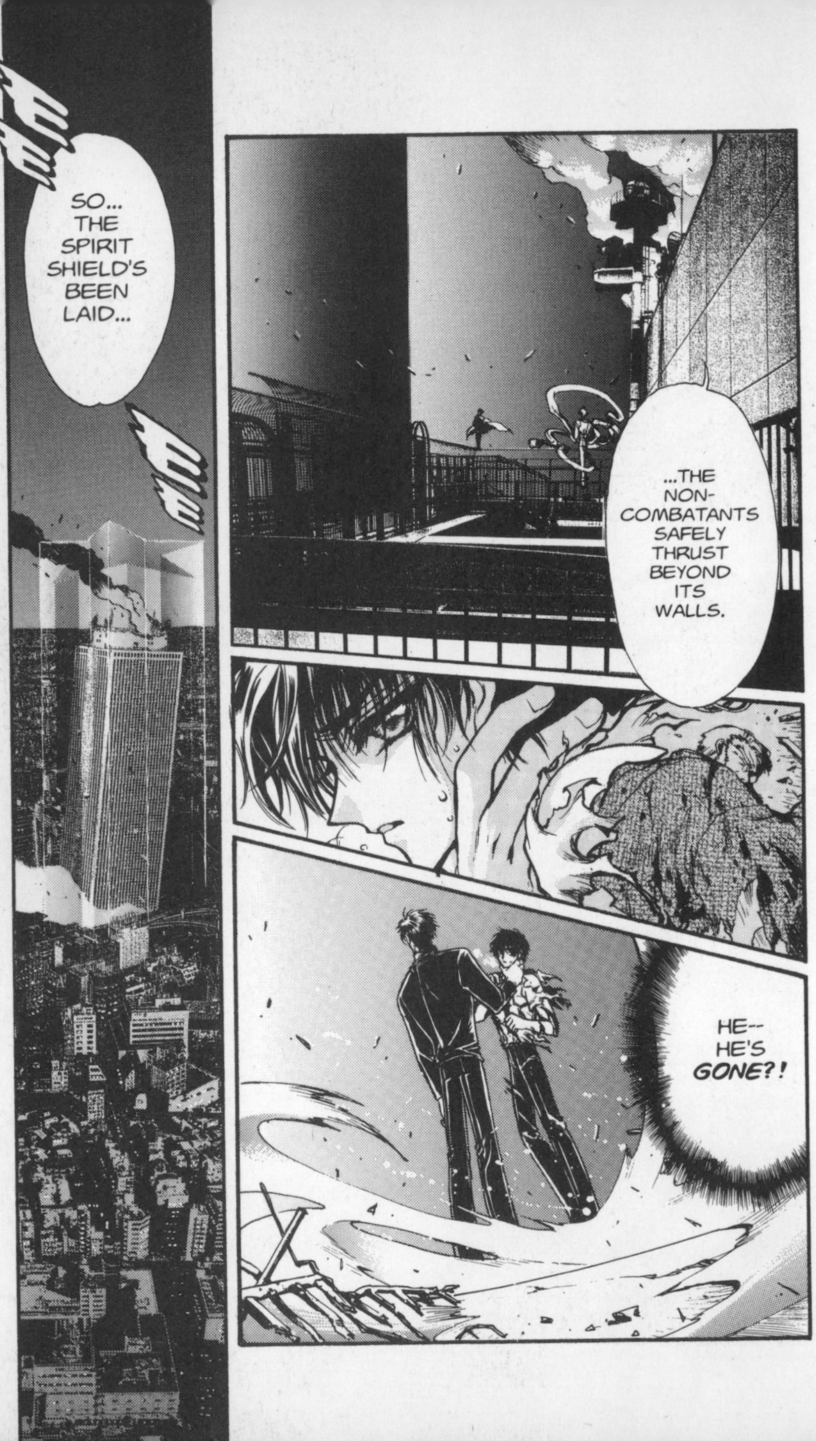
SO... THE SPIRIT SHIELD'S BEEN LAID...
...THE NON-COMBATANTS SAFELY THRUST BEYOND ITS WALLS.
HE-- HE'S *GONE?!*

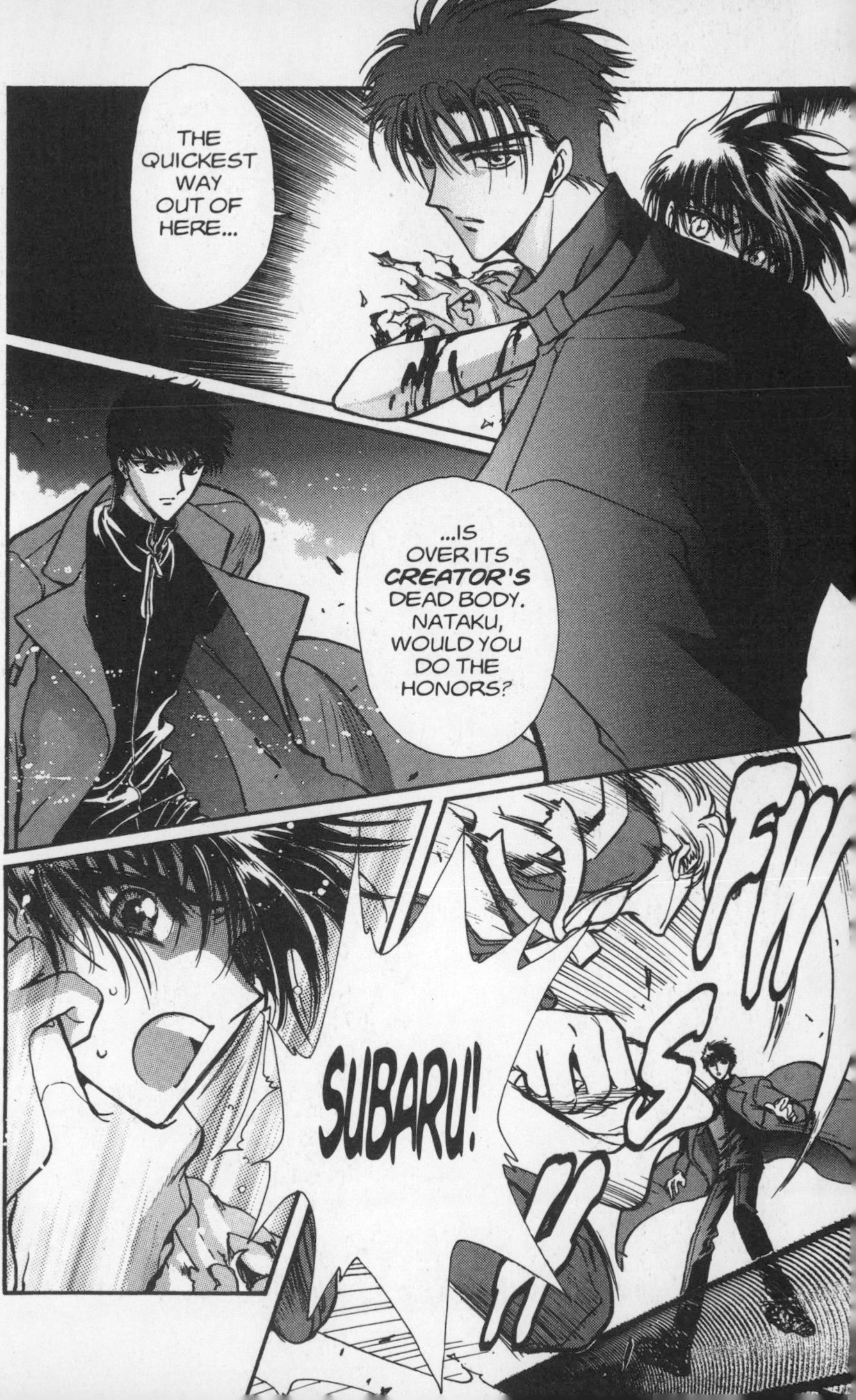
THE QUICKEST WAY OUT OF HERE...
...IS OVER ITS CREATOR'S DEAD BODY. NATAKU, WOULD YOU DO THE HONORS?
FW
SUBARU!

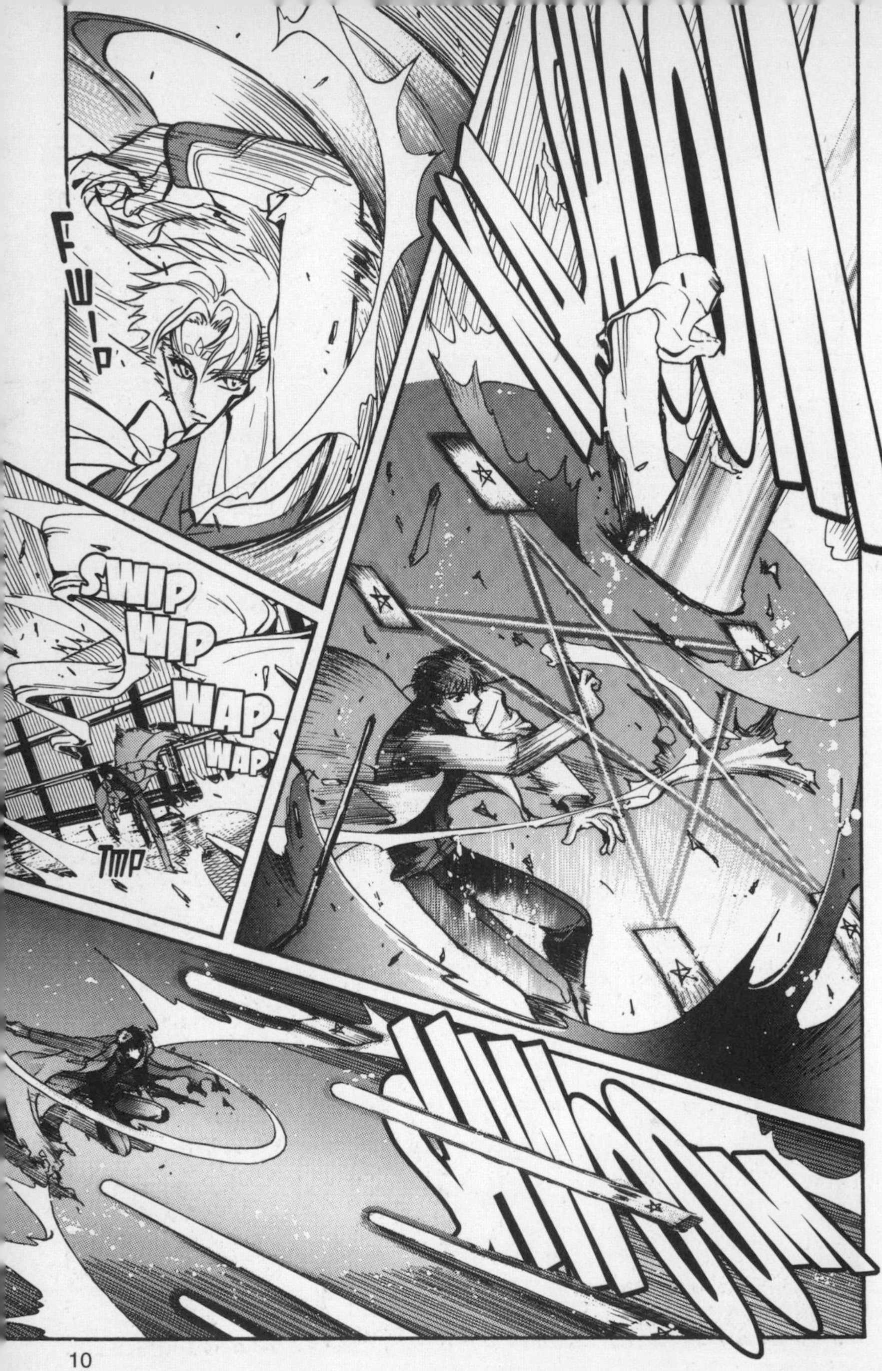
FWIP
SWIP
WIP
WAP
WAP
TMP

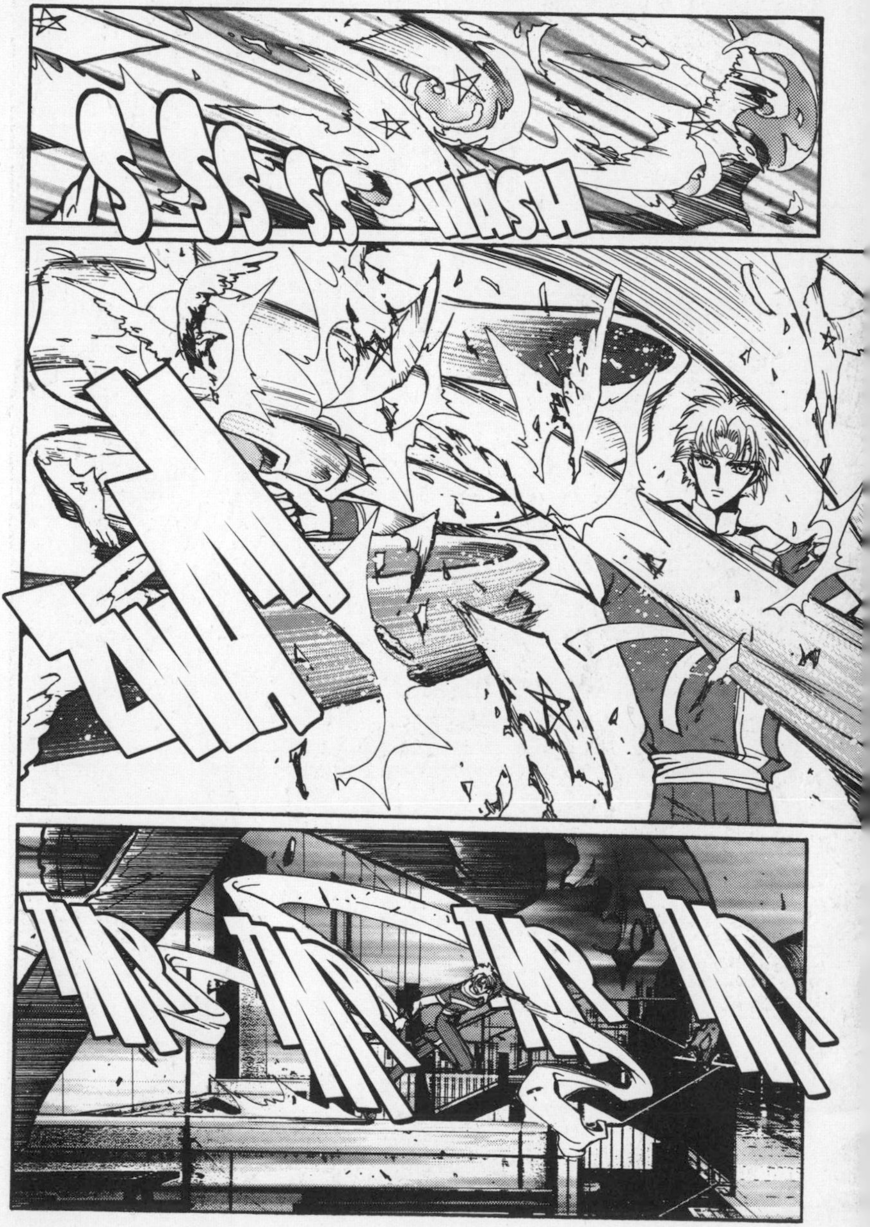
SSSSSS WASH

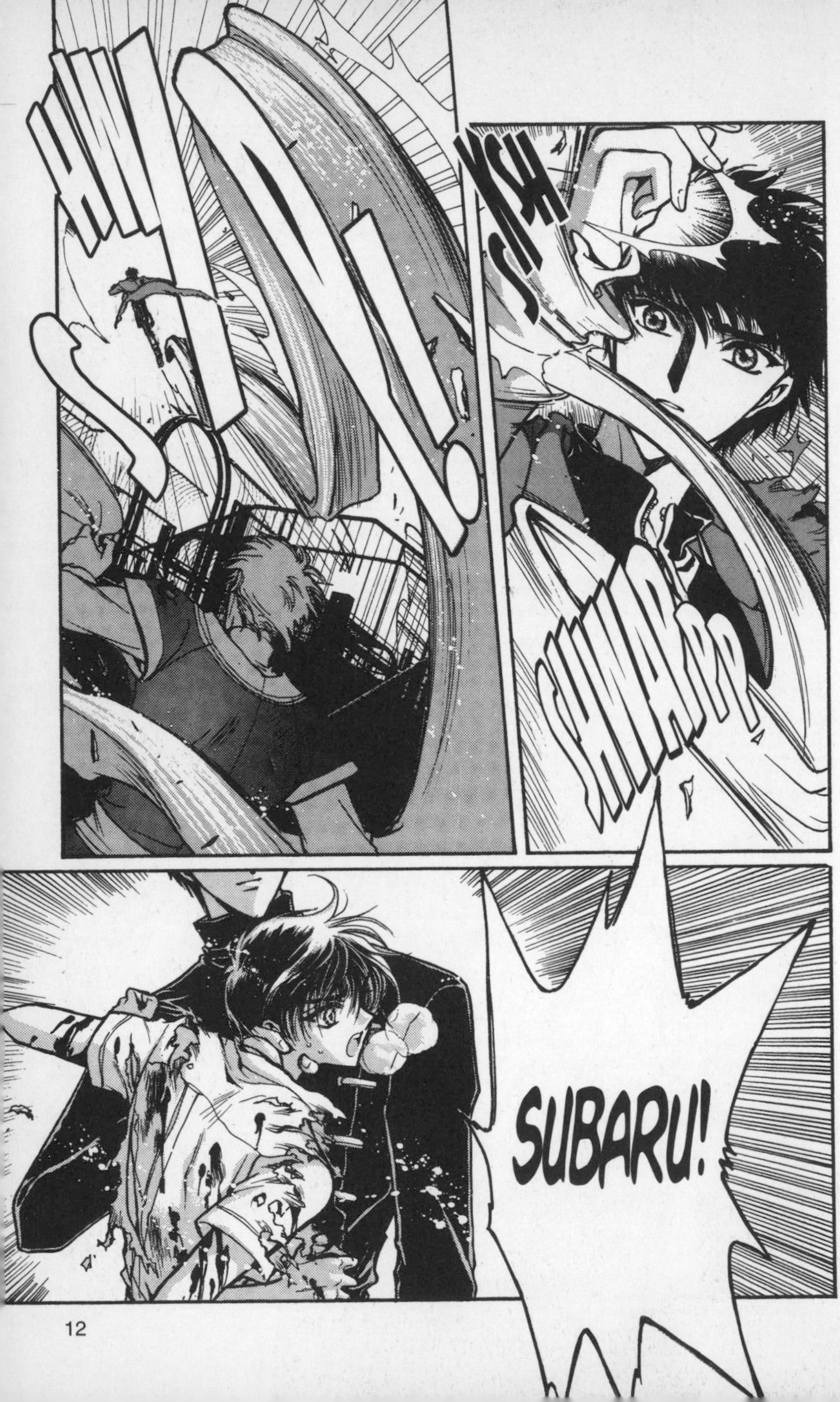
SUBARU!

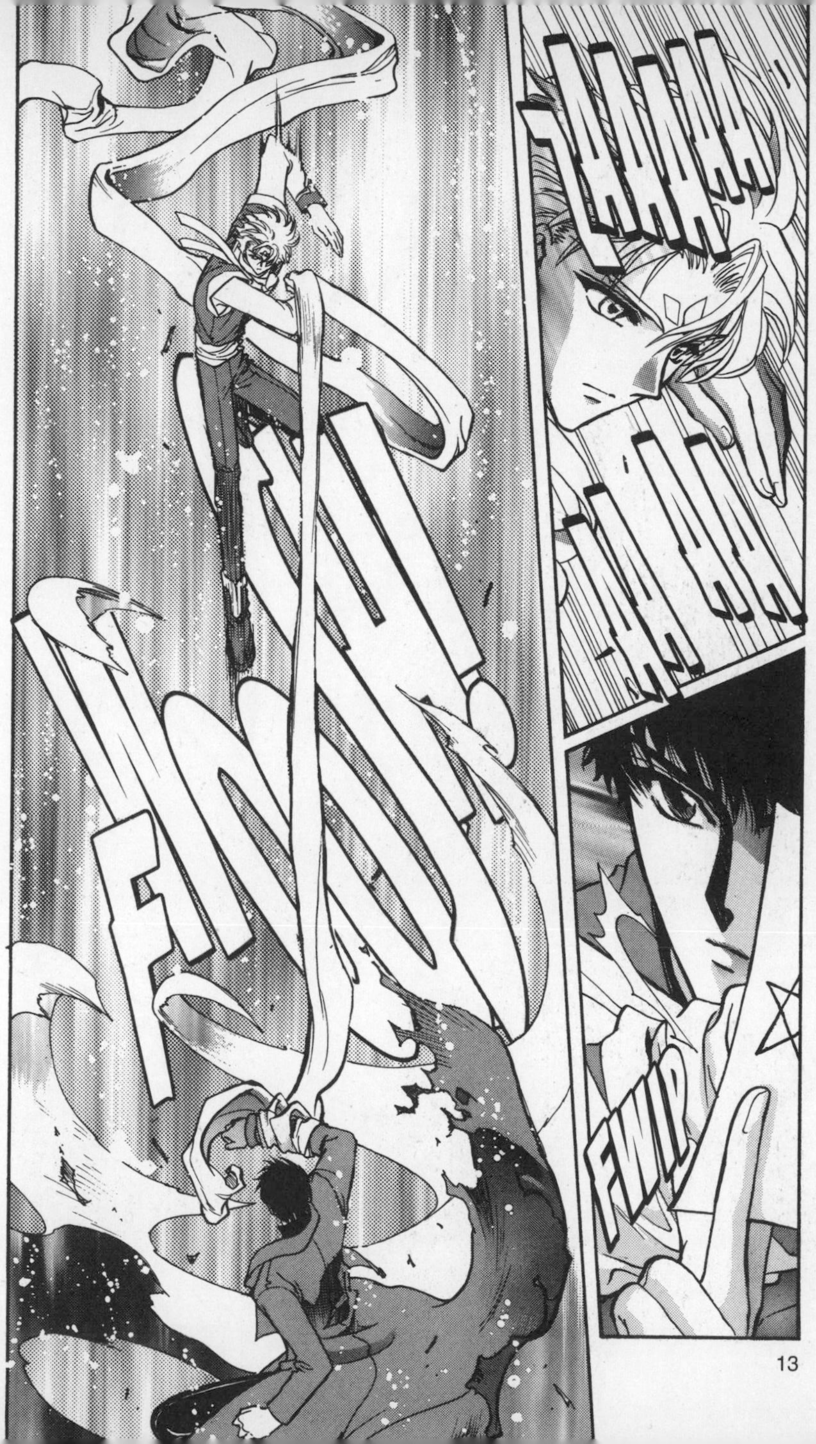
FWIP

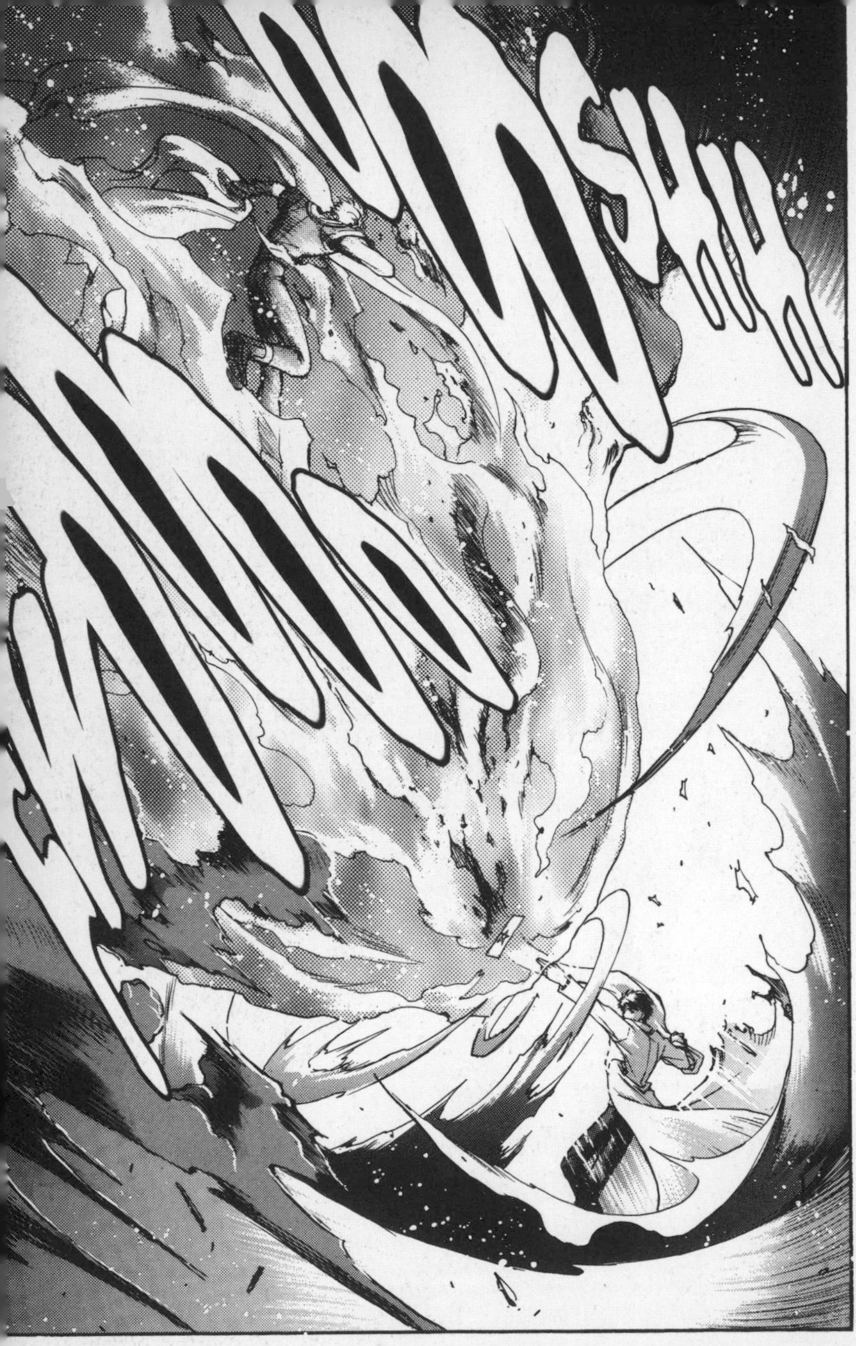

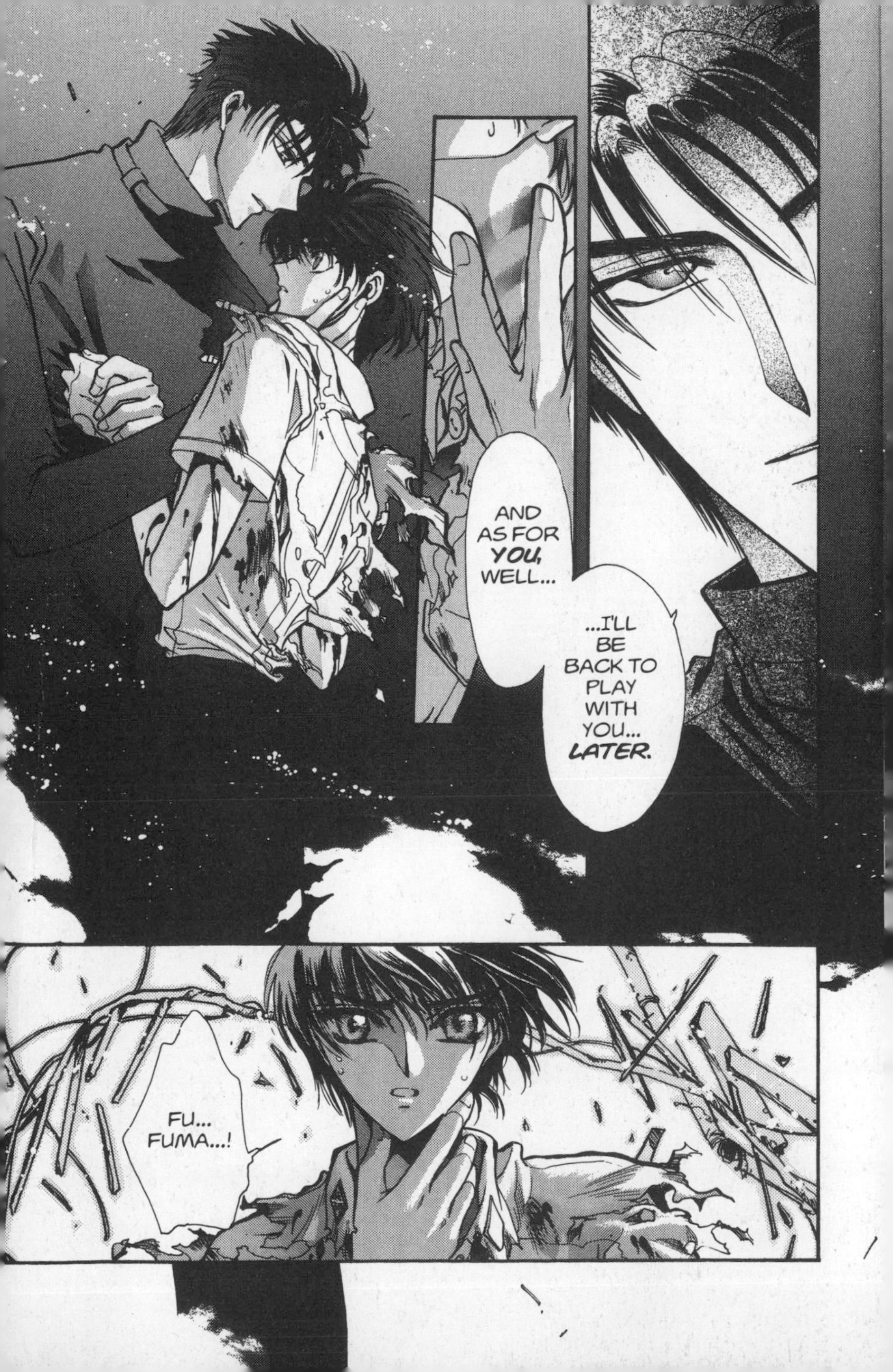
AND AS FOR YOU, WELL...
...I'LL BE BACK TO PLAY WITH YOU... LATER.
FU... FUMA...!

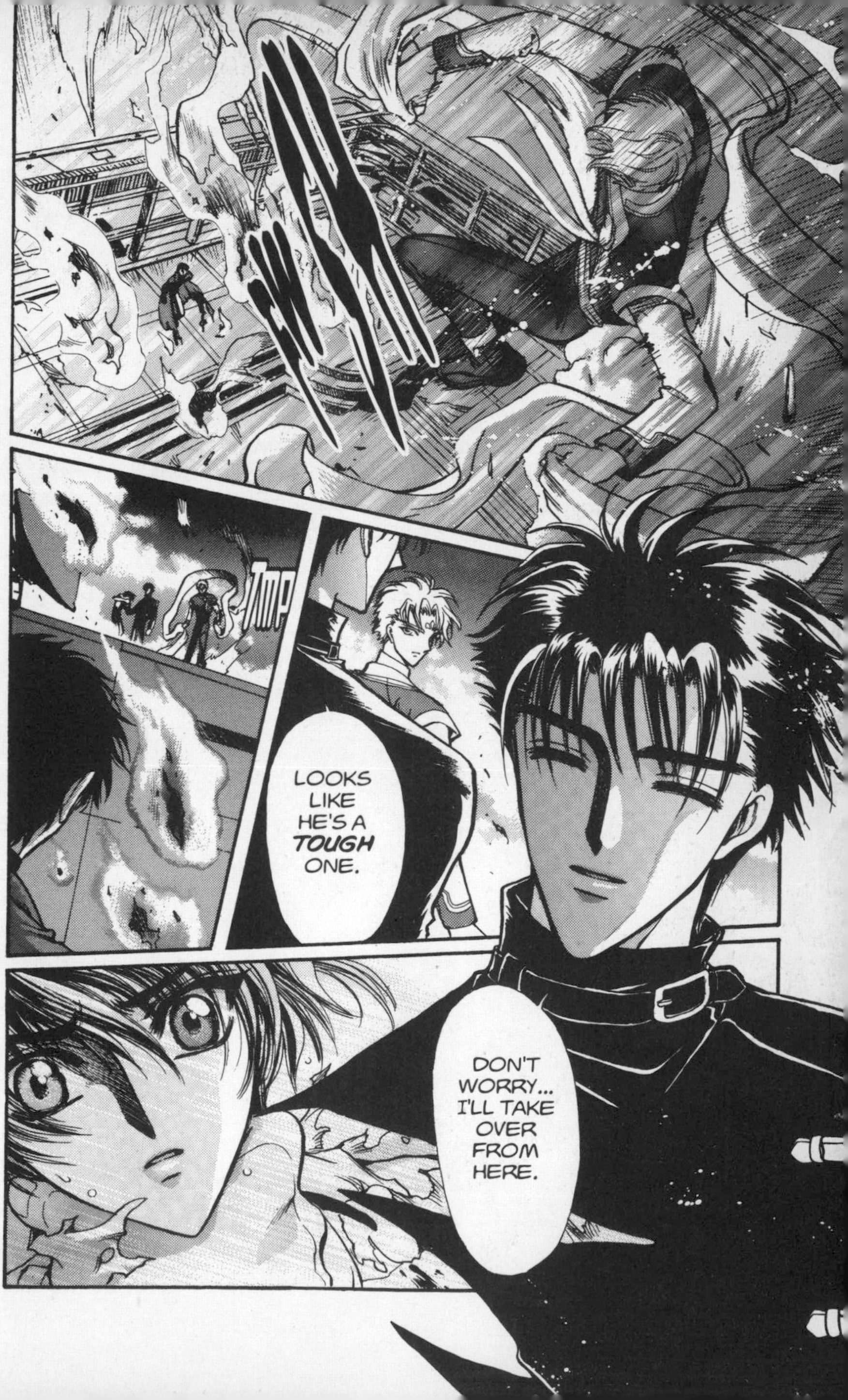
TMP
LOOKS LIKE HE'S A **TOUGH** ONE.
DON'T WORRY... I'LL TAKE OVER FROM HERE.

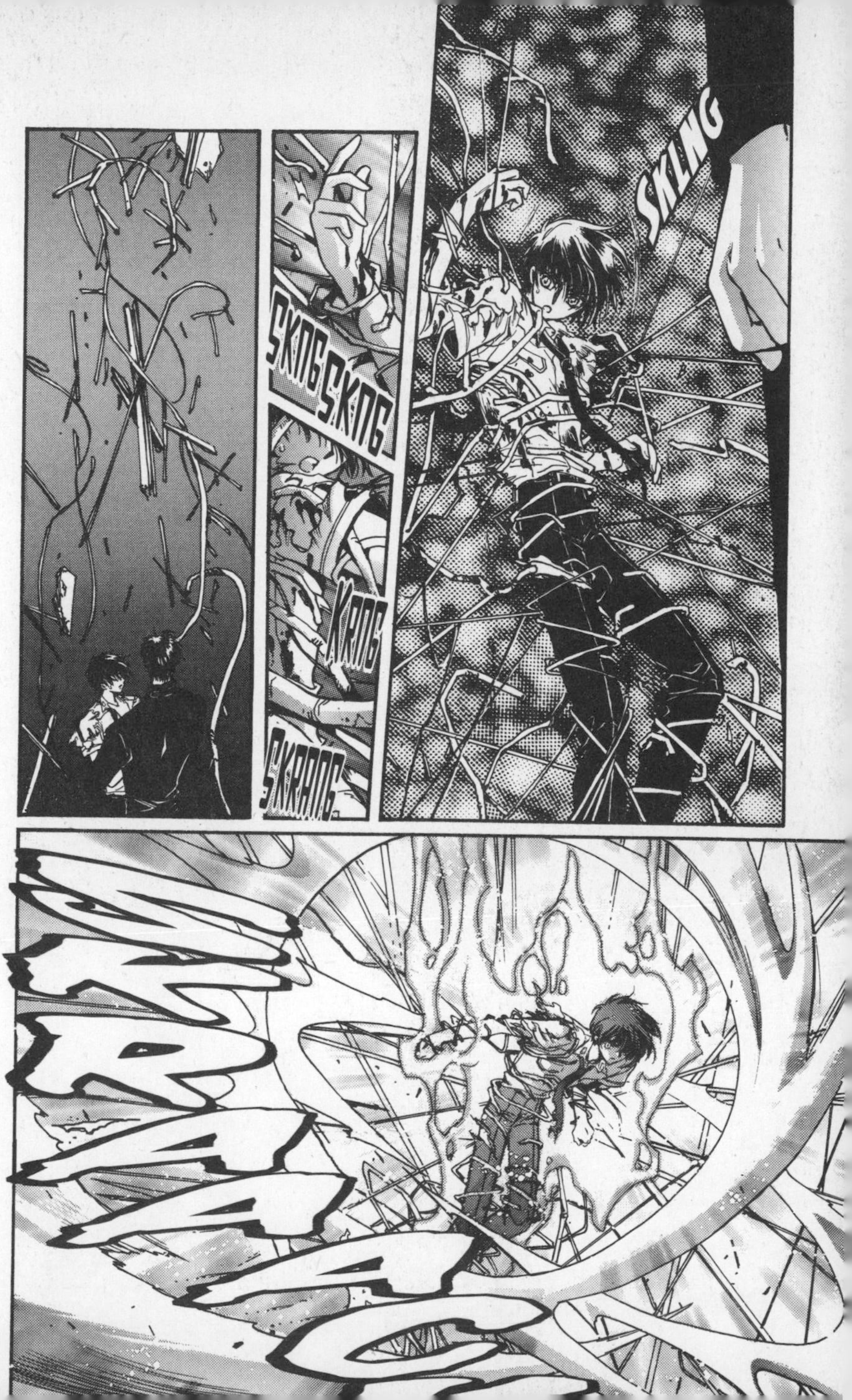
SKLNG
SKNG
SKNG
KRNG
SKRANG

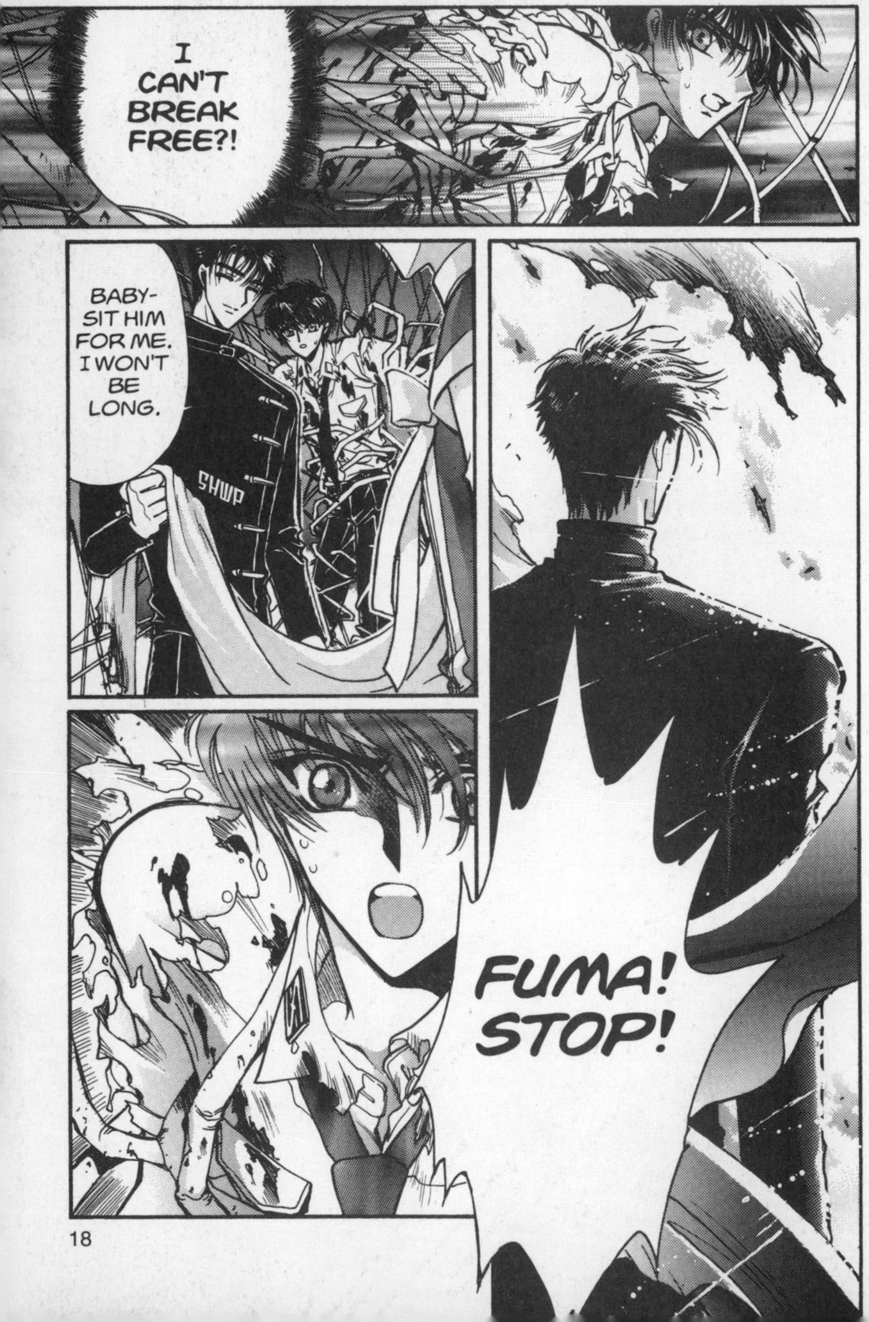
I CAN'T BREAK FREE?!
BABY-SIT HIM FOR ME. I WON'T BE LONG.
FUMA! STOP!

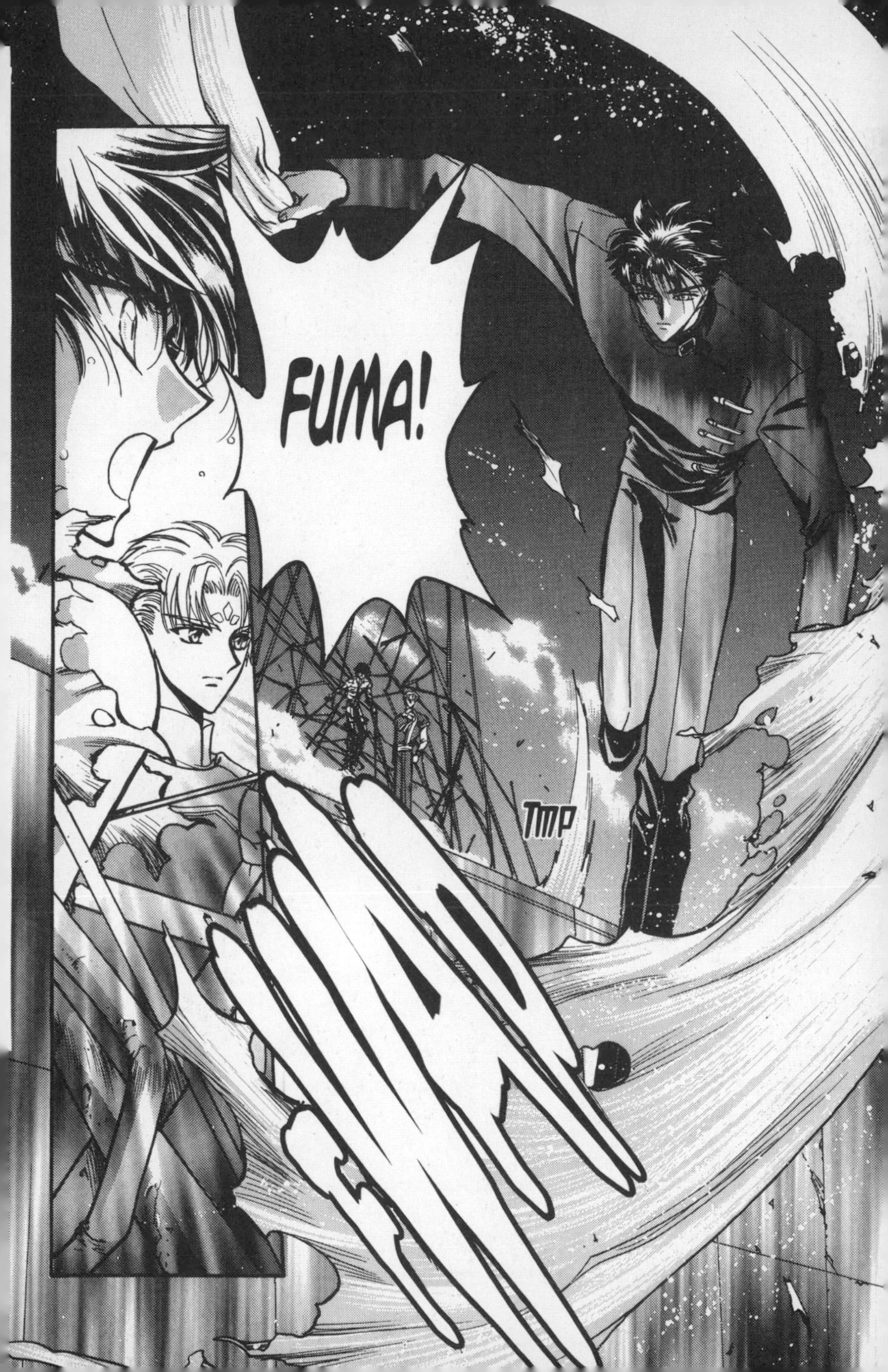
FUMA!
TMP

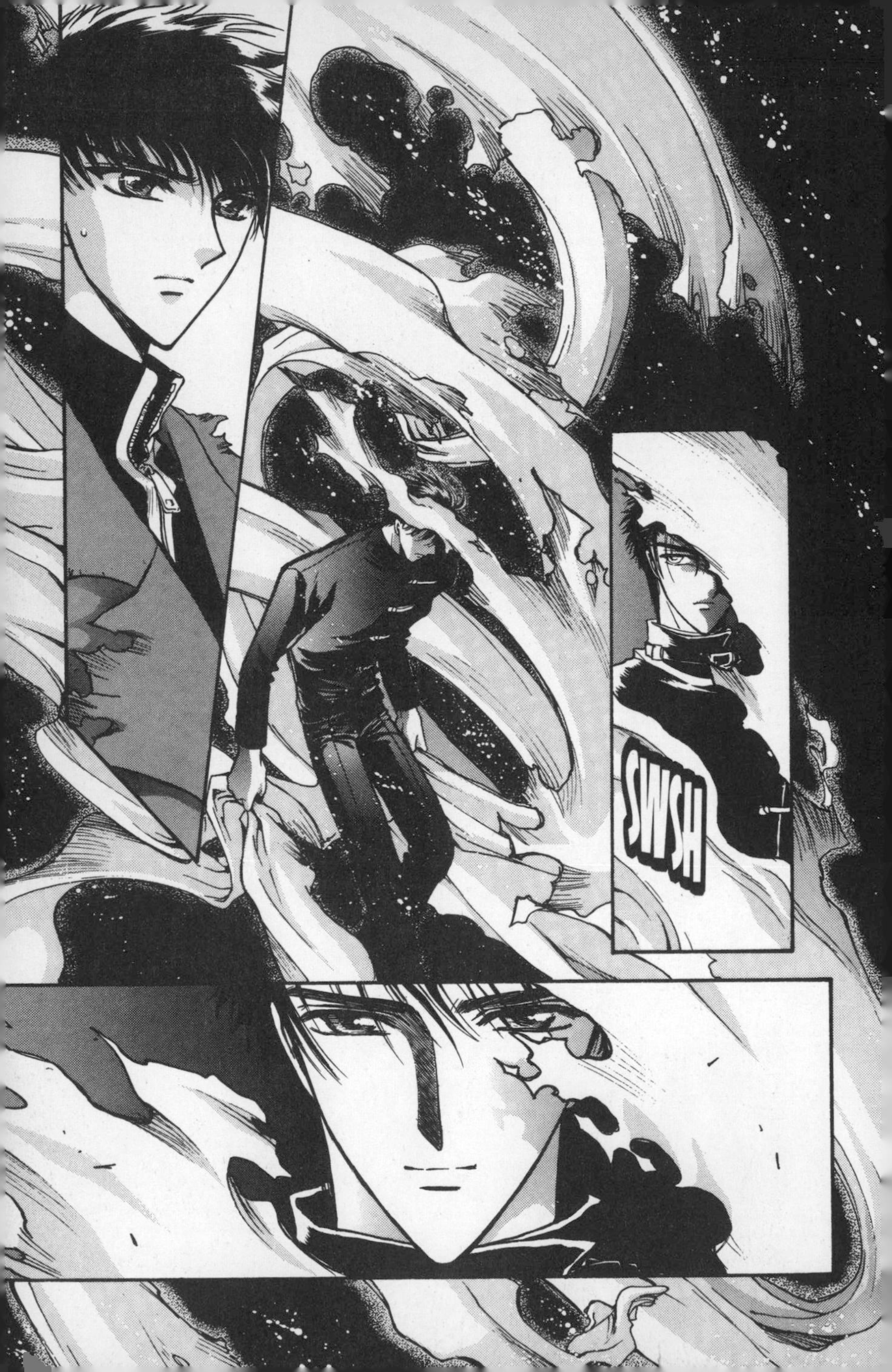
SWISH

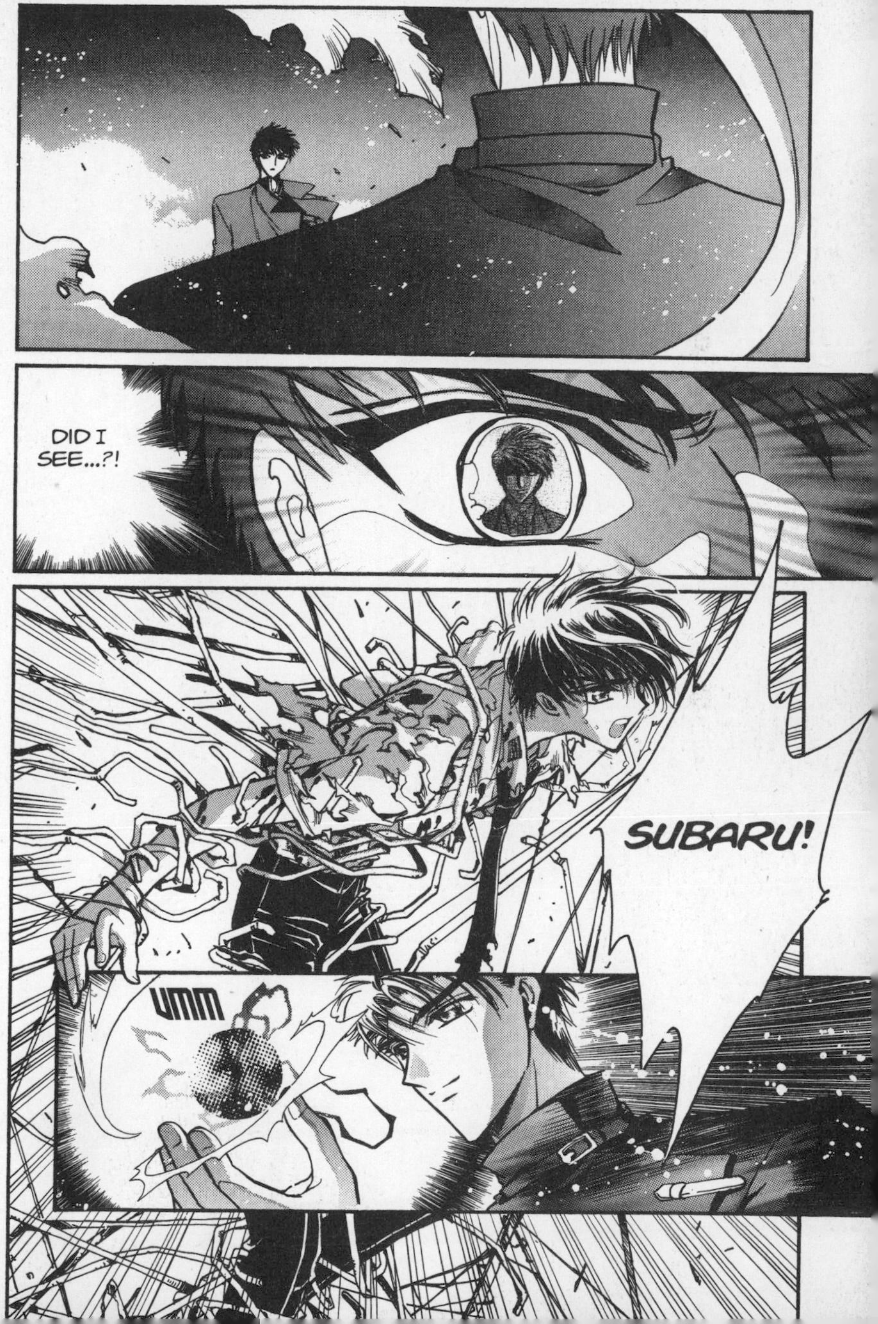
DID I SEE...?!
SUBARU!
UMM

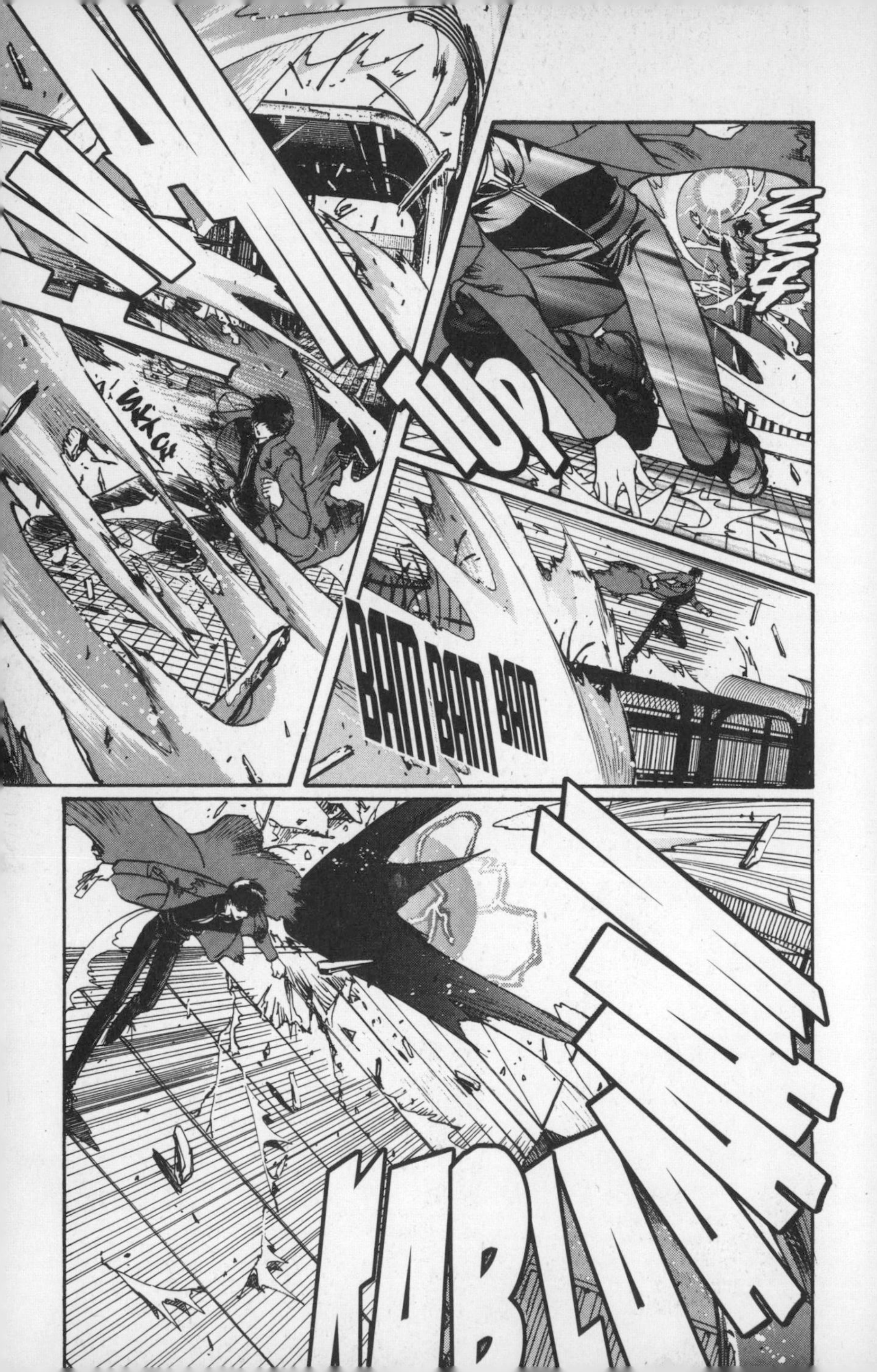
TUP
BAM BAM BAM

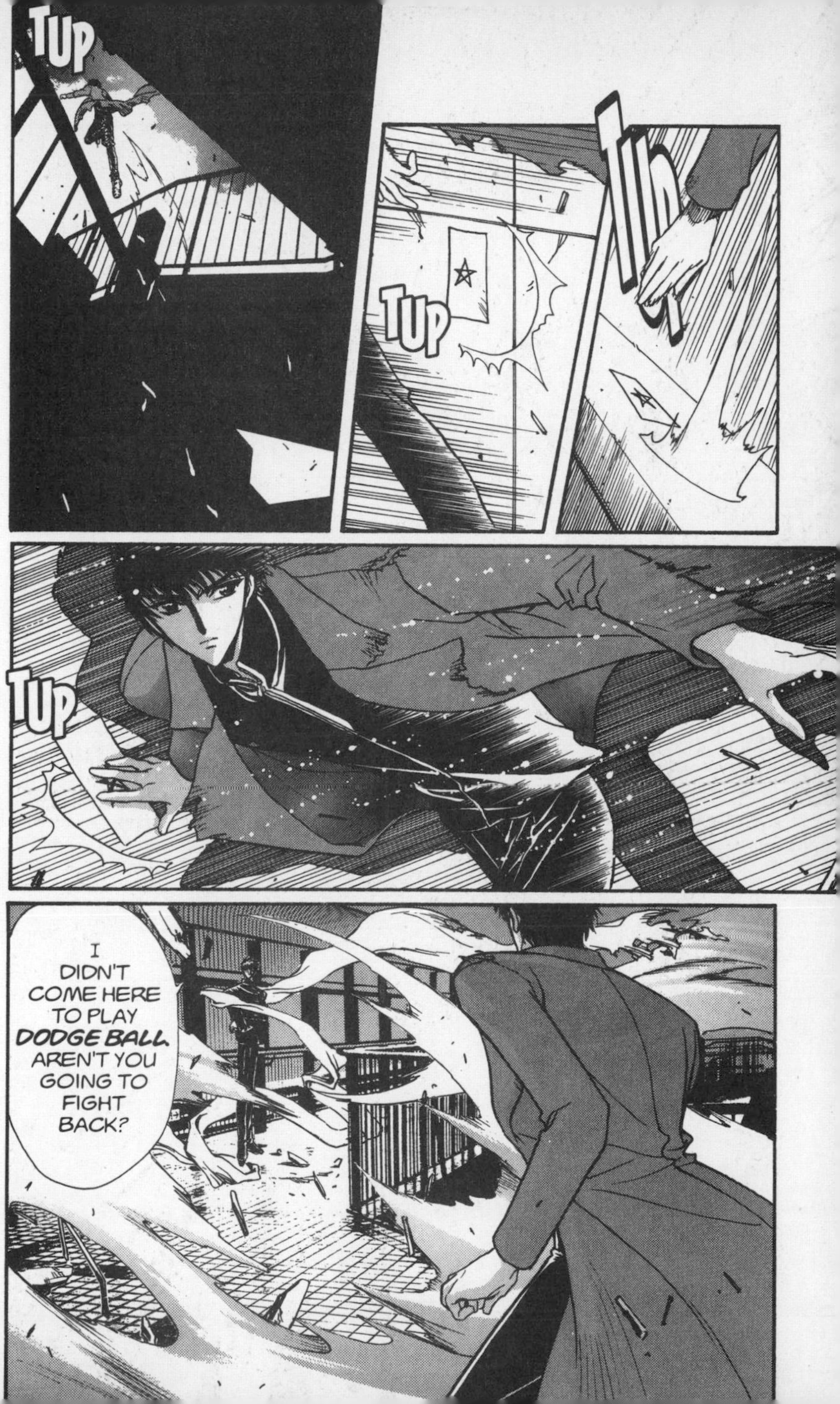
TUP
TUP
TUP
TUP
I DIDN'T COME HERE TO PLAY DODGE BALL. AREN'T YOU GOING TO FIGHT BACK?

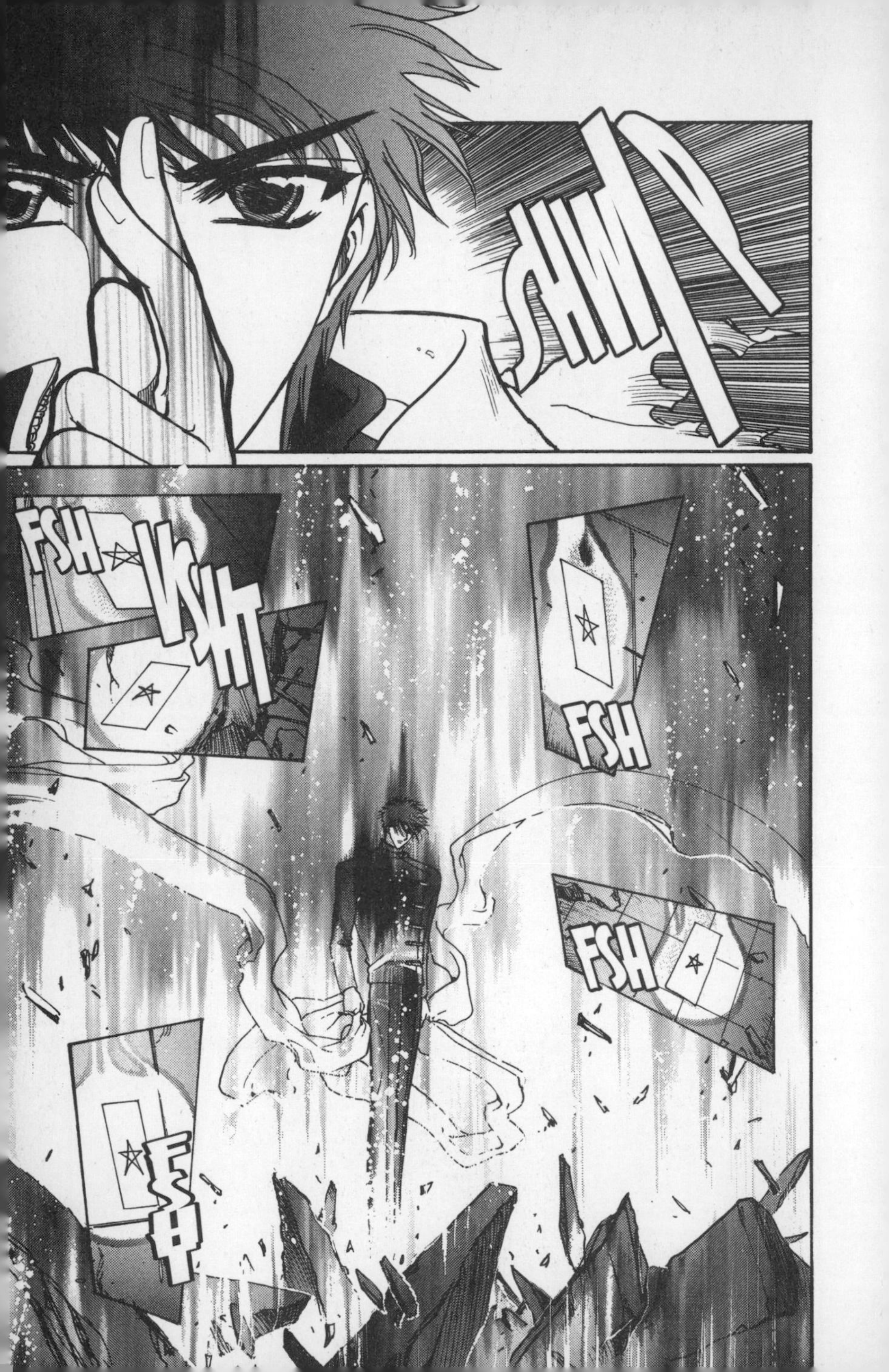
FSH
FSH
FSH
FSH

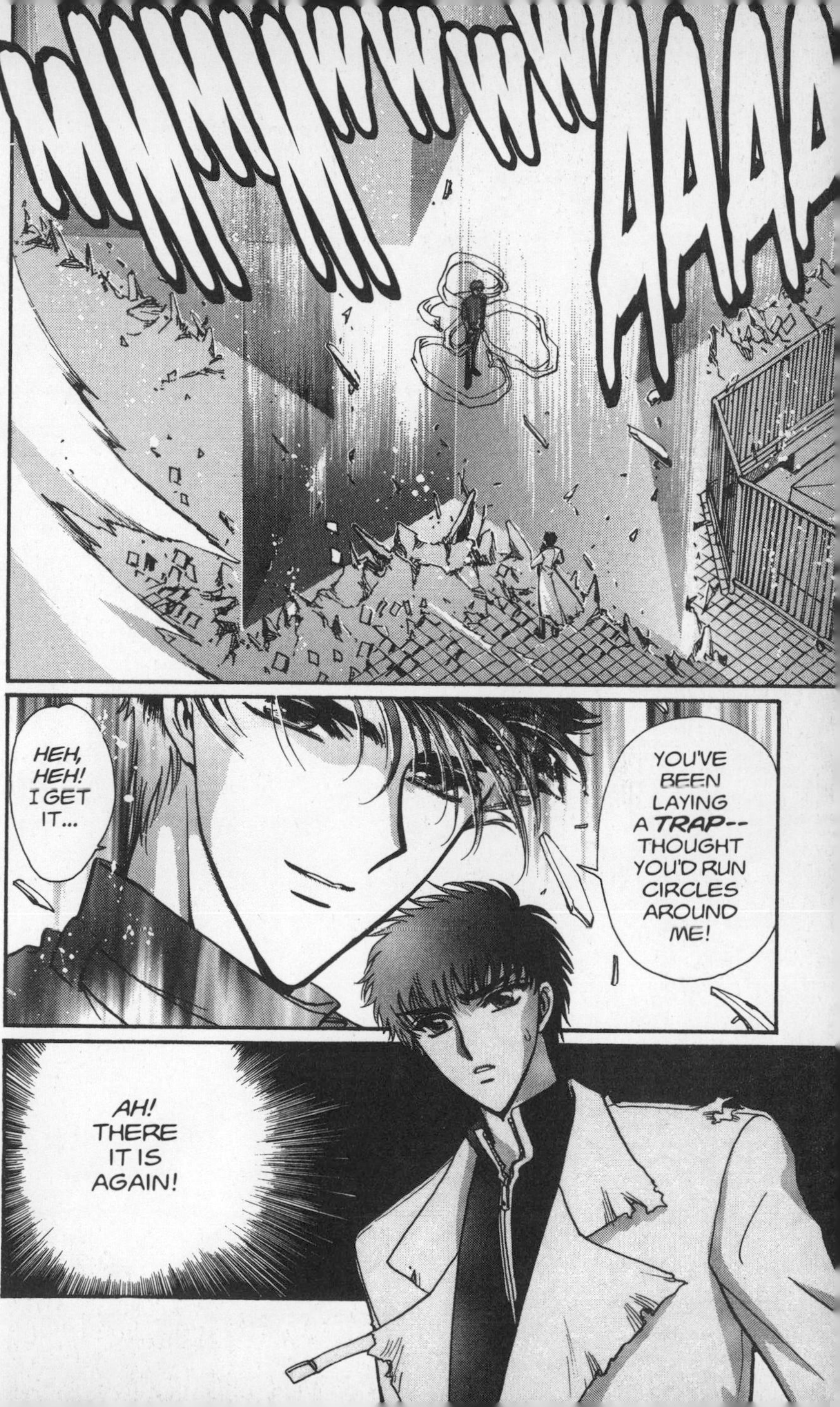
MMMMMWWWWWAAAA
YOU'VE BEEN LAYING A TRAP-- THOUGHT YOU'D RUN CIRCLES AROUND ME!
HEH, HEH! I GET IT...
AH! THERE IT IS AGAIN!

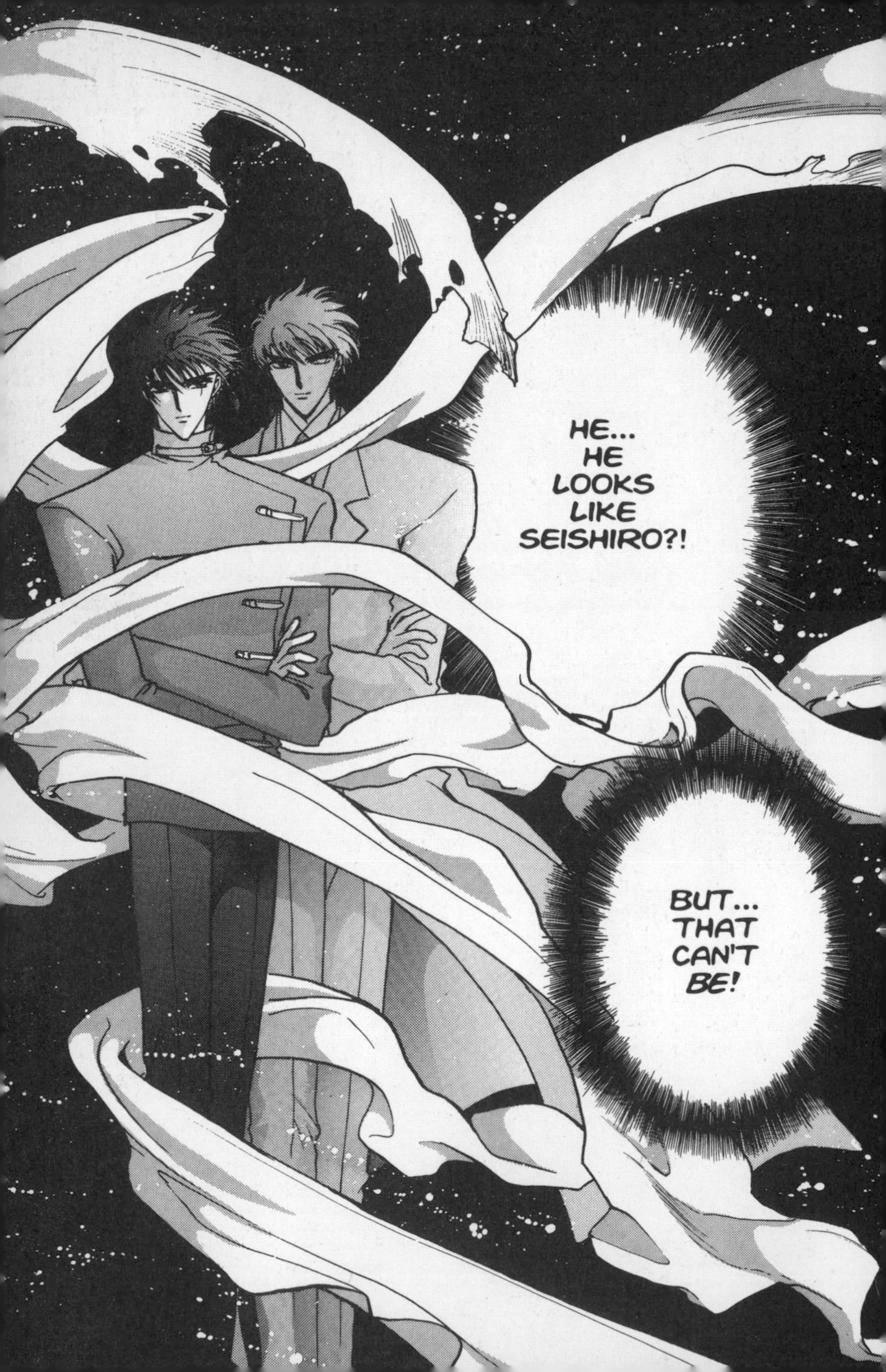
HE... HE LOOKS LIKE SEISHIRO?!
BUT... THAT CAN'T BE!

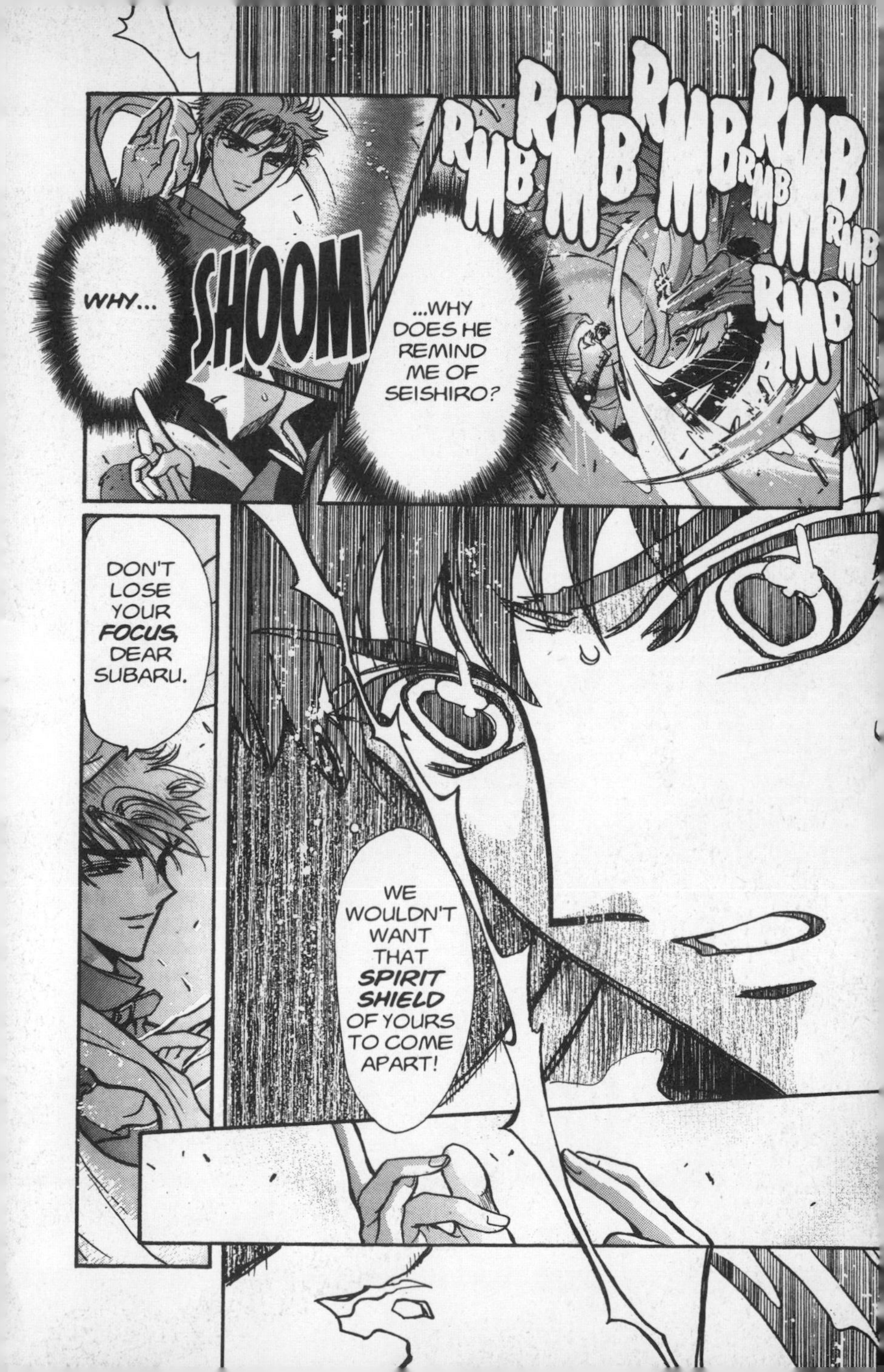
WHY...
SHOOM
...WHY DOES HE REMIND ME OF SEISHIRO?
RMB RMB RMB RMB RMB RMB RMB RMB
DON'T LOSE YOUR **FOCUS**, DEAR SUBARU.
WE WOULDN'T WANT THAT **SPIRIT SHIELD** OF YOURS TO COME APART!

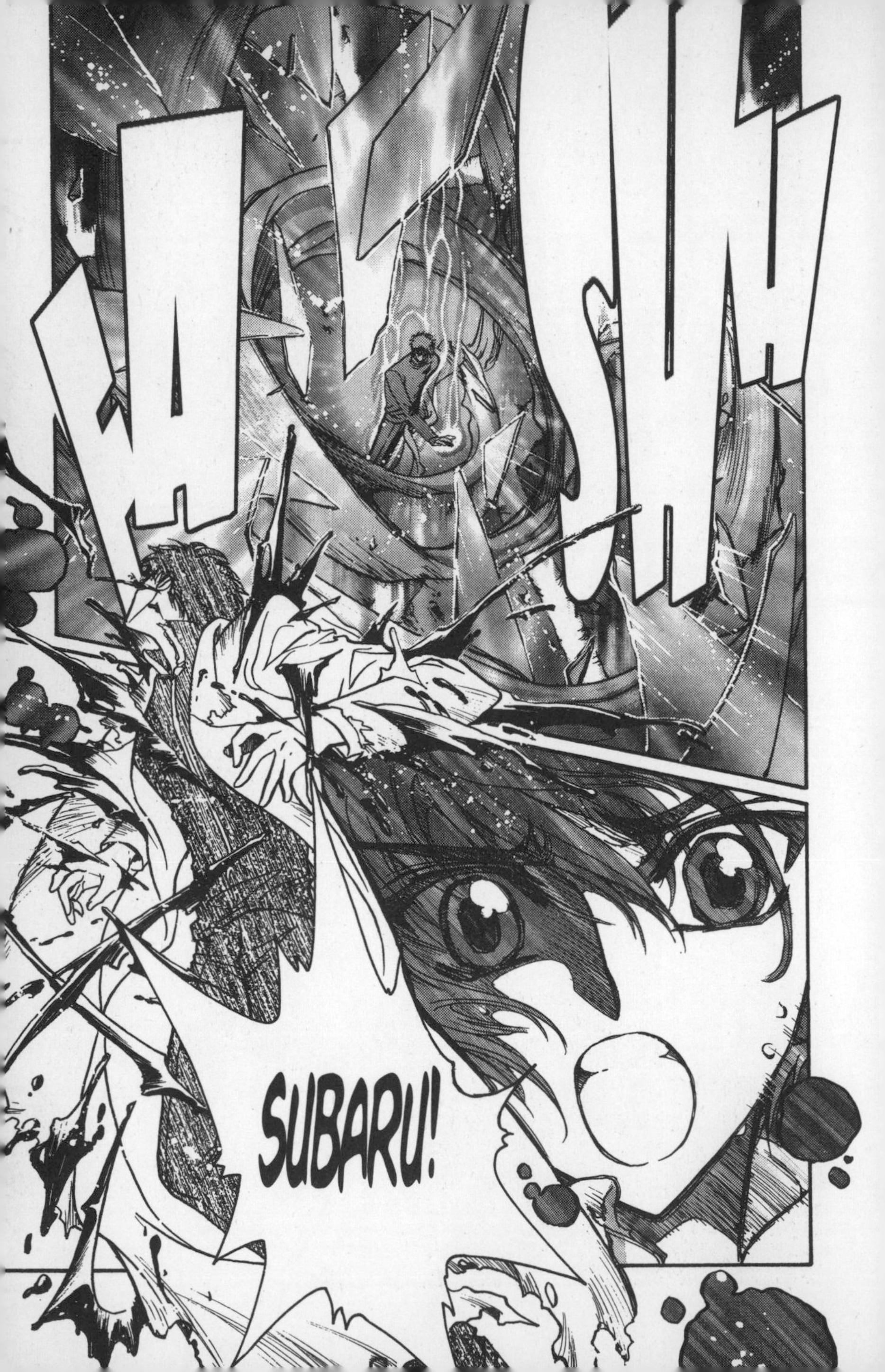
SUBARU!

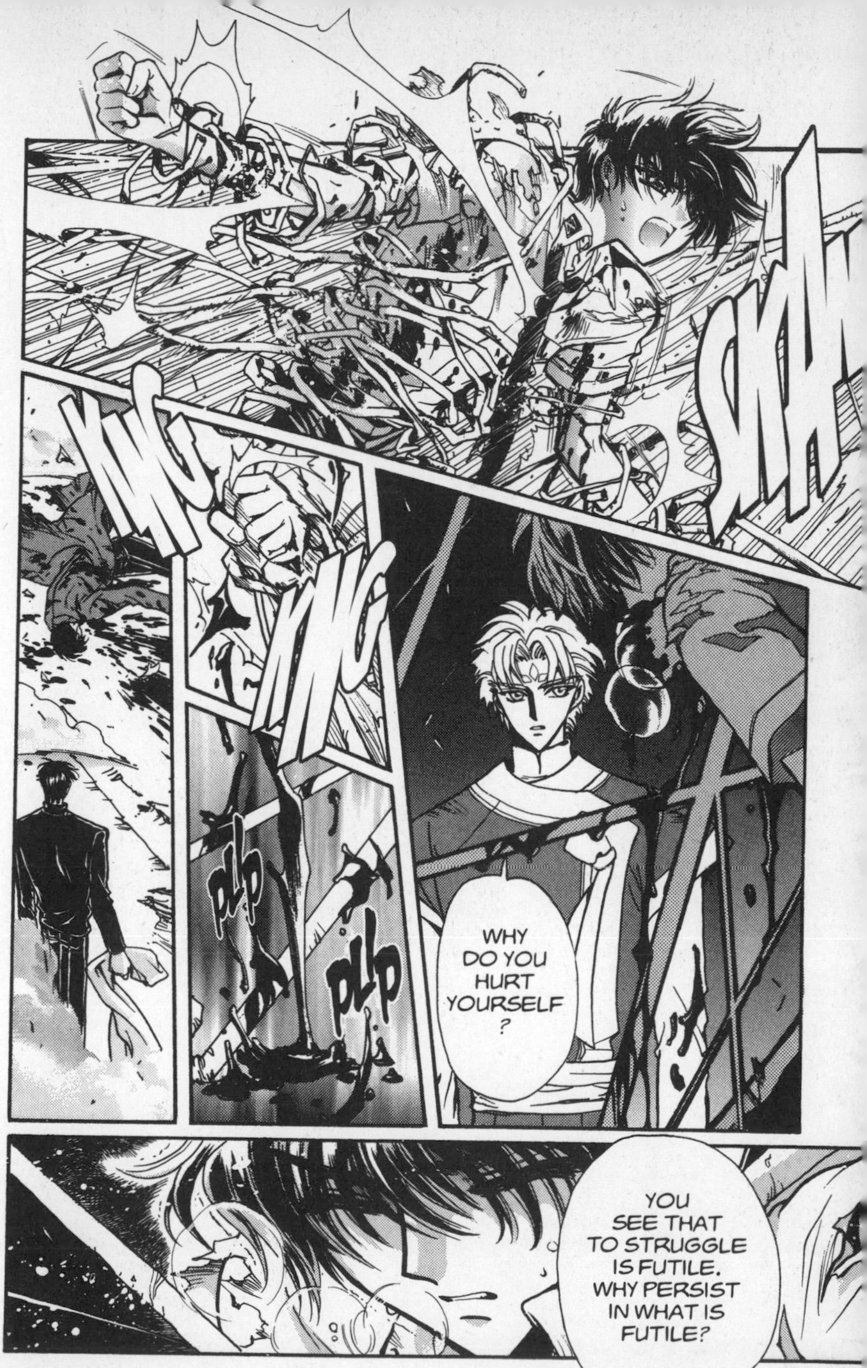
WHY DO YOU HURT YOURSELF?
PLIP
PLIP
YOU SEE THAT TO STRUGGLE IS FUTILE. WHY PERSIST IN WHAT IS FUTILE?

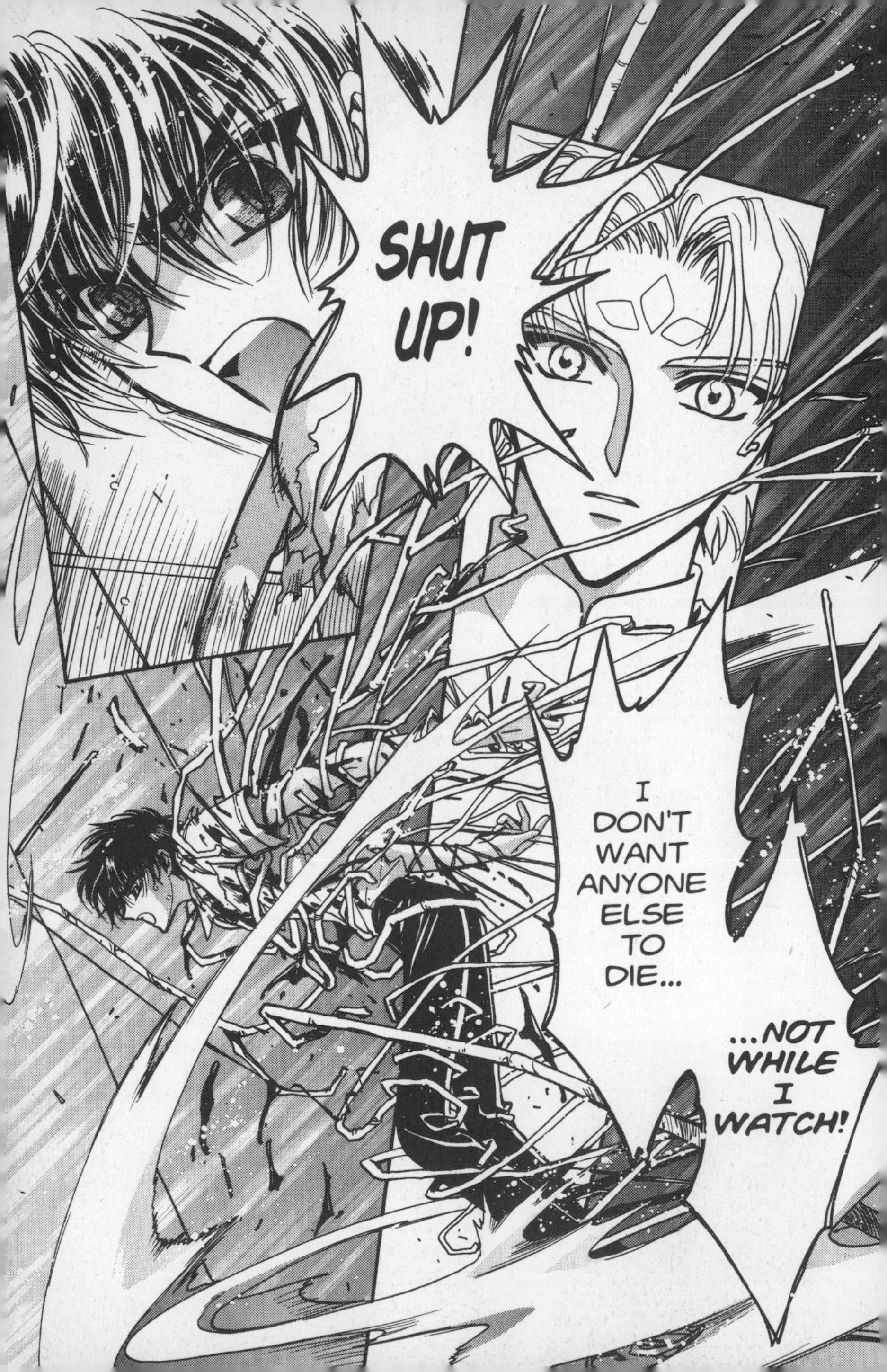
SHUT UP!
I DON'T WANT ANYONE ELSE TO DIE...
...NOT WHILE I WATCH!

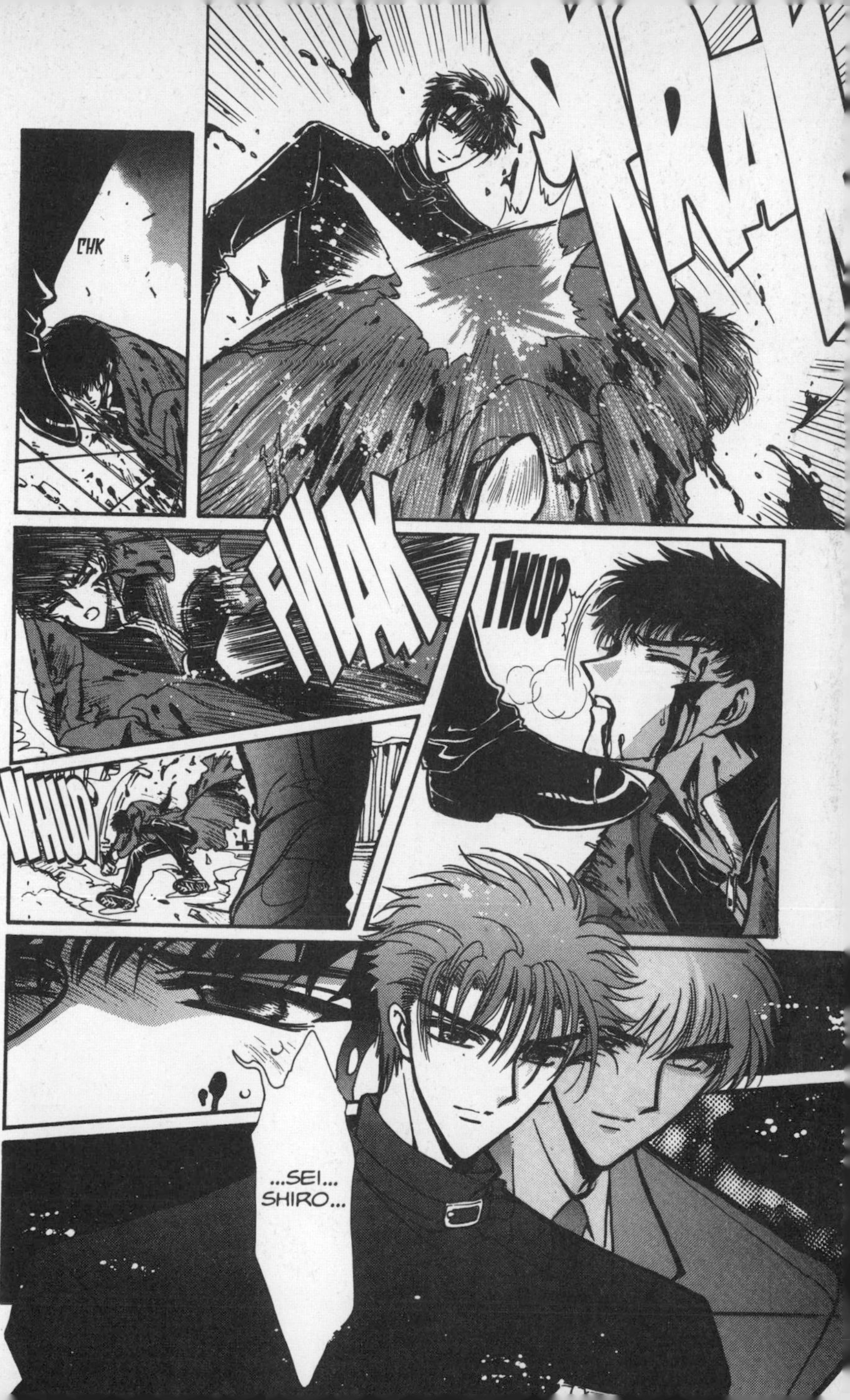
WRA
CHK
TWUP
FWAK
WHUD
...SEI... SHIRO...

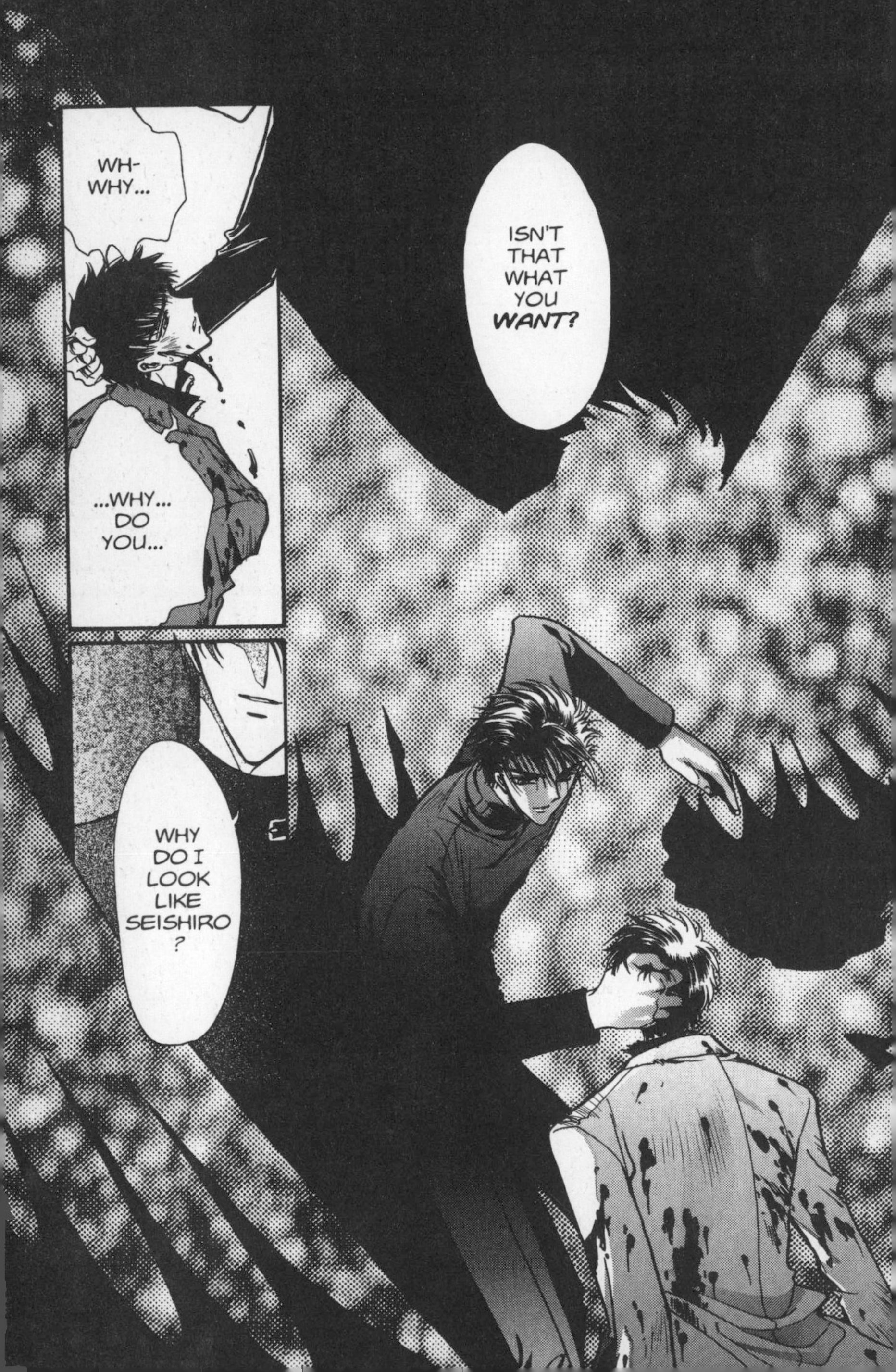
WH- WHY...
...WHY... DO YOU...
WHY DO I LOOK LIKE SEISHIRO ?
ISN'T THAT WHAT YOU **WANT?**

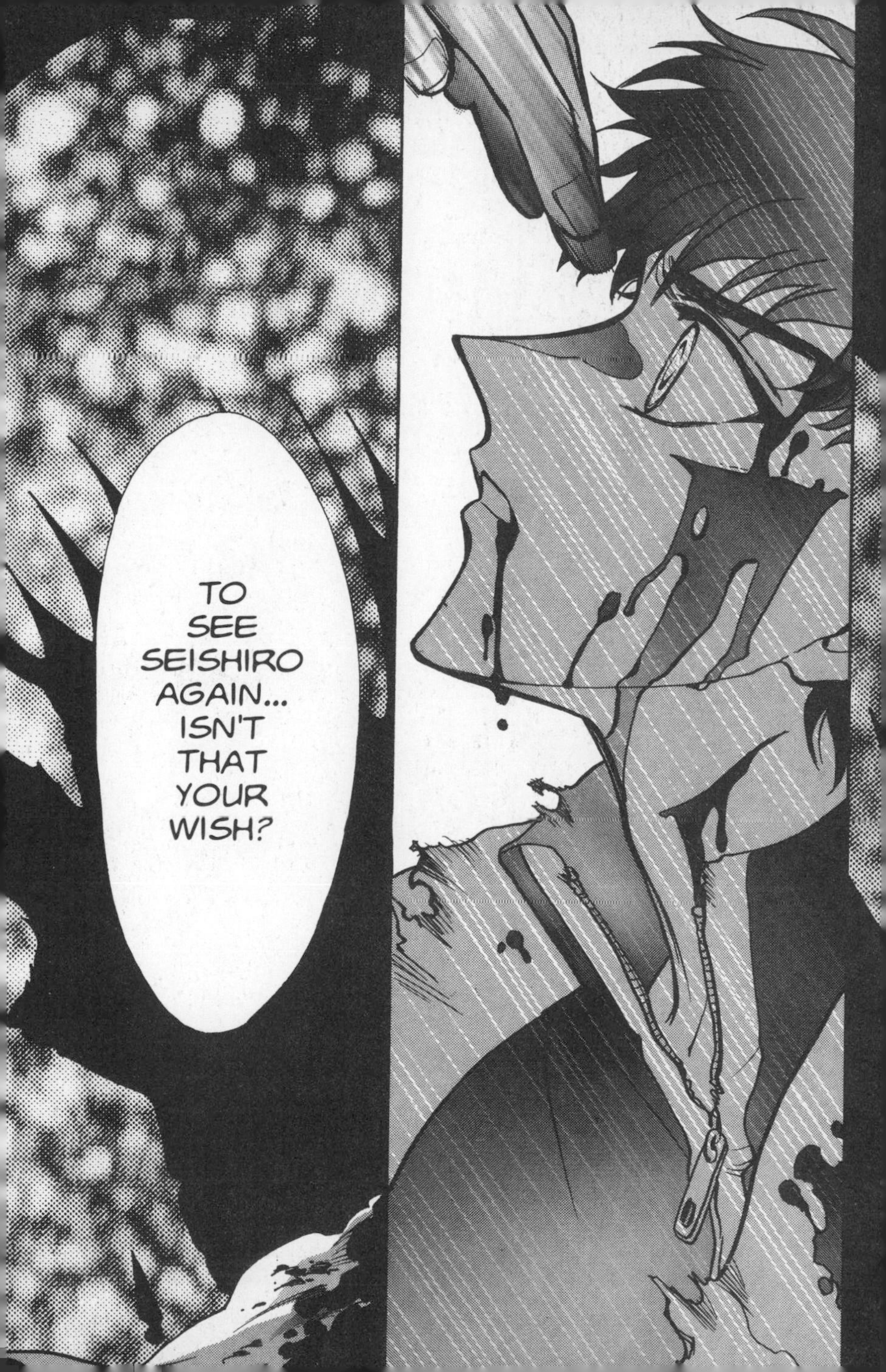
TO SEE SEISHIRO AGAIN... ISN'T THAT YOUR WISH?

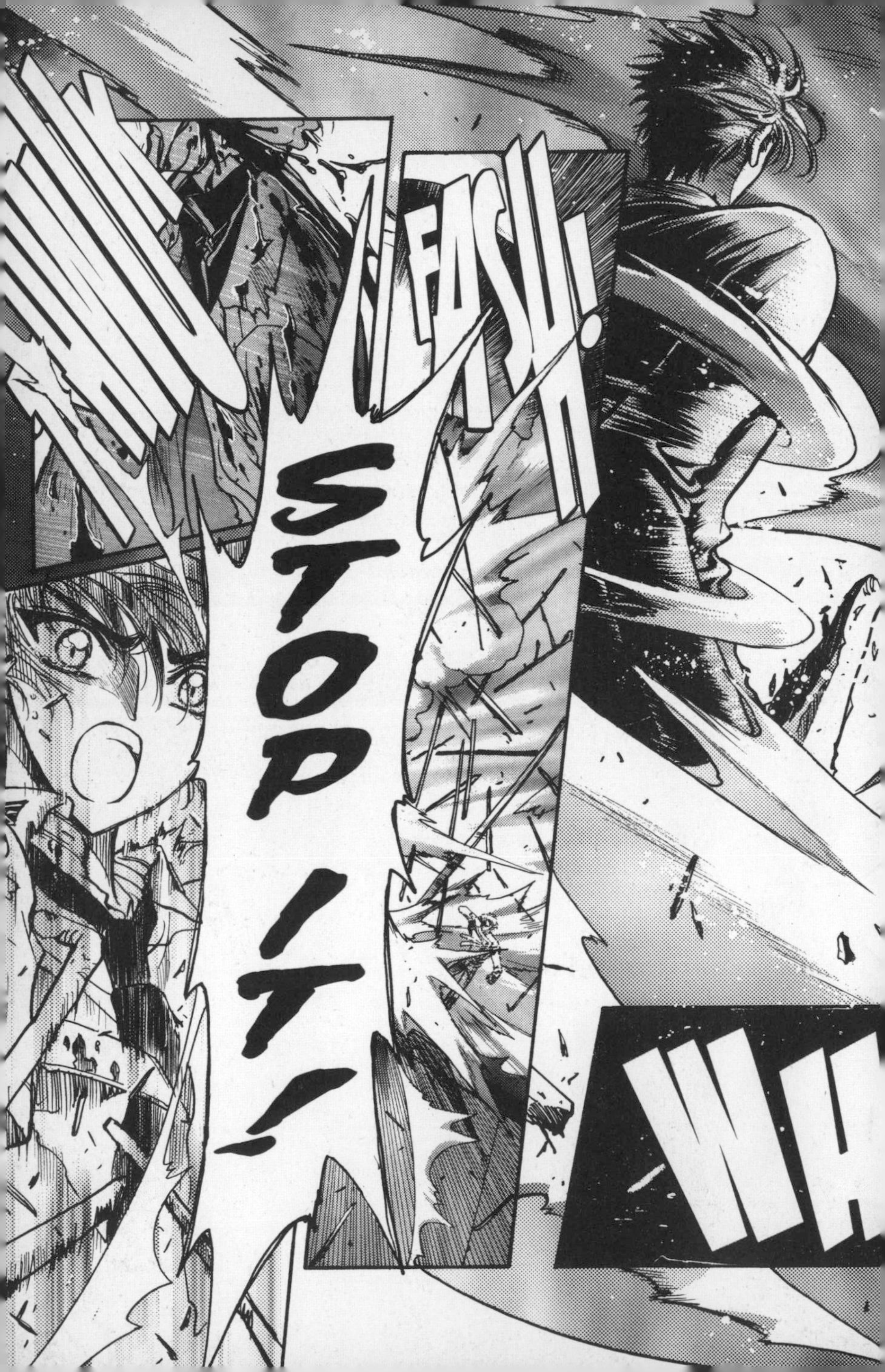
FASH!
STOP IT!
WHA

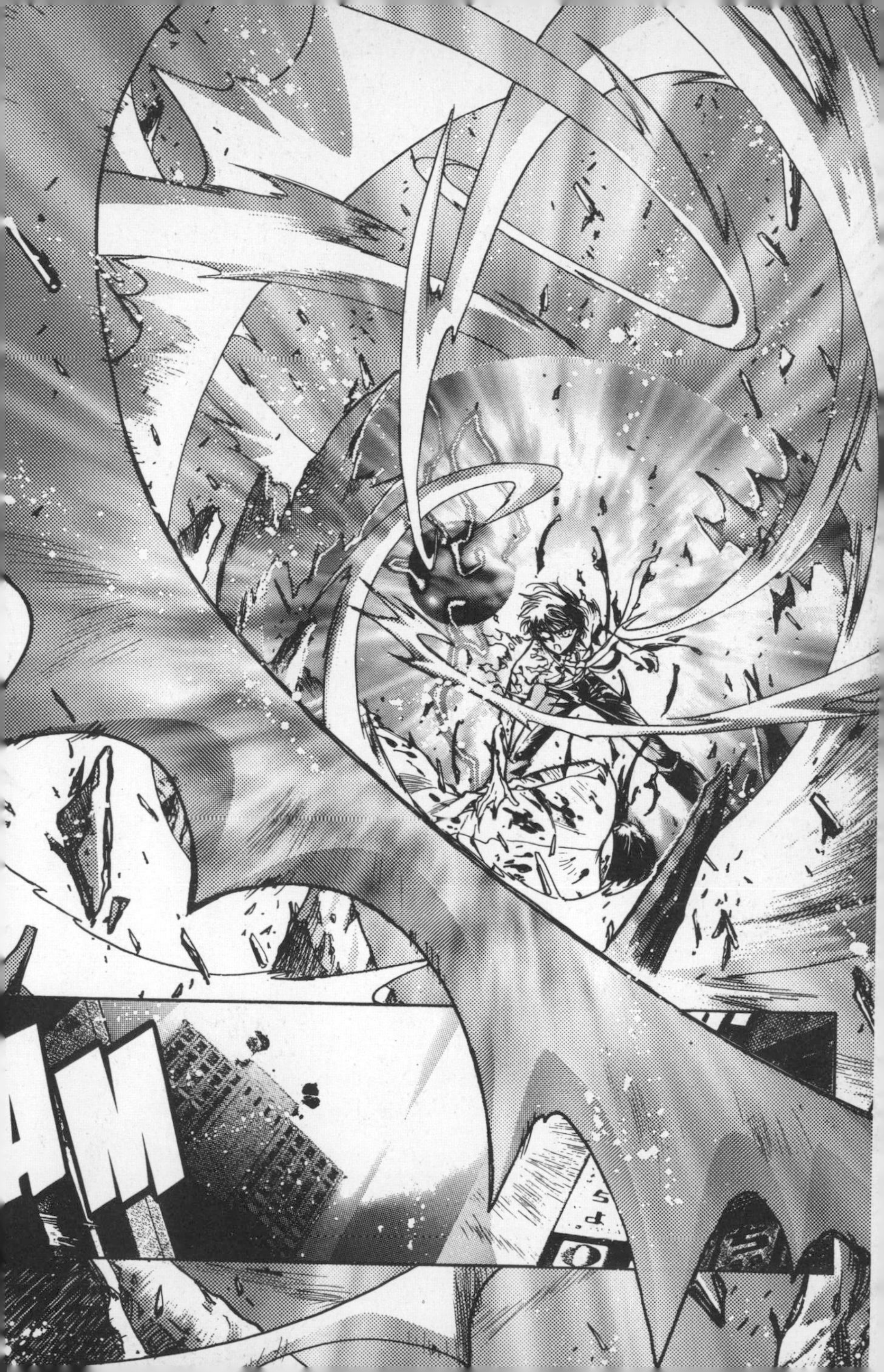
AM

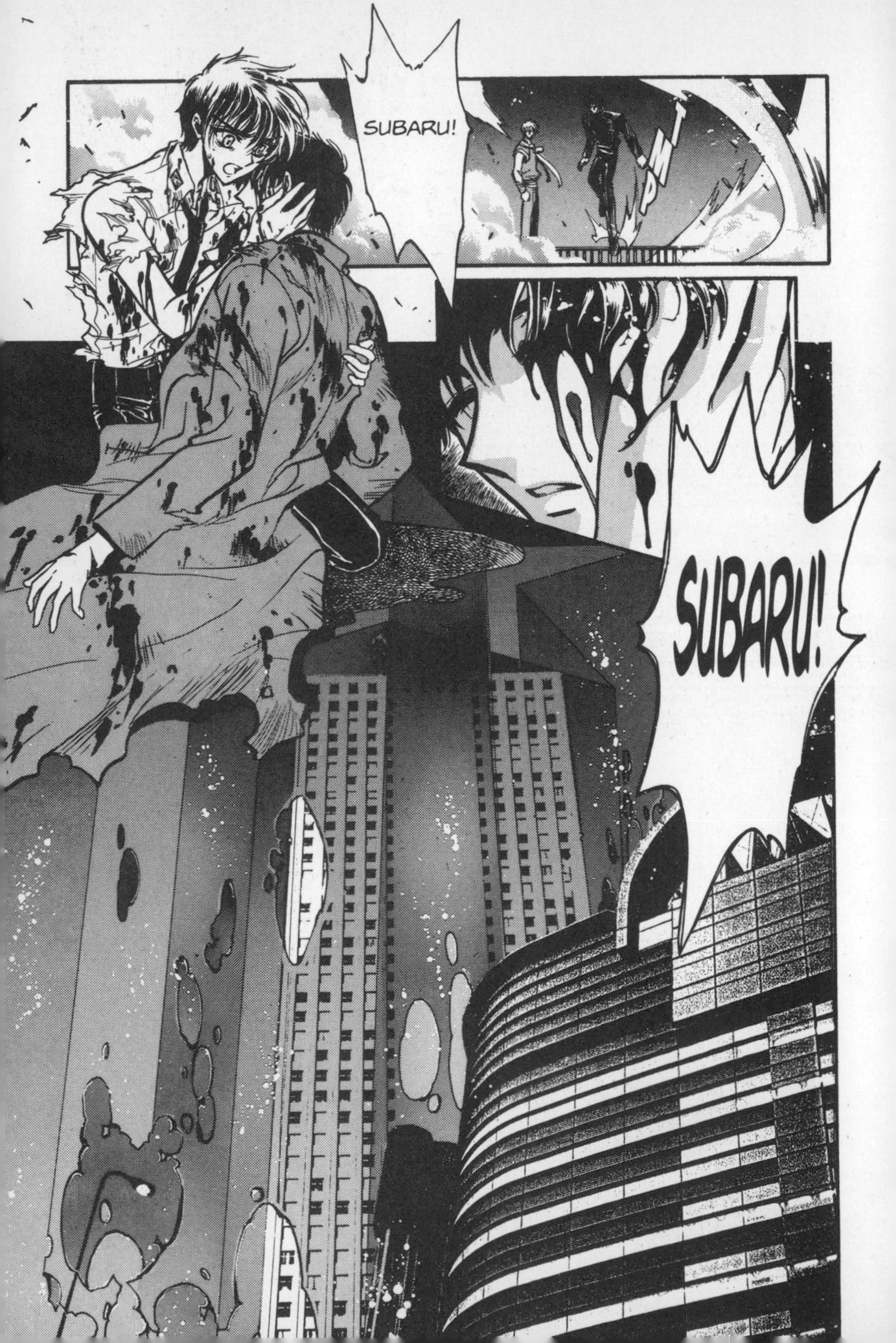
PMT
SUBARU!
SUBARU!

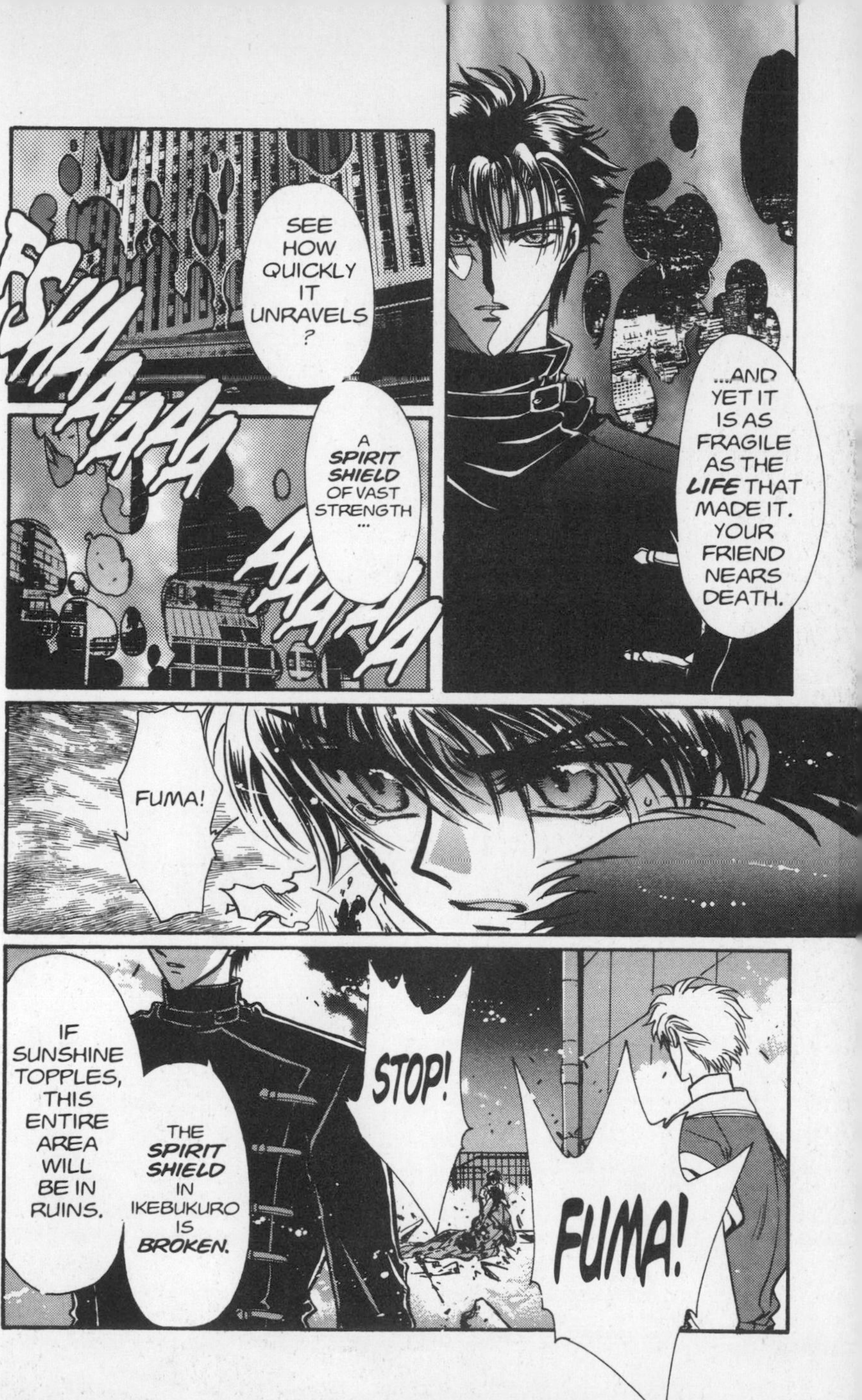

SEE HOW QUICKLY IT UNRAVELS?
FSHAAAAAAAAAA
A *SPIRIT SHIELD* OF VAST STRENGTH...
...AND YET IT IS AS FRAGILE AS THE *LIFE* THAT MADE IT. YOUR FRIEND NEARS DEATH.
FUMA!
STOP!
FUMA!
THE *SPIRIT SHIELD* IN IKEBUKURO IS *BROKEN.*
IF SUNSHINE TOPPLES, THIS ENTIRE AREA WILL BE IN RUINS.

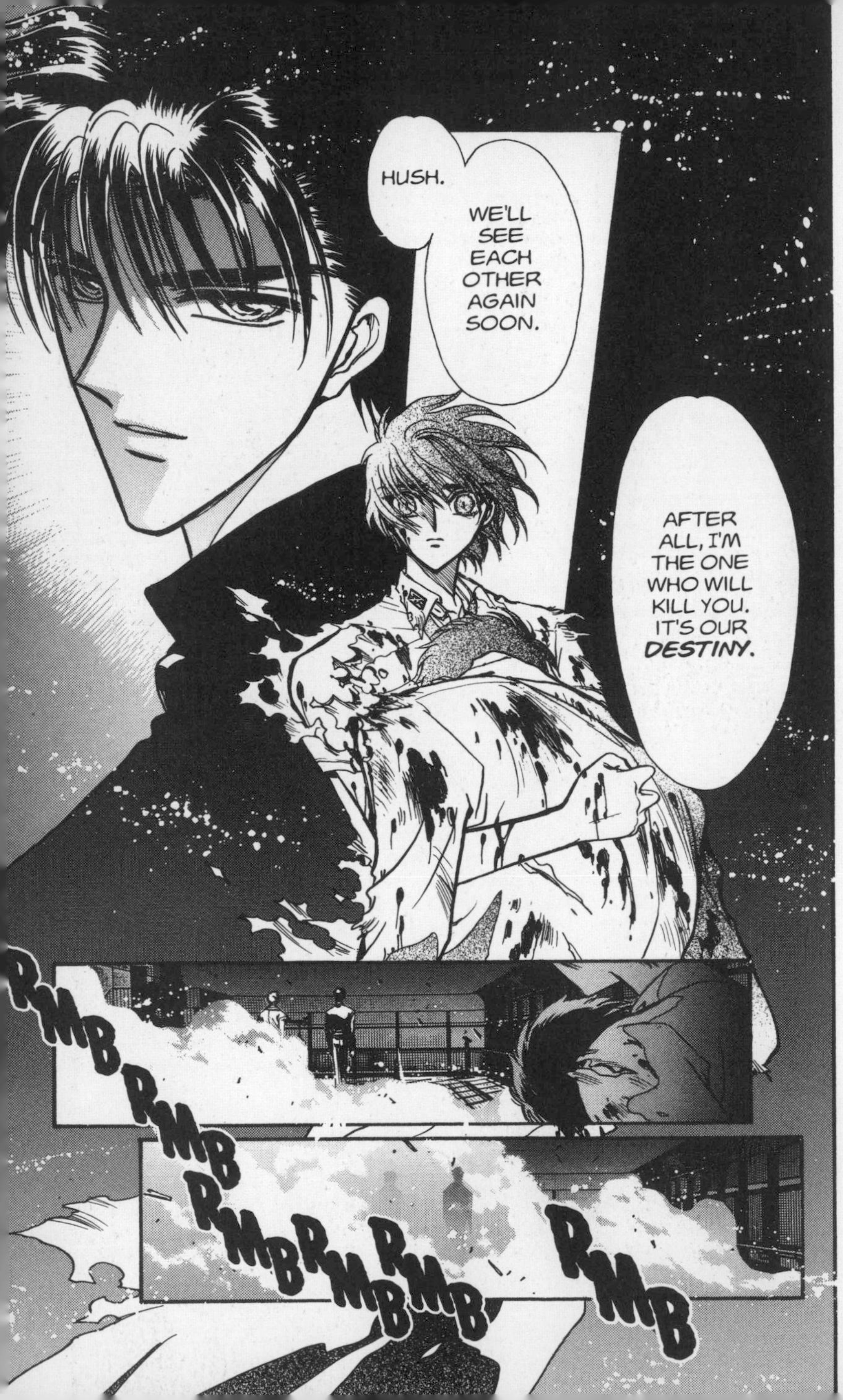
HUSH.
WE'LL SEE EACH OTHER AGAIN SOON.
AFTER ALL, I'M THE ONE WHO WILL KILL YOU. IT'S OUR DESTINY.
RMB RMB RMB RMB RMB RMB RMB

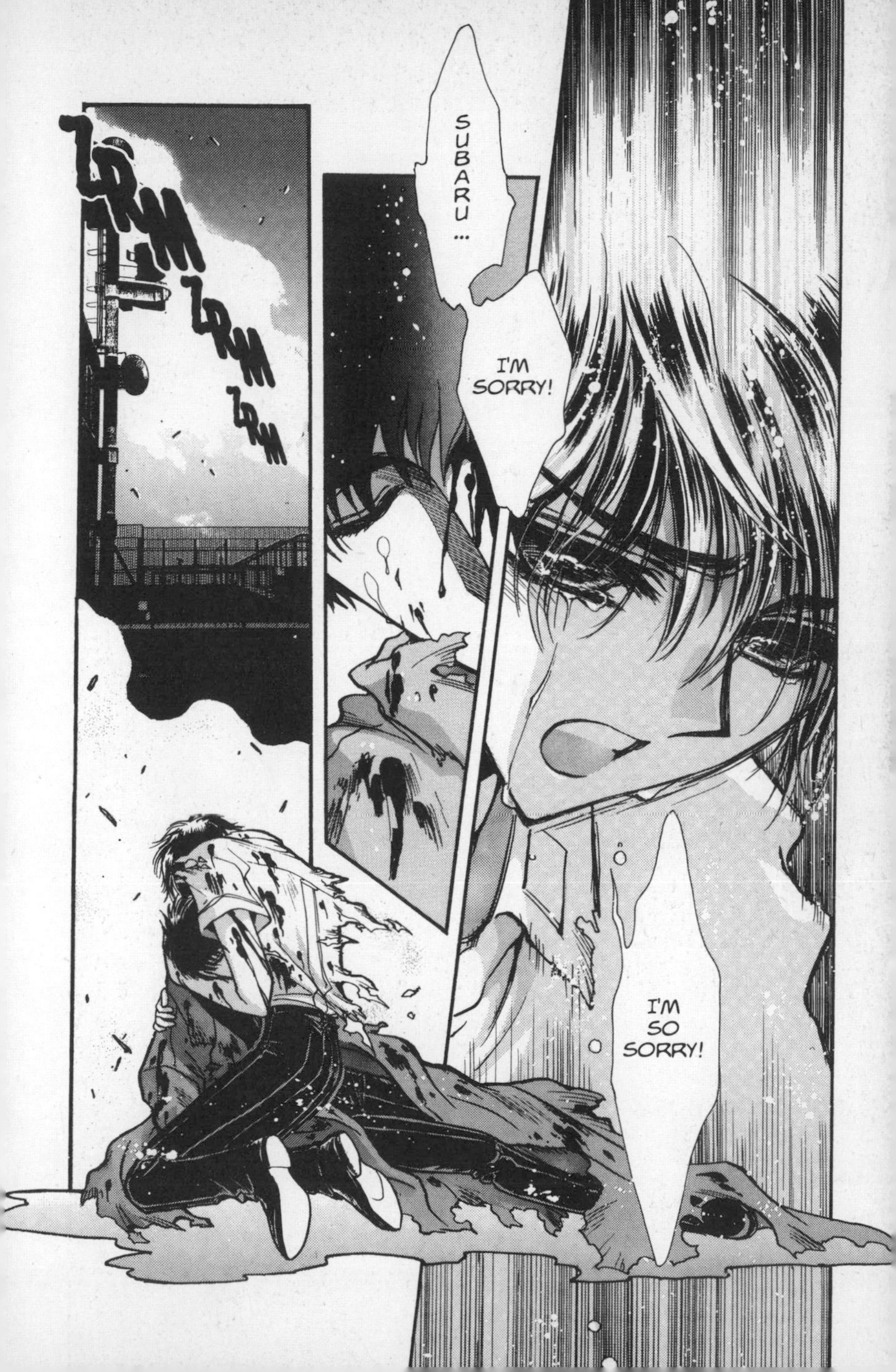
SUBARU...
I'M SORRY!
I'M SO SORRY!
ZRRM
ZRRM
ZRRM
ZRRM

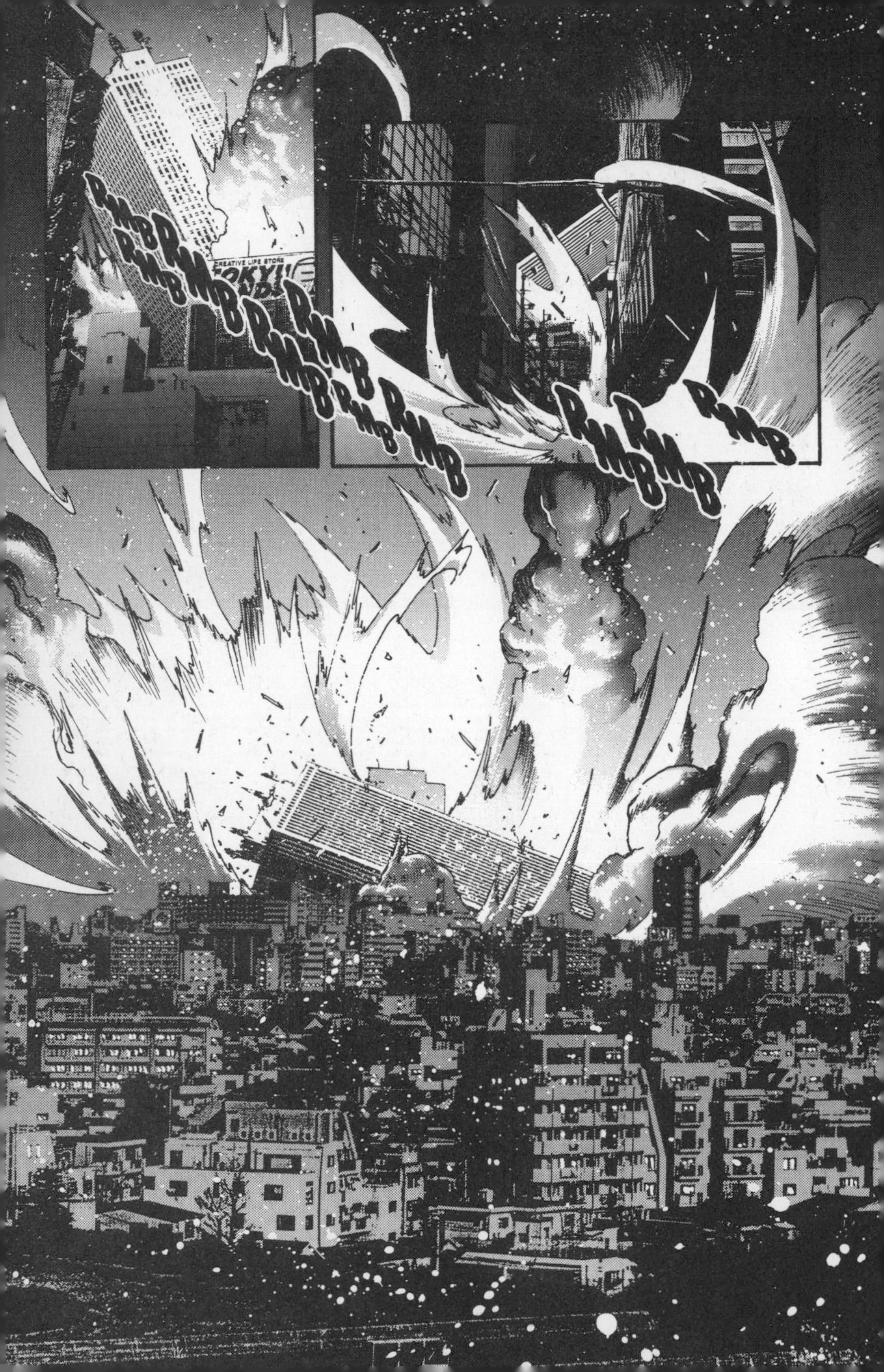
RUMB RUMB RUMB
RUMB RUMB RUMB RUMB RUMB RUMB RUMB
CREATIVE LIFE STORE

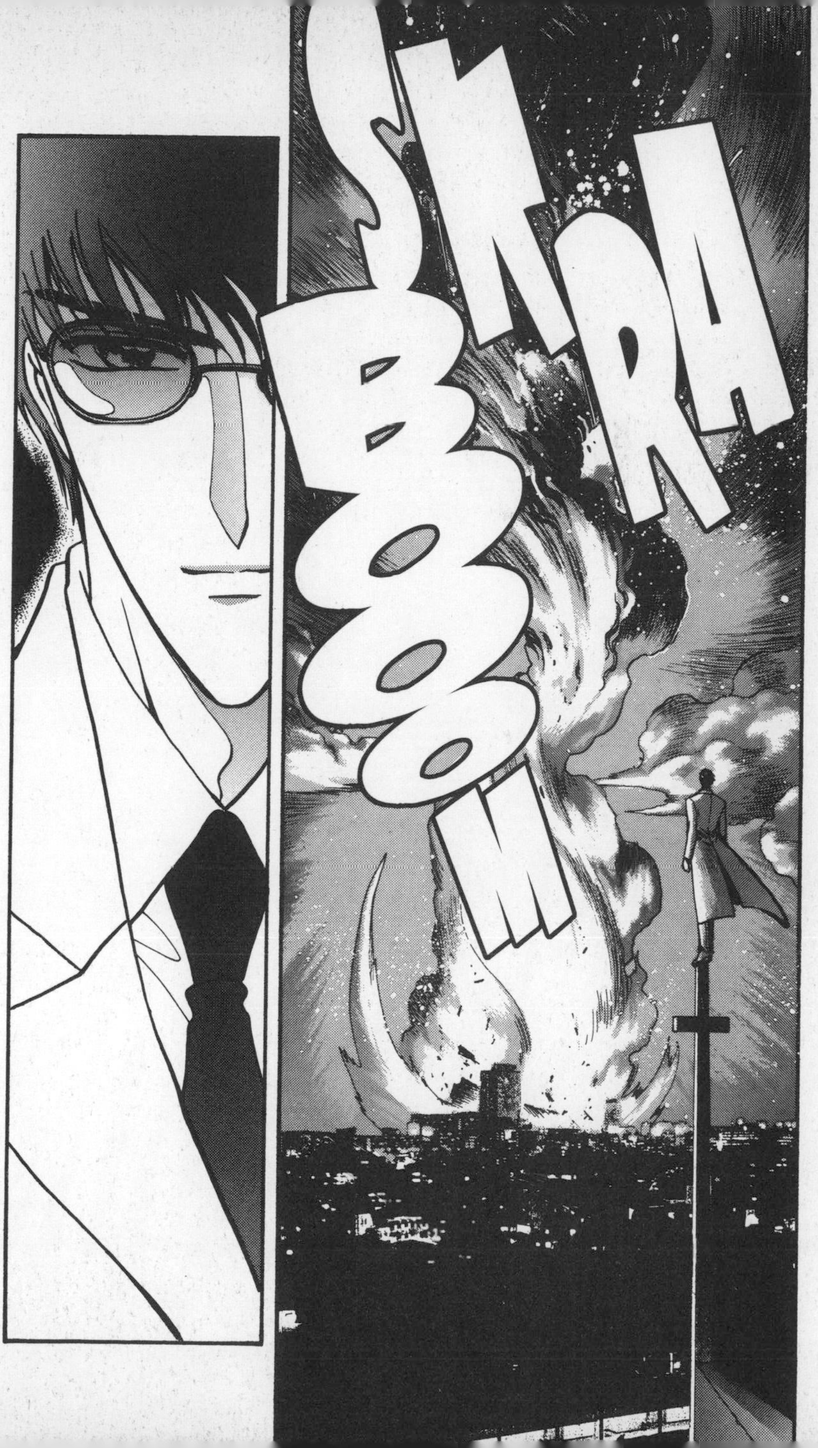
BOOOOM

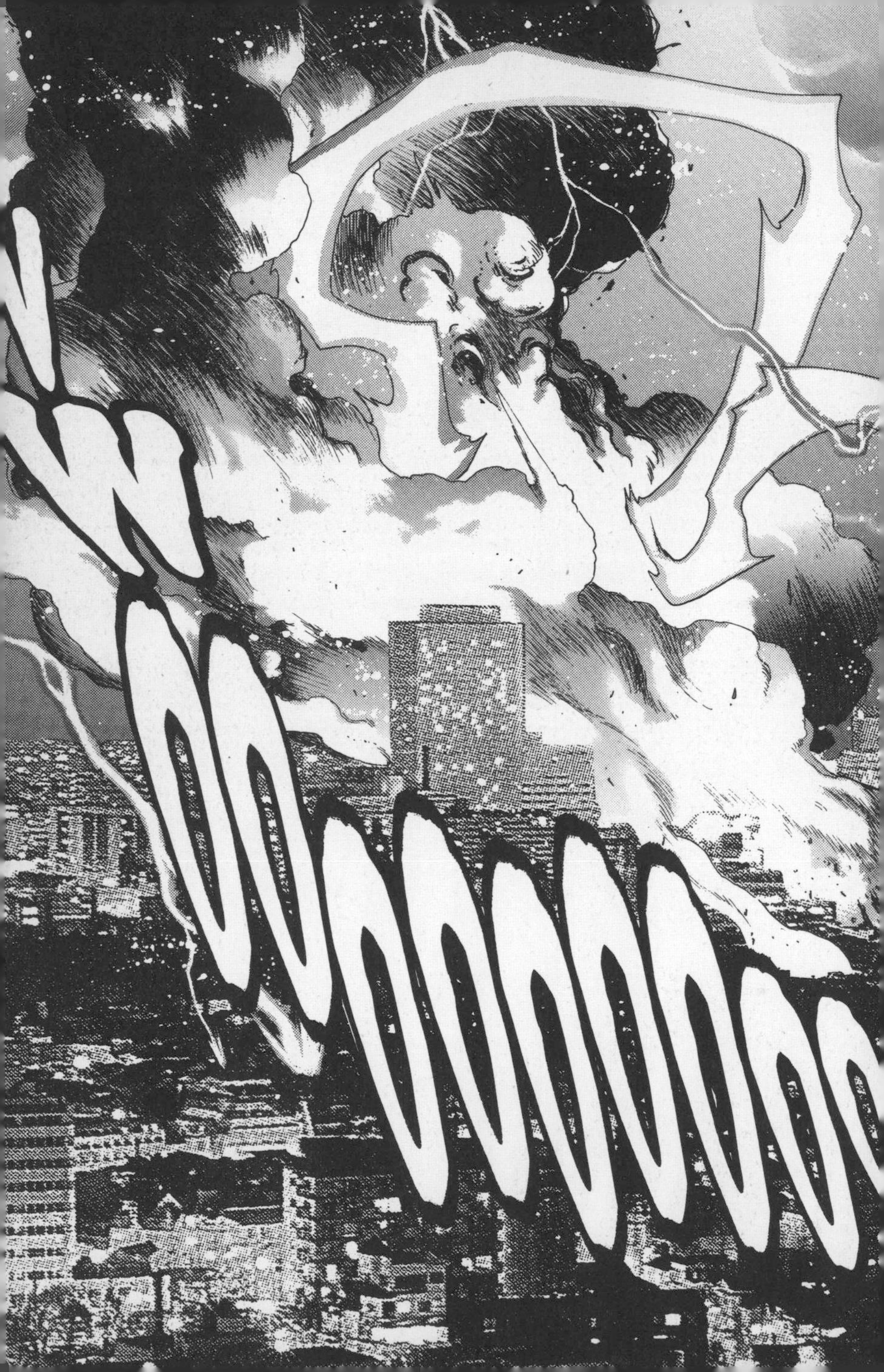
WOOOOOOOOOOOO

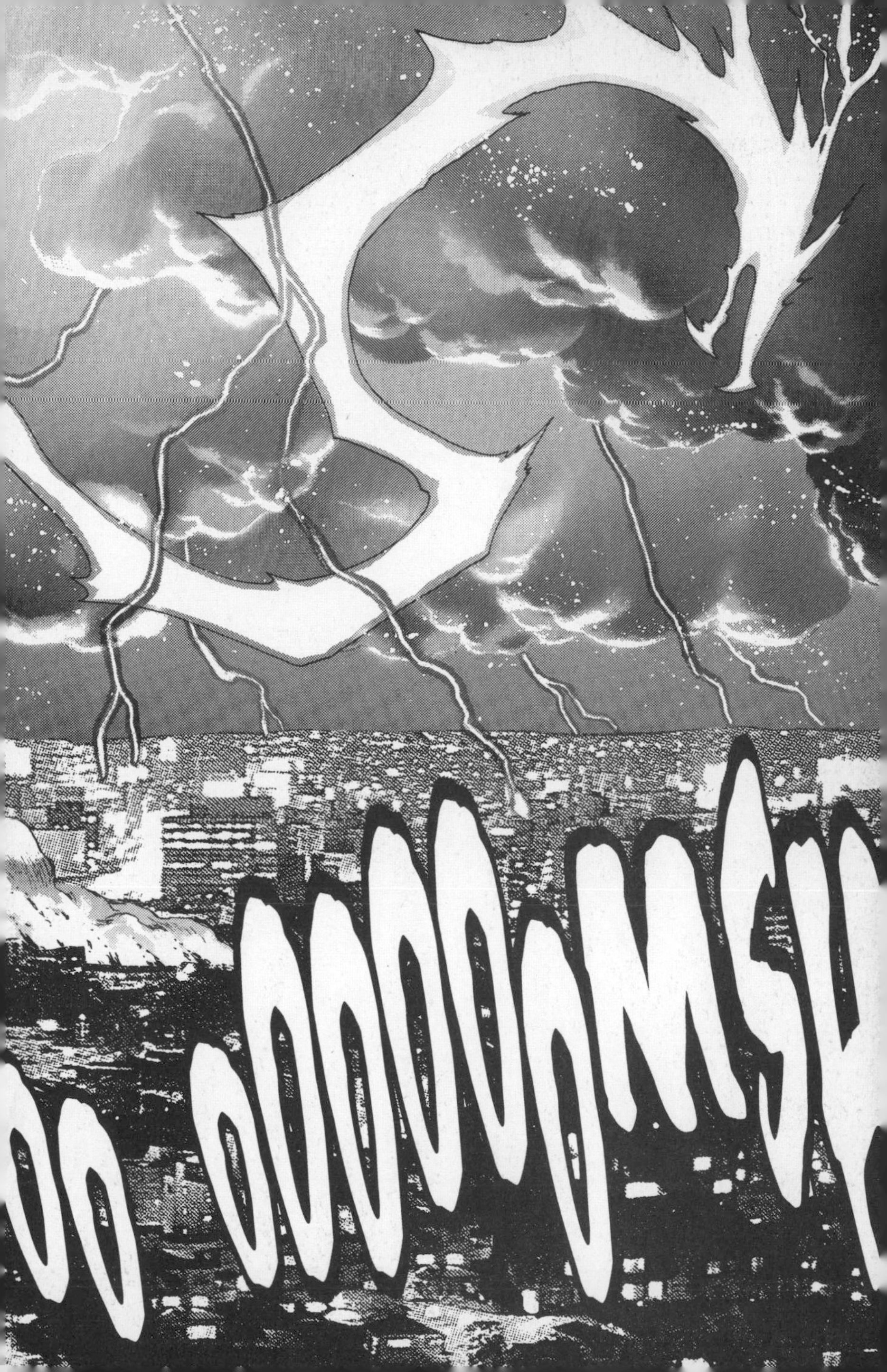

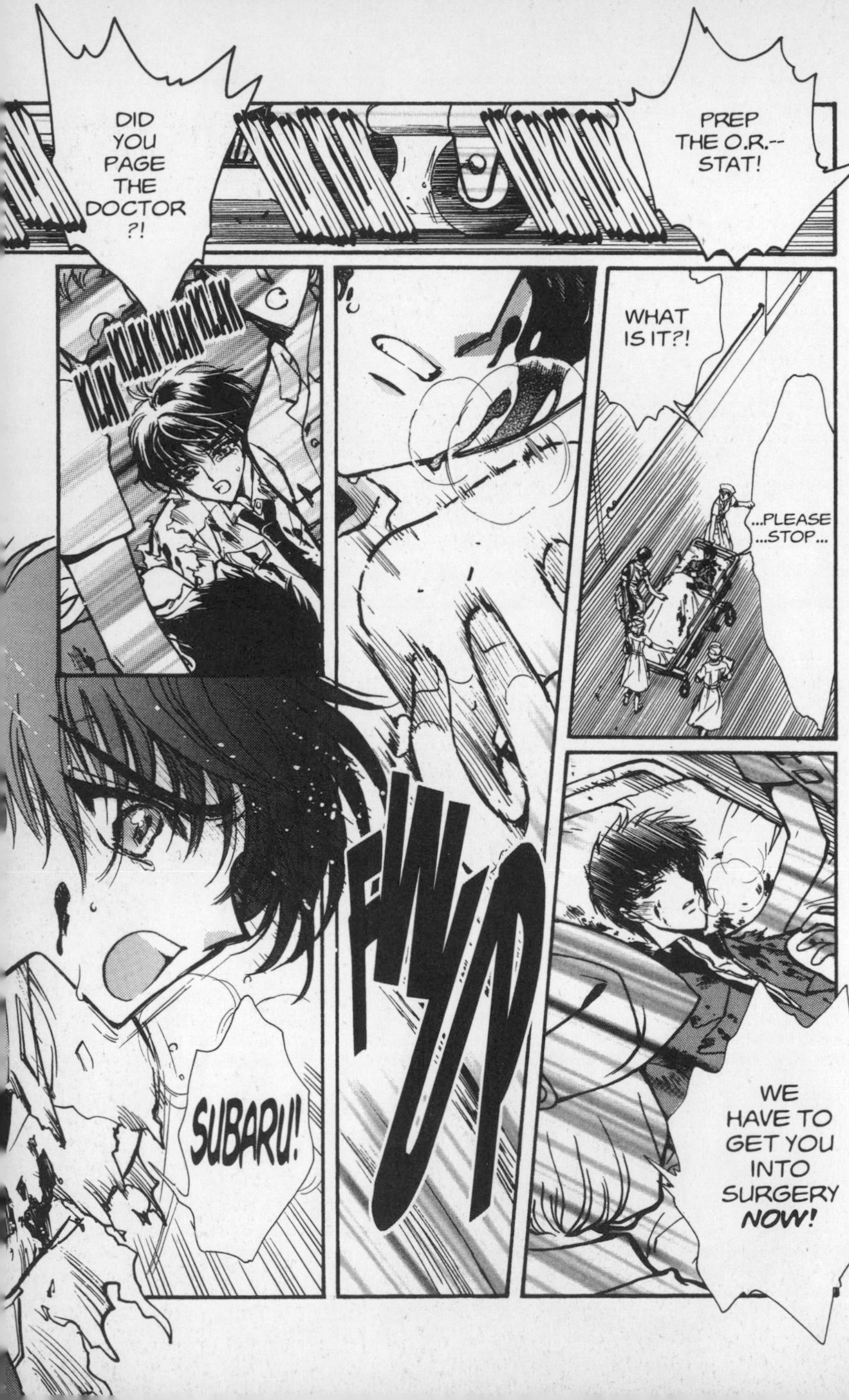
PREP THE O.R.-- STAT!
DID YOU PAGE THE DOCTOR ?!
WHAT IS IT?!
...PLEASE ...STOP...
KLAK KLAK KLAK KLAK
WE HAVE TO GET YOU INTO SURGERY *NOW!*
FWUP
SUBARU!

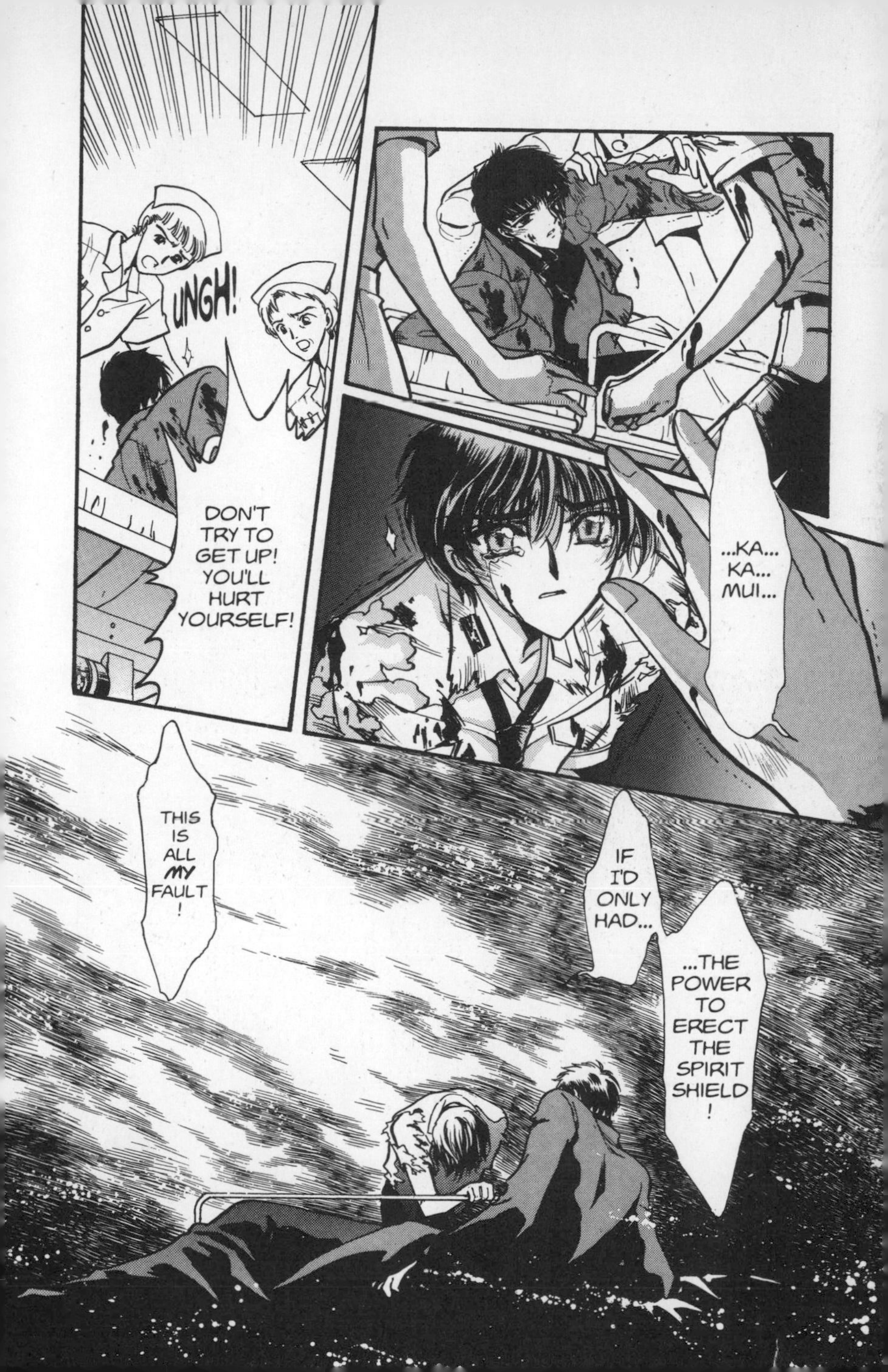
...KA... KA... MUI...
UNGH!
DON'T TRY TO GET UP! YOU'LL HURT YOURSELF!
IF I'D ONLY HAD...
...THE POWER TO ERECT THE SPIRIT SHIELD!
THIS IS ALL MY FAULT!

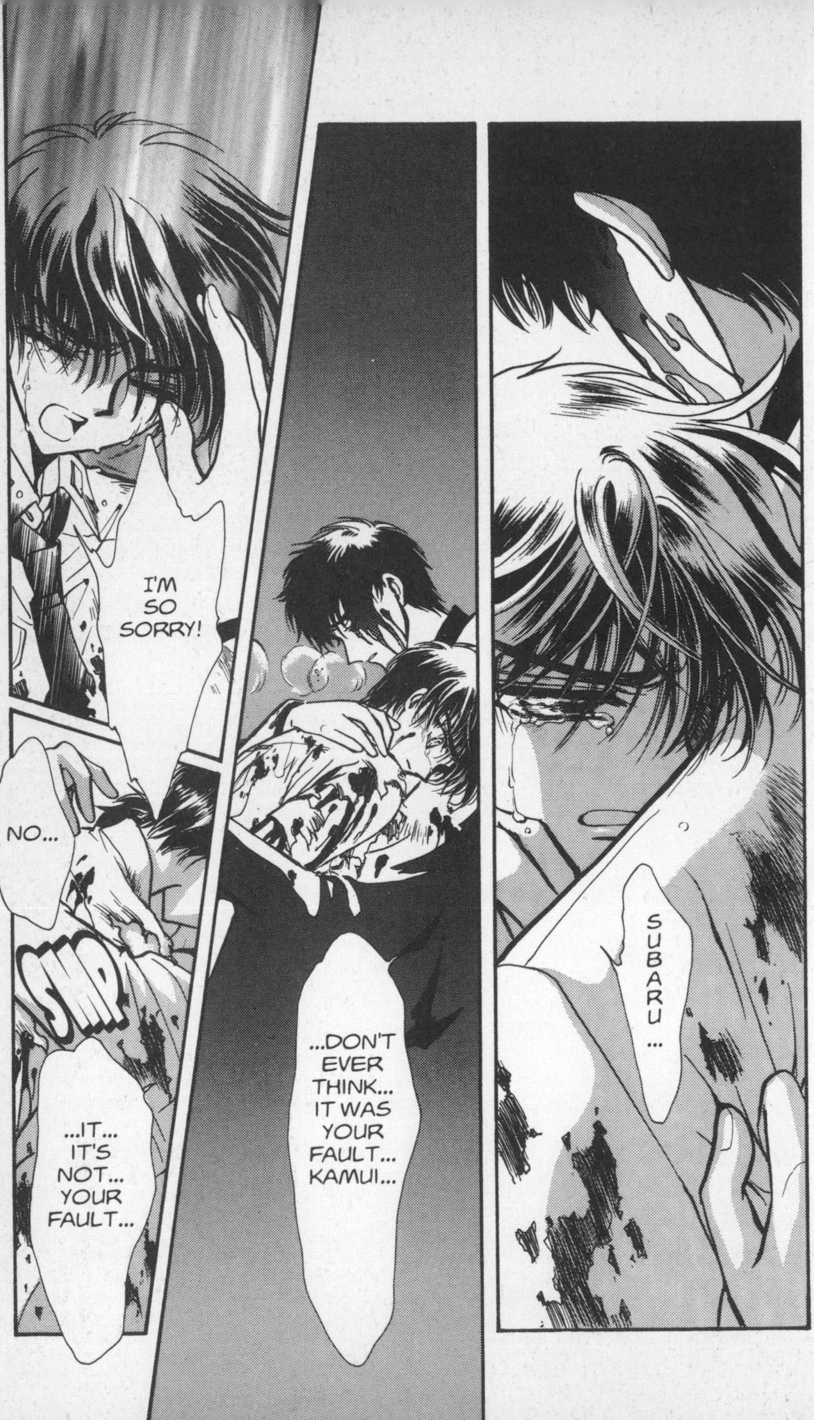
SUBARU ...
...DON'T EVER THINK... IT WAS YOUR FAULT... KAMUI...
I'M SO SORRY!
NO...
SMP
...IT... IT'S NOT... YOUR FAULT...

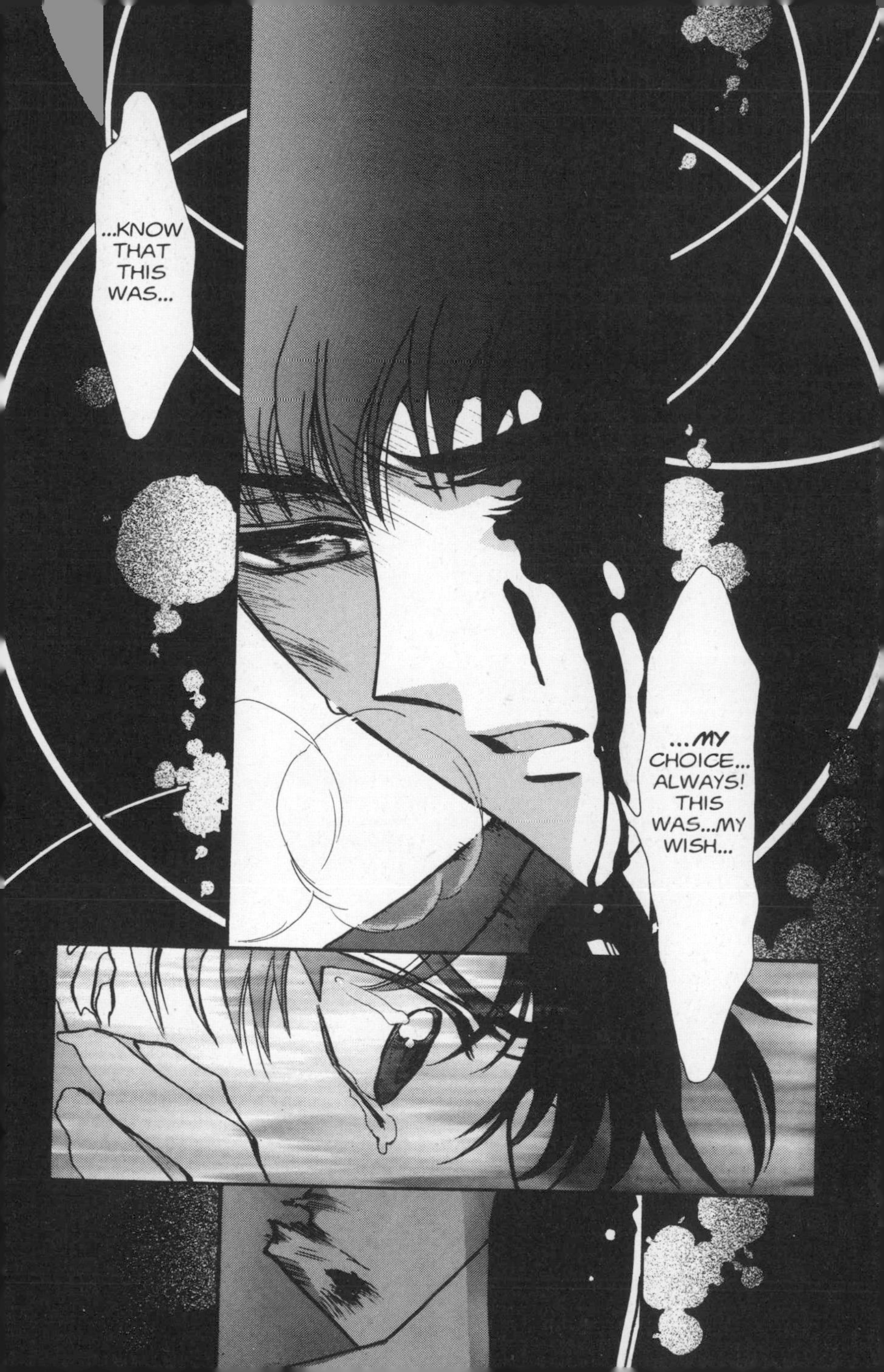
...KNOW THAT THIS WAS...
...MY CHOICE... ALWAYS! THIS WAS...MY WISH...

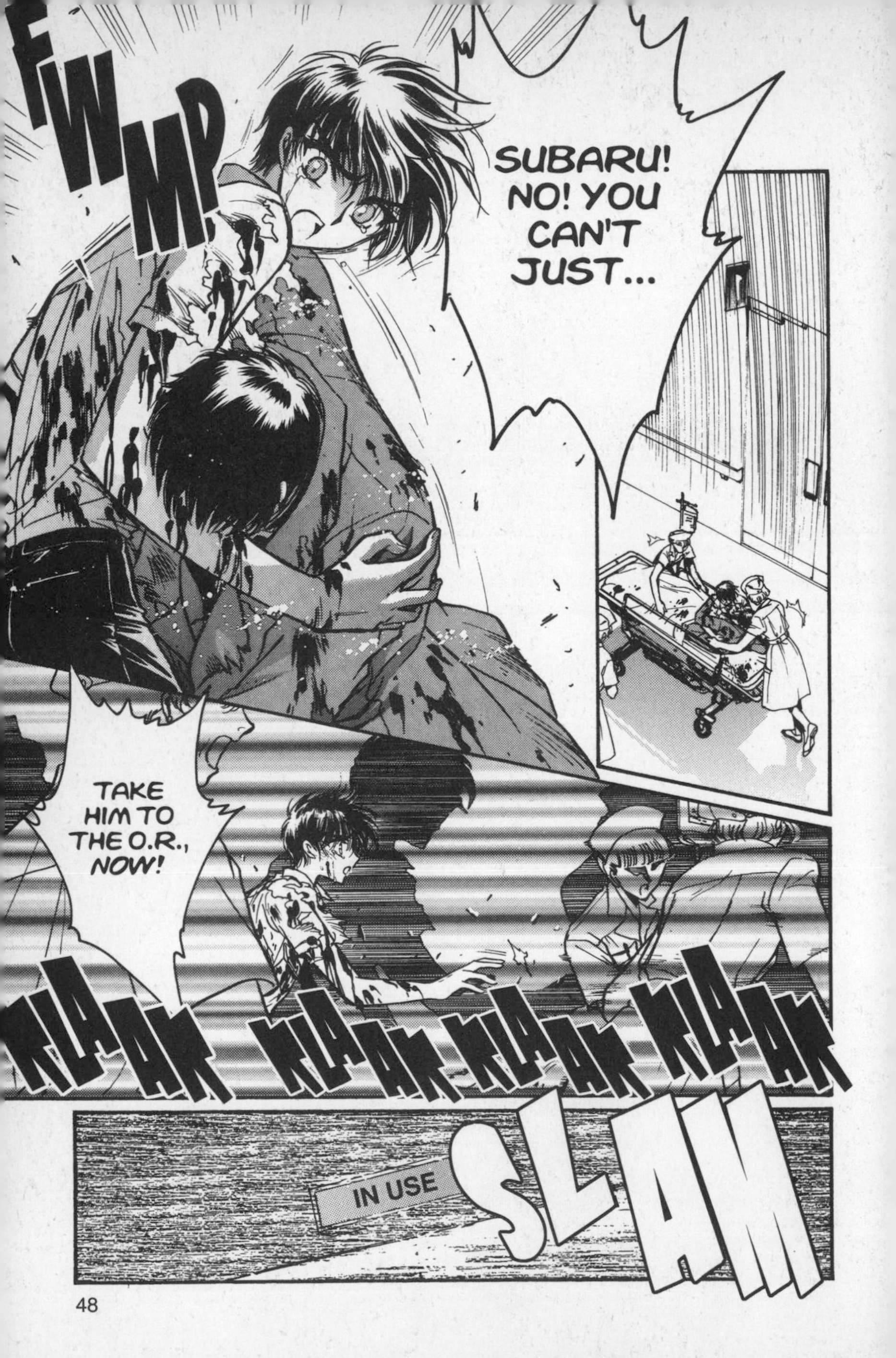
SUBARU! NO! YOU CAN'T JUST...
FWMP
TAKE HIM TO THE O.R., NOW!
KLAAK KLAAK KLAAK KLAAK
IN USE
SLAM

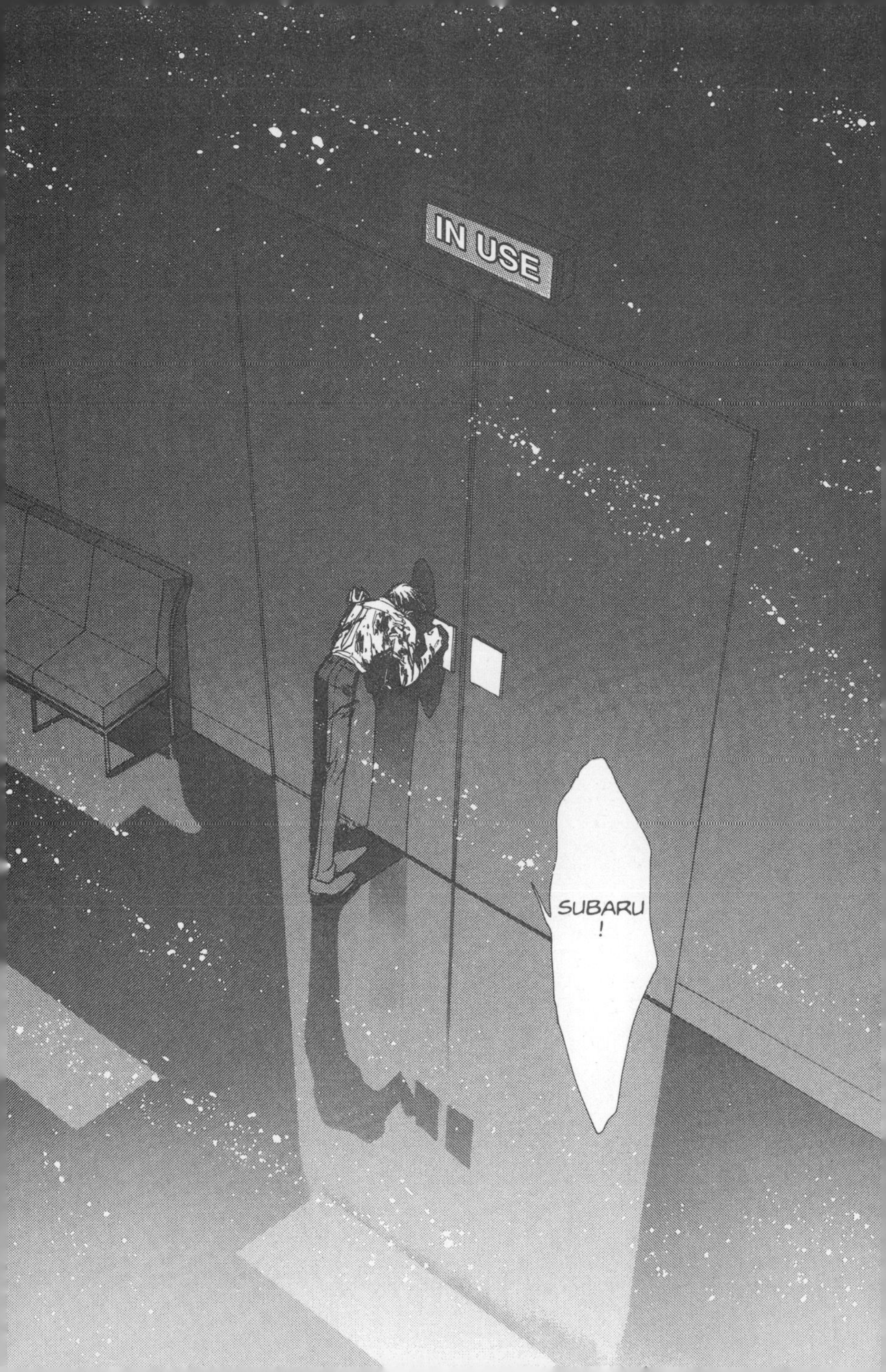
IN USE
SUBARU
!

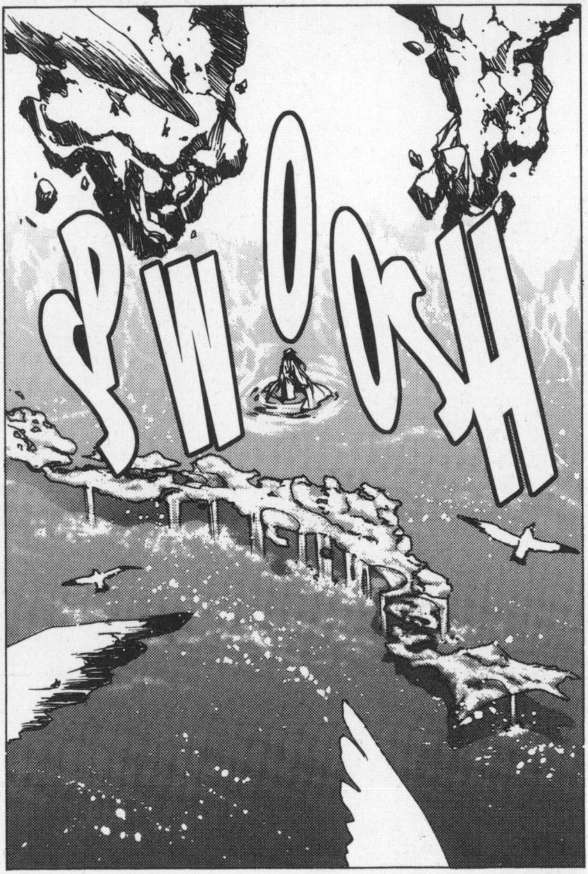
SWOOSH
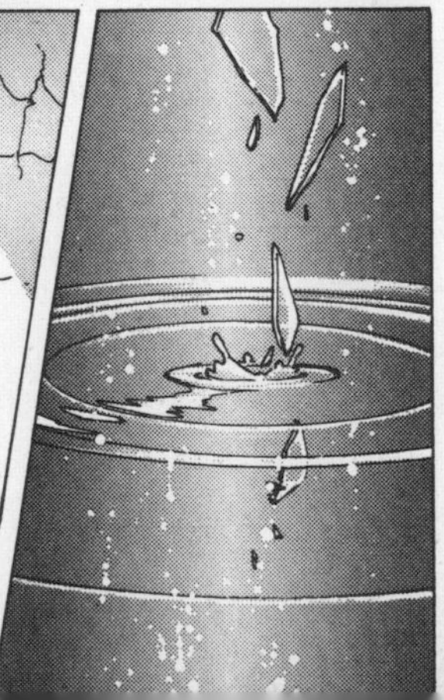
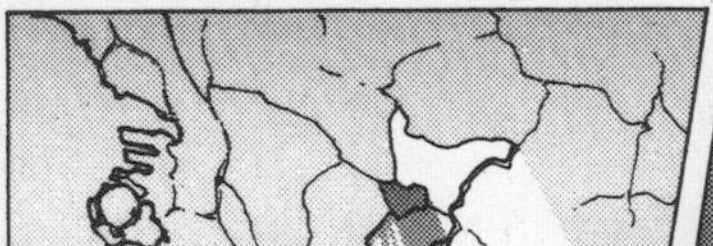
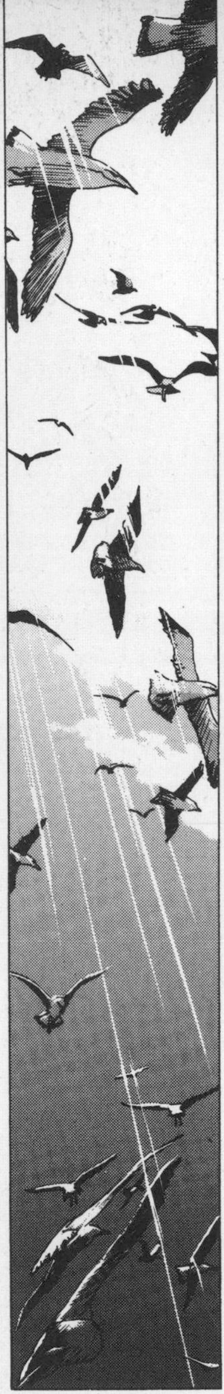

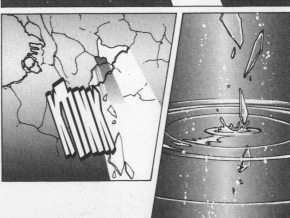

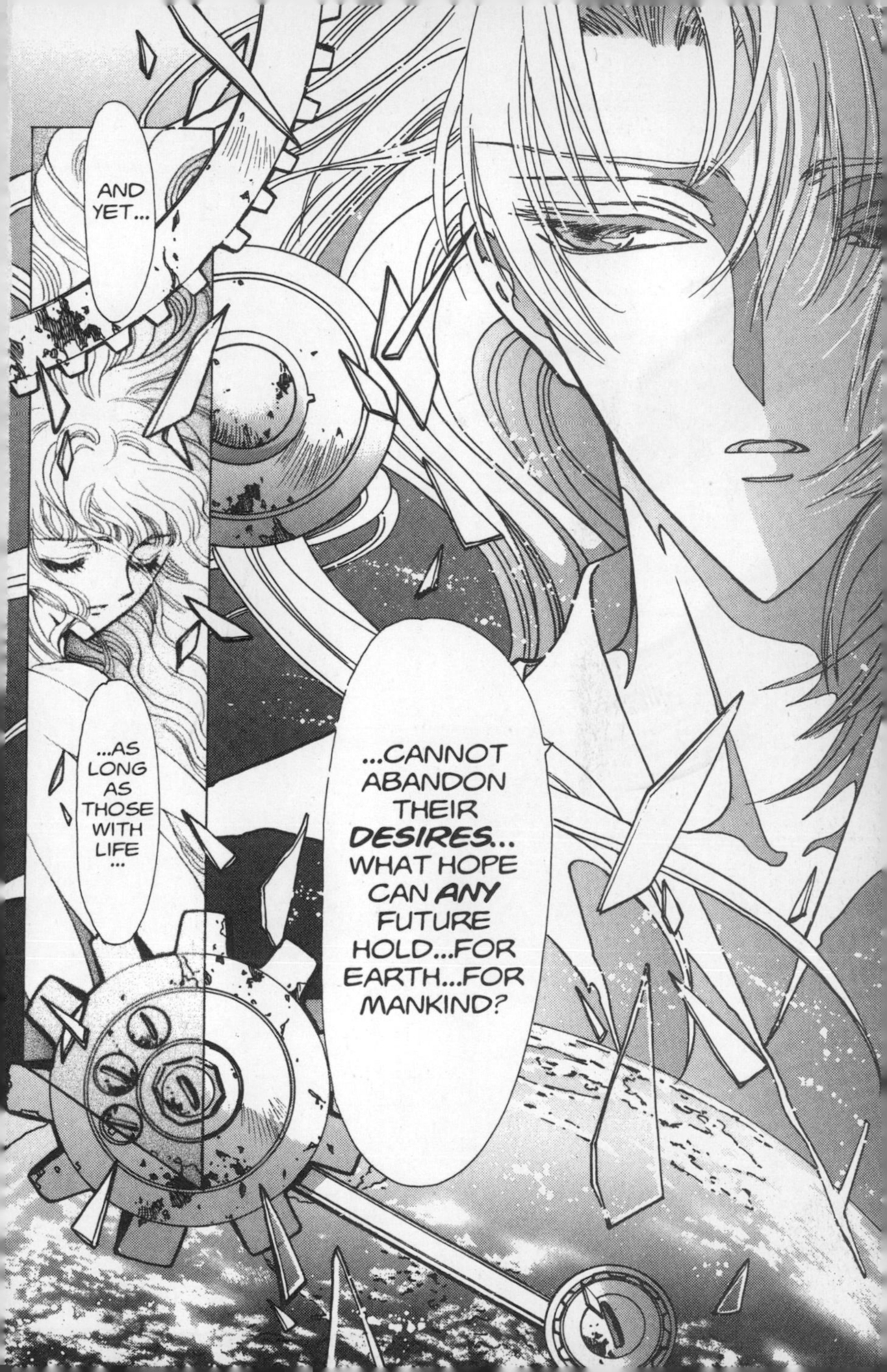
AND YET...
...AS LONG AS THOSE WITH LIFE ...
...CANNOT ABANDON THEIR DESIRES... WHAT HOPE CAN ANY FUTURE HOLD...FOR EARTH...FOR MANKIND?

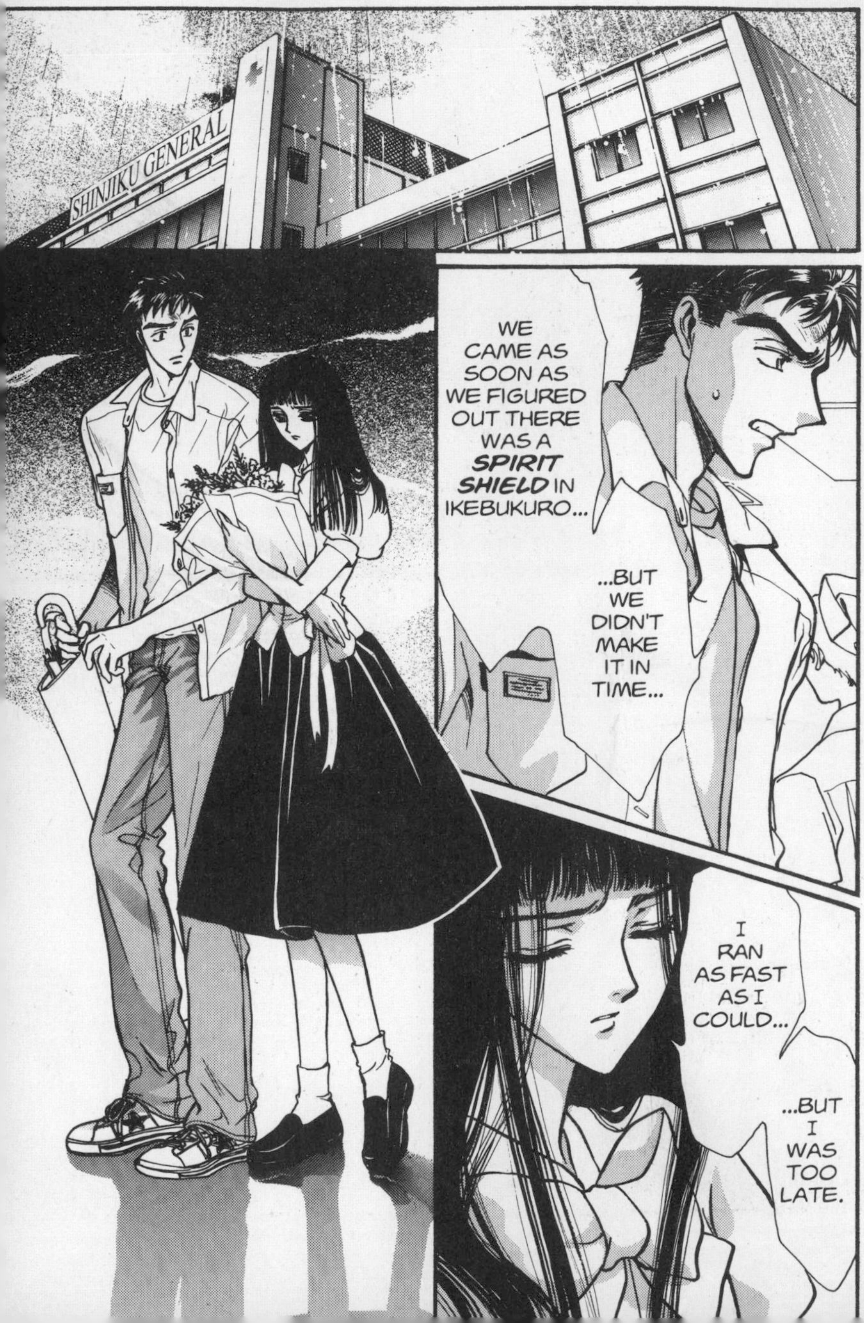
SHINJIKU GENERAL
WE CAME AS SOON AS WE FIGURED OUT THERE WAS A SPIRIT SHIELD IN IKEBUKURO...
...BUT WE DIDN'T MAKE IT IN TIME...
I RAN AS FAST AS I COULD...
...BUT I WAS TOO LATE.

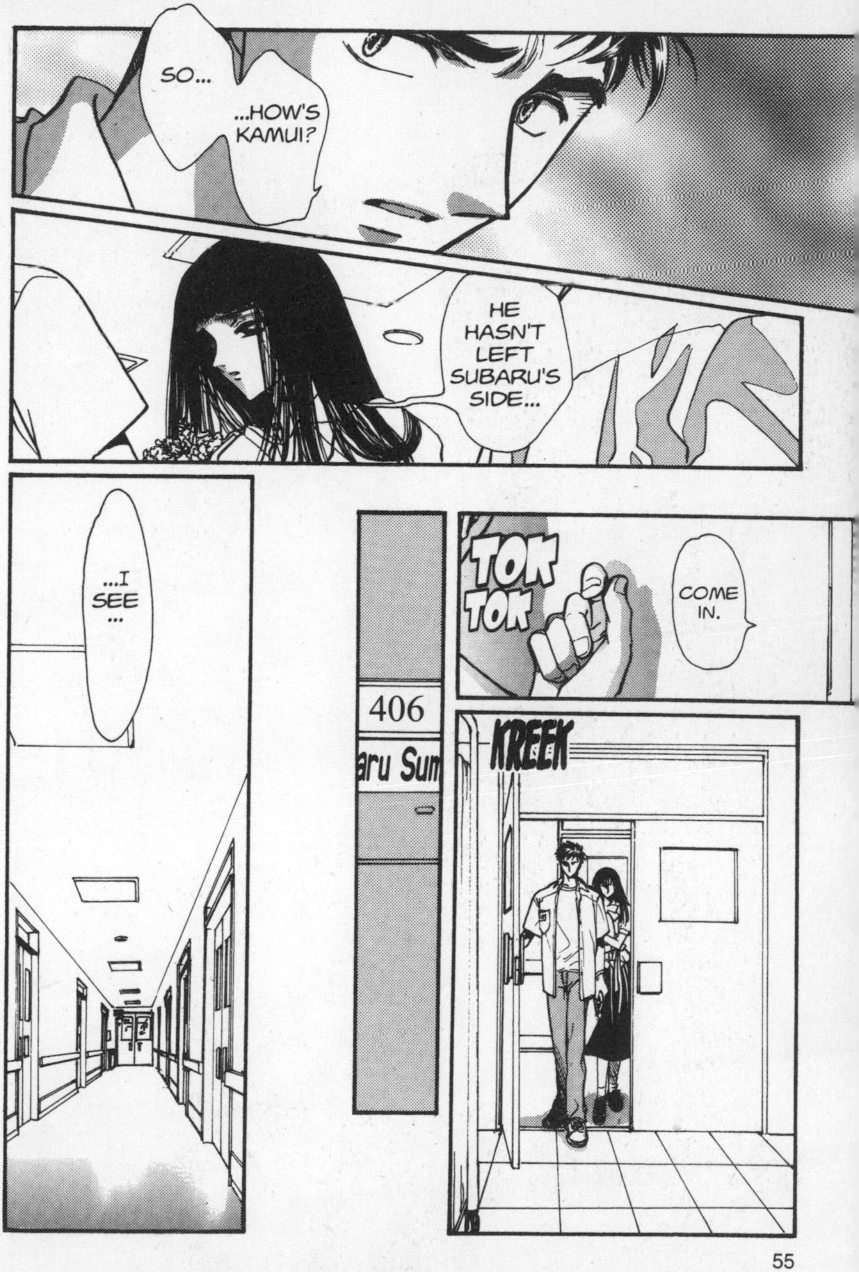
SO... ...HOW'S KAMUI?
HE HASN'T LEFT SUBARU'S SIDE...
...I SEE ...
406
aru Sum
TOK TOK
COME IN.
KREEK

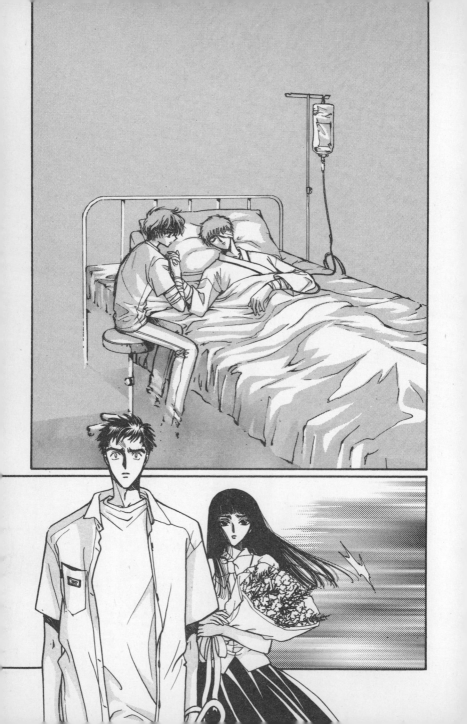

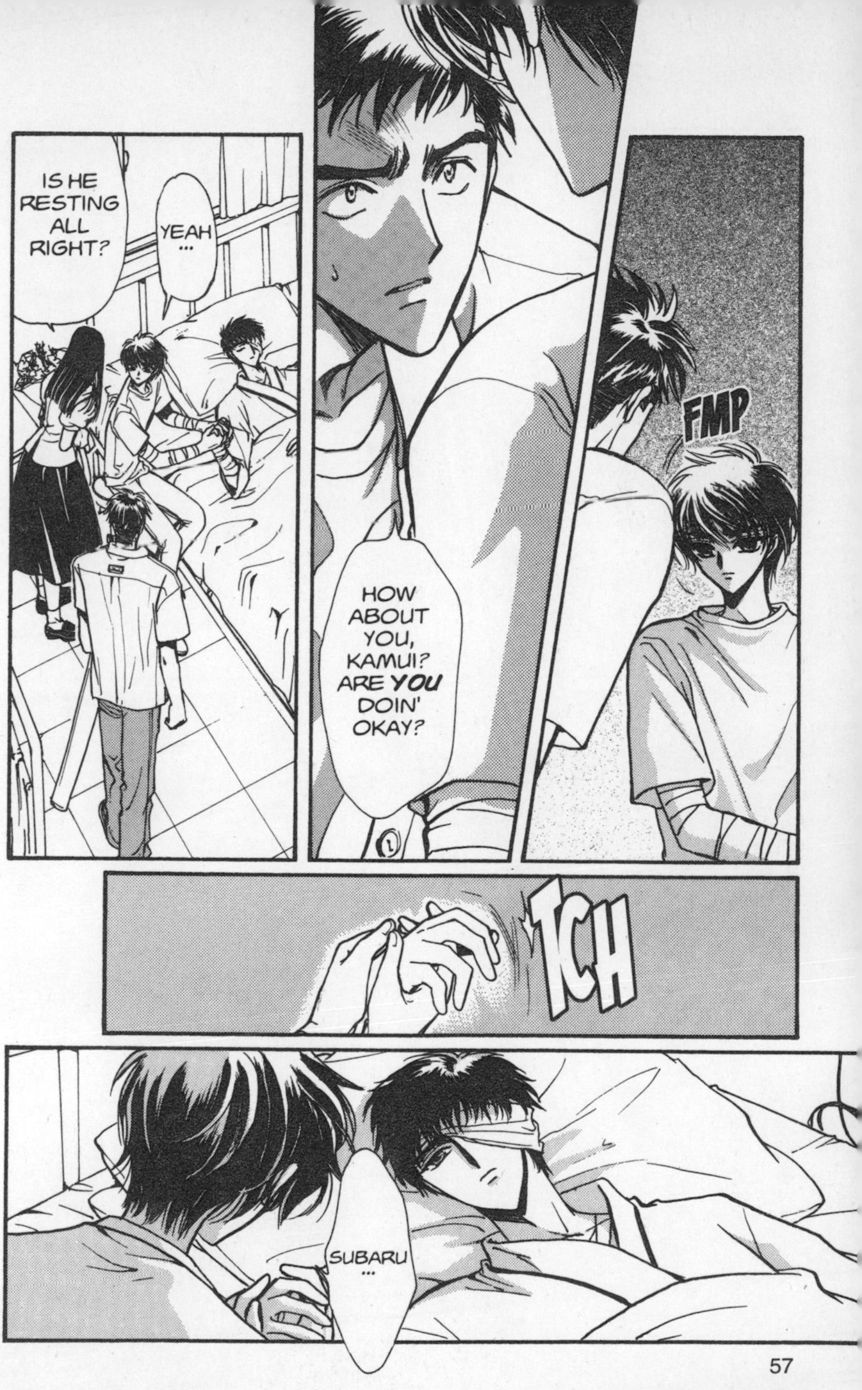
IS HE RESTING ALL RIGHT?
YEAH ...
HOW ABOUT YOU, KAMUI? ARE **YOU** DOIN' OKAY?
FMP
TCH
SUBARU ...

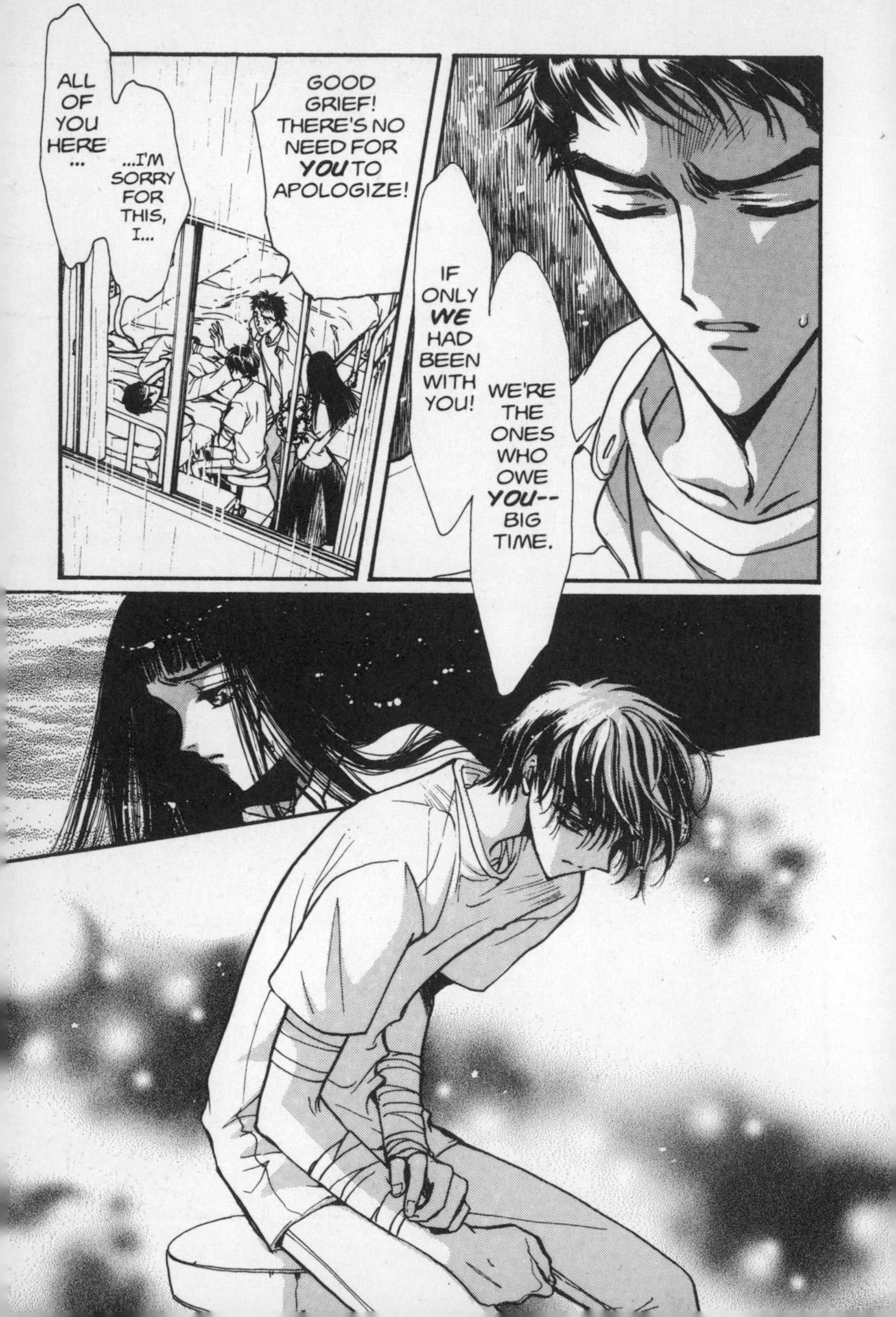
ALL OF YOU HERE ...
...I'M SORRY FOR THIS, I...
GOOD GRIEF! THERE'S NO NEED FOR YOU TO APOLOGIZE!
IF ONLY WE HAD BEEN WITH YOU!
WE'RE THE ONES WHO OWE YOU-- BIG TIME.

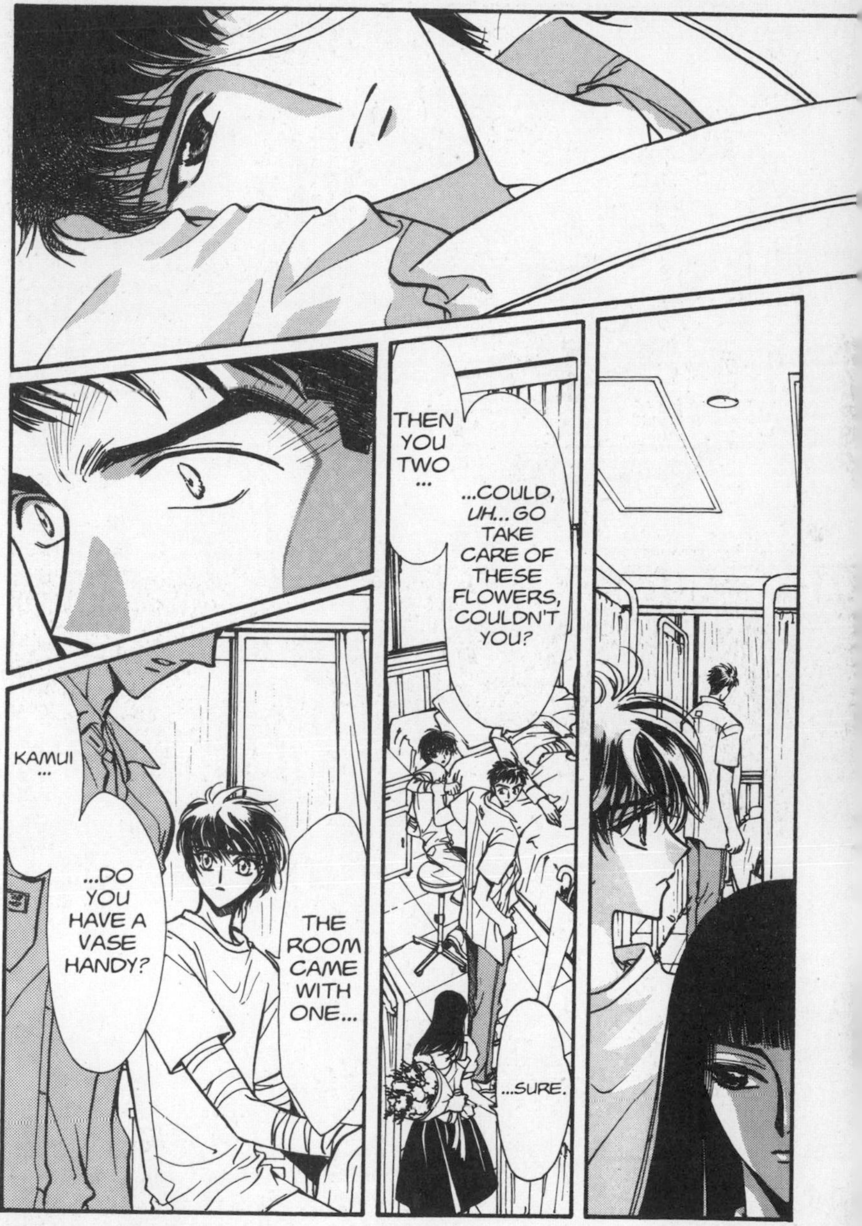
THEN YOU TWO...
...COULD, UH...GO TAKE CARE OF THESE FLOWERS, COULDN'T YOU?
...SURE.
KAMUI...
...DO YOU HAVE A VASE HANDY?
THE ROOM CAME WITH ONE...

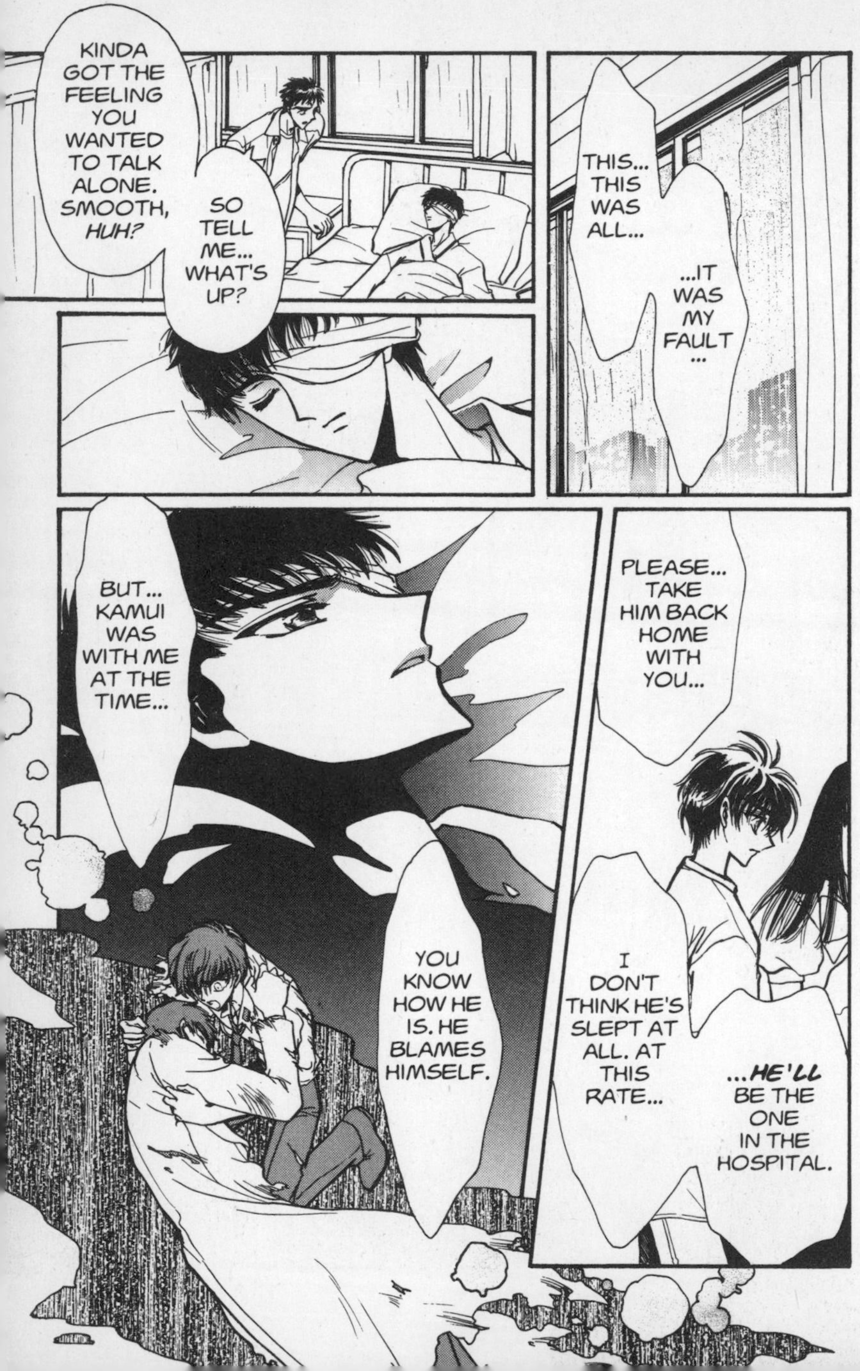
KINDA GOT THE FEELING YOU WANTED TO TALK ALONE. SMOOTH, *HUH?*
SO TELL ME... WHAT'S UP?
THIS... THIS WAS ALL...
...IT WAS MY FAULT ...
BUT... KAMUI WAS WITH ME AT THE TIME...
YOU KNOW HOW HE IS. HE BLAMES HIMSELF.
PLEASE... TAKE HIM BACK HOME WITH YOU...
I DON'T THINK HE'S SLEPT AT ALL. AT THIS RATE...
...***HE'LL*** BE THE ONE IN THE HOSPITAL.

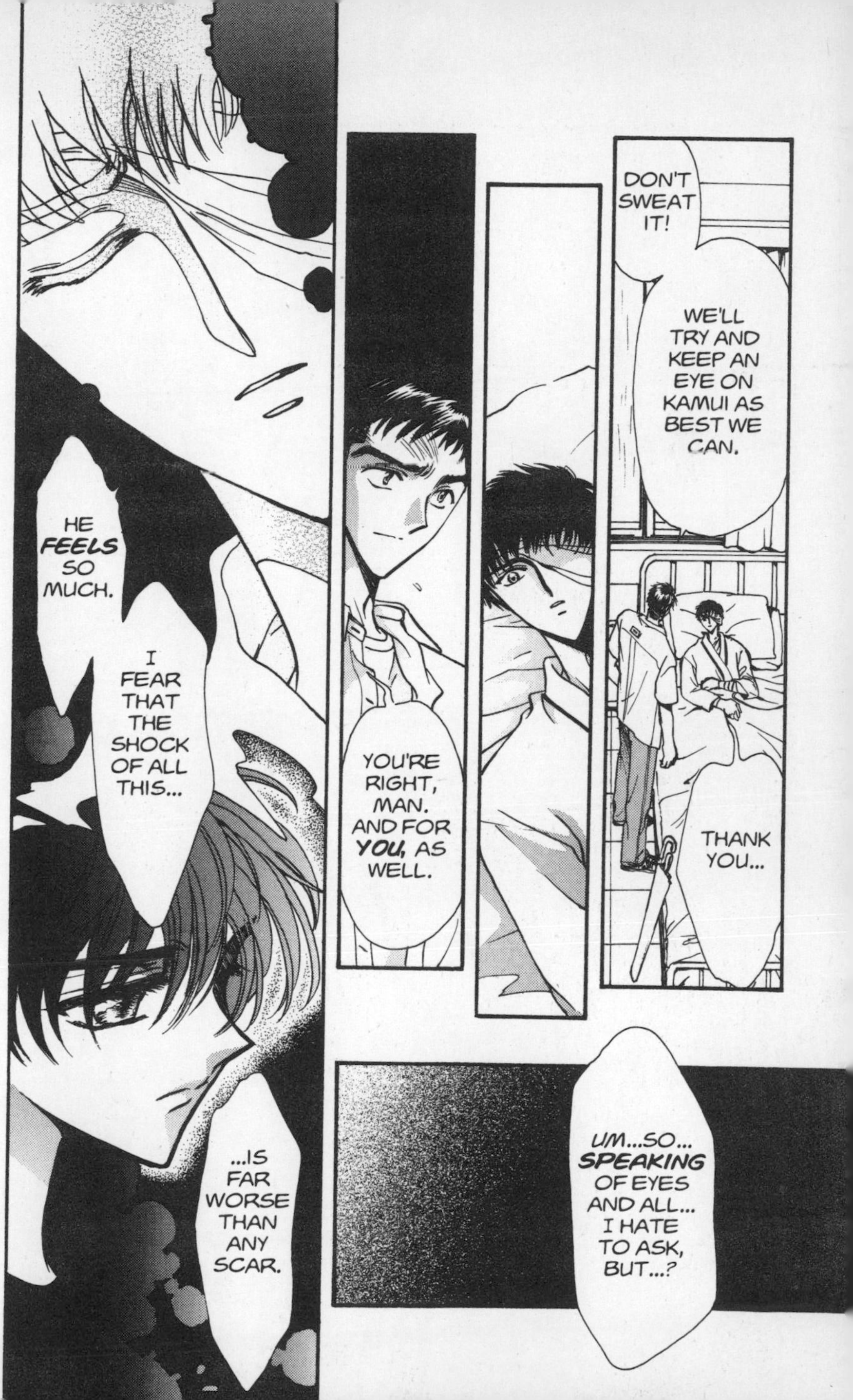
DON'T SWEAT IT!
WE'LL TRY AND KEEP AN EYE ON KAMUI AS BEST WE CAN.
THANK YOU...
YOU'RE RIGHT, MAN. AND FOR **YOU,** AS WELL.
UM...SO... **SPEAKING** OF EYES AND ALL... I HATE TO ASK, BUT...?
HE **FEELS** SO MUCH.
I FEAR THAT THE SHOCK OF ALL THIS...
...IS FAR WORSE THAN ANY SCAR.

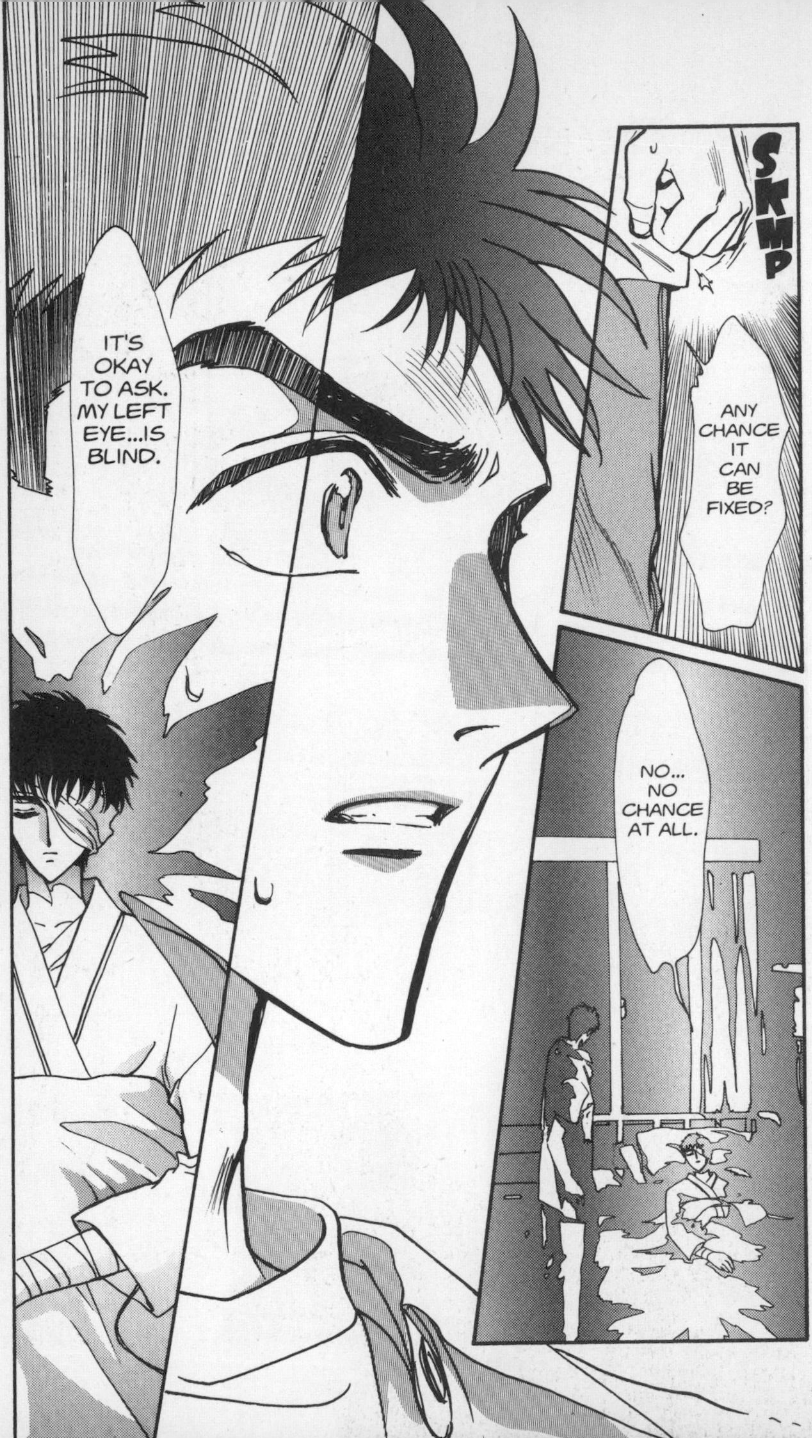
IT'S OKAY TO ASK. MY LEFT EYE...IS BLIND.
SKMP
ANY CHANCE IT CAN BE FIXED?
NO... NO CHANCE AT ALL.

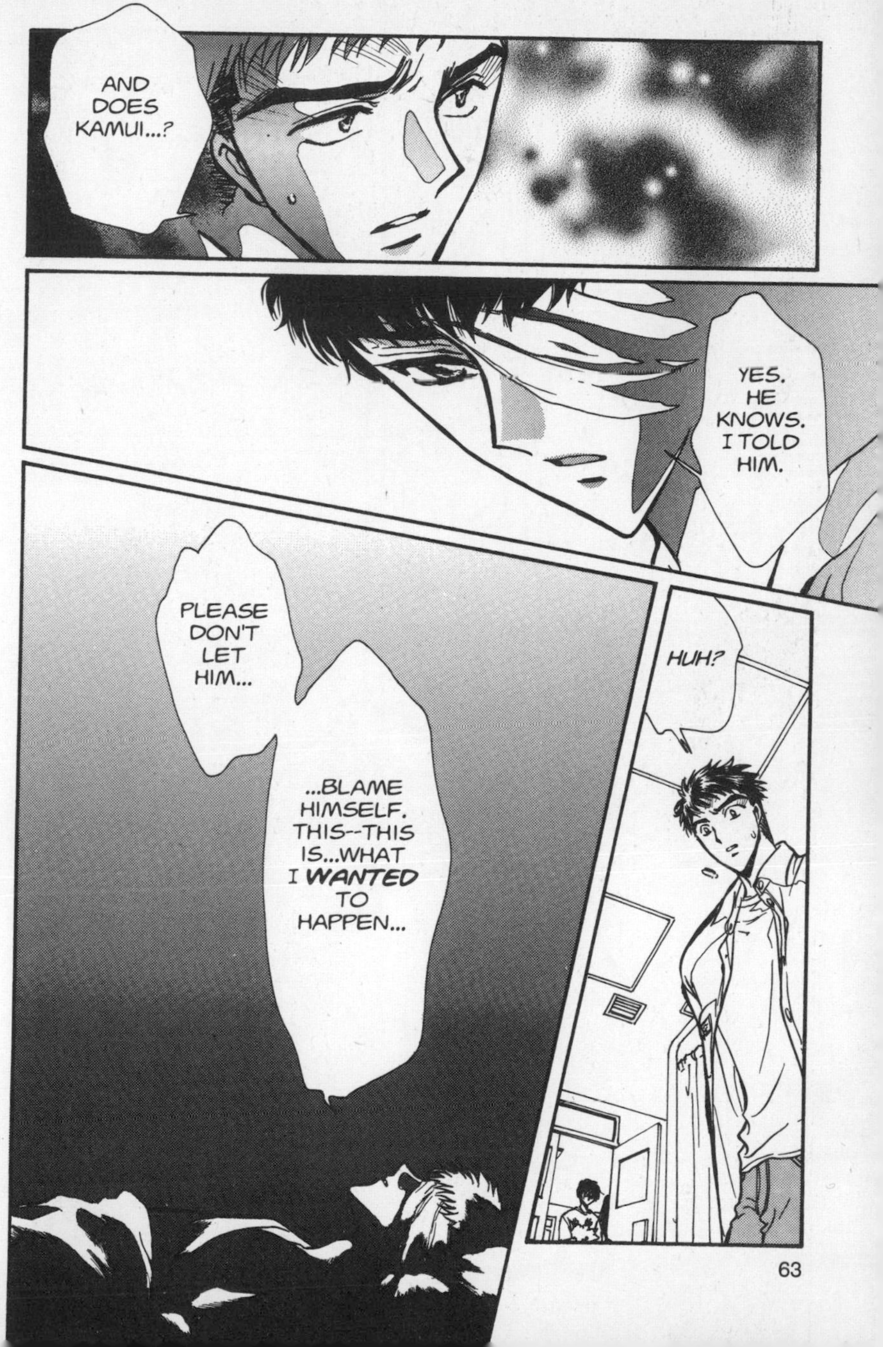
AND DOES KAMUI...?
YES. HE KNOWS. I TOLD HIM.
HUH?
PLEASE DON'T LET HIM...
...BLAME HIMSELF. THIS--THIS IS...WHAT I *WANTED* TO HAPPEN...

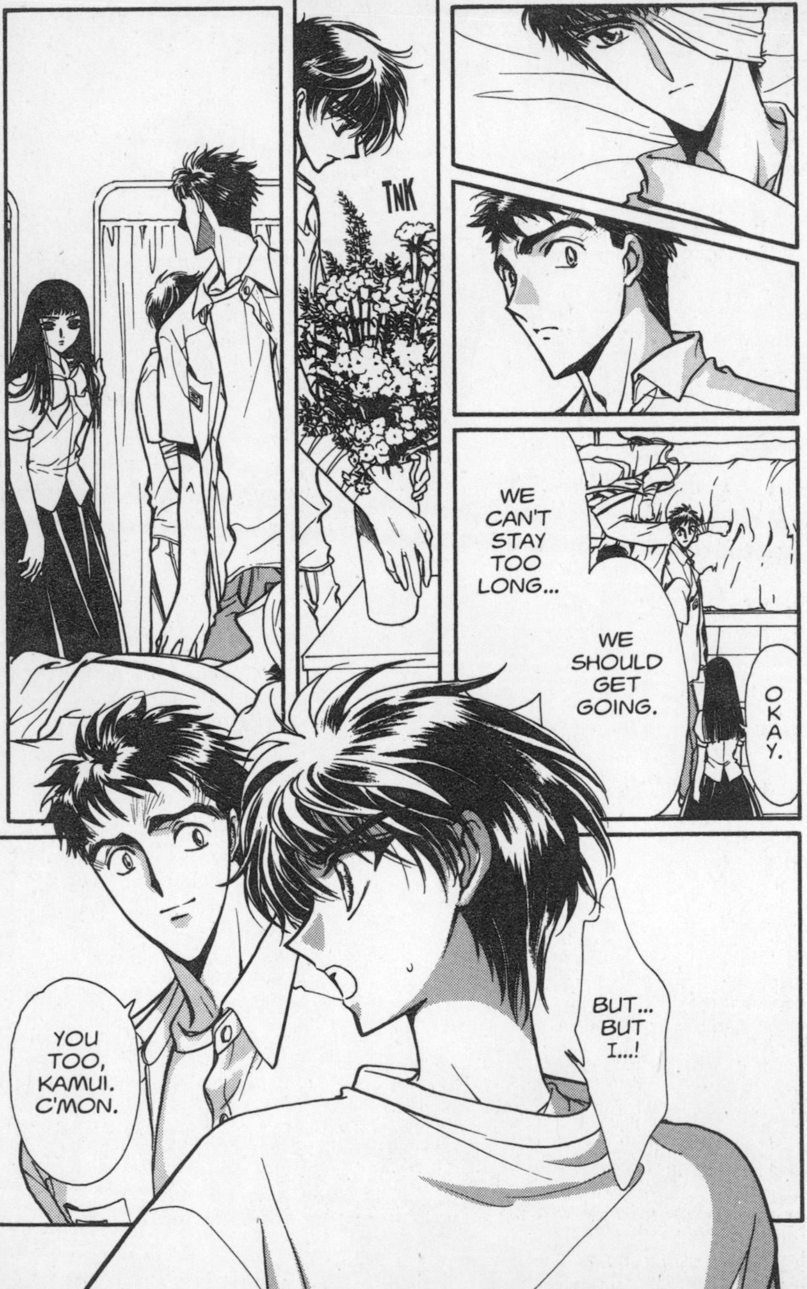
WE CAN'T STAY TOO LONG...
WE SHOULD GET GOING.
OKAY.
TNK
YOU TOO, KAMUI. C'MON.
BUT... BUT I...!

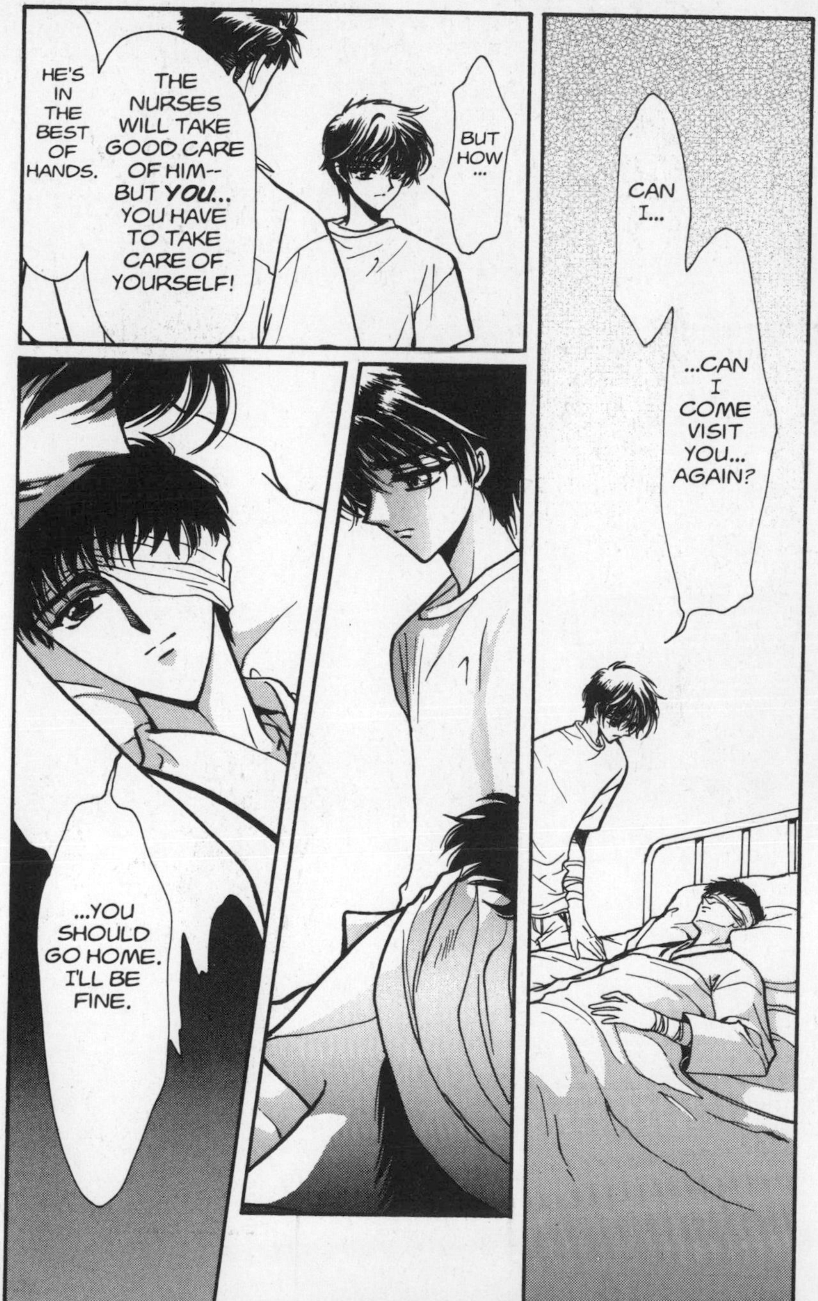
HE'S IN THE BEST OF HANDS.
THE NURSES WILL TAKE GOOD CARE OF HIM-- BUT *YOU*... YOU HAVE TO TAKE CARE OF YOURSELF!
BUT HOW ...
...YOU SHOULD GO HOME. I'LL BE FINE.
CAN I...
...CAN I COME VISIT YOU... AGAIN?

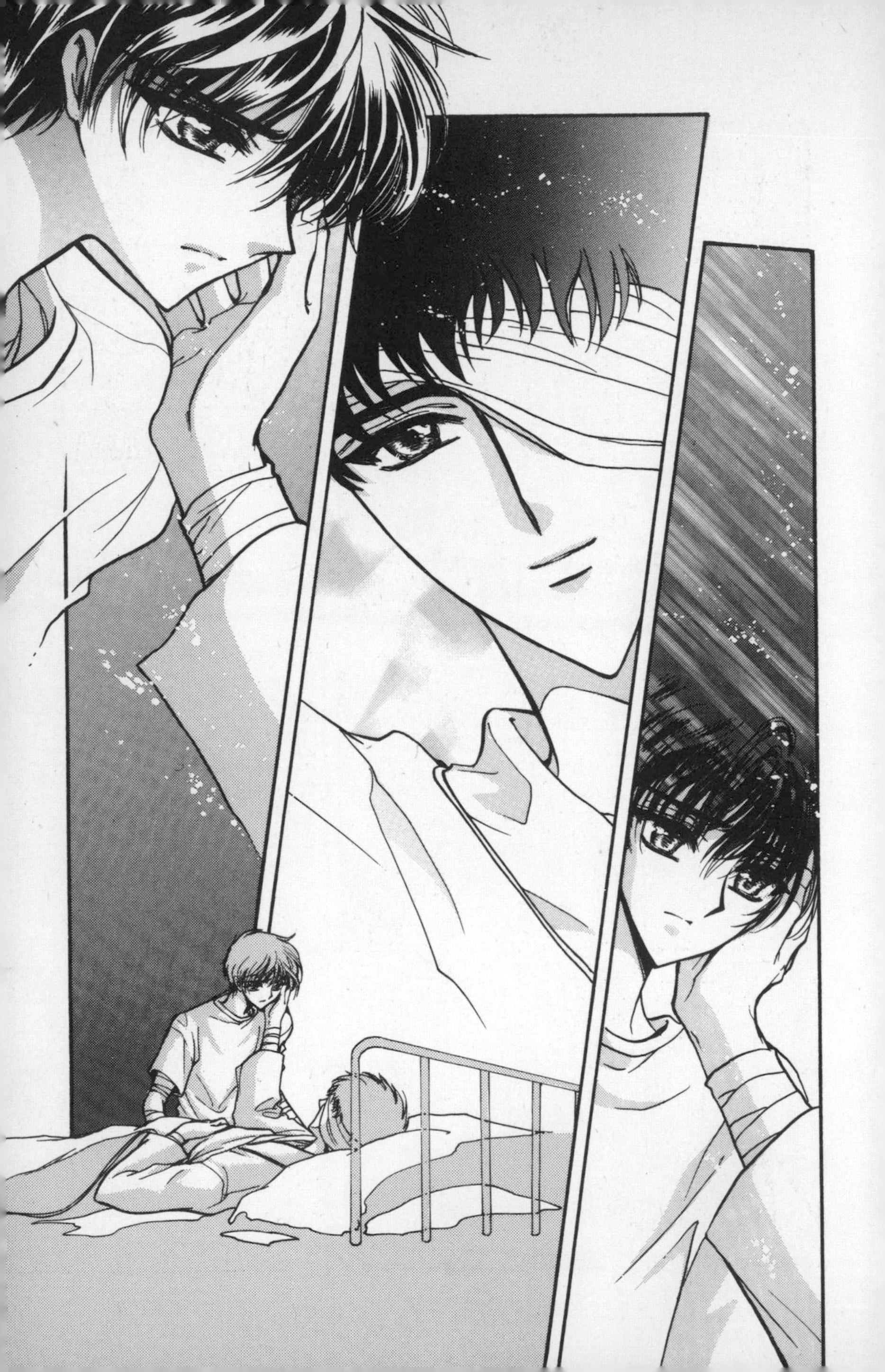

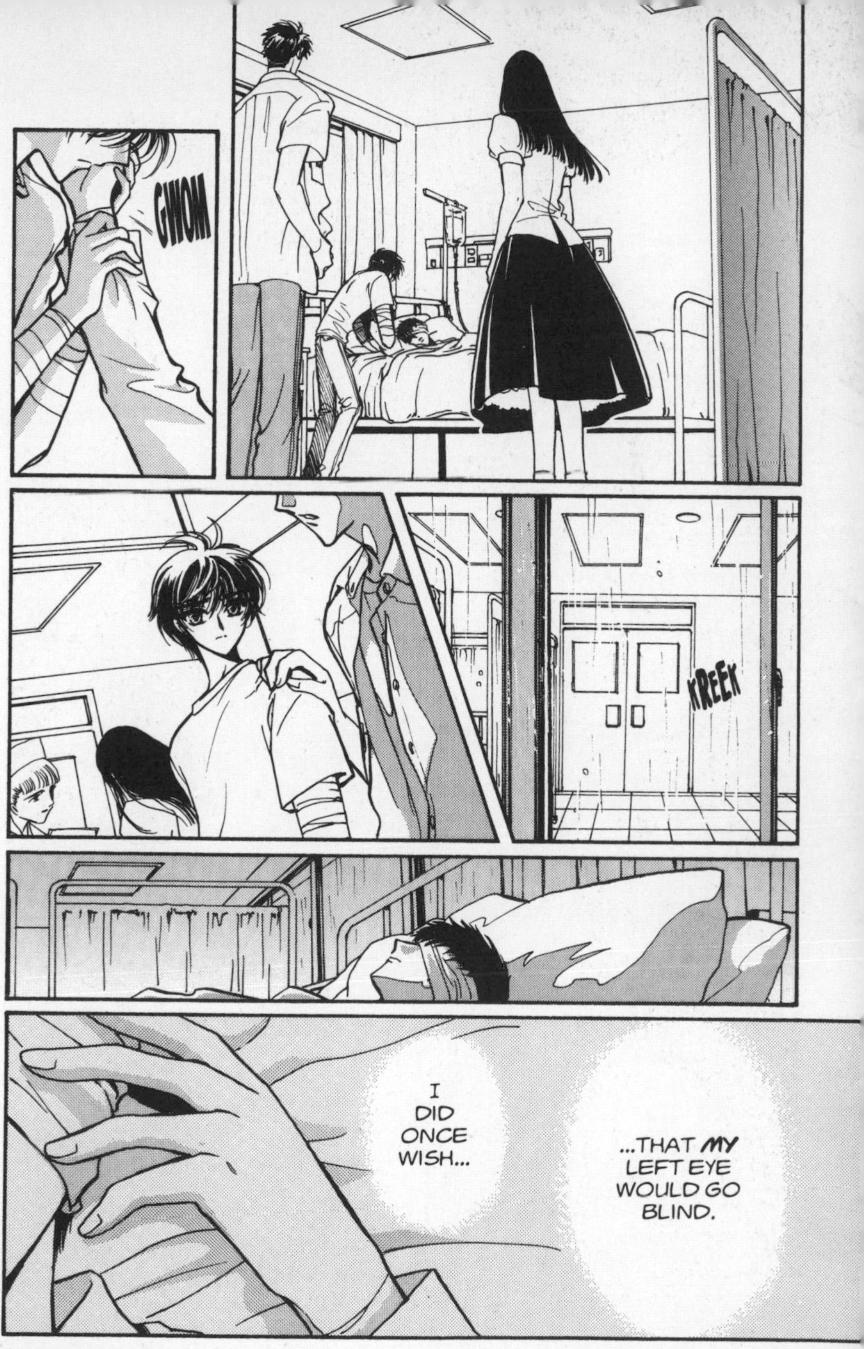
GWOM
KREEK
I DID ONCE WISH...
...THAT *MY* LEFT EYE WOULD GO BLIND.

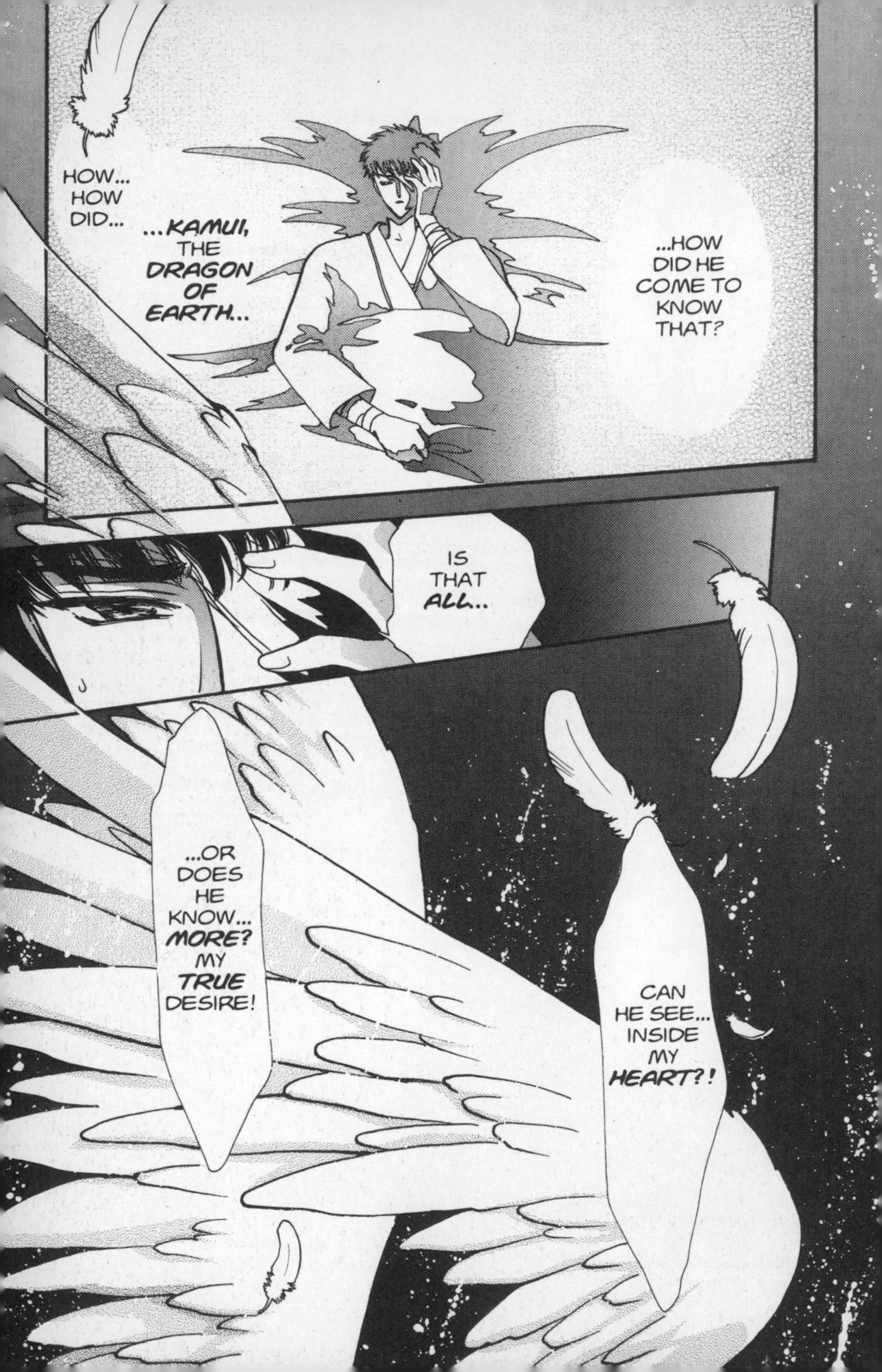

HOW... HOW DID...
...KAMUI, THE DRAGON OF EARTH...
...HOW DID HE COME TO KNOW THAT?
IS THAT ALL...
...OR DOES HE KNOW... MORE? MY TRUE DESIRE!
CAN HE SEE... INSIDE MY HEART?!

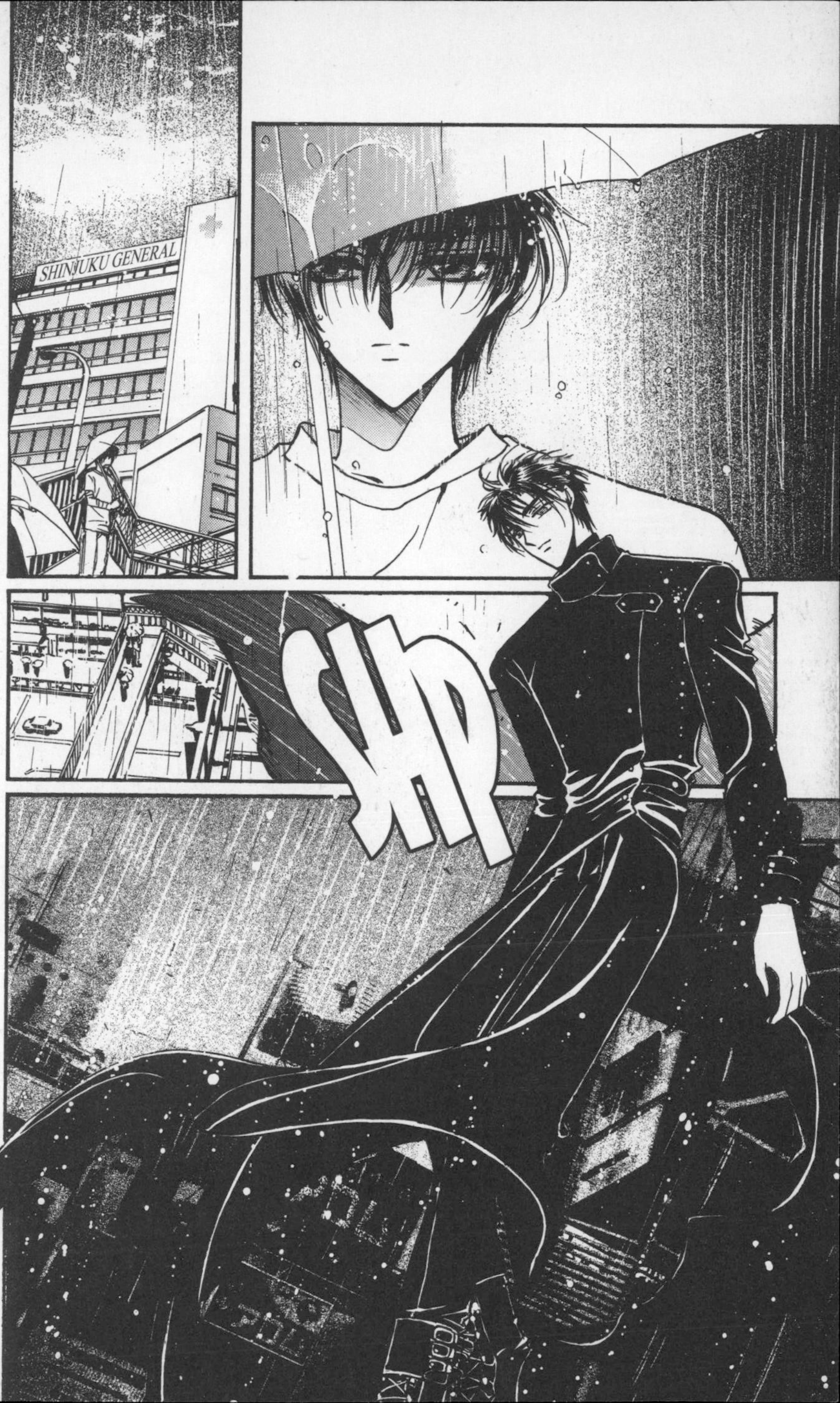
SHINJUKU GENERAL
SHP

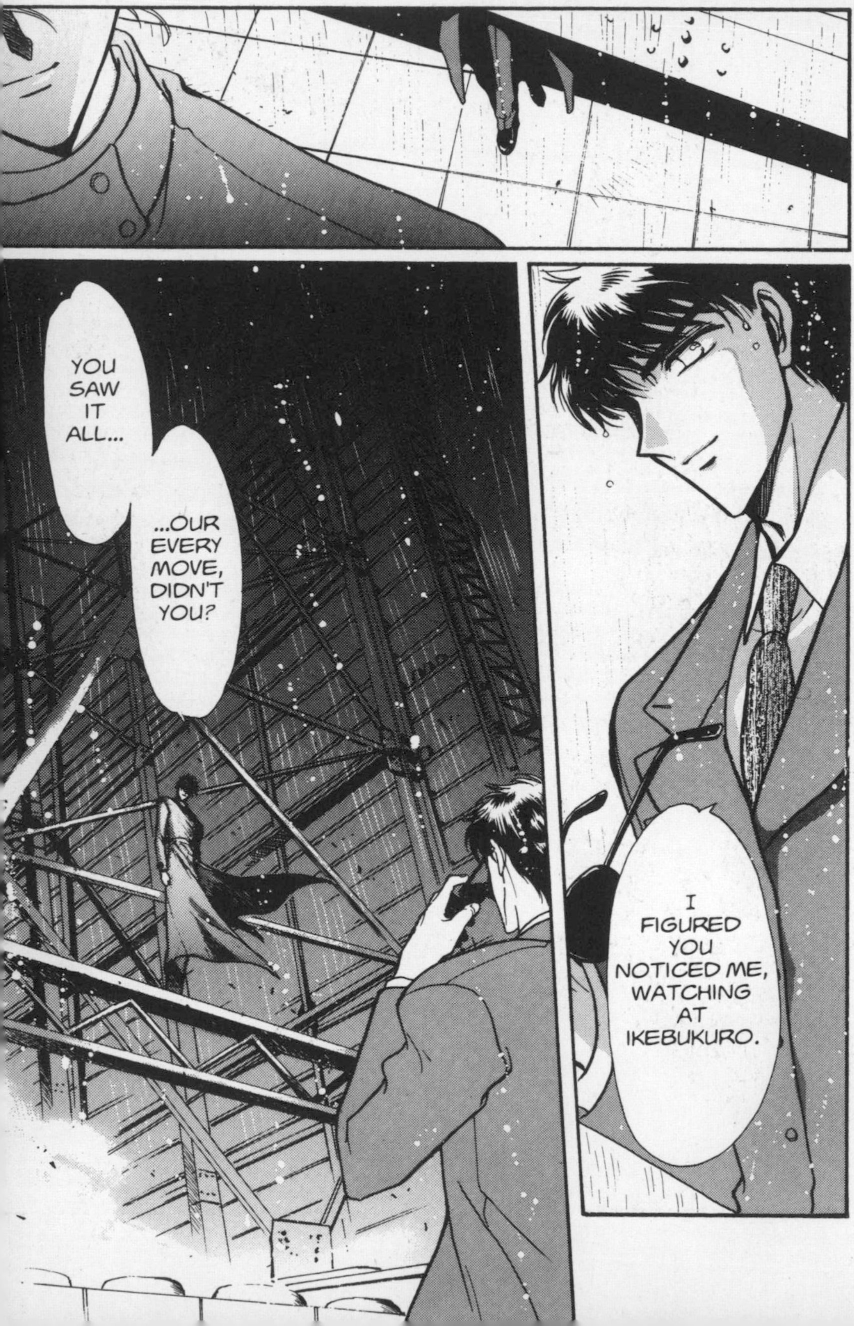
I FIGURED YOU NOTICED ME, WATCHING AT IKEBUKURO.
YOU SAW IT ALL...
...OUR EVERY MOVE, DIDN'T YOU?

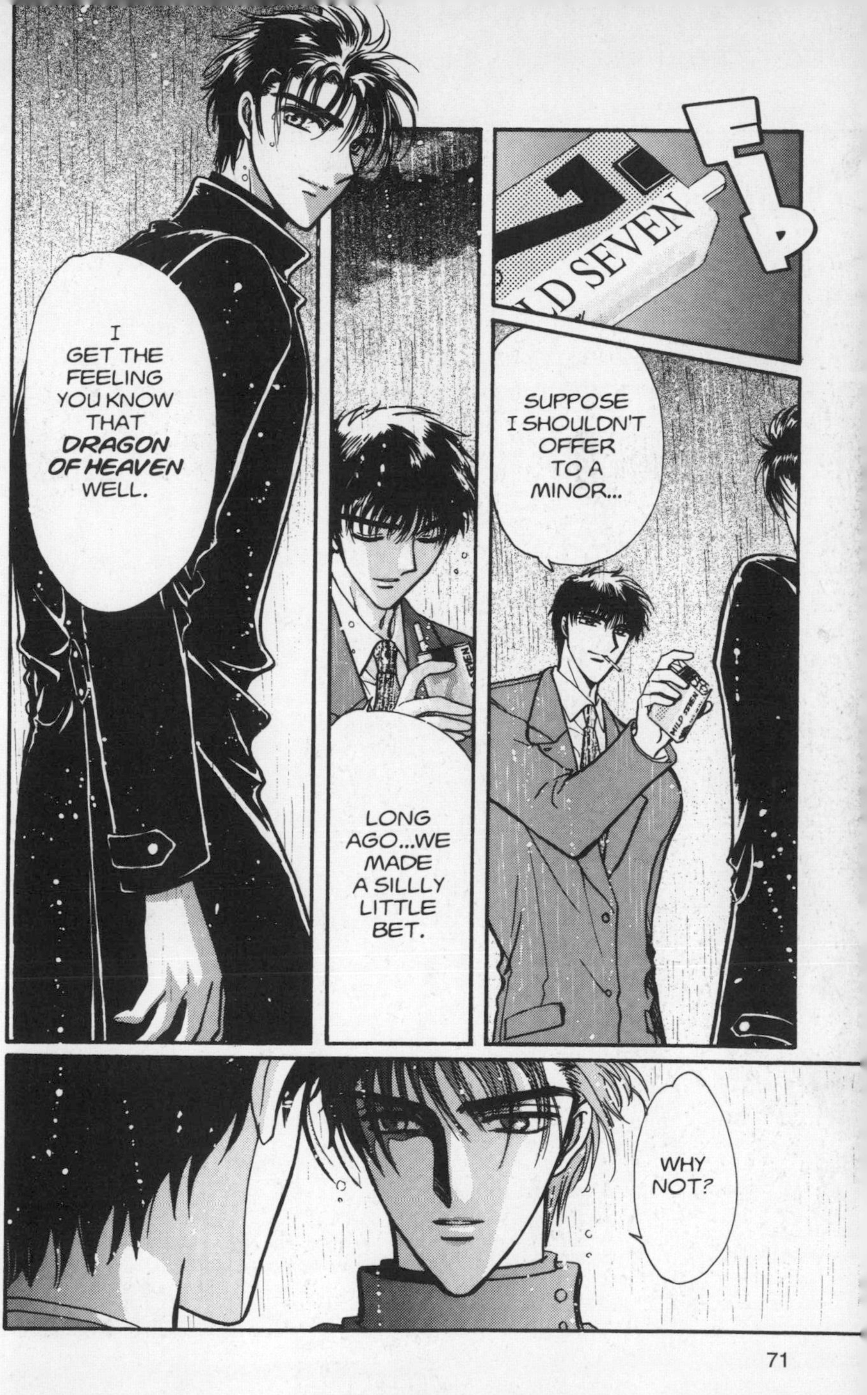
SUPPOSE I SHOULDN'T OFFER TO A MINOR...
LONG AGO...WE MADE A SILLLY LITTLE BET.
I GET THE FEELING YOU KNOW THAT **DRAGON OF HEAVEN** WELL.
WHY NOT?

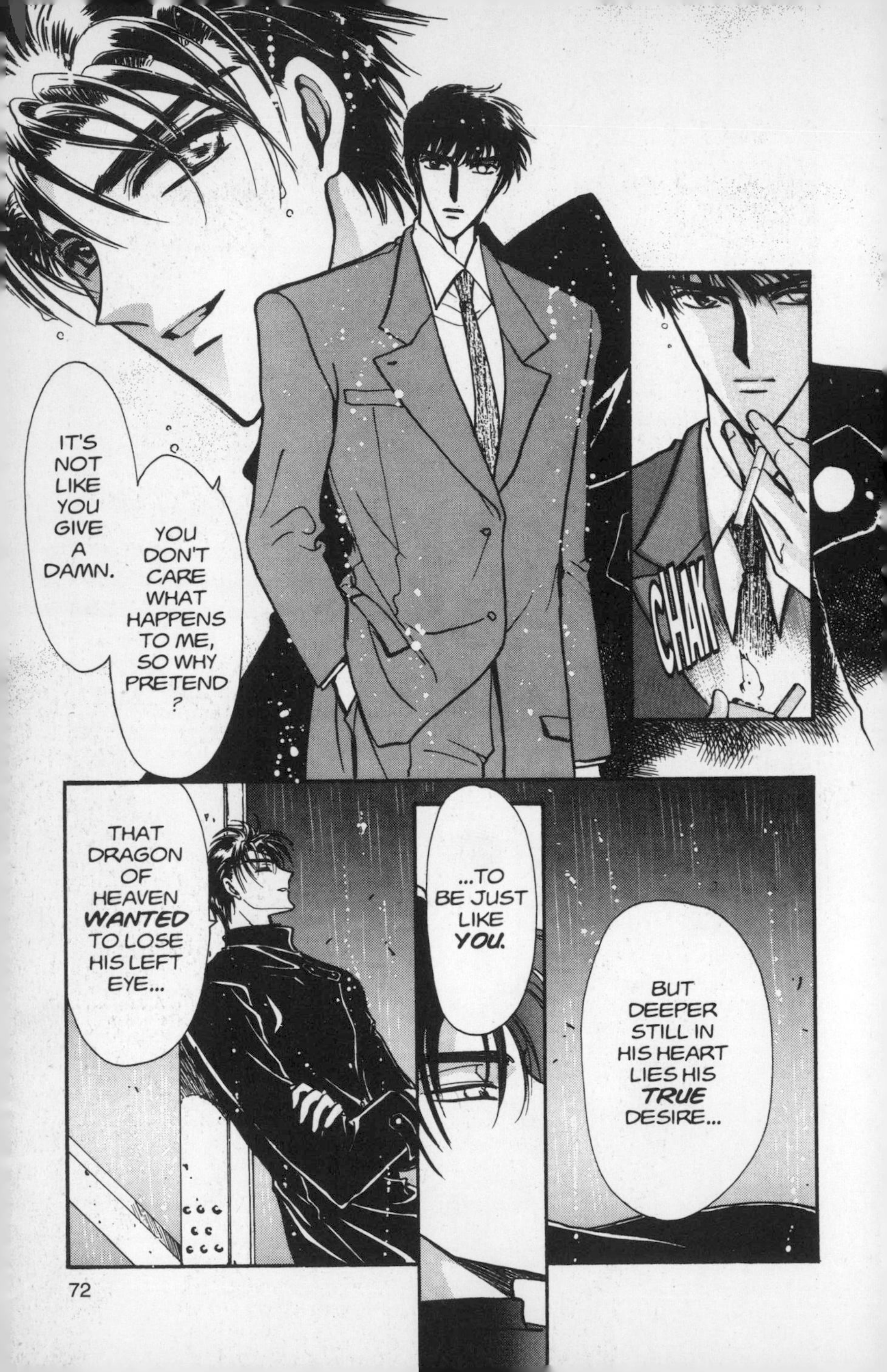
IT'S NOT LIKE YOU GIVE A DAMN.
YOU DON'T CARE WHAT HAPPENS TO ME, SO WHY PRETEND?
CHAK
THAT DRAGON OF HEAVEN **WANTED** TO LOSE HIS LEFT EYE...
...TO BE JUST LIKE **YOU.**
BUT DEEPER STILL IN HIS HEART LIES HIS **TRUE** DESIRE...

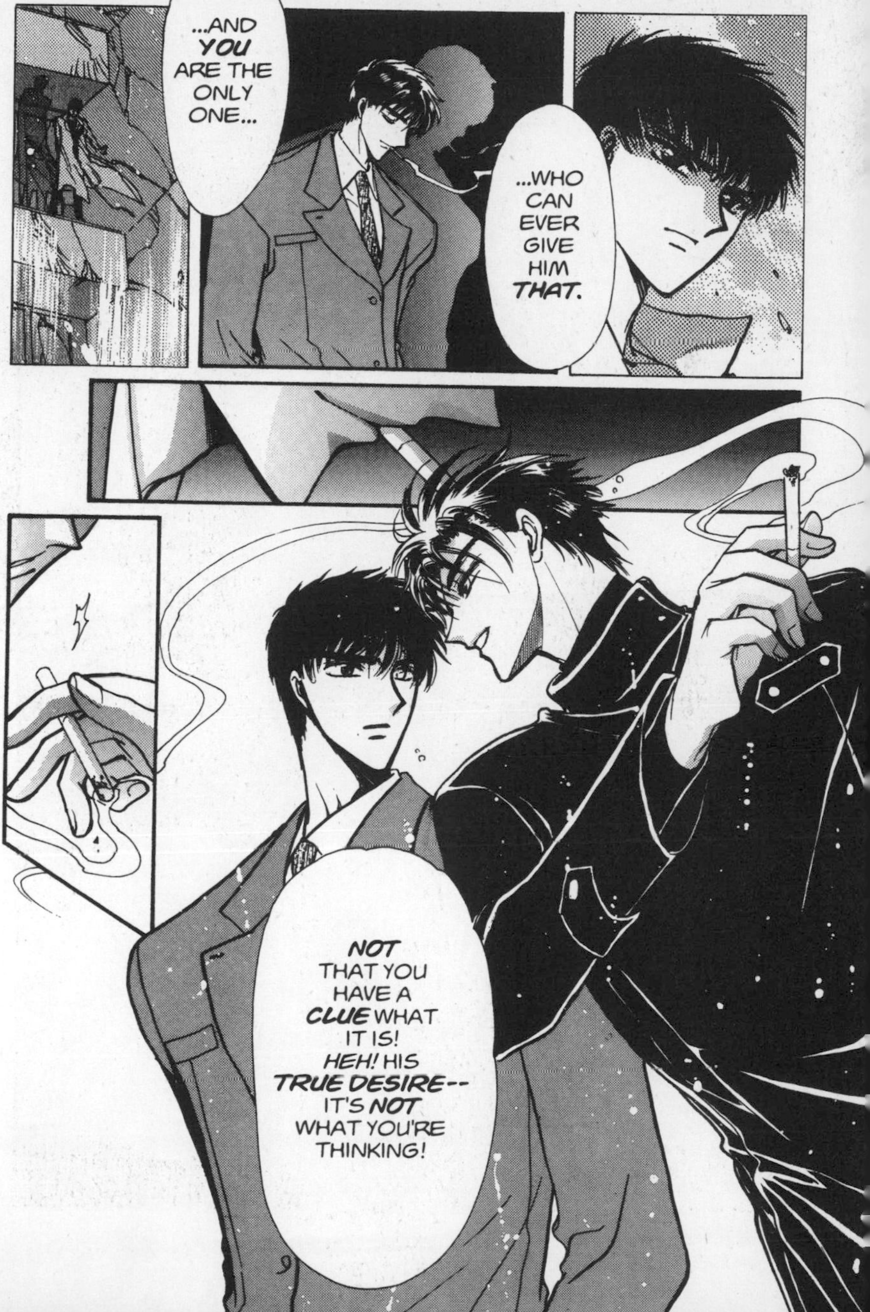
...AND YOU ARE THE ONLY ONE...
...WHO CAN EVER GIVE HIM THAT.
NOT THAT YOU HAVE A CLUE WHAT IT IS! HEH! HIS TRUE DESIRE-- IT'S NOT WHAT YOU'RE THINKING!

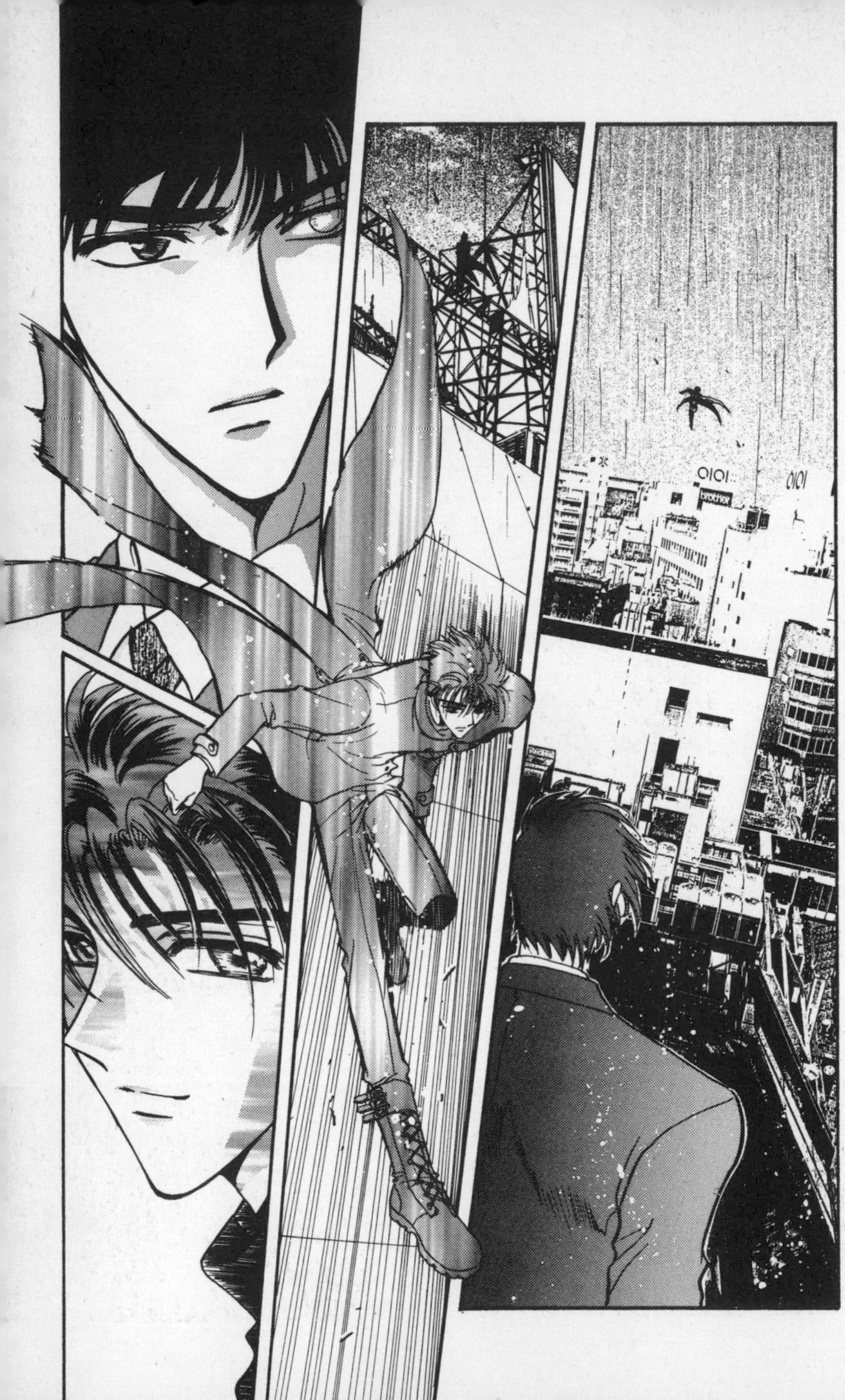
brother

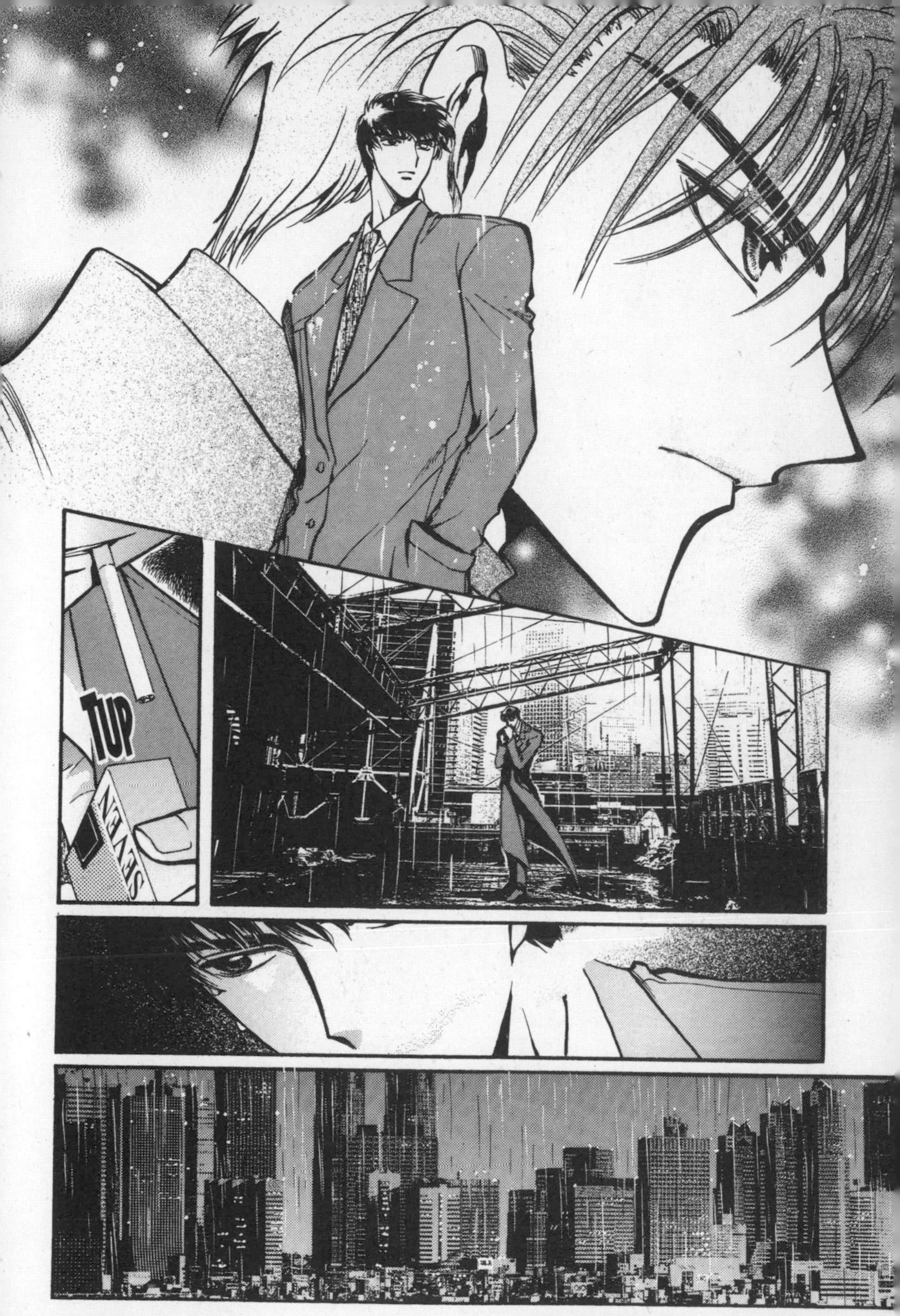
TUP
SEVEN

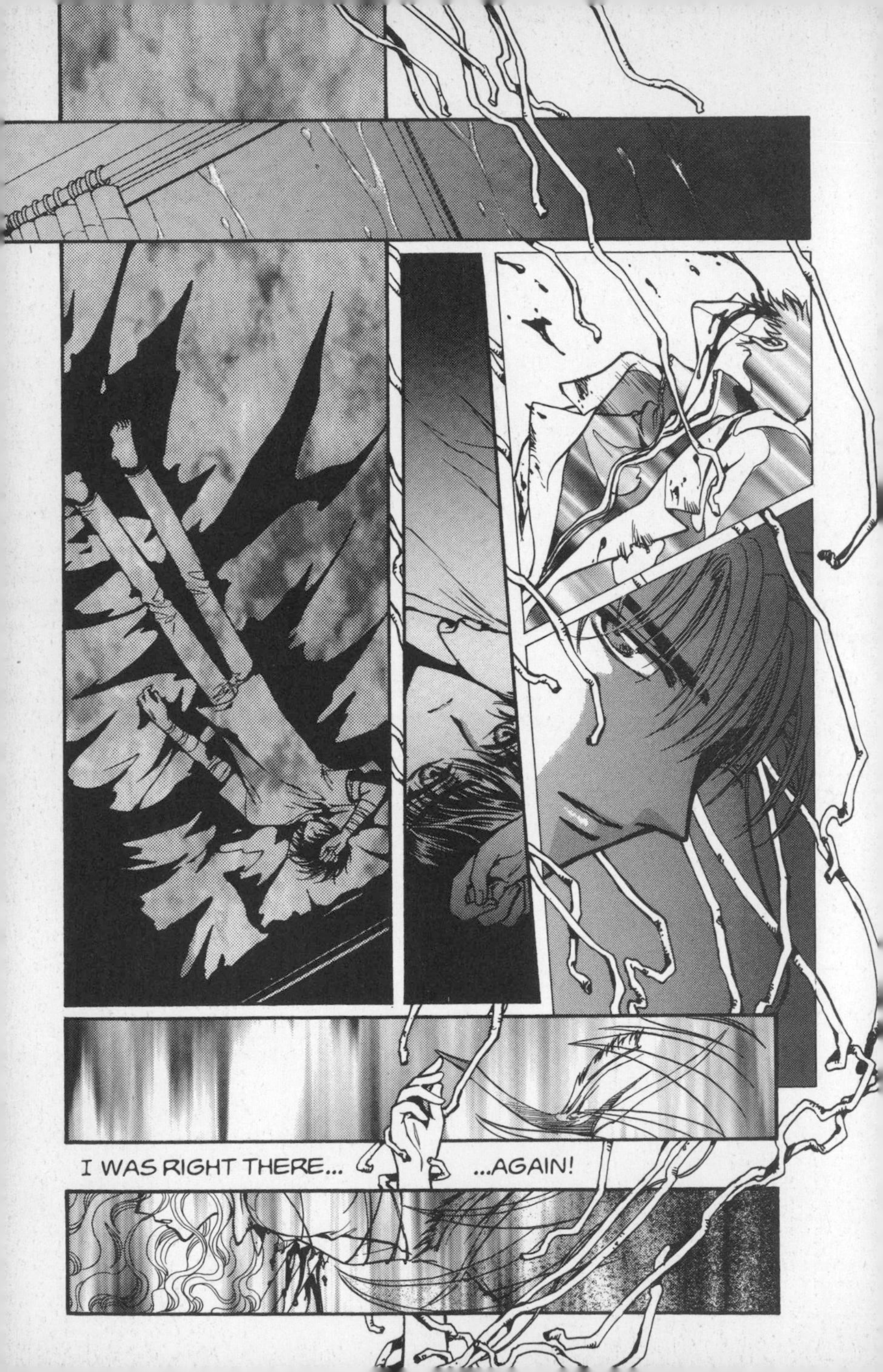
I WAS RIGHT THERE...
...AGAIN!

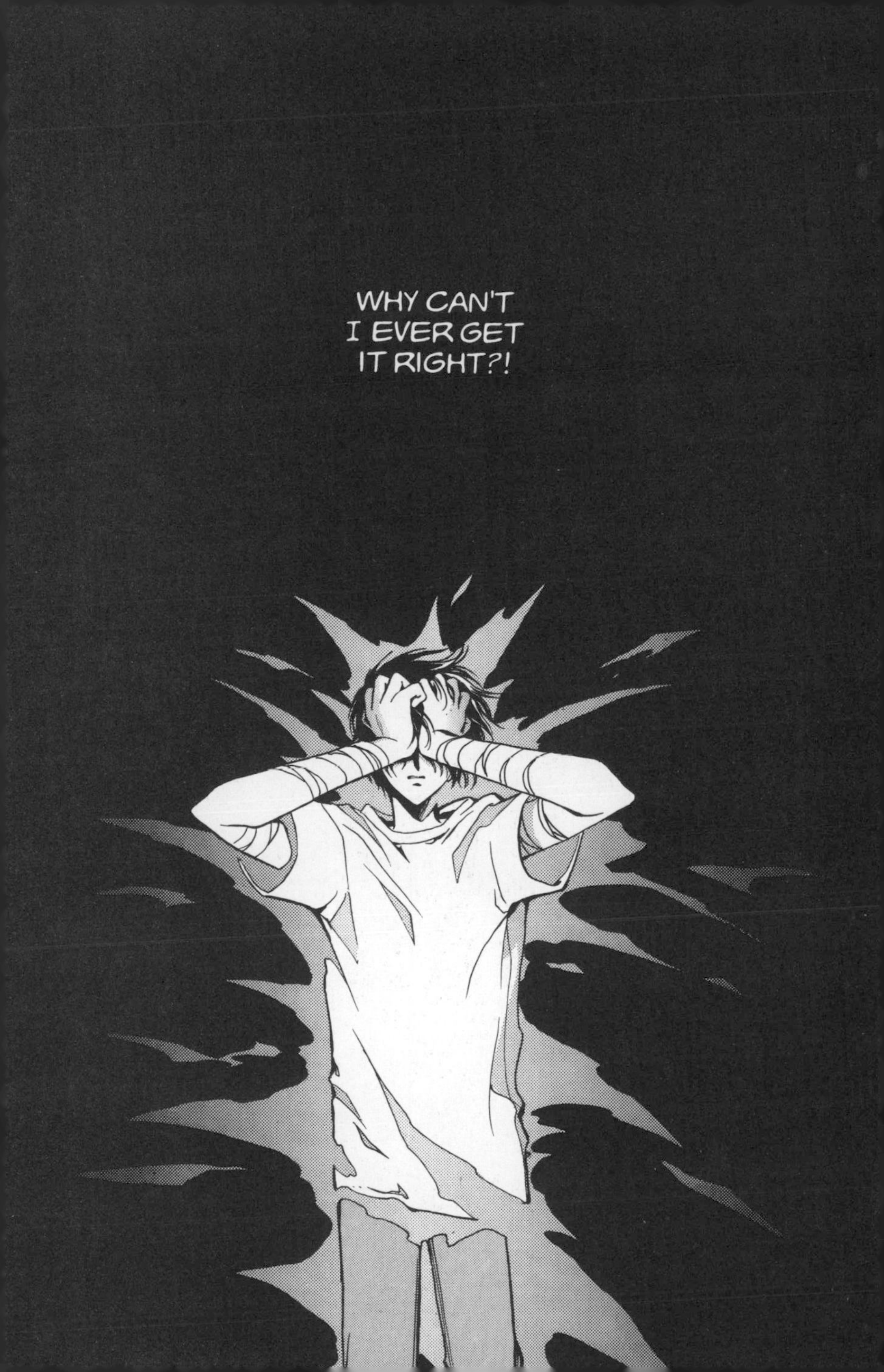
WHY CAN'T I EVER GET IT RIGHT?!

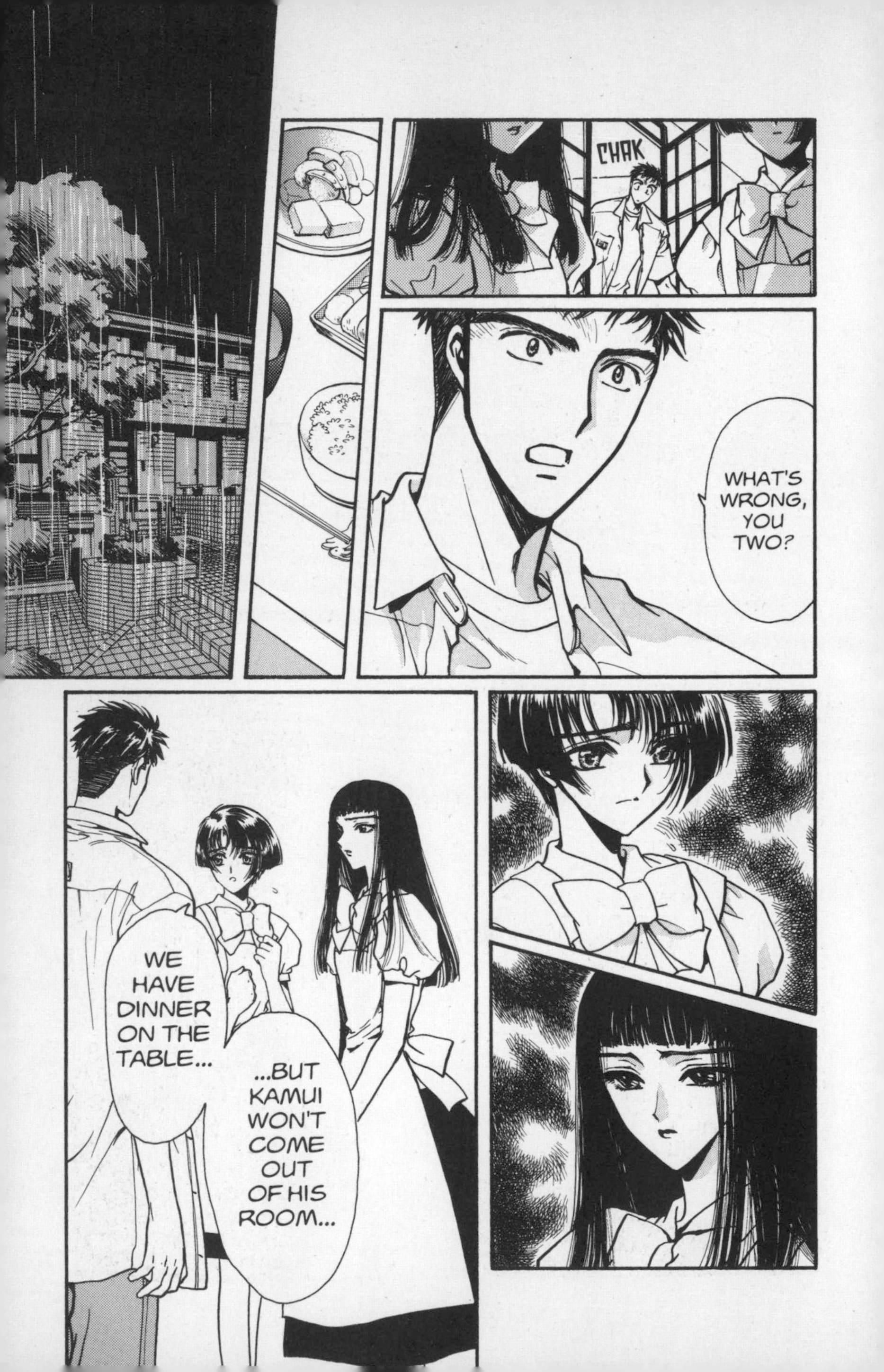
CHAK
WHAT'S WRONG, YOU TWO?
WE HAVE DINNER ON THE TABLE...
...BUT KAMUI WON'T COME OUT OF HIS ROOM...

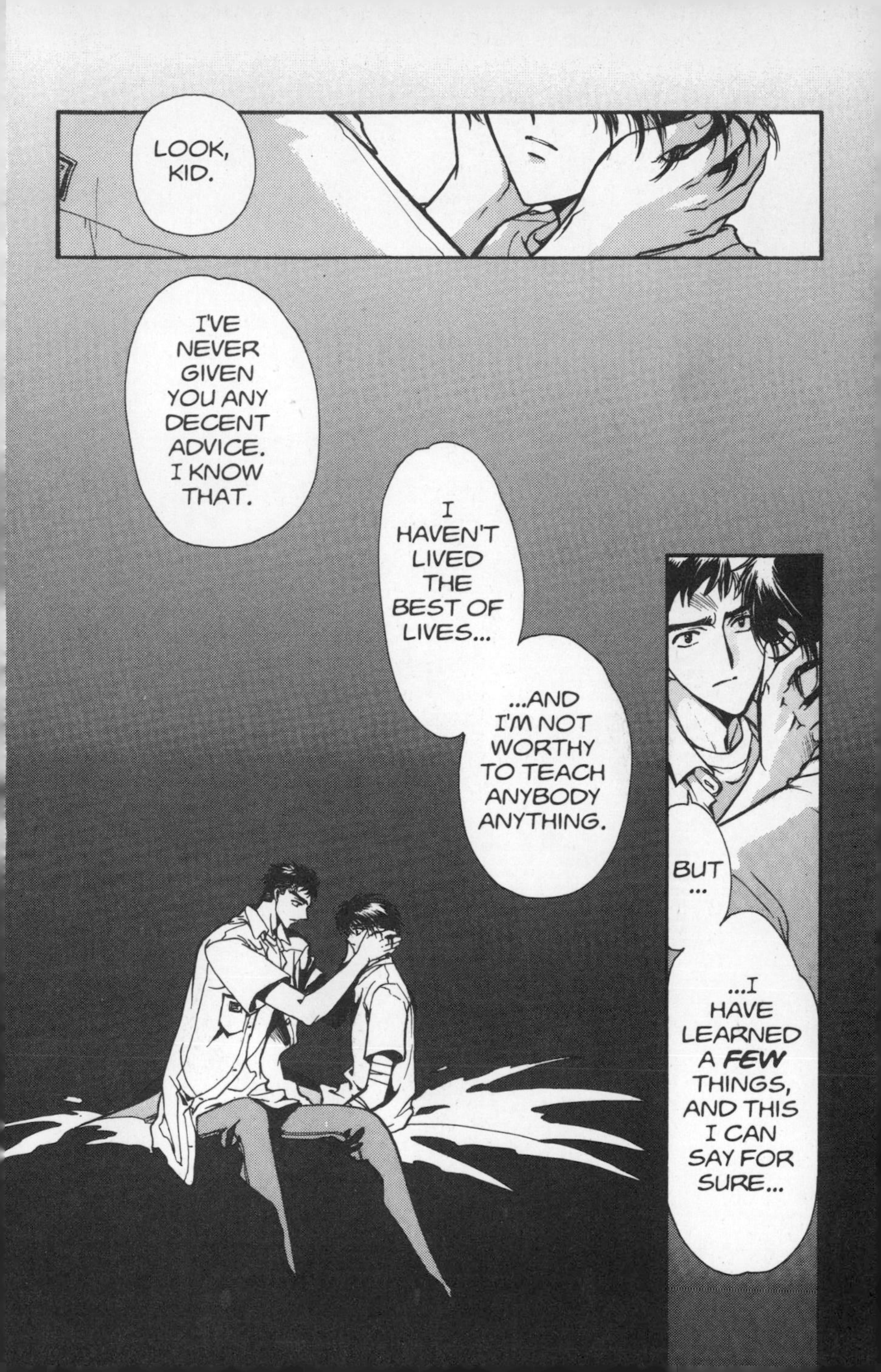
LOOK, KID.
I'VE NEVER GIVEN YOU ANY DECENT ADVICE. I KNOW THAT.
I HAVEN'T LIVED THE BEST OF LIVES...
...AND I'M NOT WORTHY TO TEACH ANYBODY ANYTHING.
BUT...
...I HAVE LEARNED A ***FEW*** THINGS, AND THIS I CAN SAY FOR SURE...

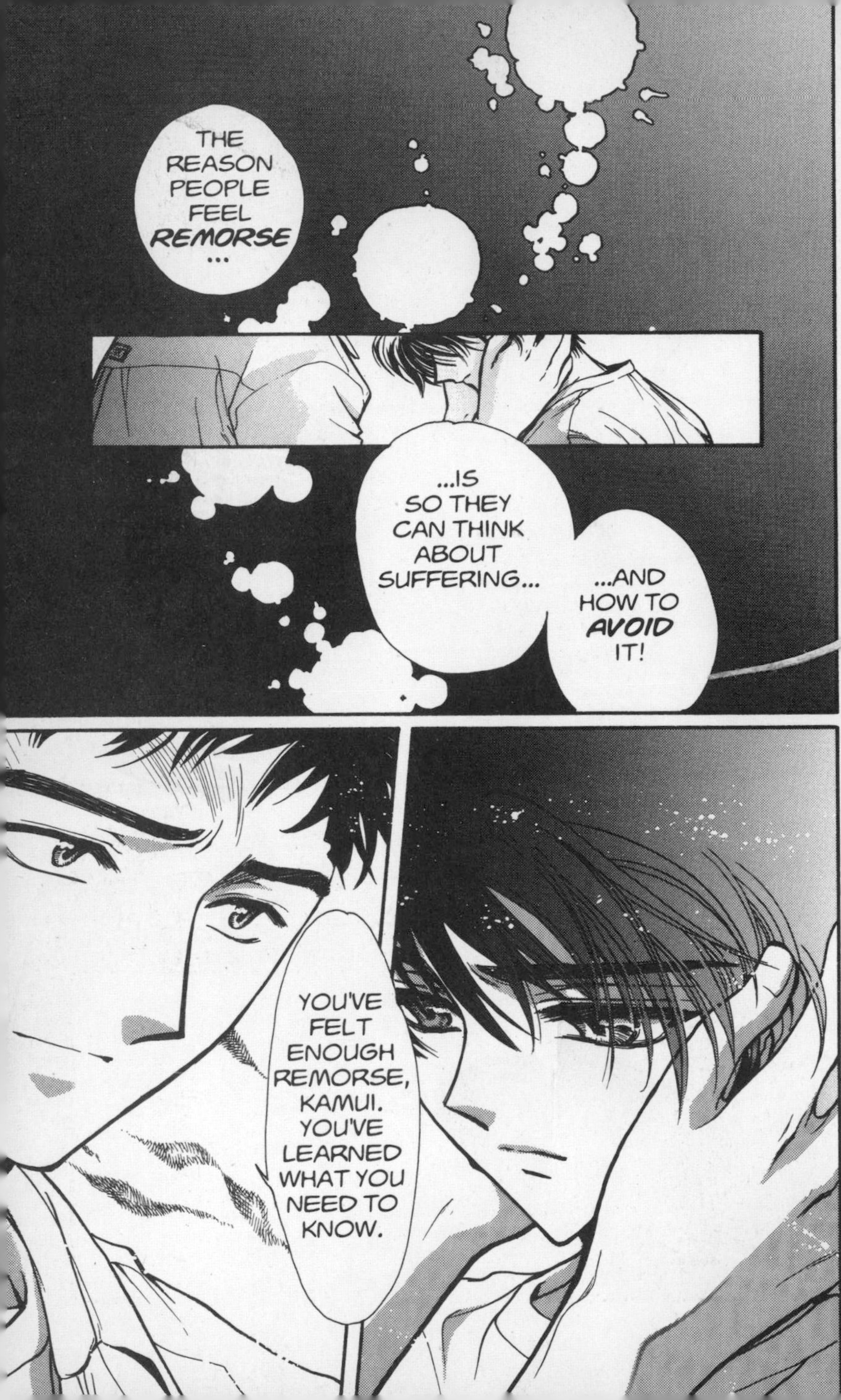
THE REASON PEOPLE FEEL REMORSE...
...IS SO THEY CAN THINK ABOUT SUFFERING...
...AND HOW TO AVOID IT!
YOU'VE FELT ENOUGH REMORSE, KAMUI. YOU'VE LEARNED WHAT YOU NEED TO KNOW.

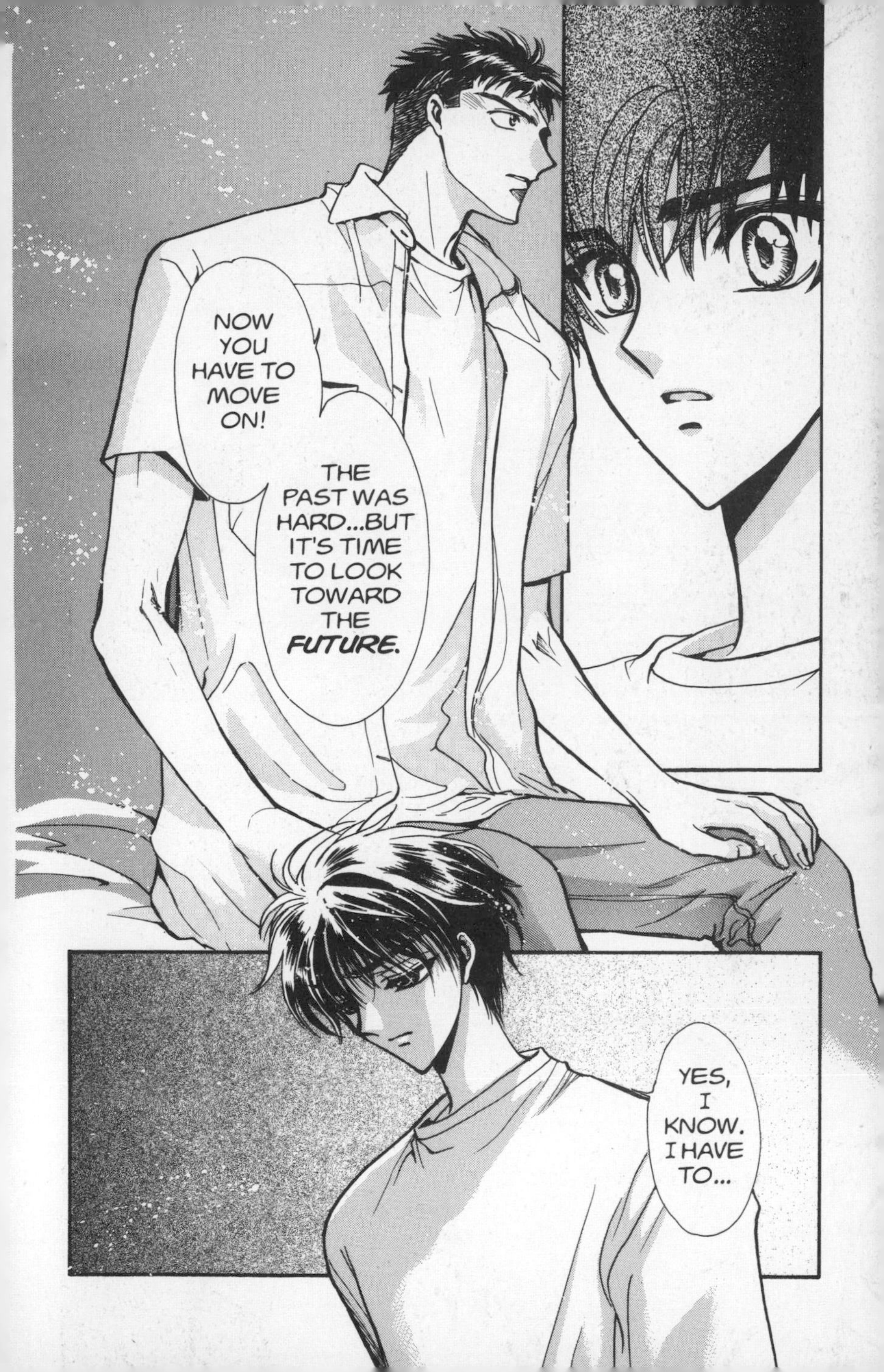
NOW YOU HAVE TO MOVE ON!
THE PAST WAS HARD...BUT IT'S TIME TO LOOK TOWARD THE *FUTURE.*
YES, I KNOW. I HAVE TO...

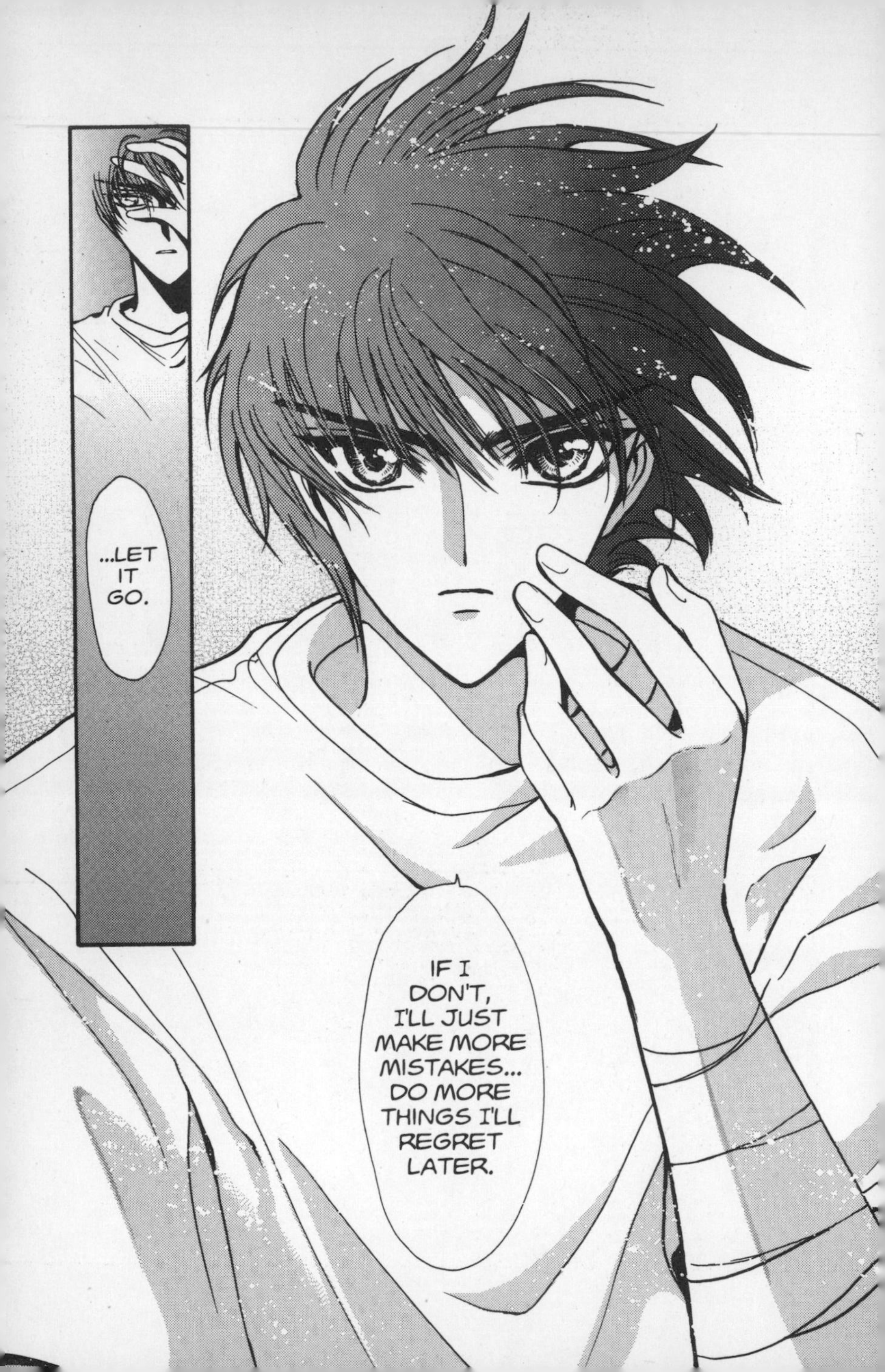
...LET IT GO.
IF I DON'T, I'LL JUST MAKE MORE MISTAKES... DO MORE THINGS I'LL REGRET LATER.

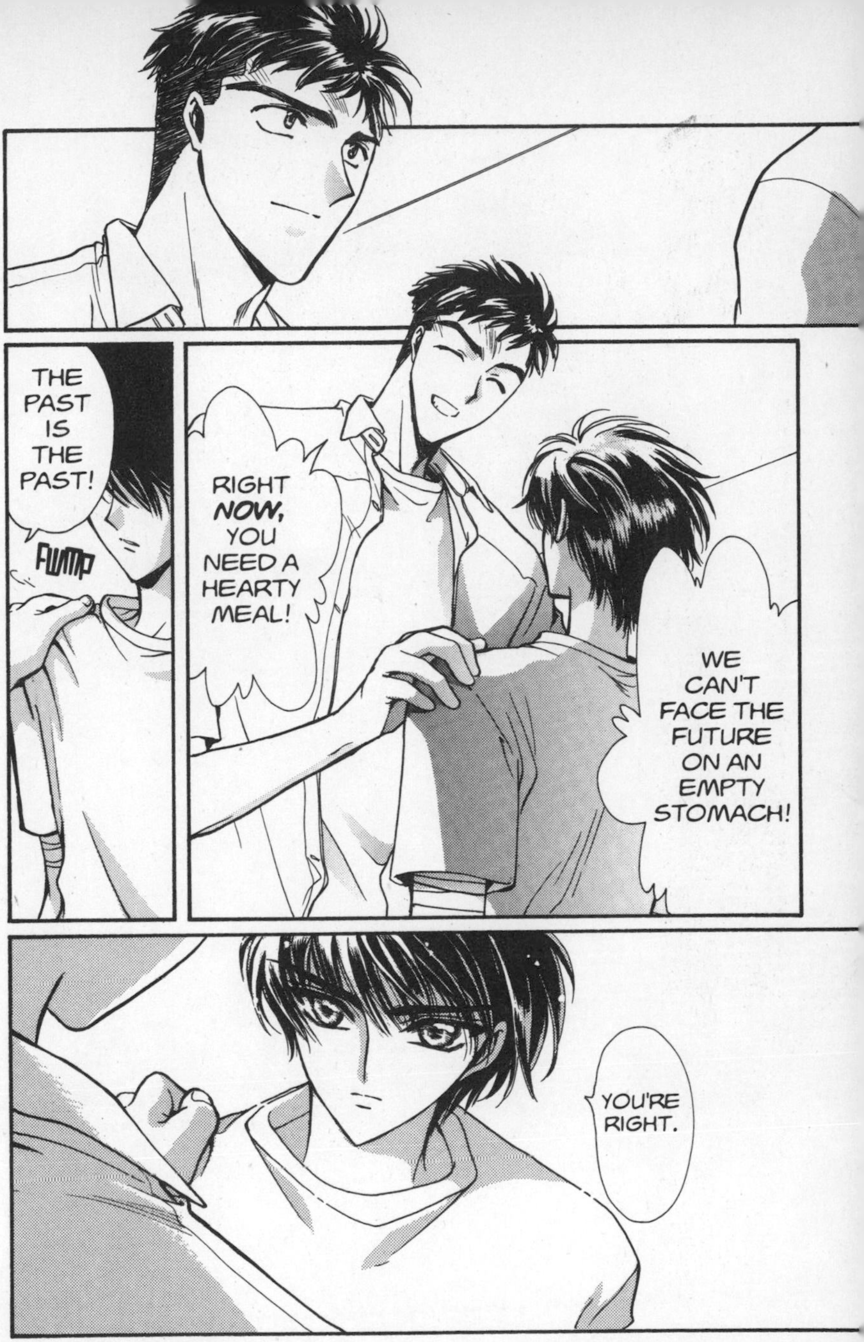
THE PAST IS THE PAST!
FLUMP
RIGHT *NOW,* YOU NEED A HEARTY MEAL!
WE CAN'T FACE THE FUTURE ON AN EMPTY STOMACH!
YOU'RE RIGHT.

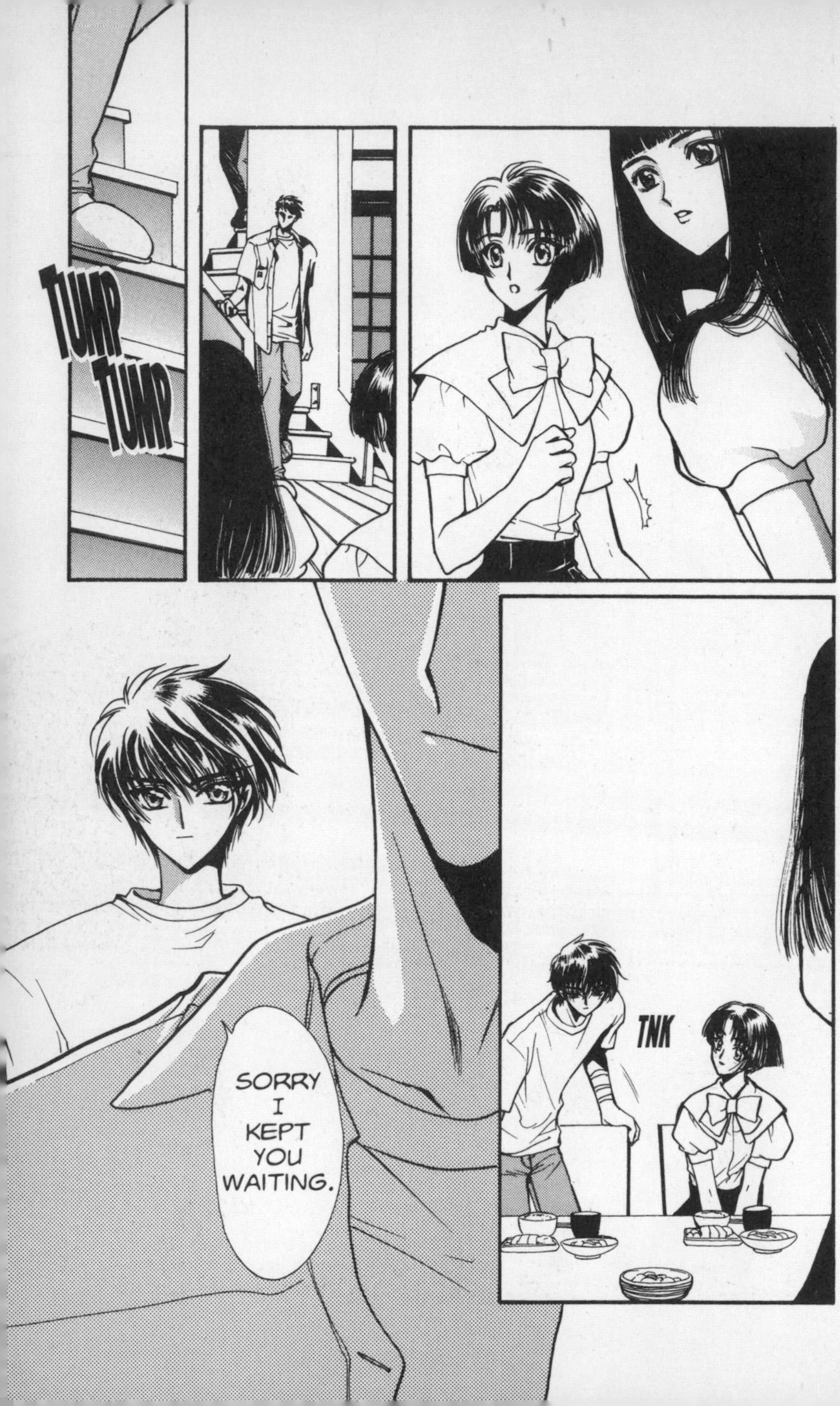
TUMP TUMP
TNK
SORRY I KEPT YOU WAITING.

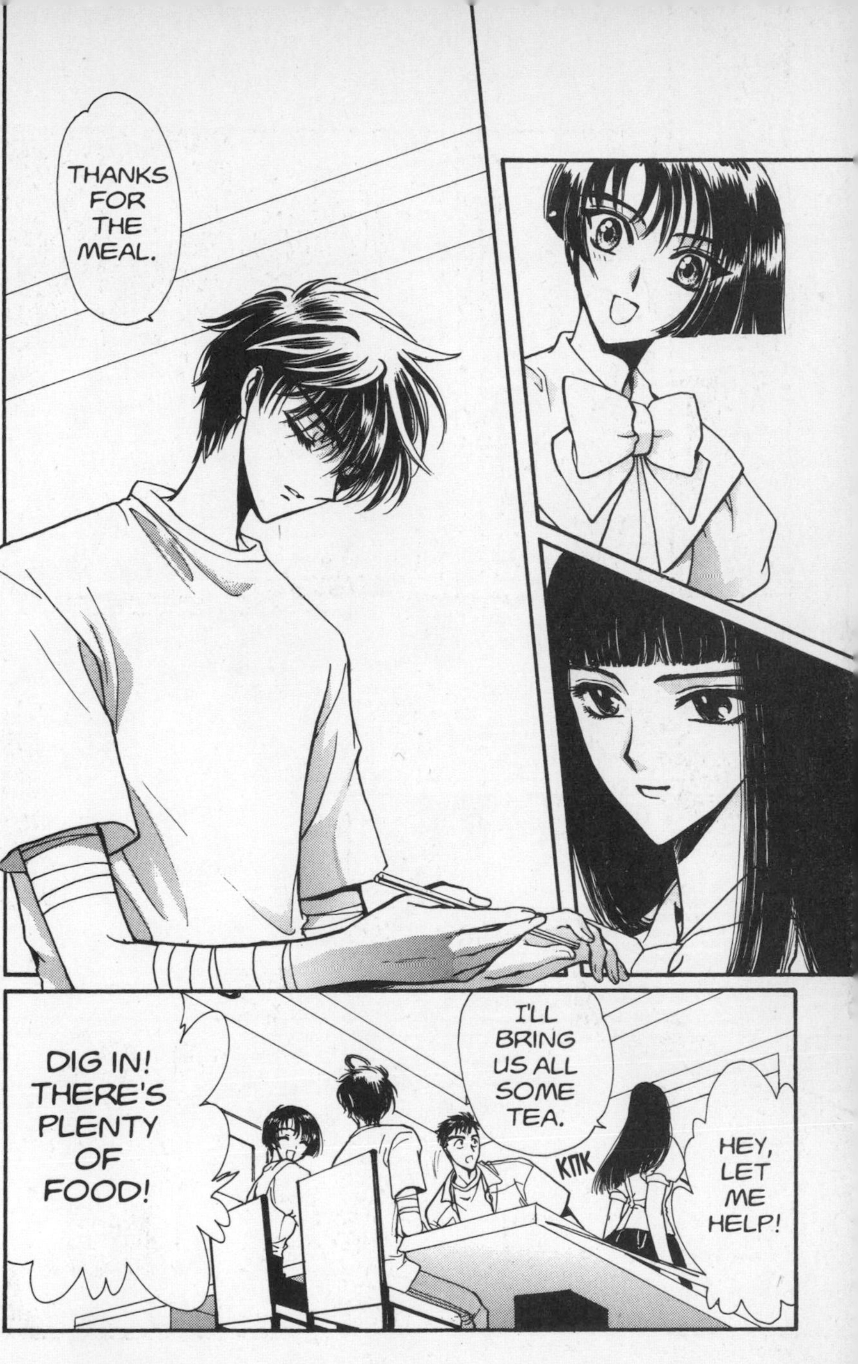
THANKS FOR THE MEAL.
HEY, LET ME HELP!
KNK
I'LL BRING US ALL SOME TEA.
DIG IN! THERE'S PLENTY OF FOOD!

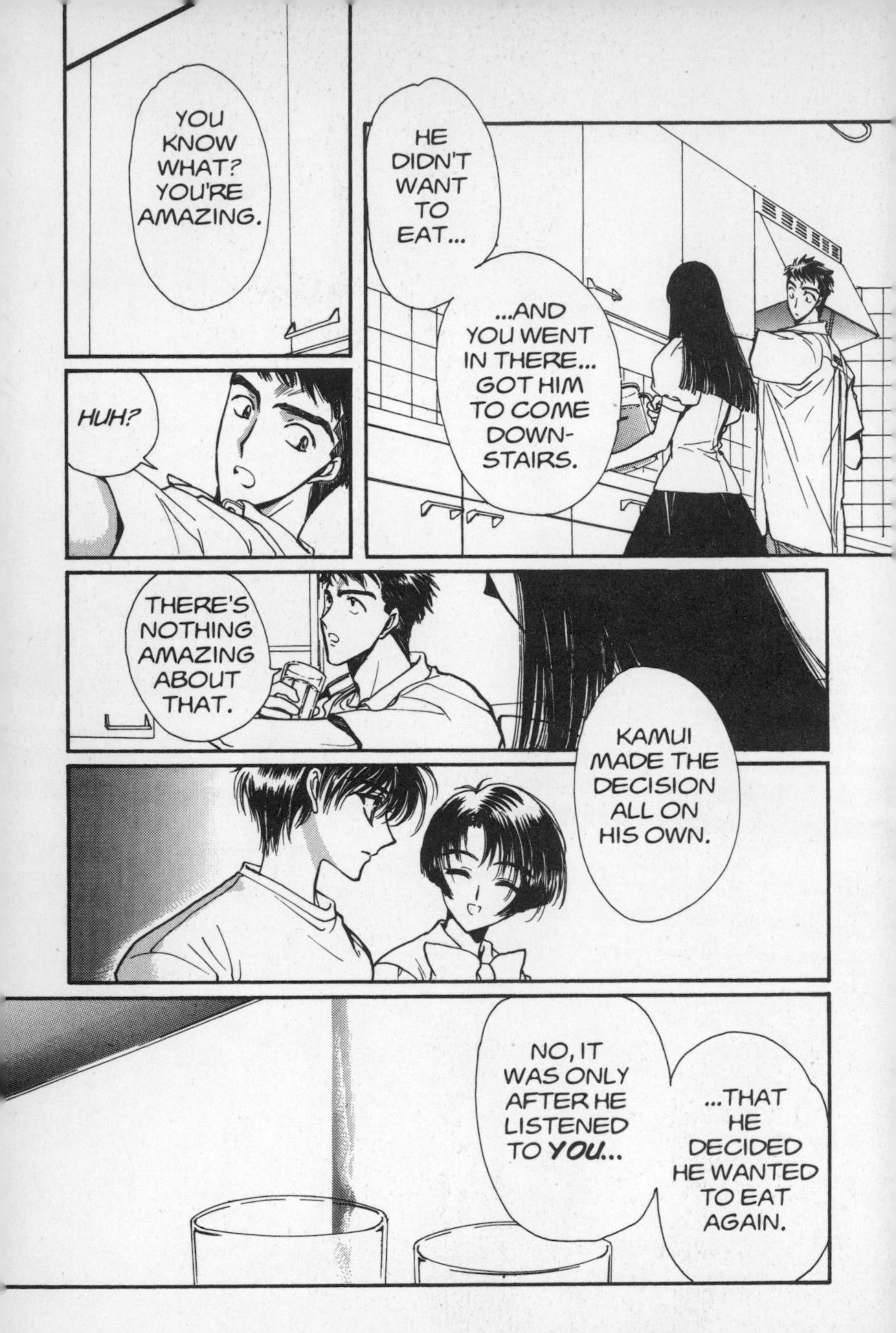
YOU KNOW WHAT? YOU'RE AMAZING.
HUH?
HE DIDN'T WANT TO EAT...
...AND YOU WENT IN THERE... GOT HIM TO COME DOWN-STAIRS.
THERE'S NOTHING AMAZING ABOUT THAT.
KAMUI MADE THE DECISION ALL ON HIS OWN.
NO, IT WAS ONLY AFTER HE LISTENED TO *YOU*...
...THAT HE DECIDED HE WANTED TO EAT AGAIN.

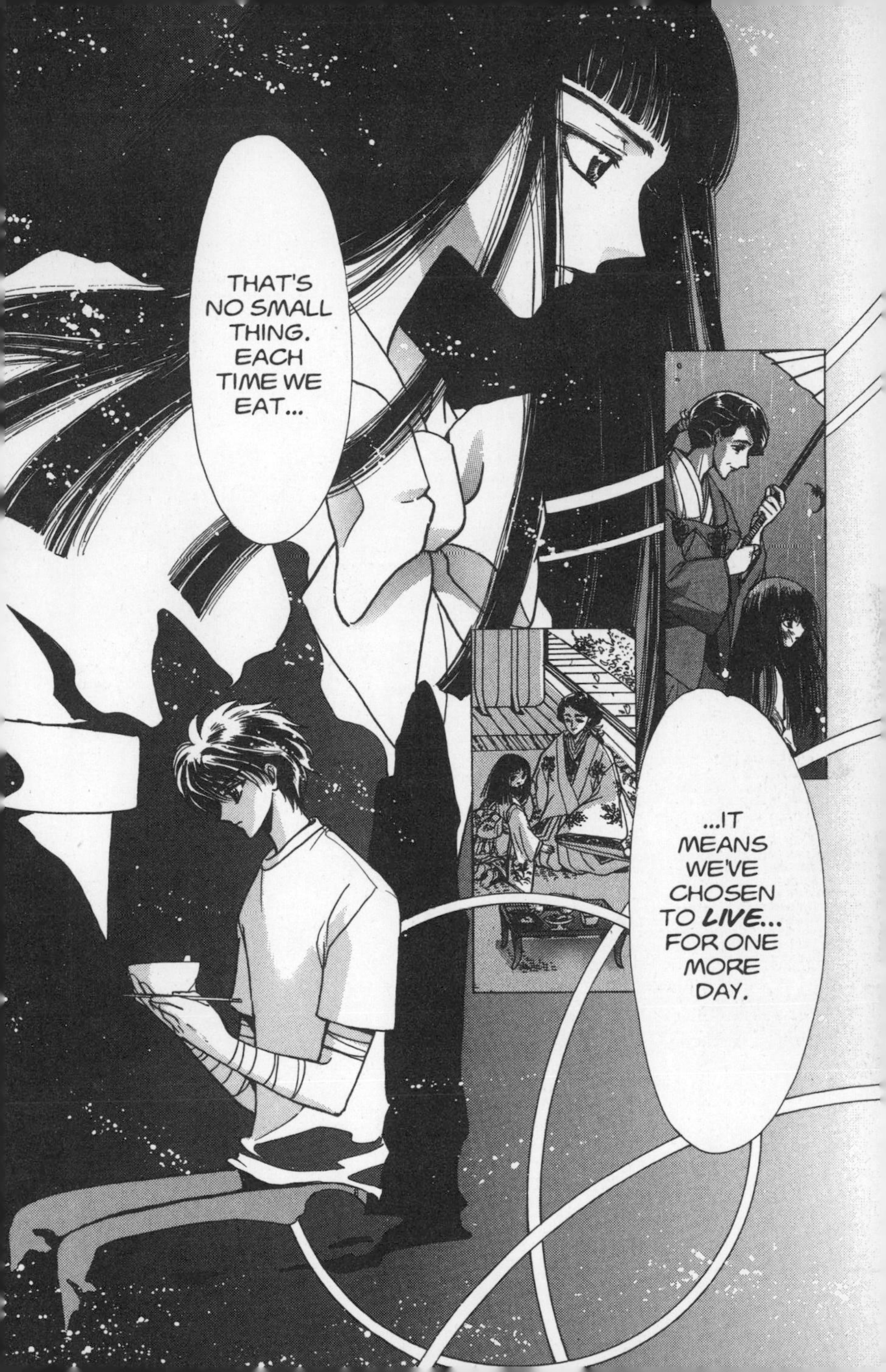
THAT'S NO SMALL THING. EACH TIME WE EAT...
...IT MEANS WE'VE CHOSEN TO LIVE... FOR ONE MORE DAY.

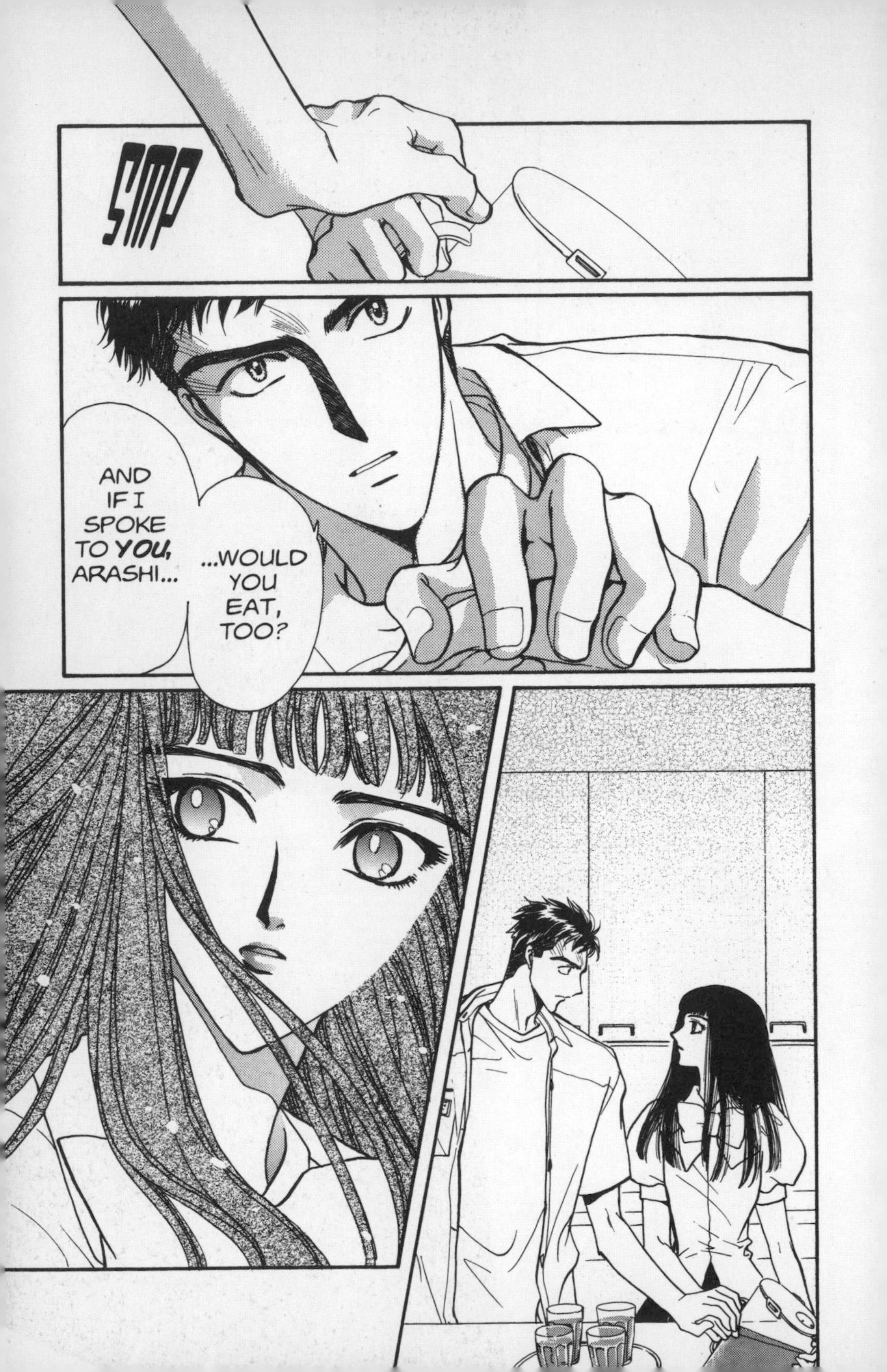
SMP
AND IF I SPOKE TO YOU, ARASHI...
...WOULD YOU EAT, TOO?

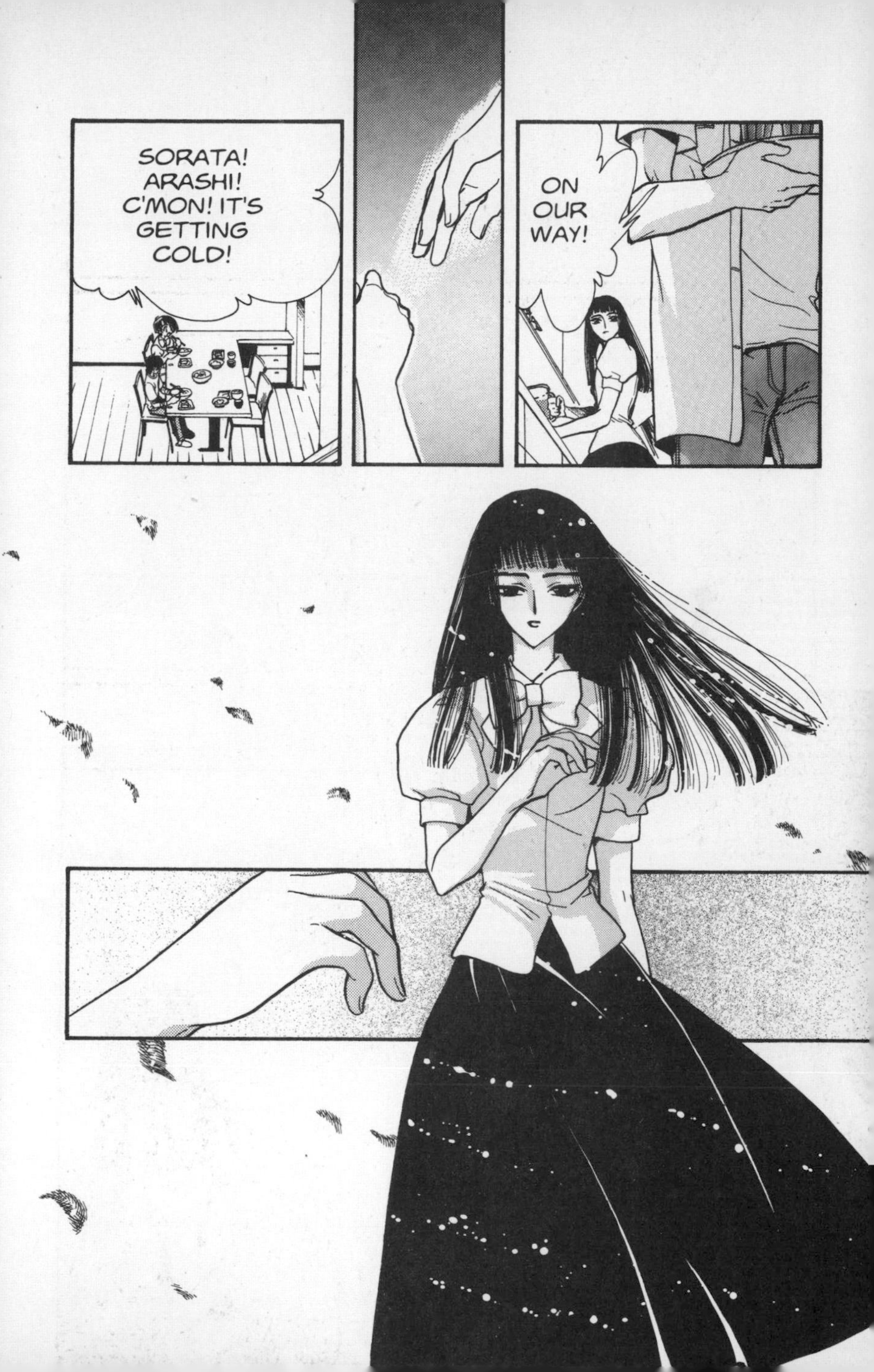
SORATA! ARASHI! C'MON! IT'S GETTING COLD!
ON OUR WAY!

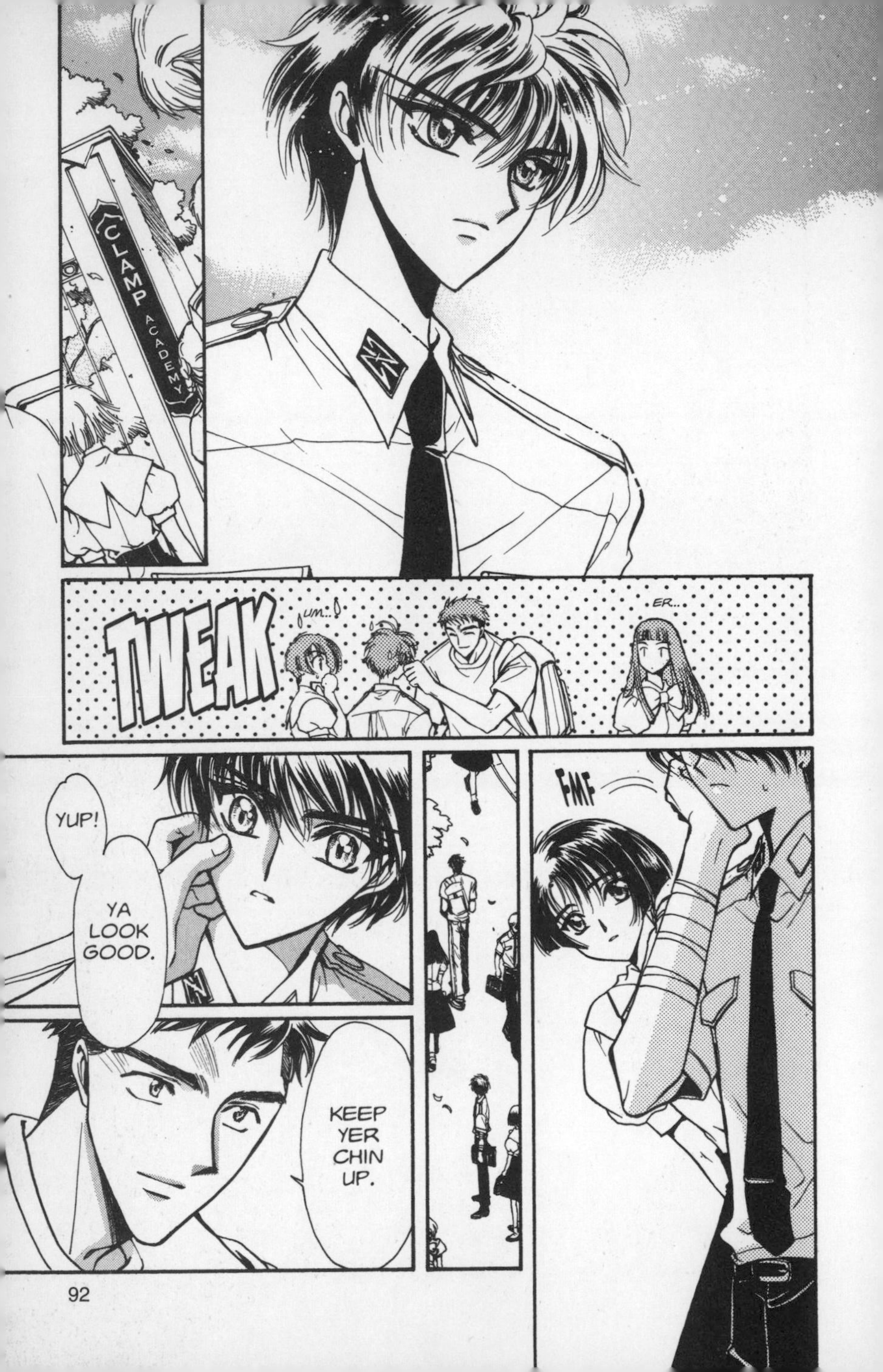
CLAMP ACADEMY
ER...
UM...
TWEAK
FMF
YUP!
YA LOOK GOOD.
KEEP YER CHIN UP.

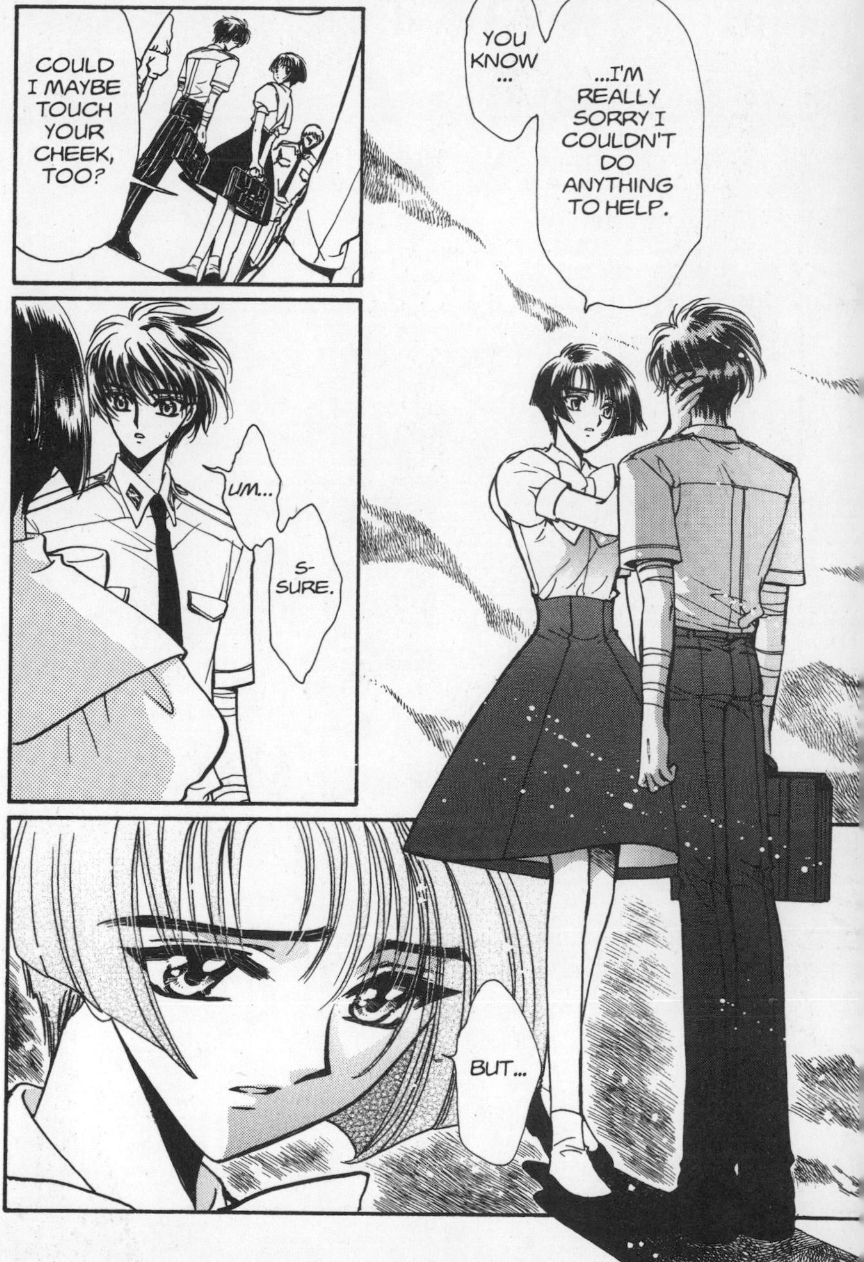
COULD I MAYBE TOUCH YOUR CHEEK, TOO?
UM...
S- SURE.
YOU KNOW ...
...I'M REALLY SORRY I COULDN'T DO ANYTHING TO HELP.
BUT...

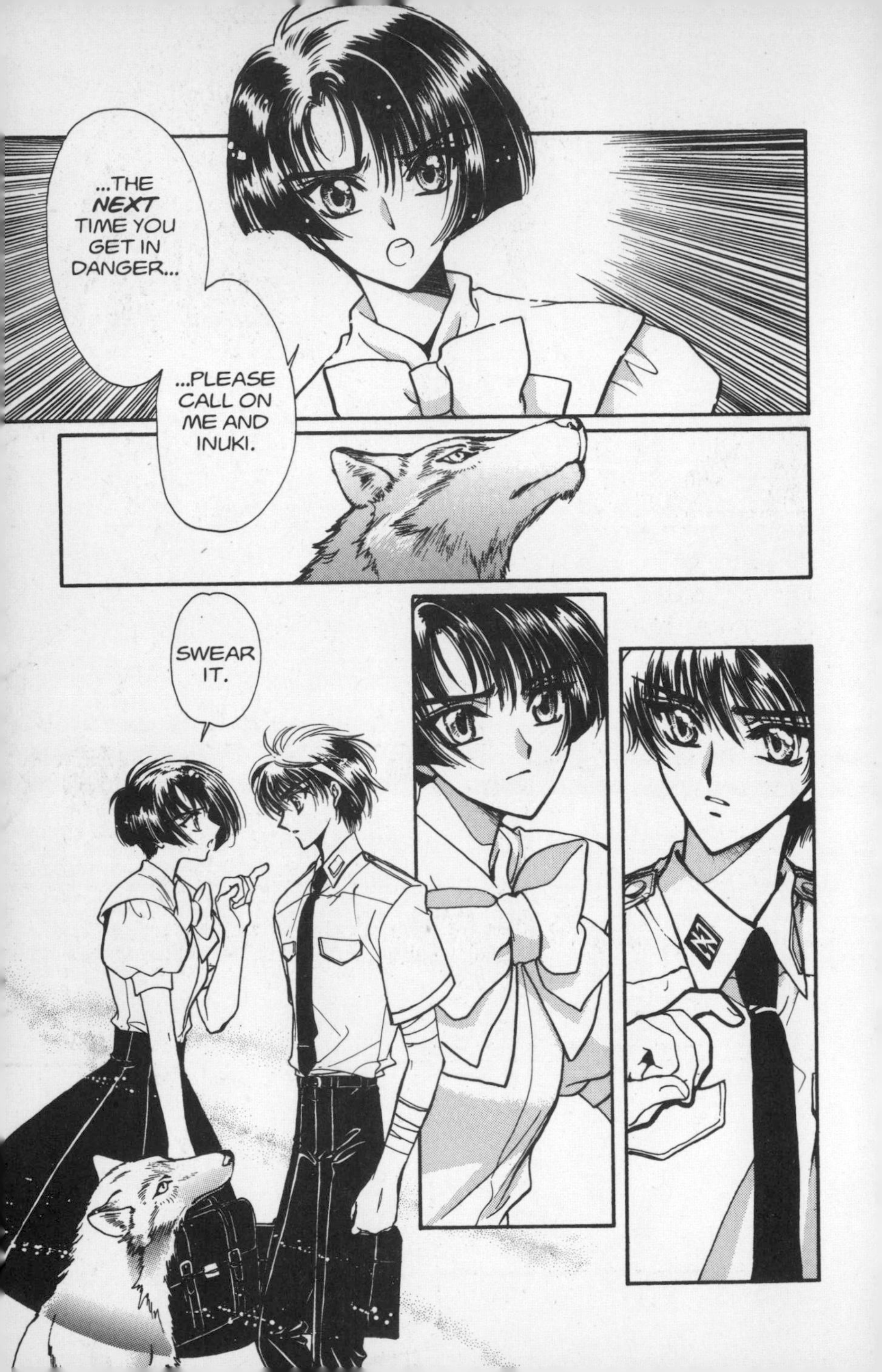
...THE ***NEXT*** TIME YOU GET IN DANGER...
...PLEASE CALL ON ME AND INUKI.
SWEAR IT.

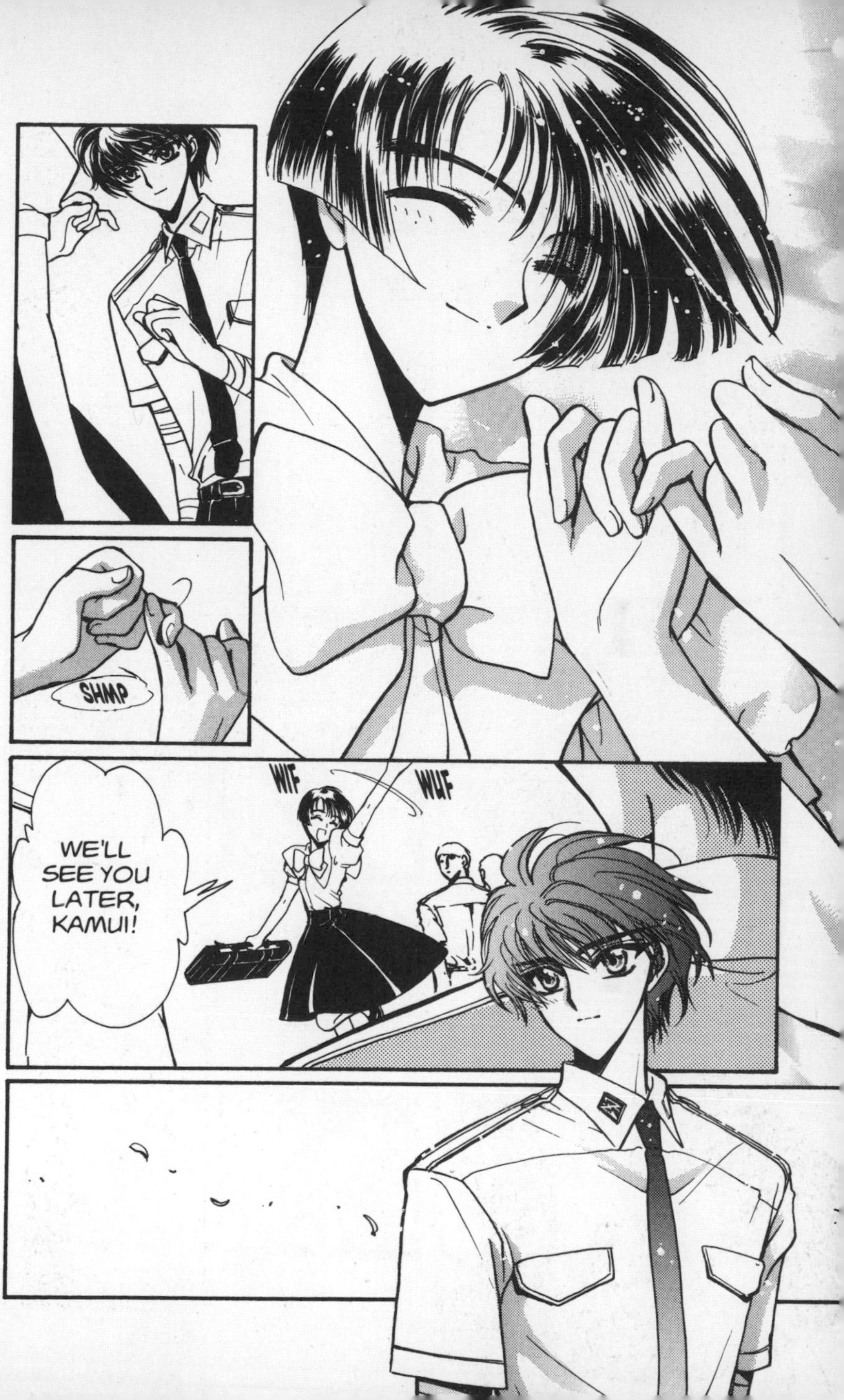
SHMP
WUF
WIF
WE'LL SEE YOU LATER, KAMUI!

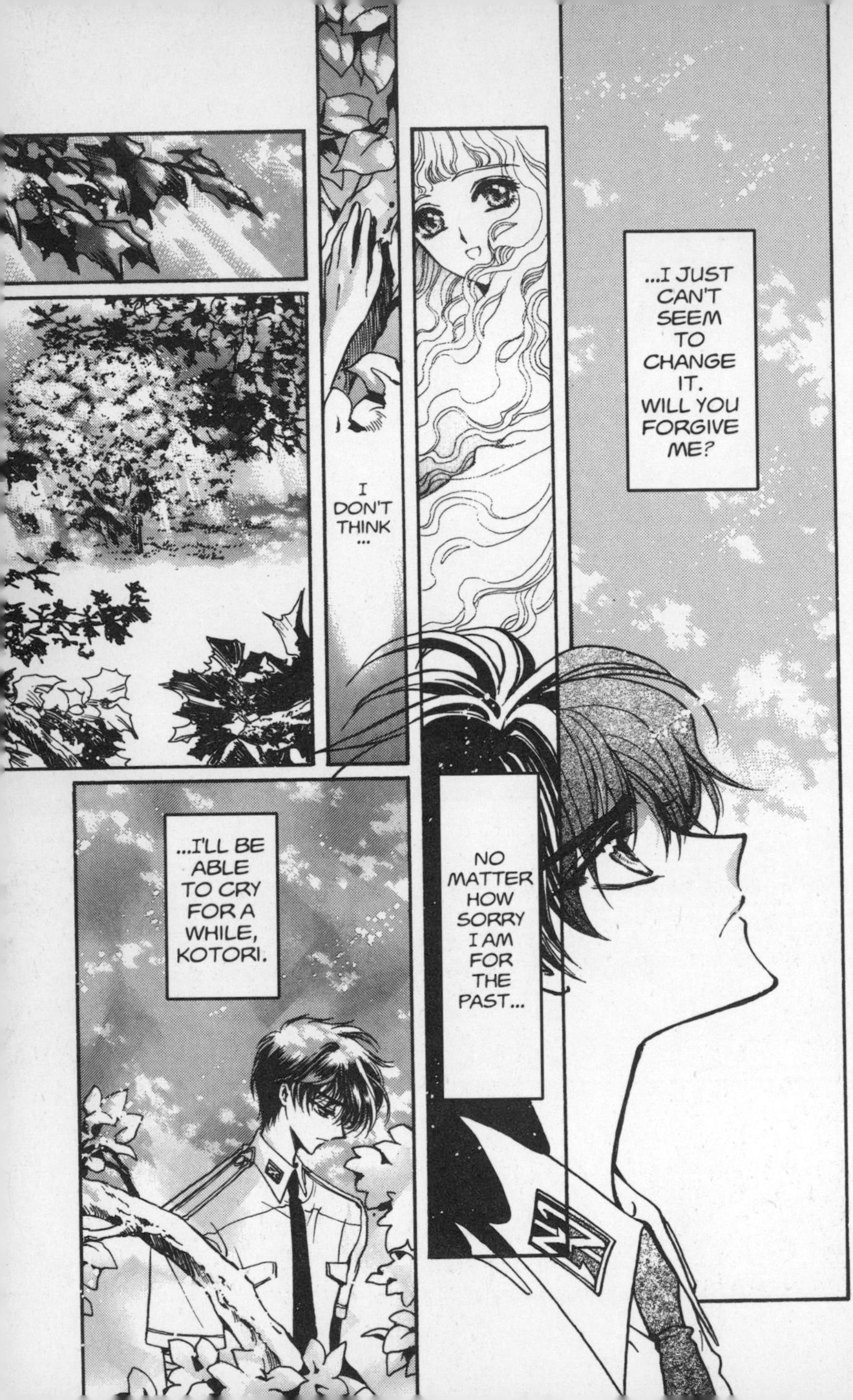
NO MATTER HOW SORRY I AM FOR THE PAST...
...I JUST CAN'T SEEM TO CHANGE IT. WILL YOU FORGIVE ME?
I DON'T THINK...
...I'LL BE ABLE TO CRY FOR A WHILE, KOTORI.

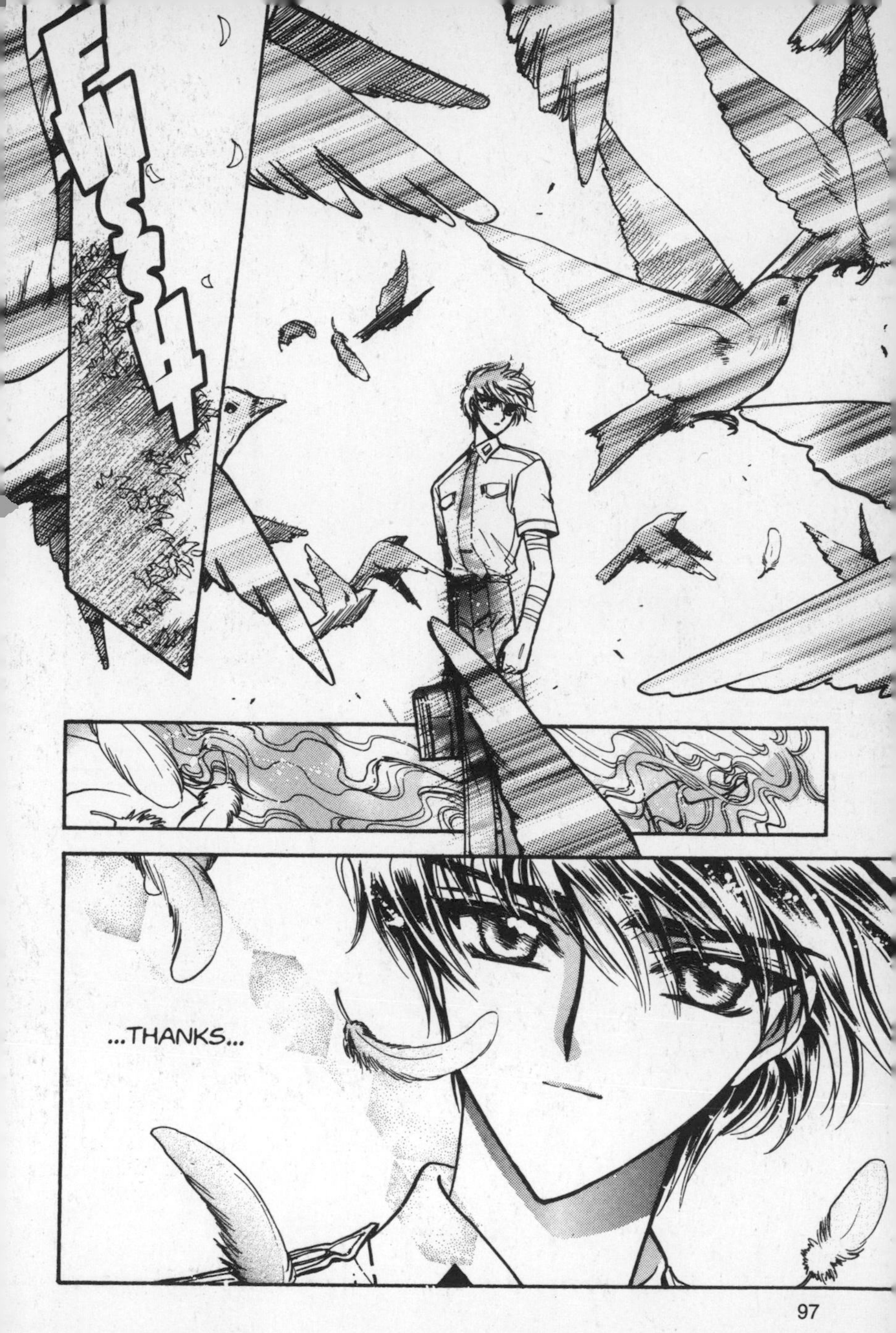
FWUSH
...THANKS...

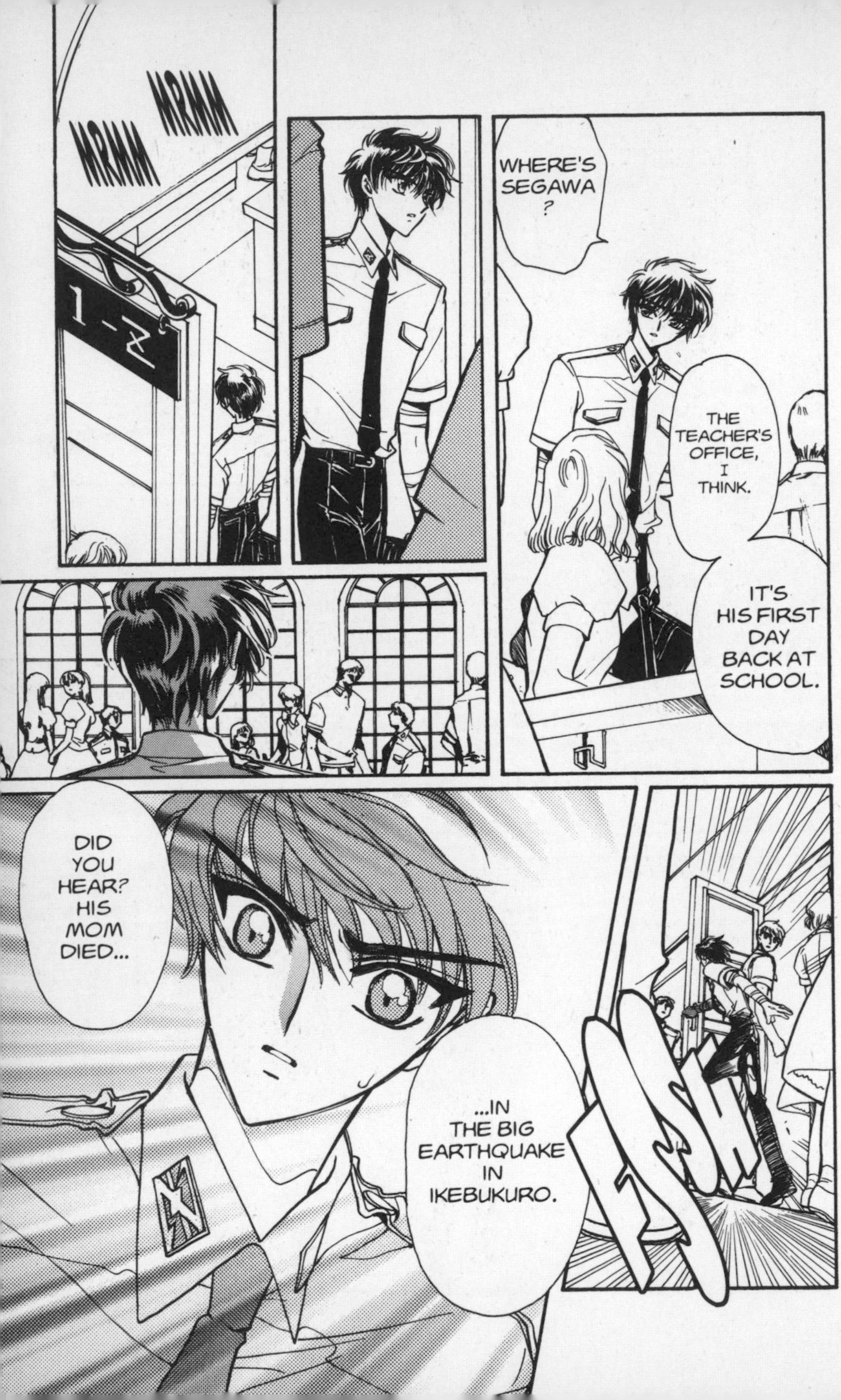
WHERE'S SEGAWA?
THE TEACHER'S OFFICE, I THINK.
IT'S HIS FIRST DAY BACK AT SCHOOL.
MRMM MRMM
DID YOU HEAR? HIS MOM DIED...
...IN THE BIG EARTHQUAKE IN IKEBUKURO.

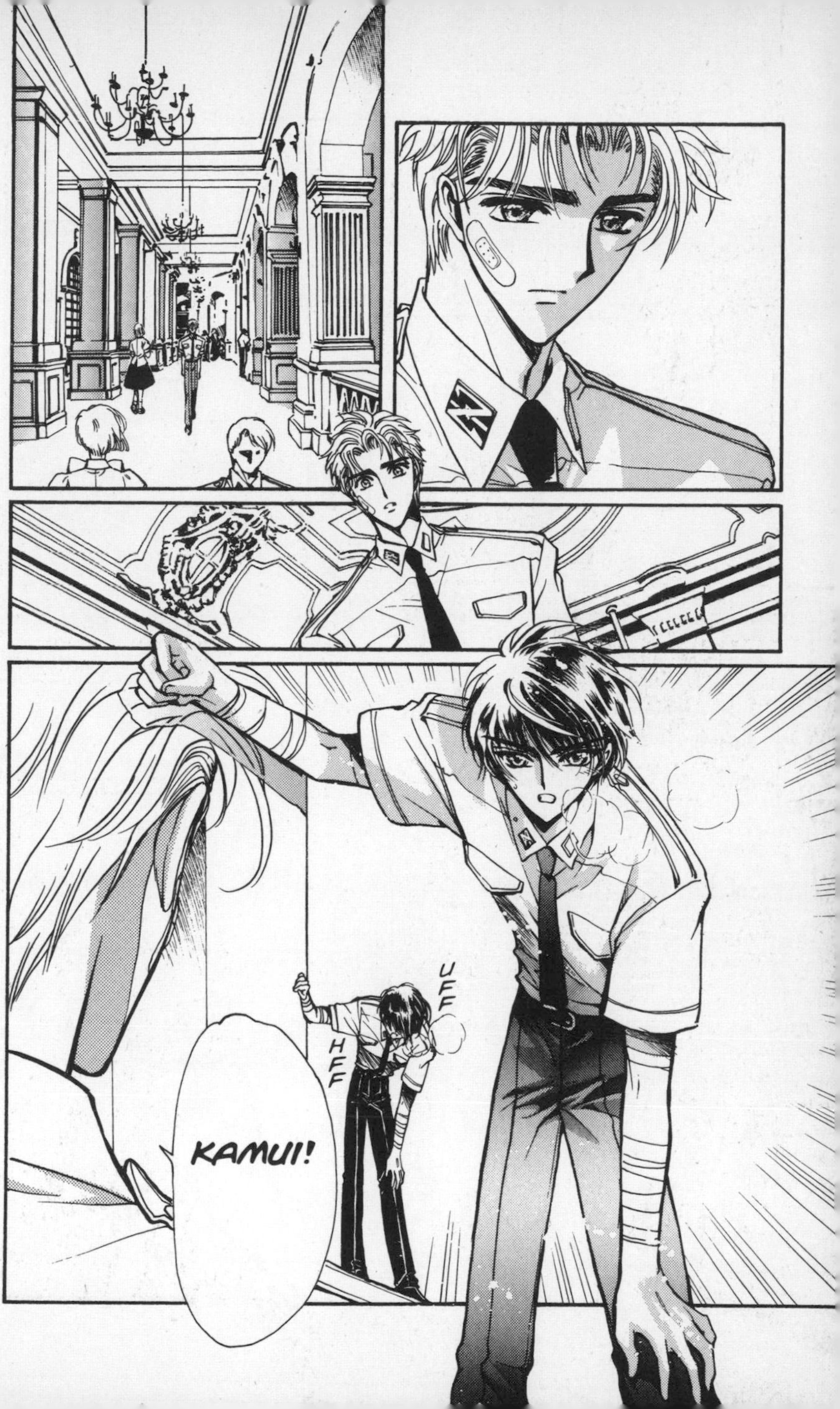

UFF
HFF
KAMUI!

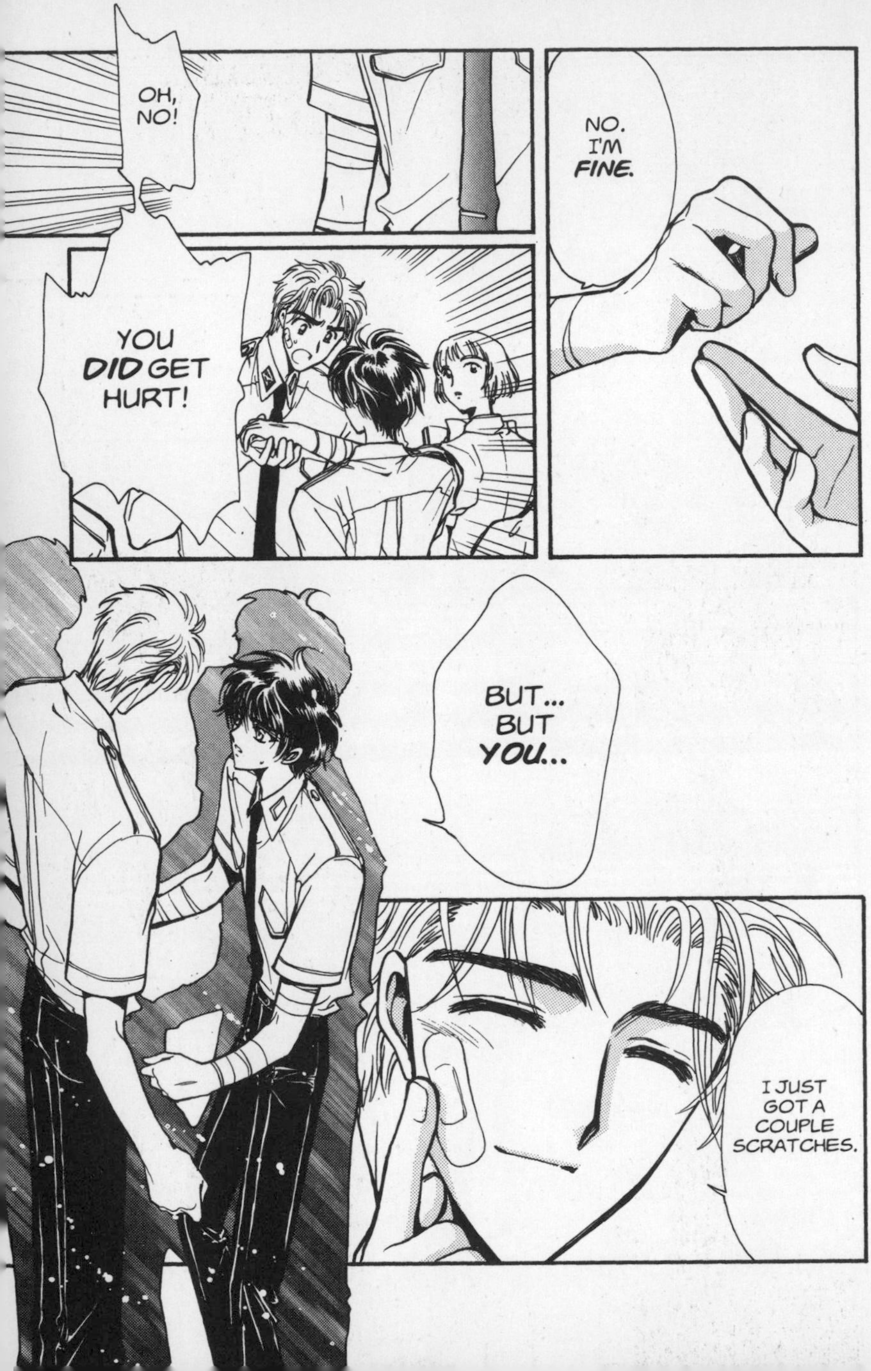
NO. I'M FINE.
OH, NO!
YOU DID GET HURT!
BUT... BUT YOU...
I JUST GOT A COUPLE SCRATCHES.

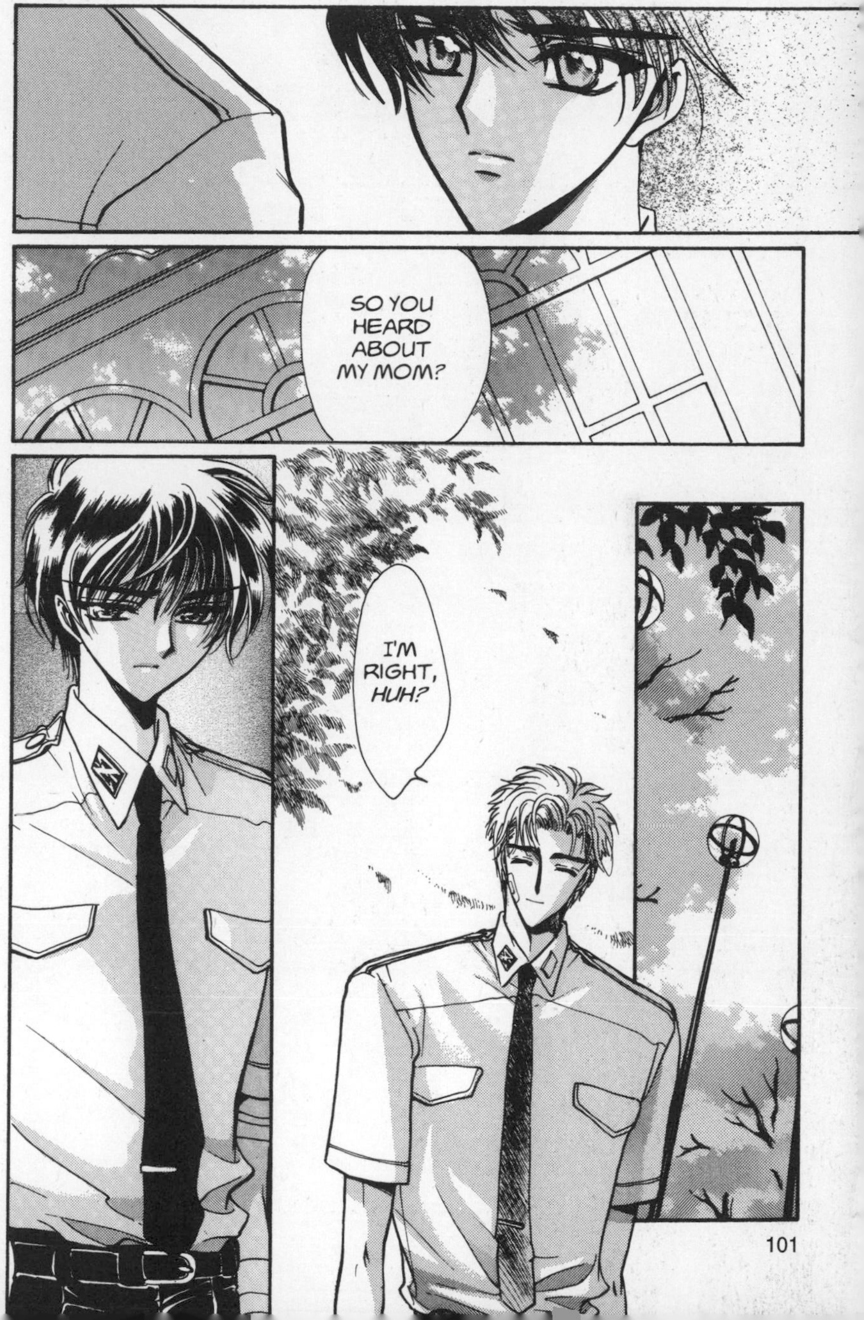
SO YOU HEARD ABOUT MY MOM?
I'M RIGHT, HUH?

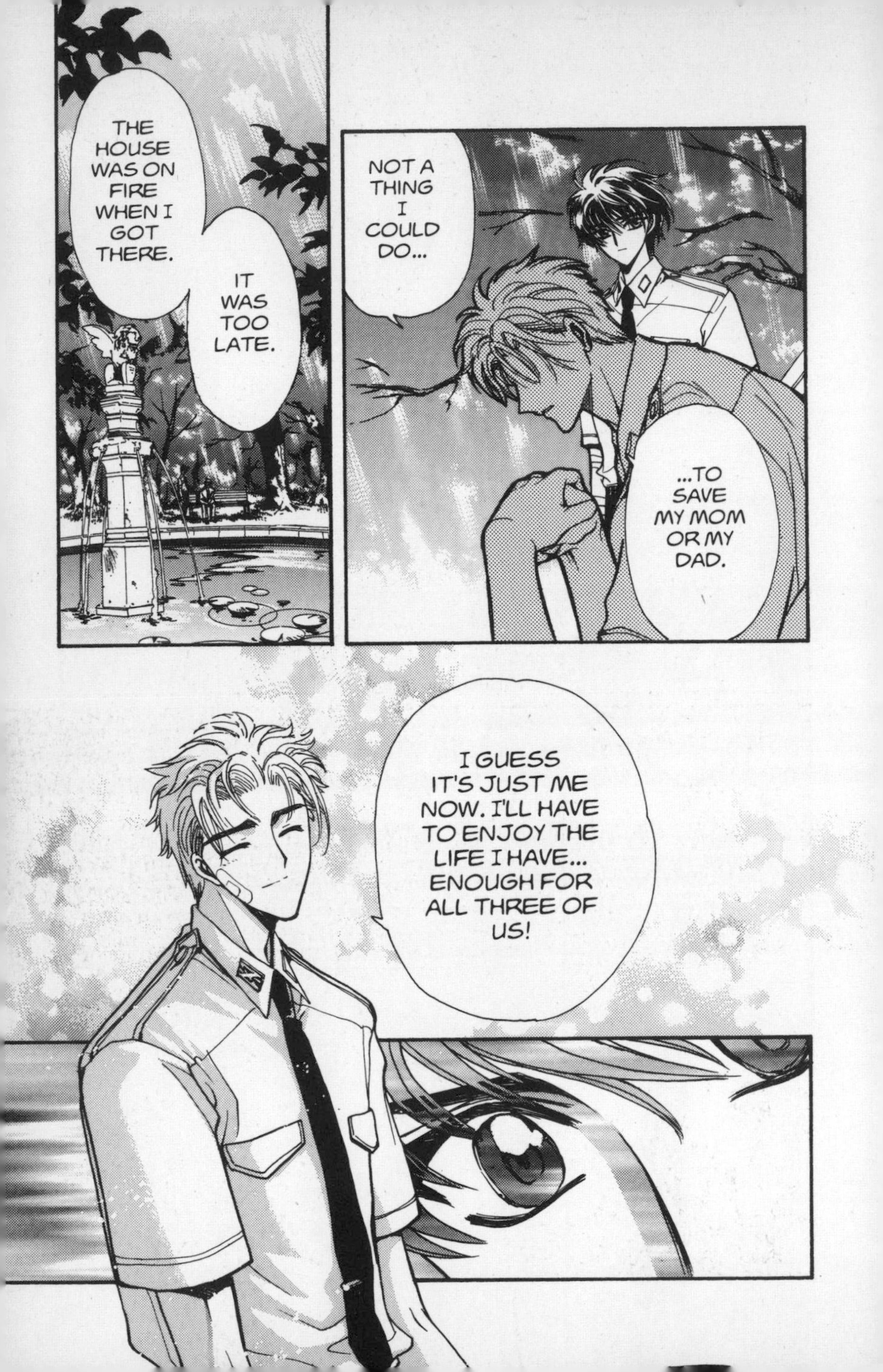
THE HOUSE WAS ON FIRE WHEN I GOT THERE.
IT WAS TOO LATE.
NOT A THING I COULD DO...
...TO SAVE MY MOM OR MY DAD.
I GUESS IT'S JUST ME NOW. I'LL HAVE TO ENJOY THE LIFE I HAVE... ENOUGH FOR ALL THREE OF US!

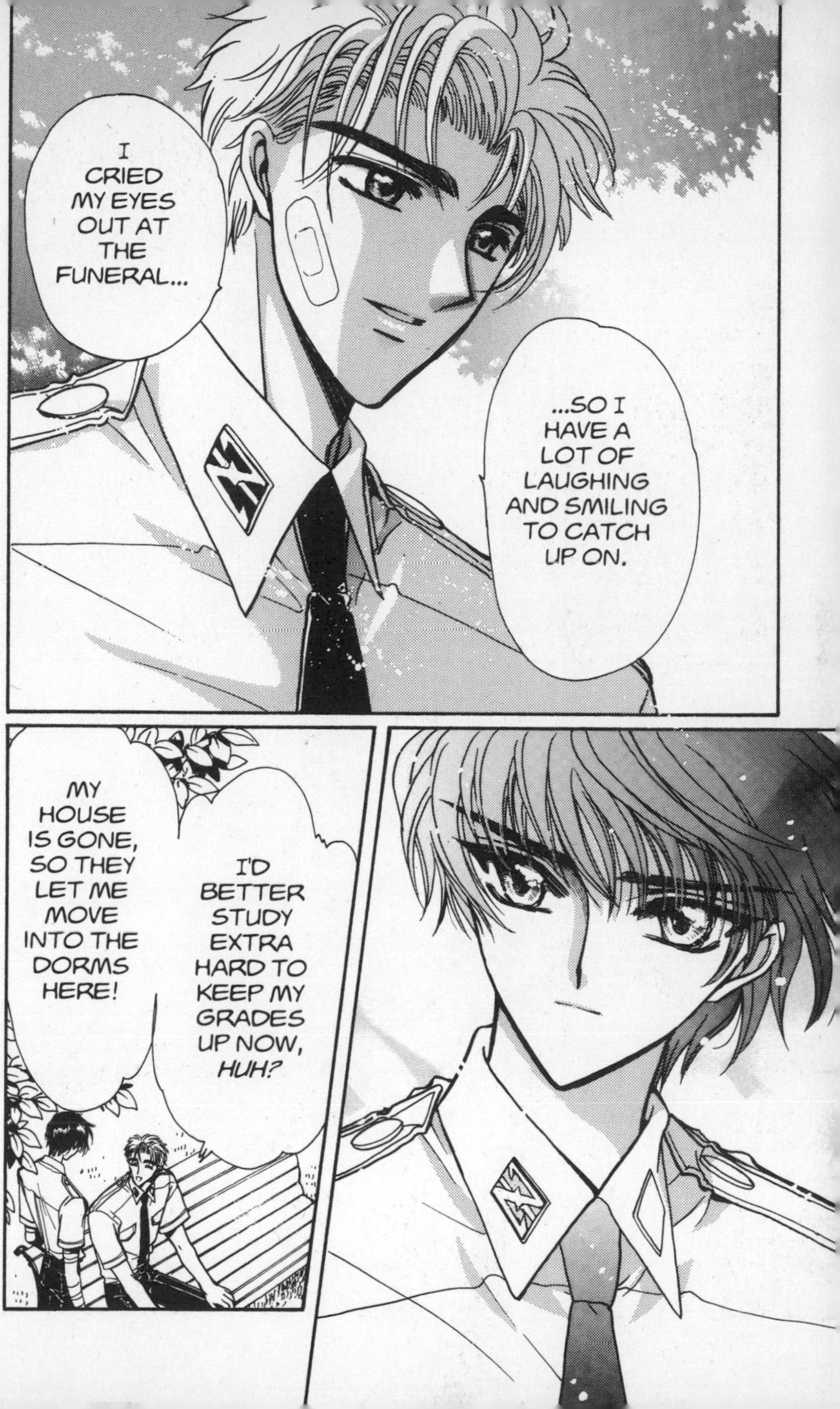
I CRIED MY EYES OUT AT THE FUNERAL...
...SO I HAVE A LOT OF LAUGHING AND SMILING TO CATCH UP ON.
MY HOUSE IS GONE, SO THEY LET ME MOVE INTO THE DORMS HERE!
I'D BETTER STUDY EXTRA HARD TO KEEP MY GRADES UP NOW, *HUH?*

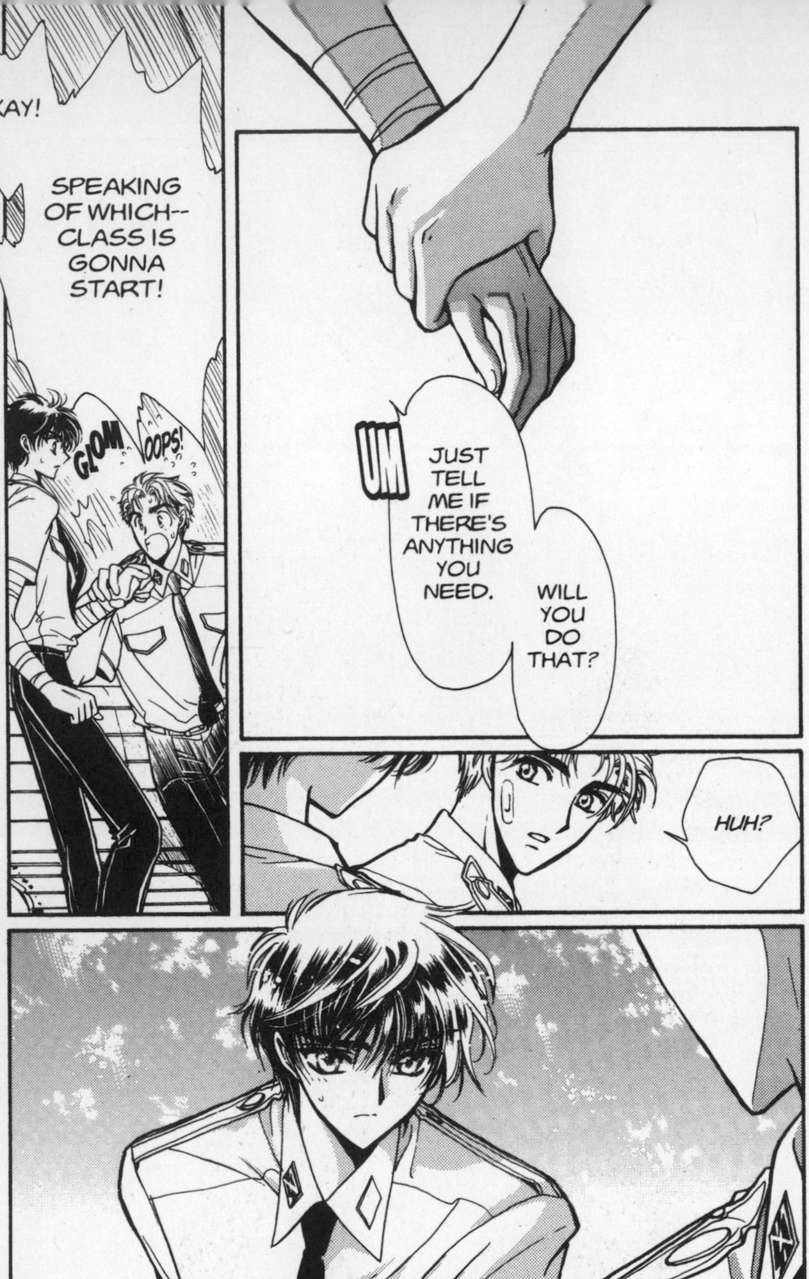
UM
JUST TELL ME IF THERE'S ANYTHING YOU NEED.
WILL YOU DO THAT?
HUH?
OKAY!
SPEAKING OF WHICH-- CLASS IS GONNA START!
GLOM
OOPS!

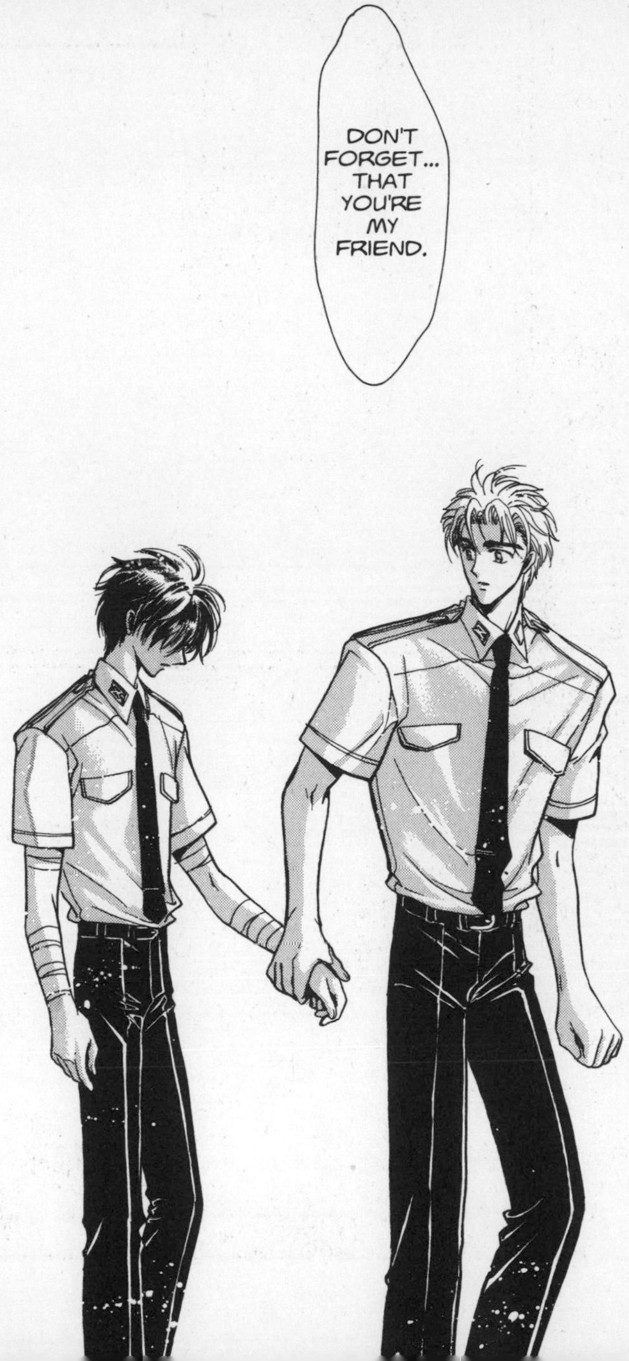
DON'T FORGET... THAT YOU'RE MY FRIEND.

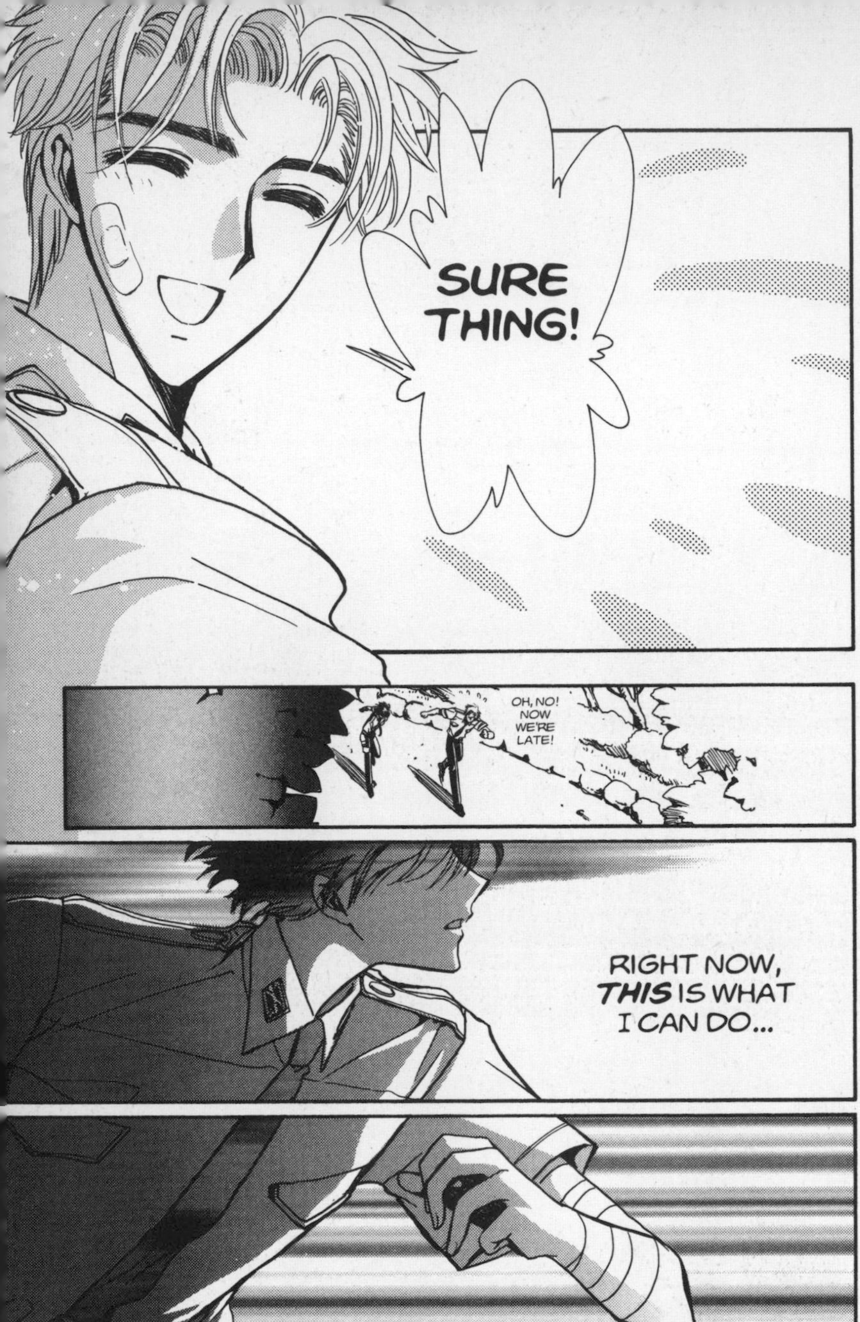
SURE THING!
OH, NO! NOW WE'RE LATE!
RIGHT NOW, *THIS* IS WHAT I CAN DO...

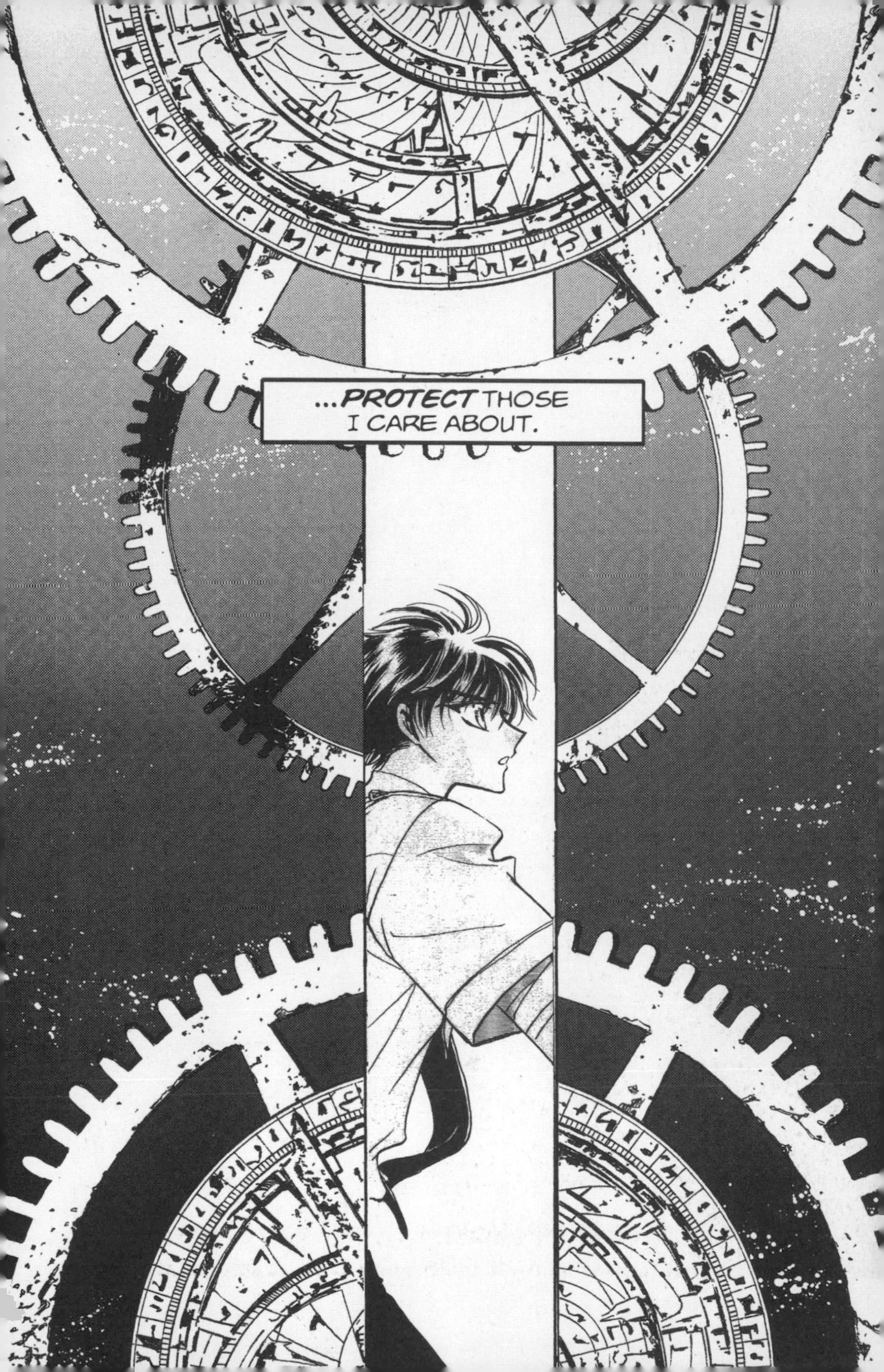
...PROTECT THOSE I CARE ABOUT.

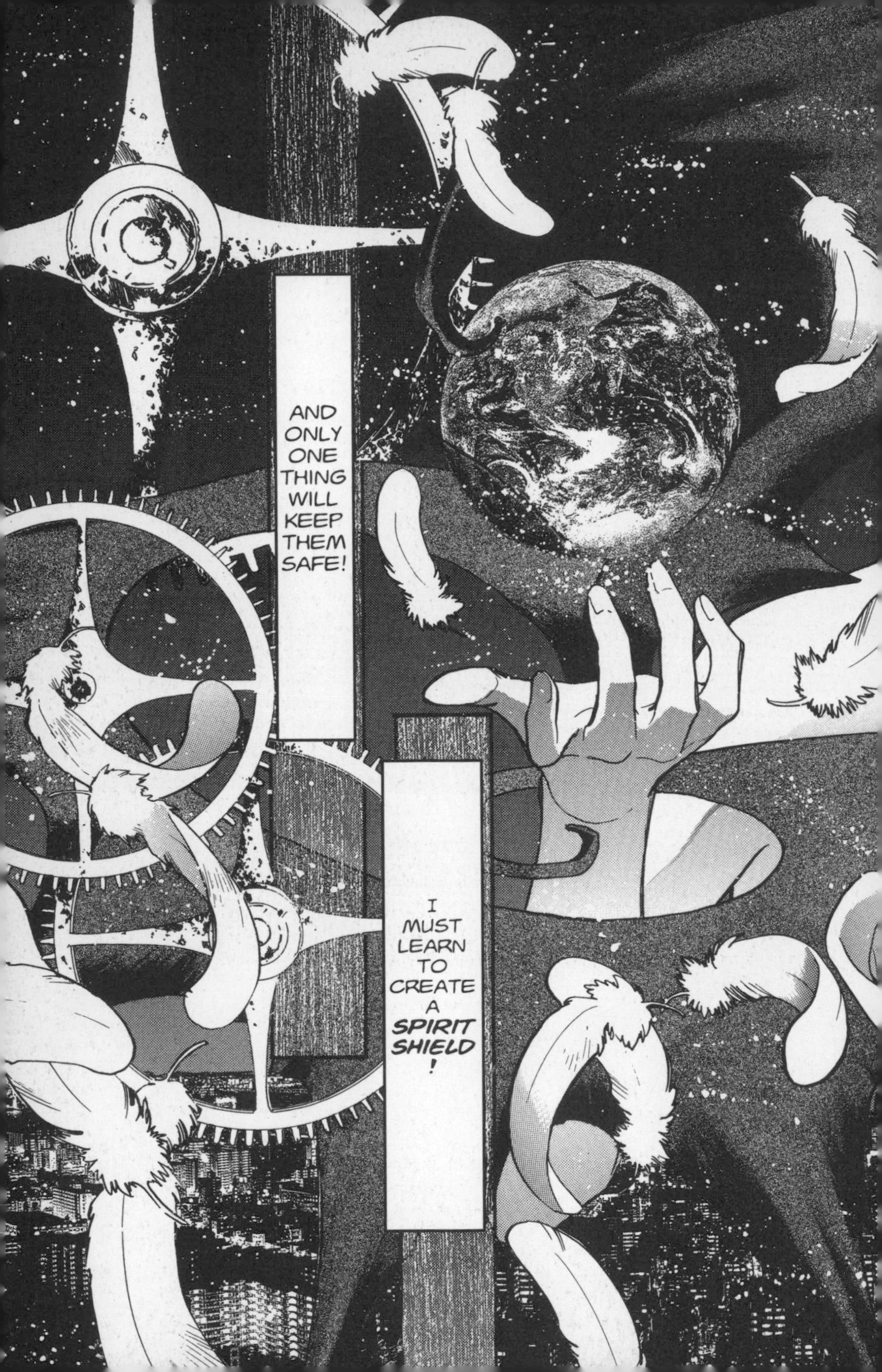
AND ONLY ONE THING WILL KEEP THEM SAFE!
I MUST LEARN TO CREATE A SPIRIT SHIELD!

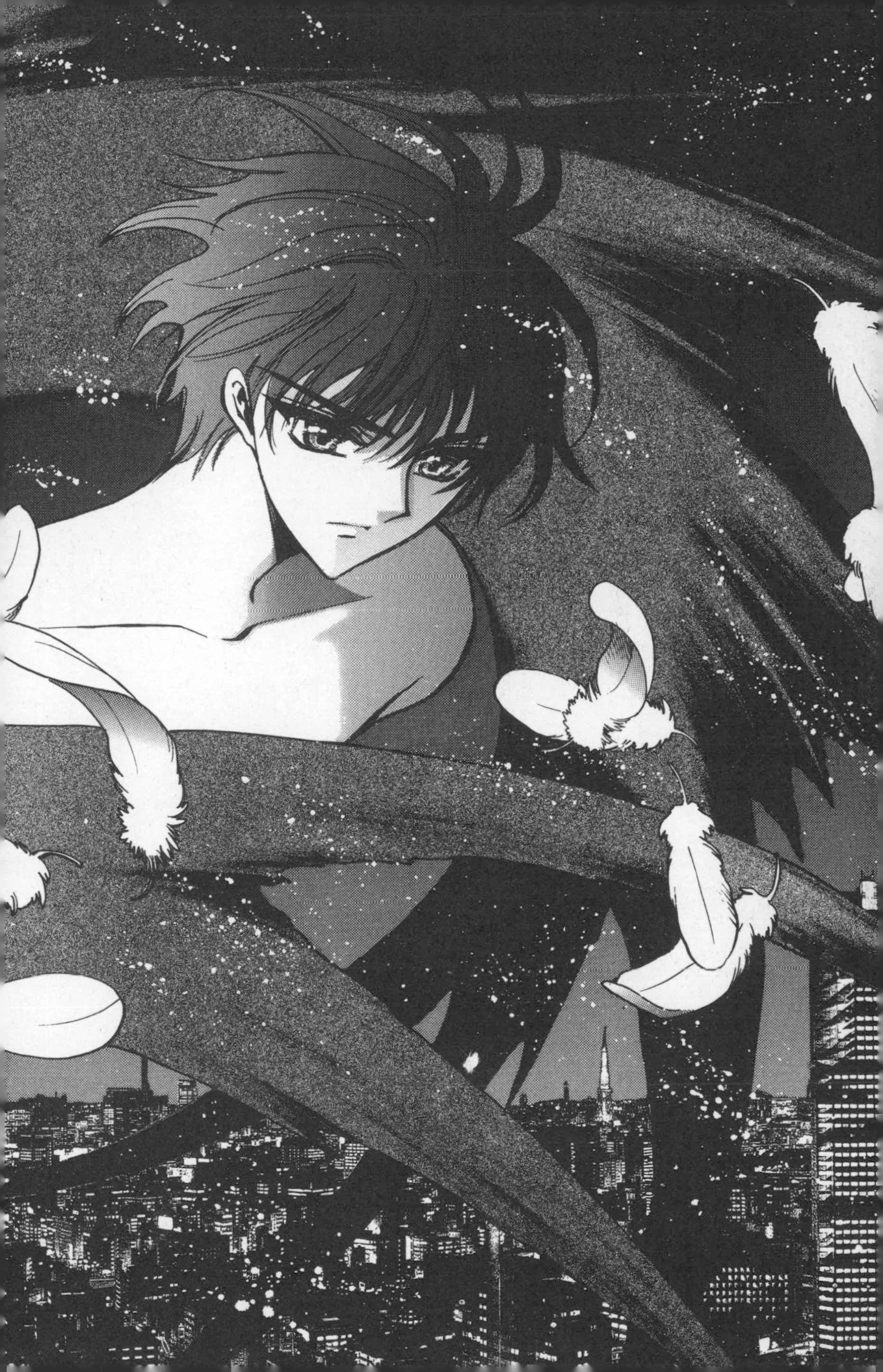

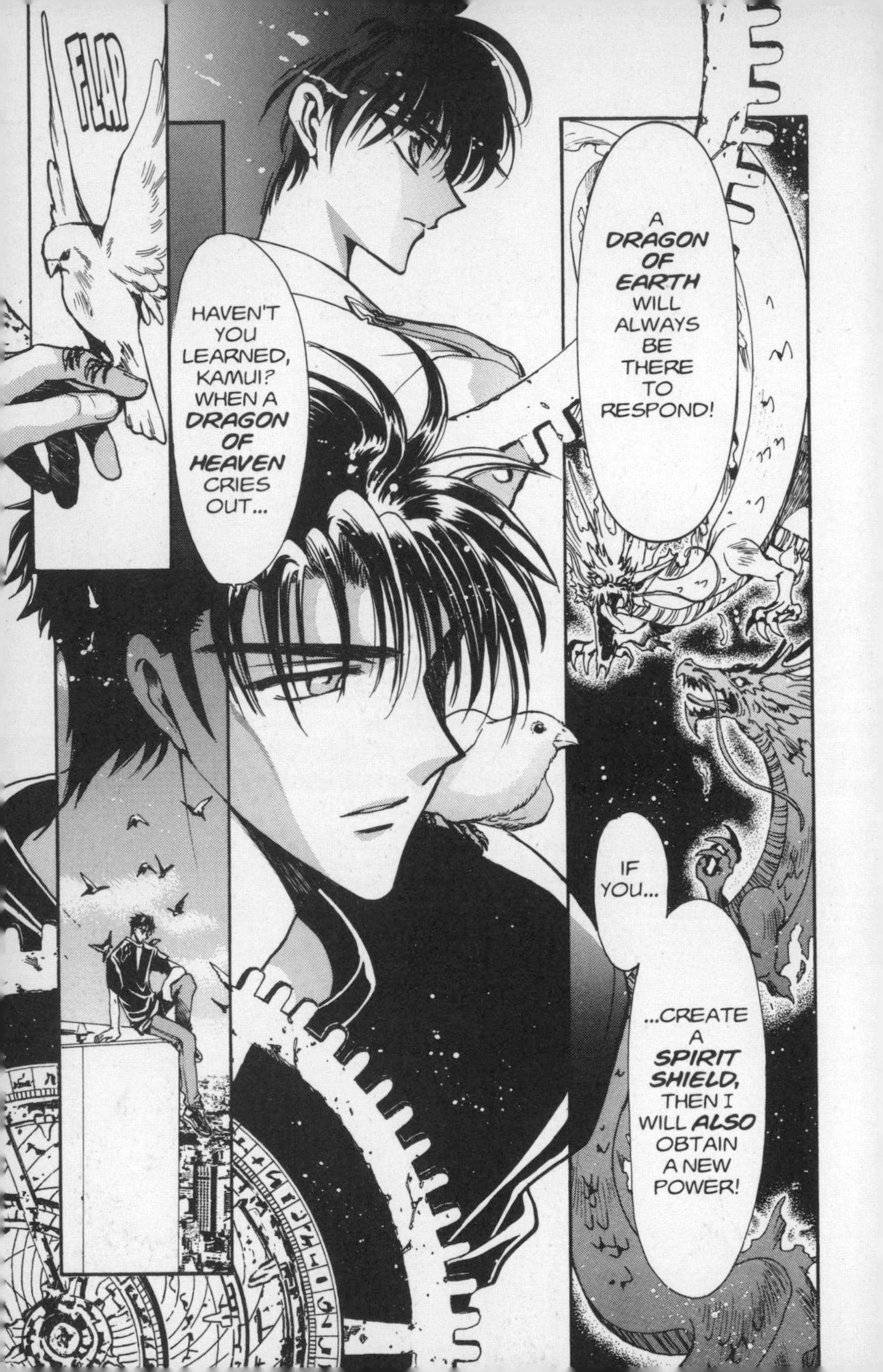
FLAP
HAVEN'T YOU LEARNED, KAMUI? WHEN A DRAGON OF HEAVEN CRIES OUT...
A DRAGON OF EARTH WILL ALWAYS BE THERE TO RESPOND!
IF YOU...
...CREATE A SPIRIT SHIELD, THEN I WILL ALSO OBTAIN A NEW POWER!

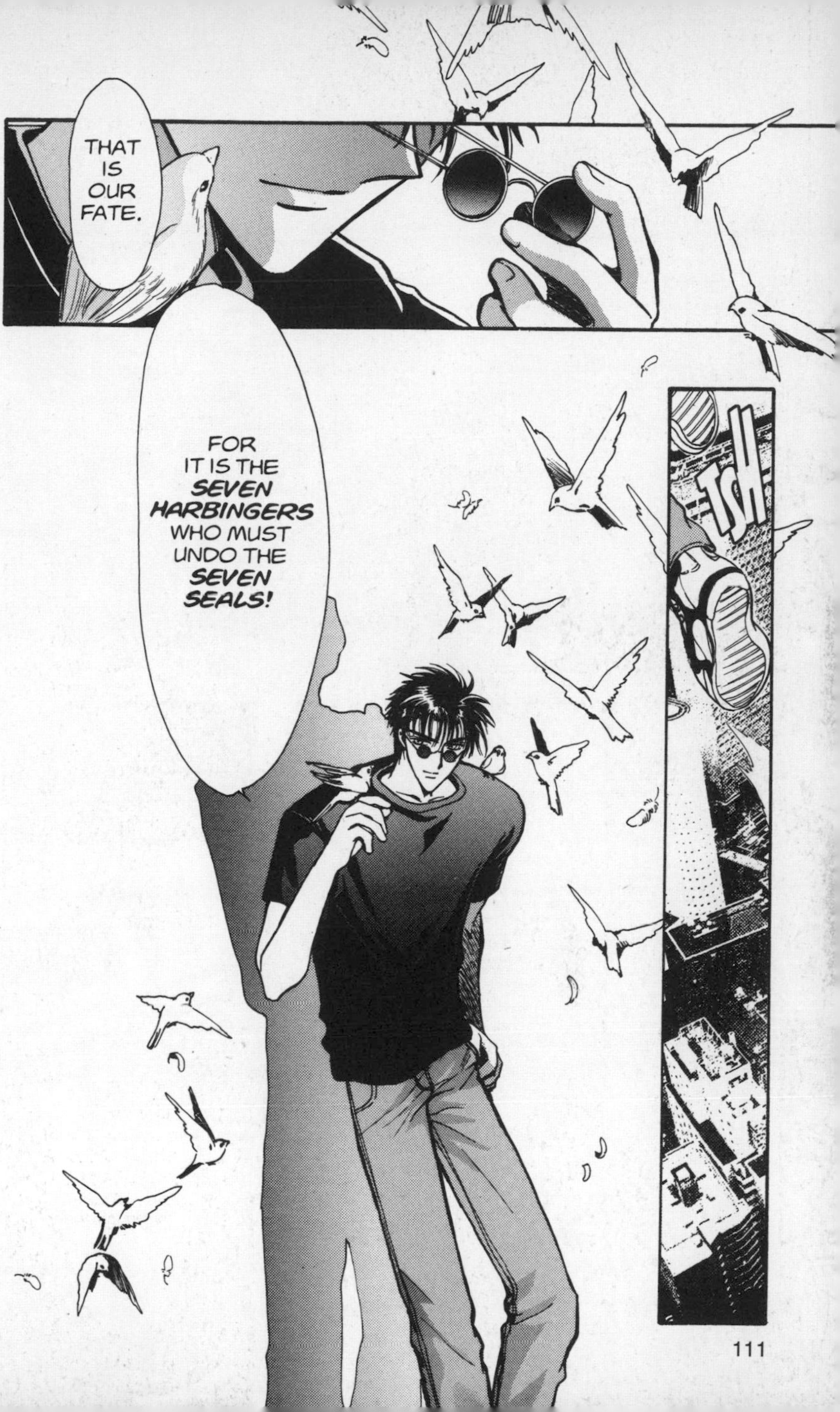
THAT IS OUR FATE.
FOR IT IS THE SEVEN HARBINGERS WHO MUST UNDO THE SEVEN SEALS!
TSH

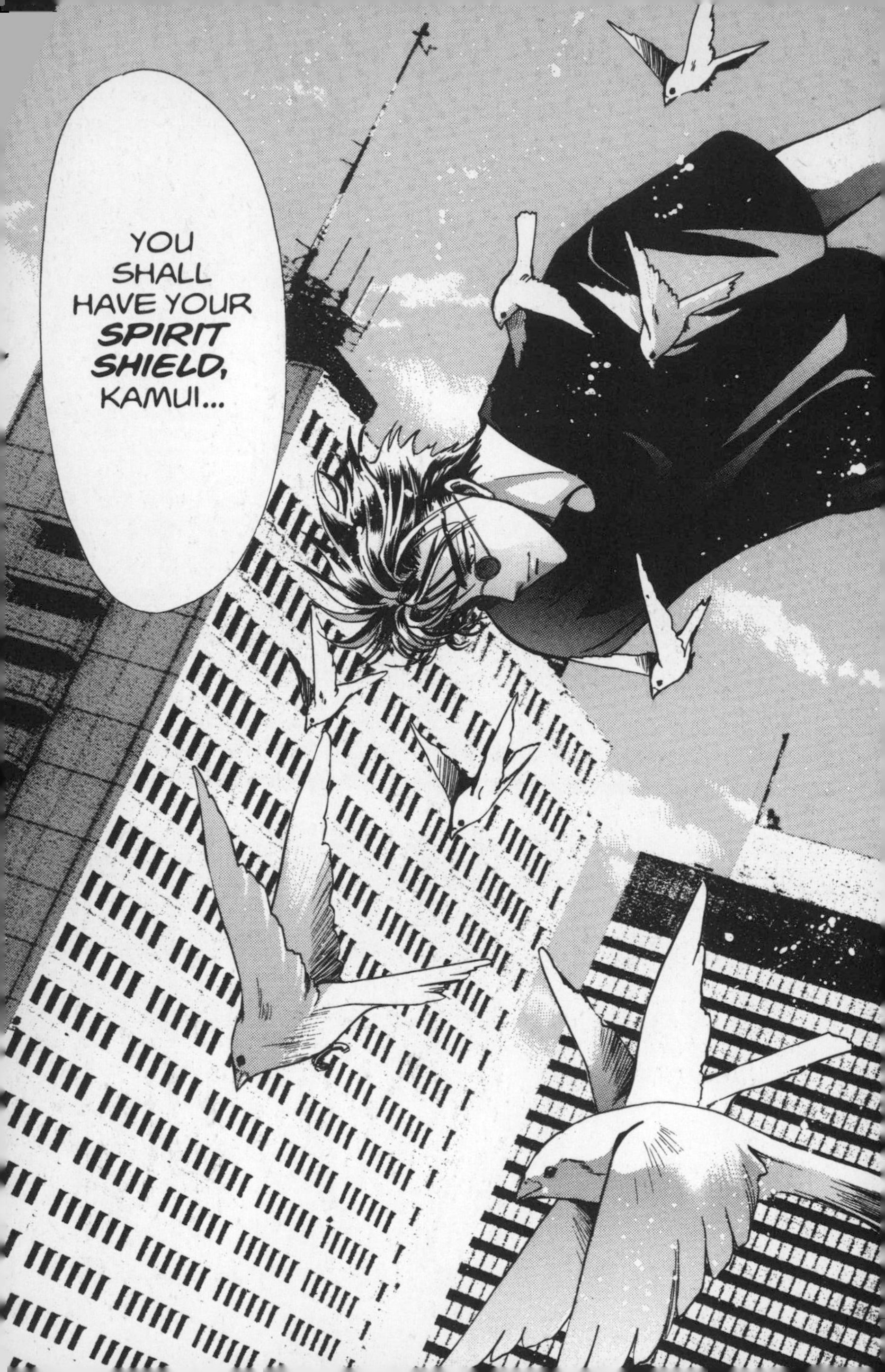
YOU SHALL HAVE YOUR SPIRIT SHIELD, KAMUI...

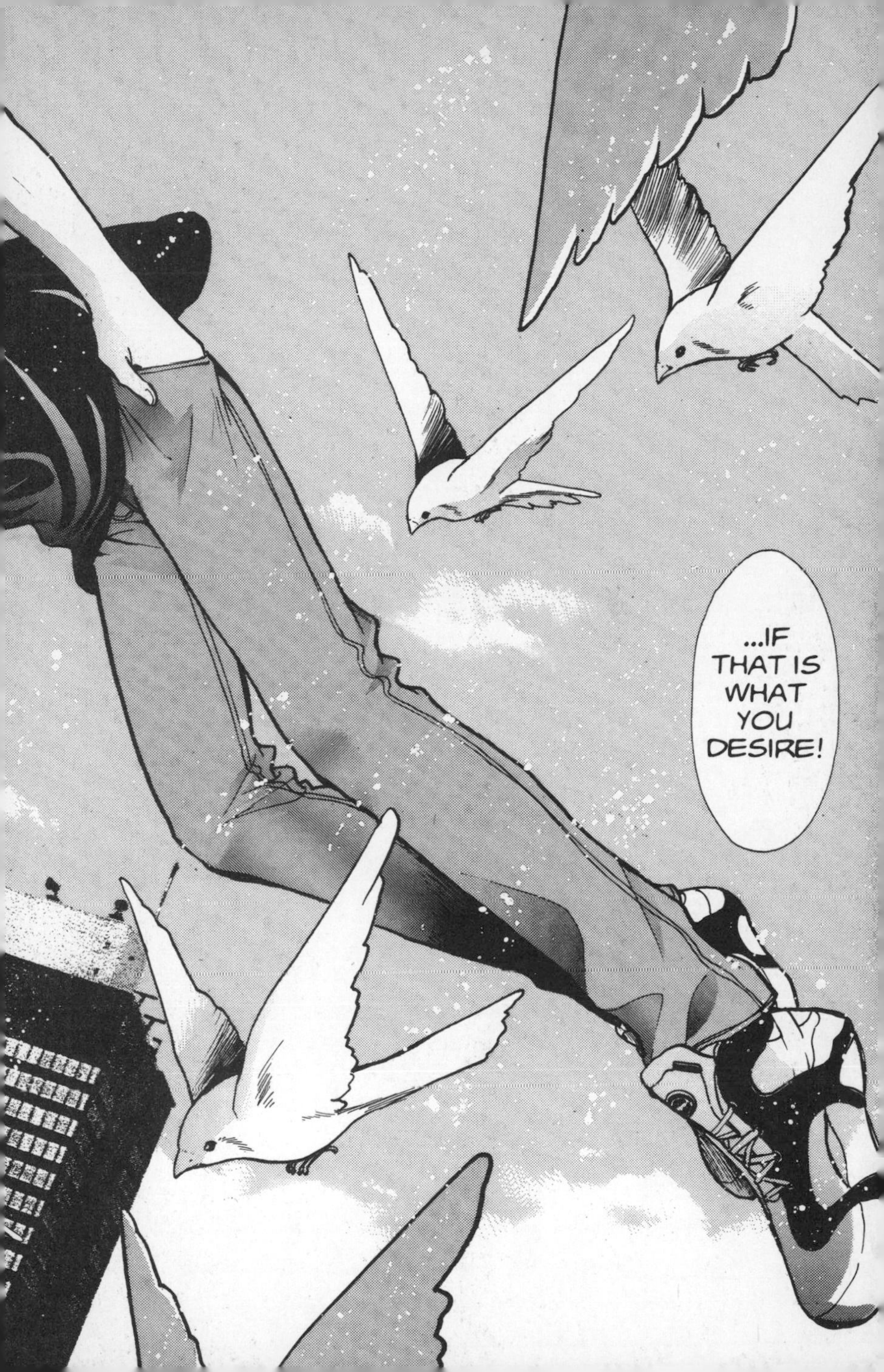
...IF THAT IS WHAT YOU DESIRE!

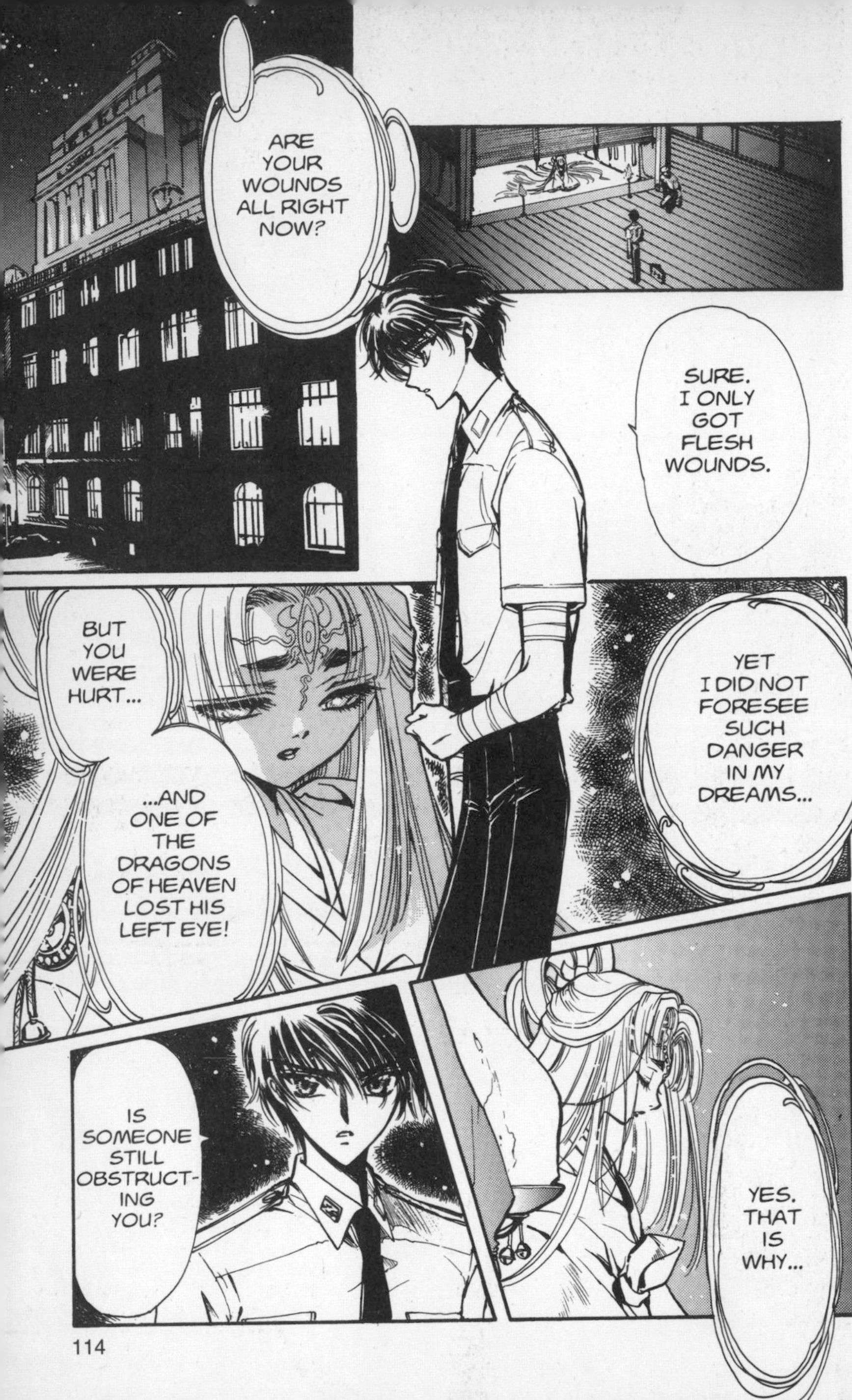
ARE YOUR WOUNDS ALL RIGHT NOW?
SURE. I ONLY GOT FLESH WOUNDS.
YET I DID NOT FORESEE SUCH DANGER IN MY DREAMS...
BUT YOU WERE HURT...
...AND ONE OF THE DRAGONS OF HEAVEN LOST HIS LEFT EYE!
IS SOMEONE STILL OBSTRUCTING YOU?
YES. THAT IS WHY...

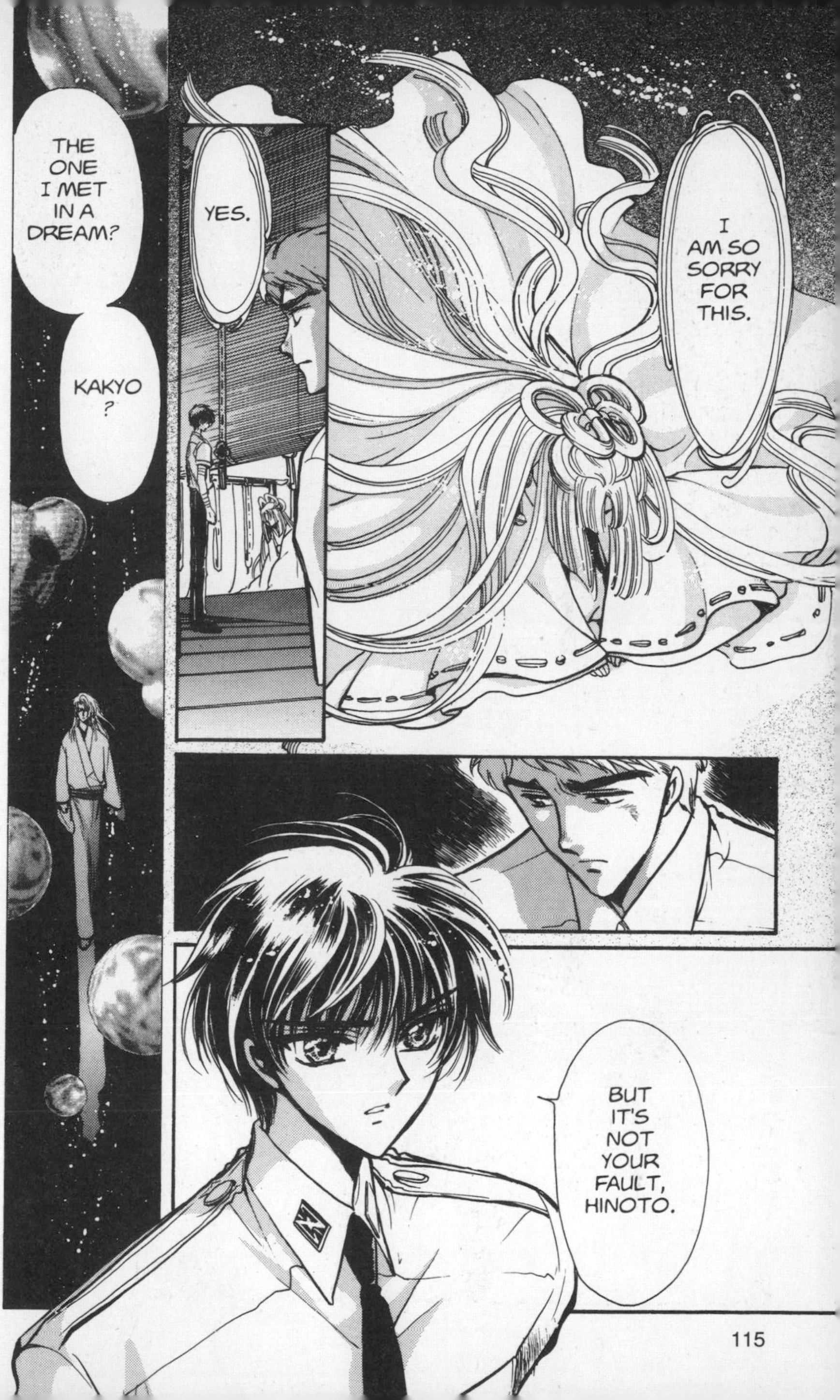
I AM SO SORRY FOR THIS.
YES.
BUT IT'S NOT YOUR FAULT, HINOTO.
THE ONE I MET IN A DREAM?
KAKYO ?

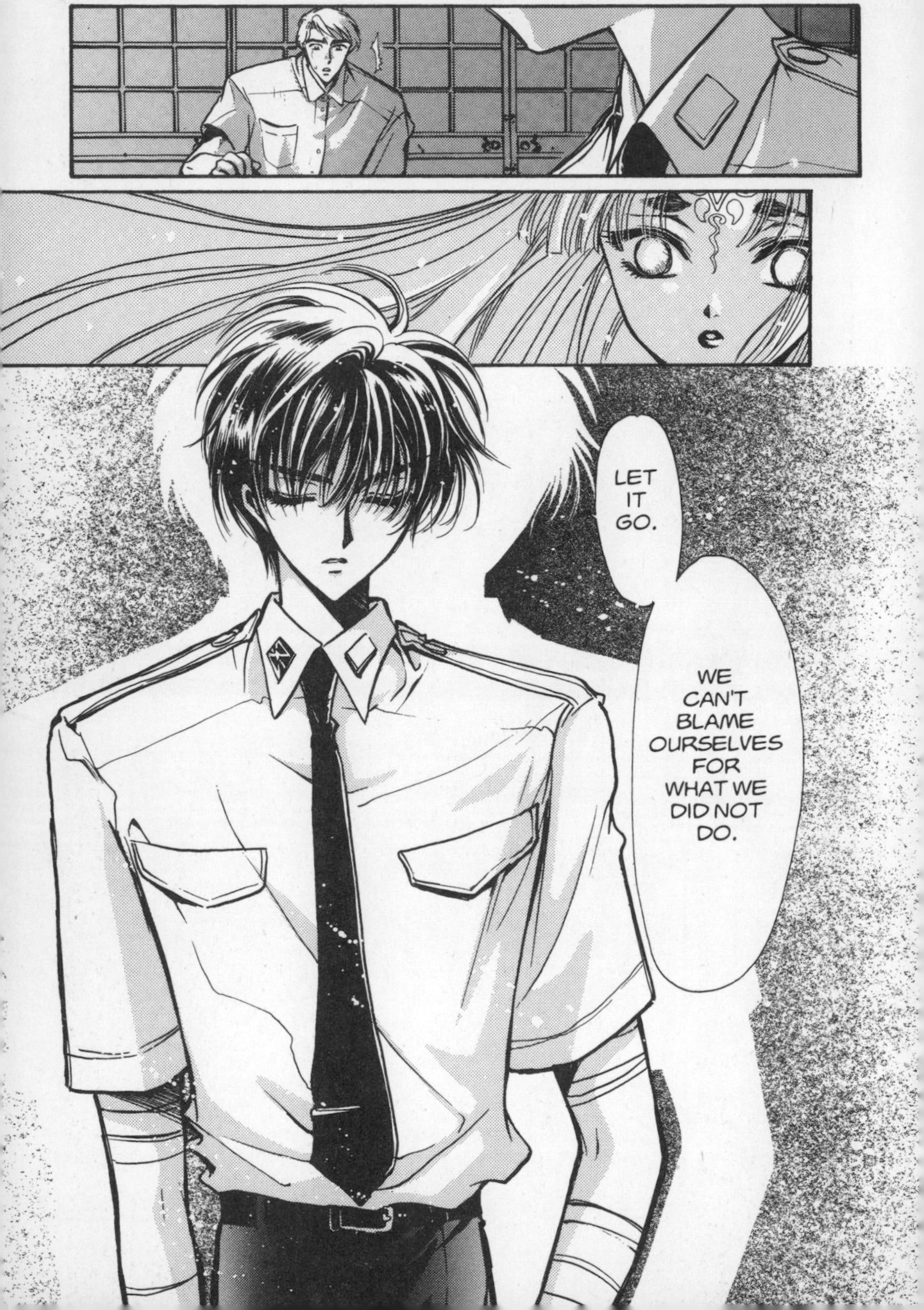
LET IT GO.
WE CAN'T BLAME OURSELVES FOR WHAT WE DID NOT DO.

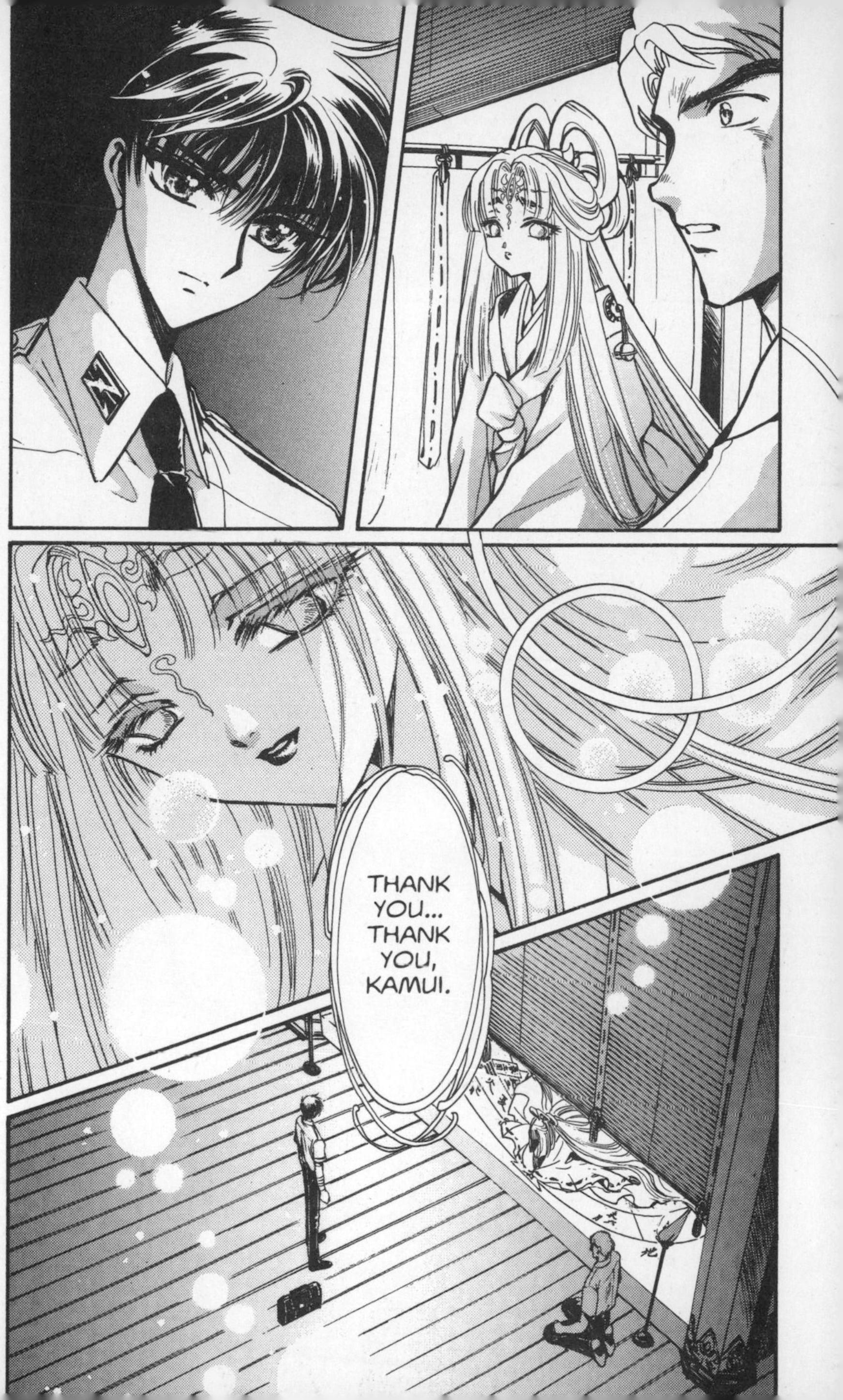
THANK YOU... THANK YOU, KAMUI.

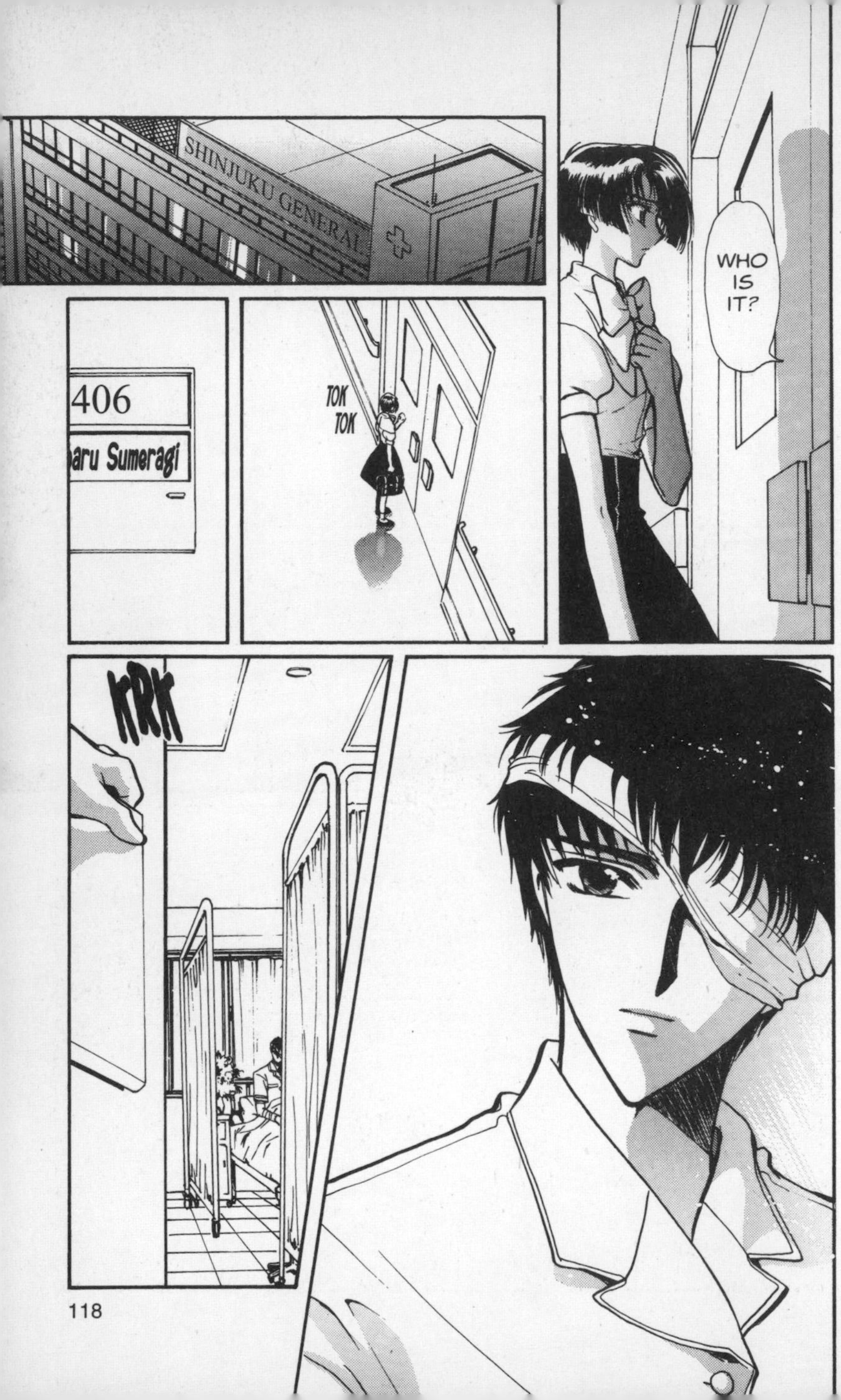
SHINJUKU GENERAL
406
aru Sumeragi
TOK TOK
WHO IS IT?
KRK

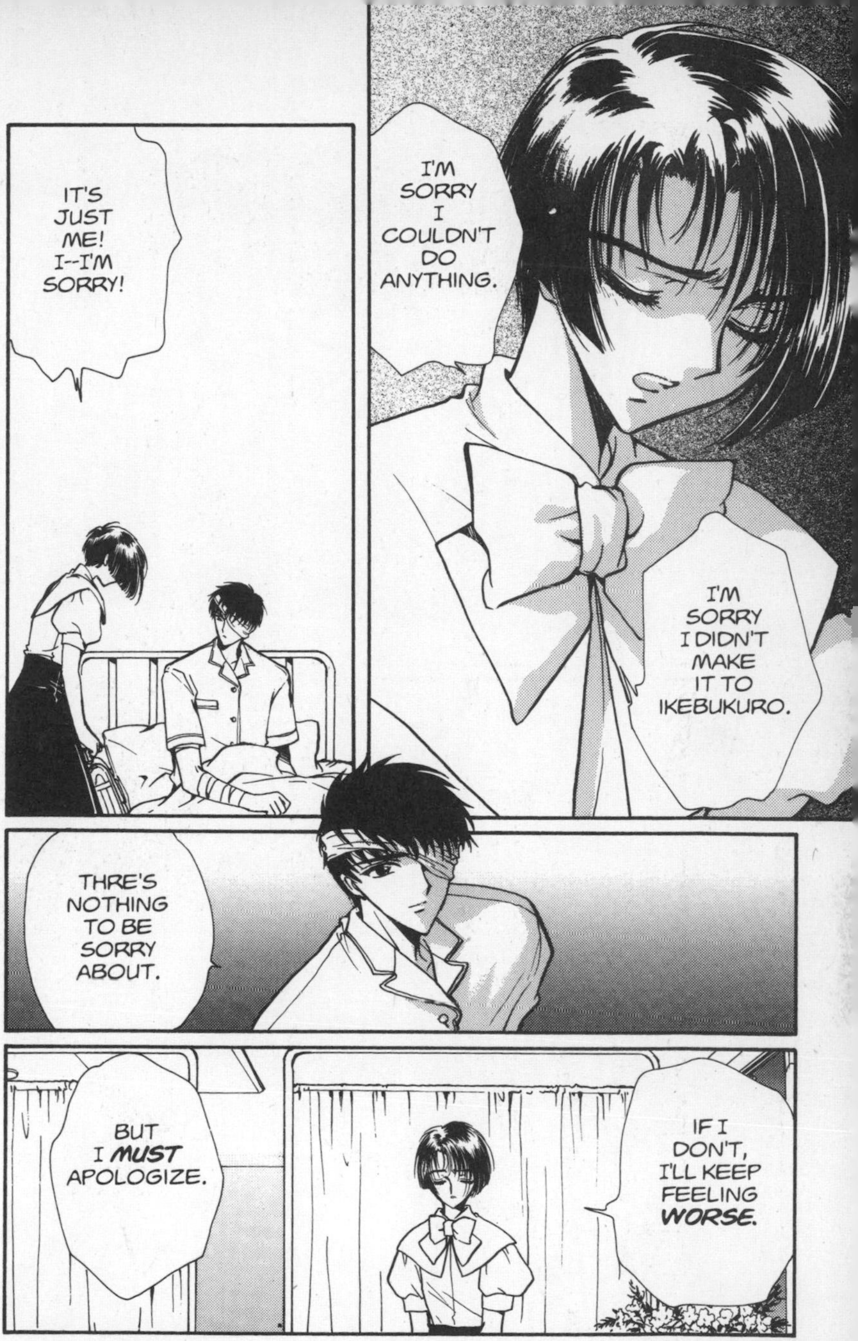

IT'S JUST ME! I--I'M SORRY!
I'M SORRY I COULDN'T DO ANYTHING.
I'M SORRY I DIDN'T MAKE IT TO IKEBUKURO.
THRE'S NOTHING TO BE SORRY ABOUT.
BUT I **MUST** APOLOGIZE.
IF I DON'T, I'LL KEEP FEELING ***WORSE.***

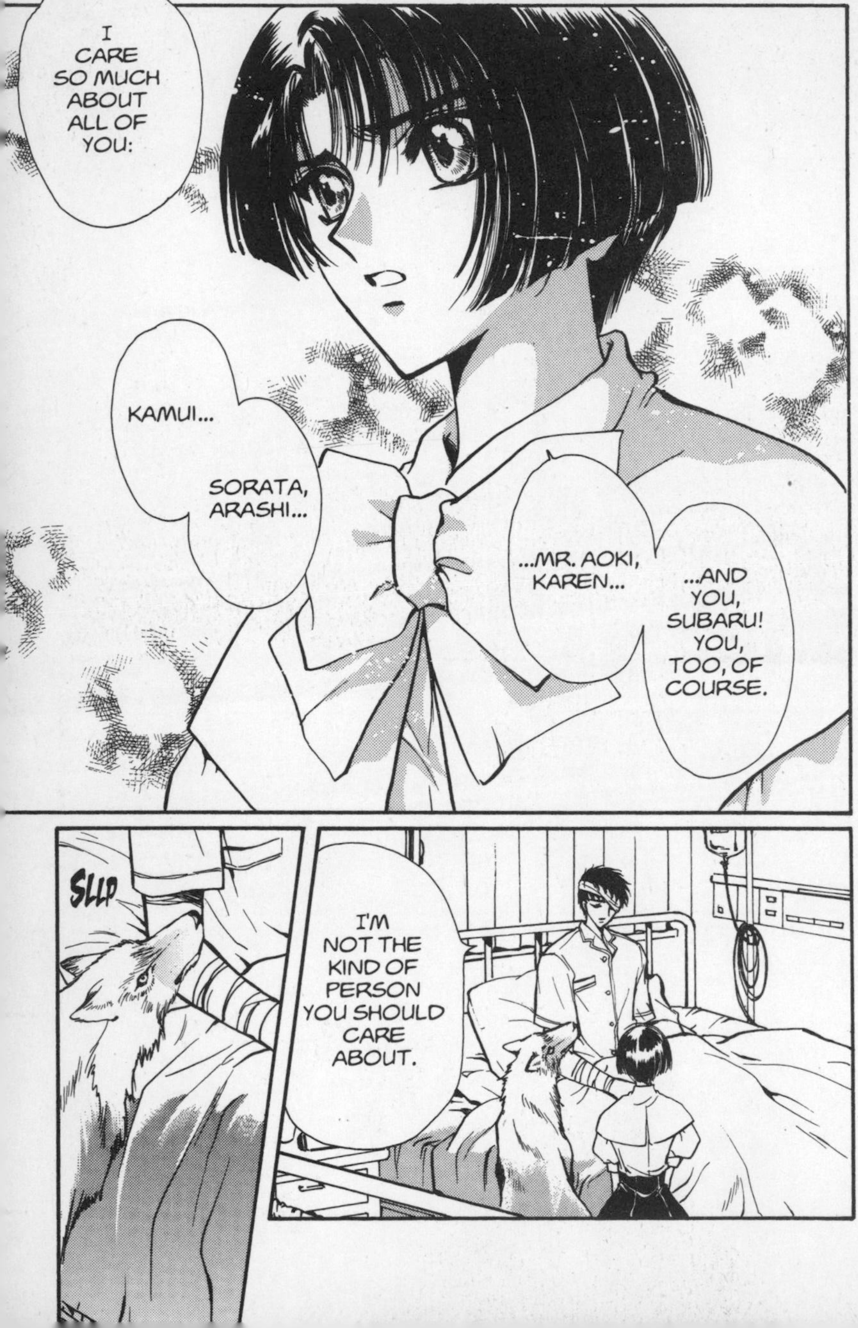
I CARE SO MUCH ABOUT ALL OF YOU:
KAMUI...
SORATA, ARASHI...
...MR. AOKI, KAREN...
...AND YOU, SUBARU! YOU, TOO, OF COURSE.
SLLP
I'M NOT THE KIND OF PERSON YOU SHOULD CARE ABOUT.

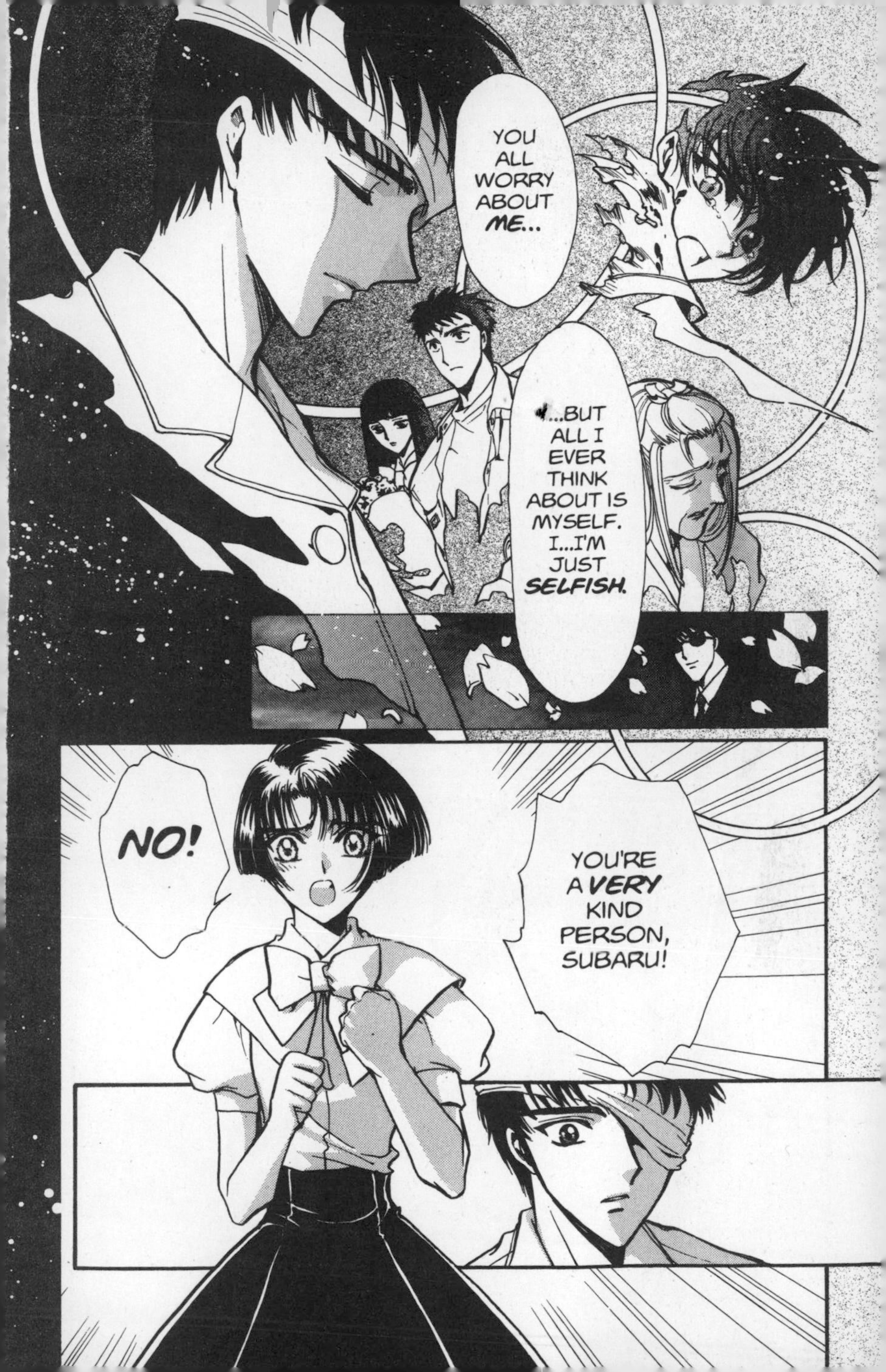
YOU ALL WORRY ABOUT ME...
...BUT ALL I EVER THINK ABOUT IS MYSELF. I...I'M JUST SELFISH.
NO!
YOU'RE A VERY KIND PERSON, SUBARU!

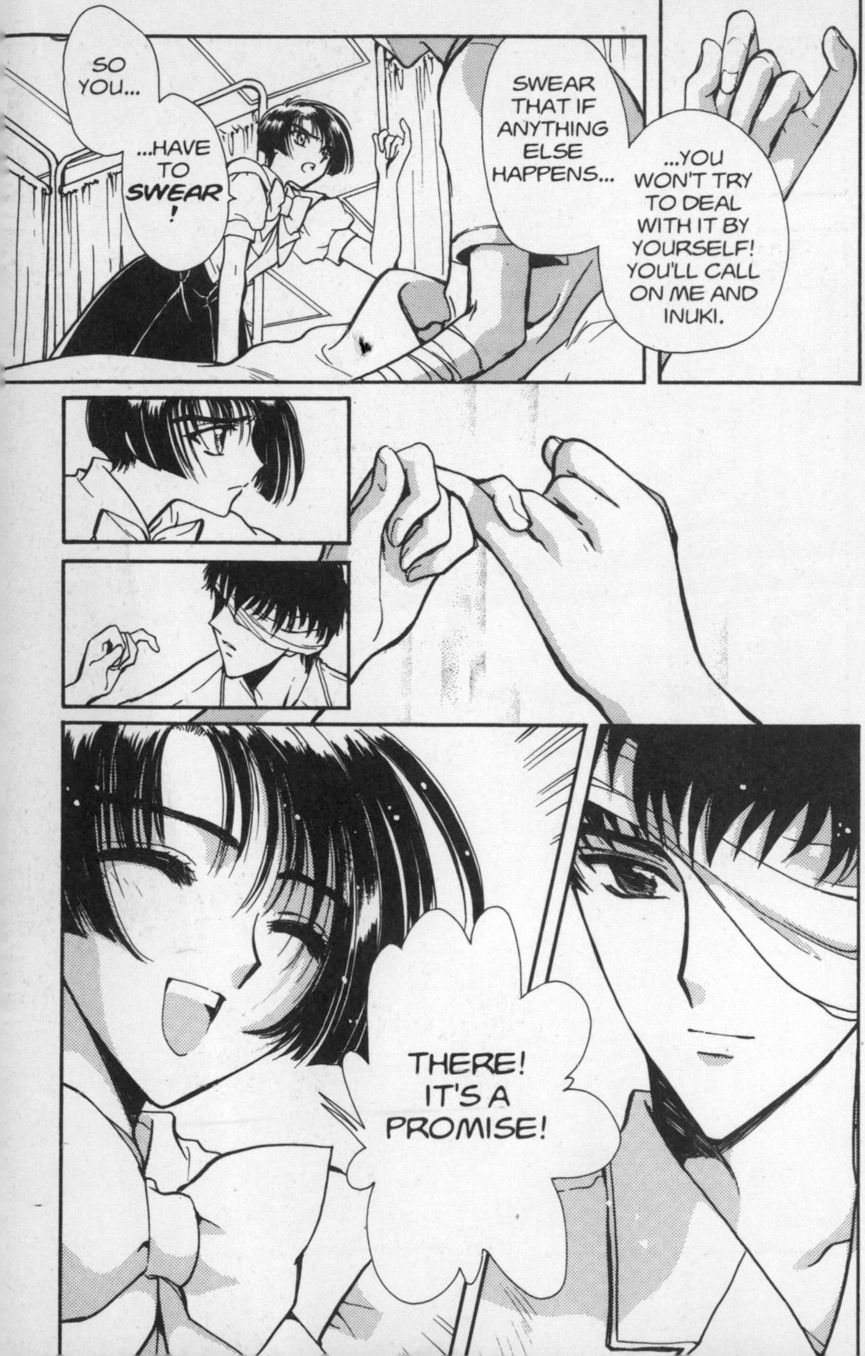
SO YOU...
...HAVE TO SWEAR!
SWEAR THAT IF ANYTHING ELSE HAPPENS...
...YOU WON'T TRY TO DEAL WITH IT BY YOURSELF! YOU'LL CALL ON ME AND INUKI.
THERE! IT'S A PROMISE!

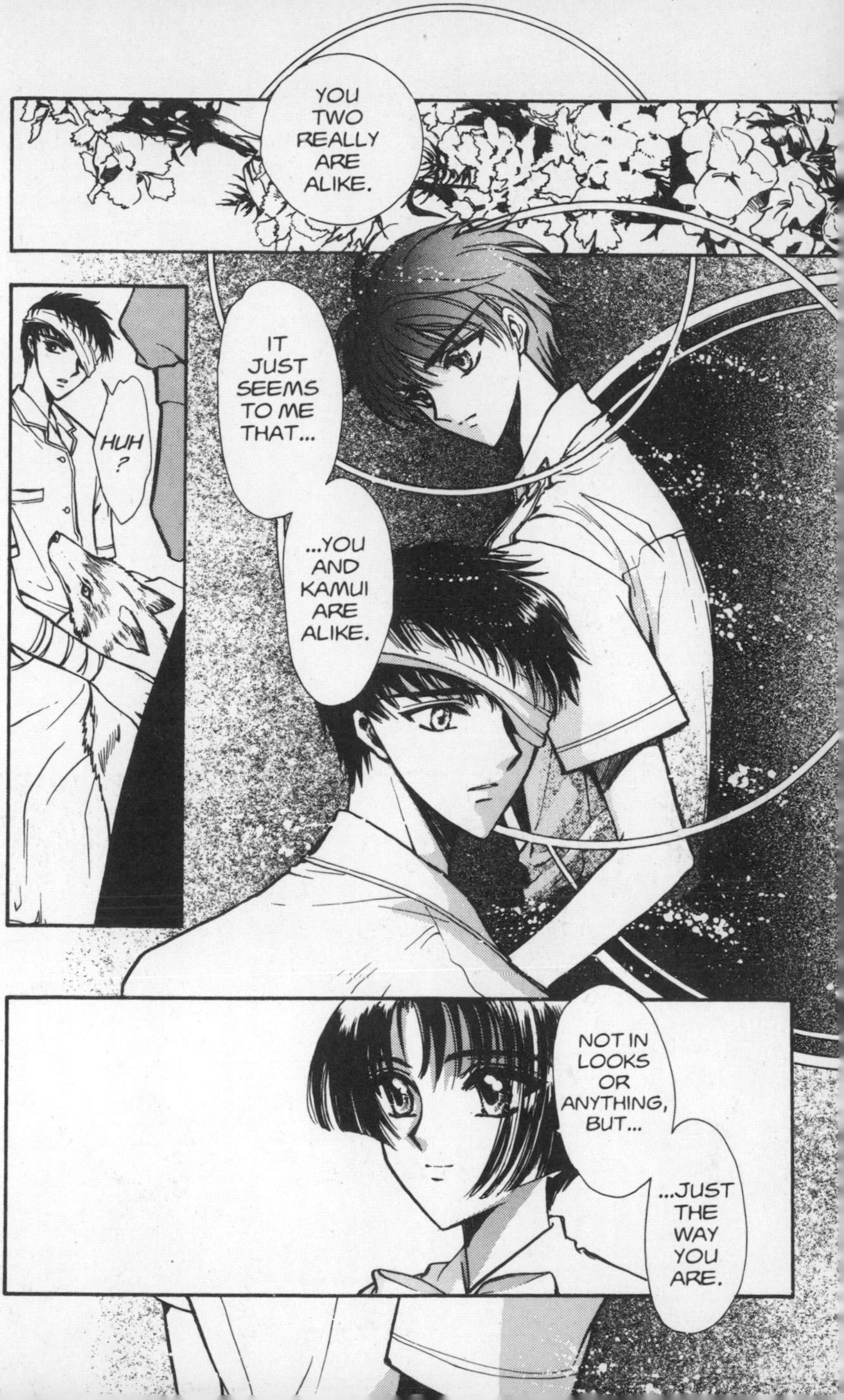
YOU TWO REALLY ARE ALIKE.
HUH?
IT JUST SEEMS TO ME THAT...
...YOU AND KAMUI ARE ALIKE.
NOT IN LOOKS OR ANYTHING, BUT...
...JUST THE WAY YOU ARE.

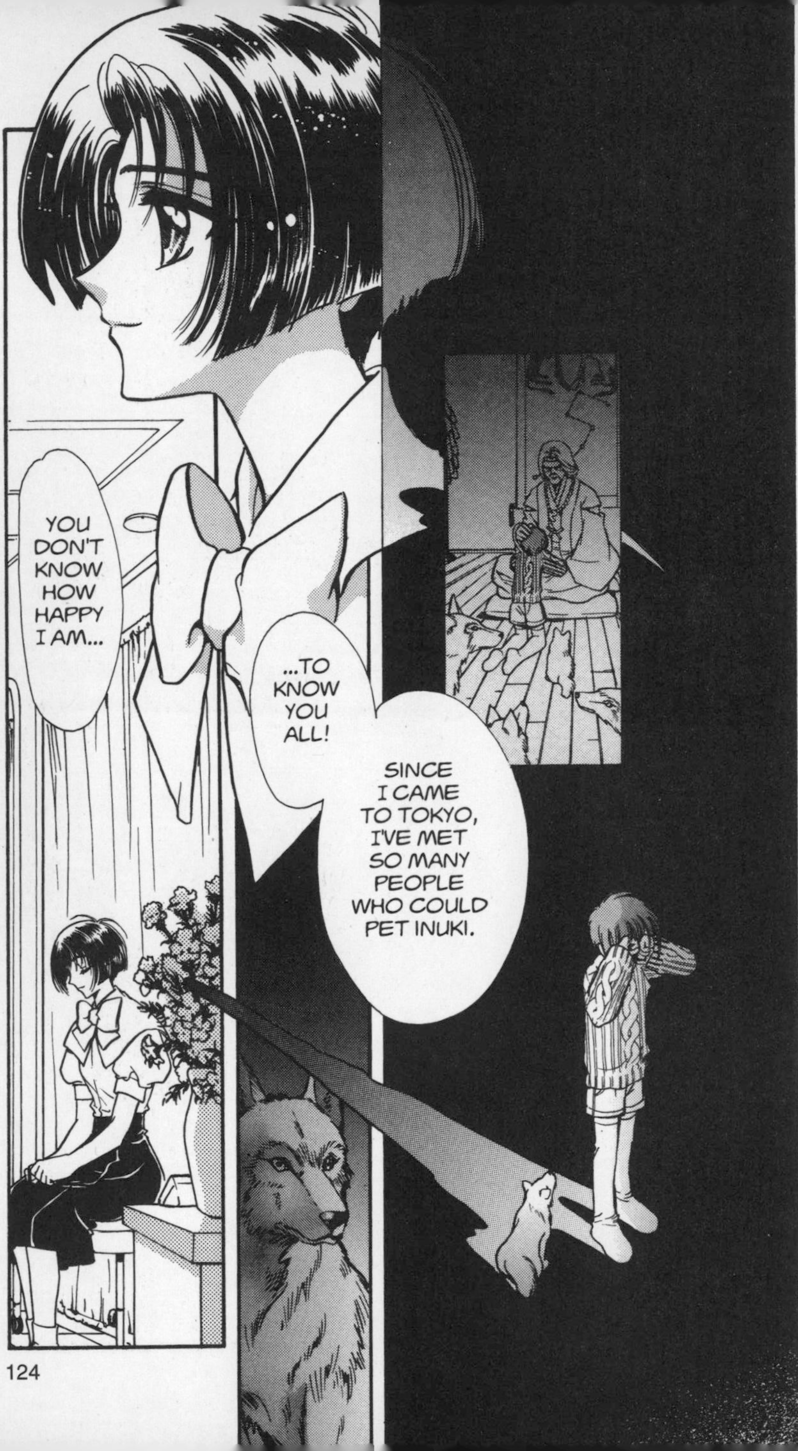
YOU DON'T KNOW HOW HAPPY I AM...
...TO KNOW YOU ALL!
SINCE I CAME TO TOKYO, I'VE MET SO MANY PEOPLE WHO COULD PET INUKI.

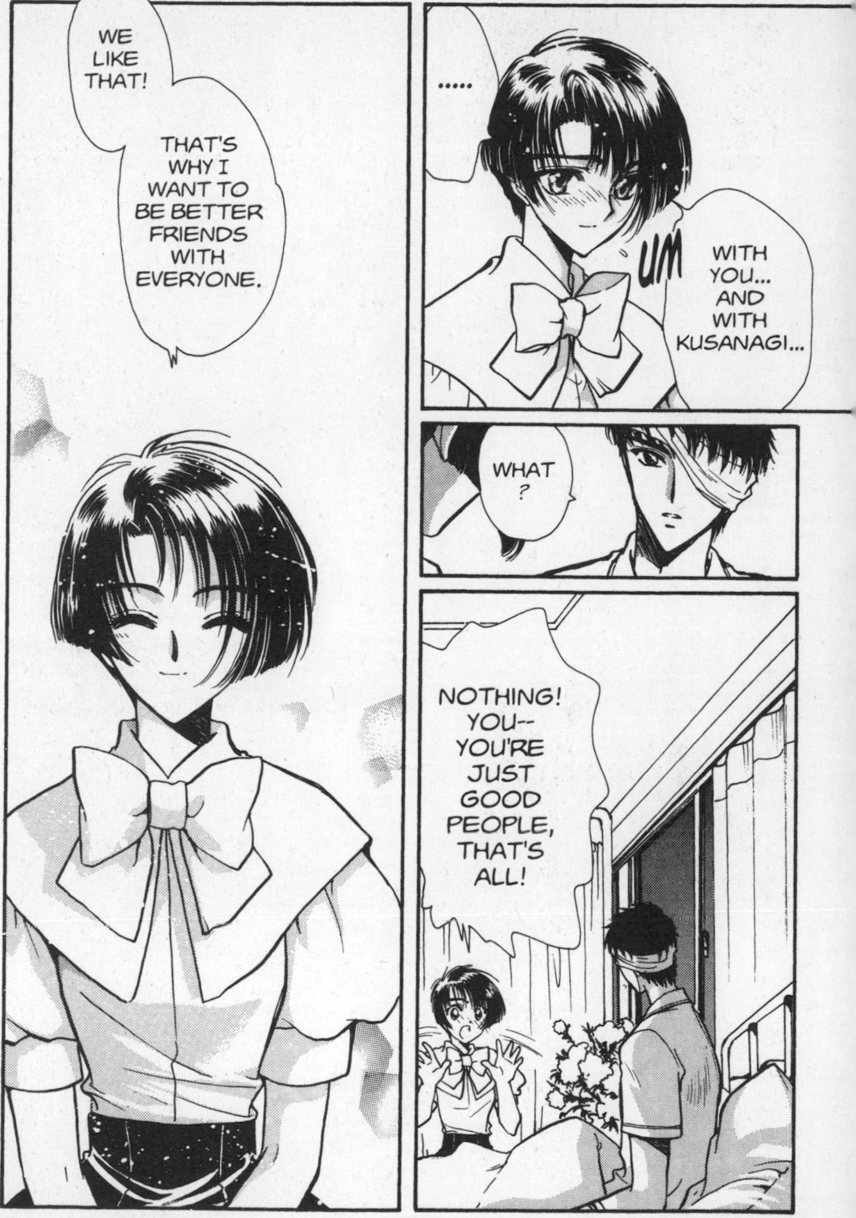
WE LIKE THAT!
THAT'S WHY I WANT TO BE BETTER FRIENDS WITH EVERYONE.
.....
UM
WITH YOU... AND WITH KUSANAGI...
WHAT?
NOTHING! YOU-- YOU'RE JUST GOOD PEOPLE, THAT'S ALL!

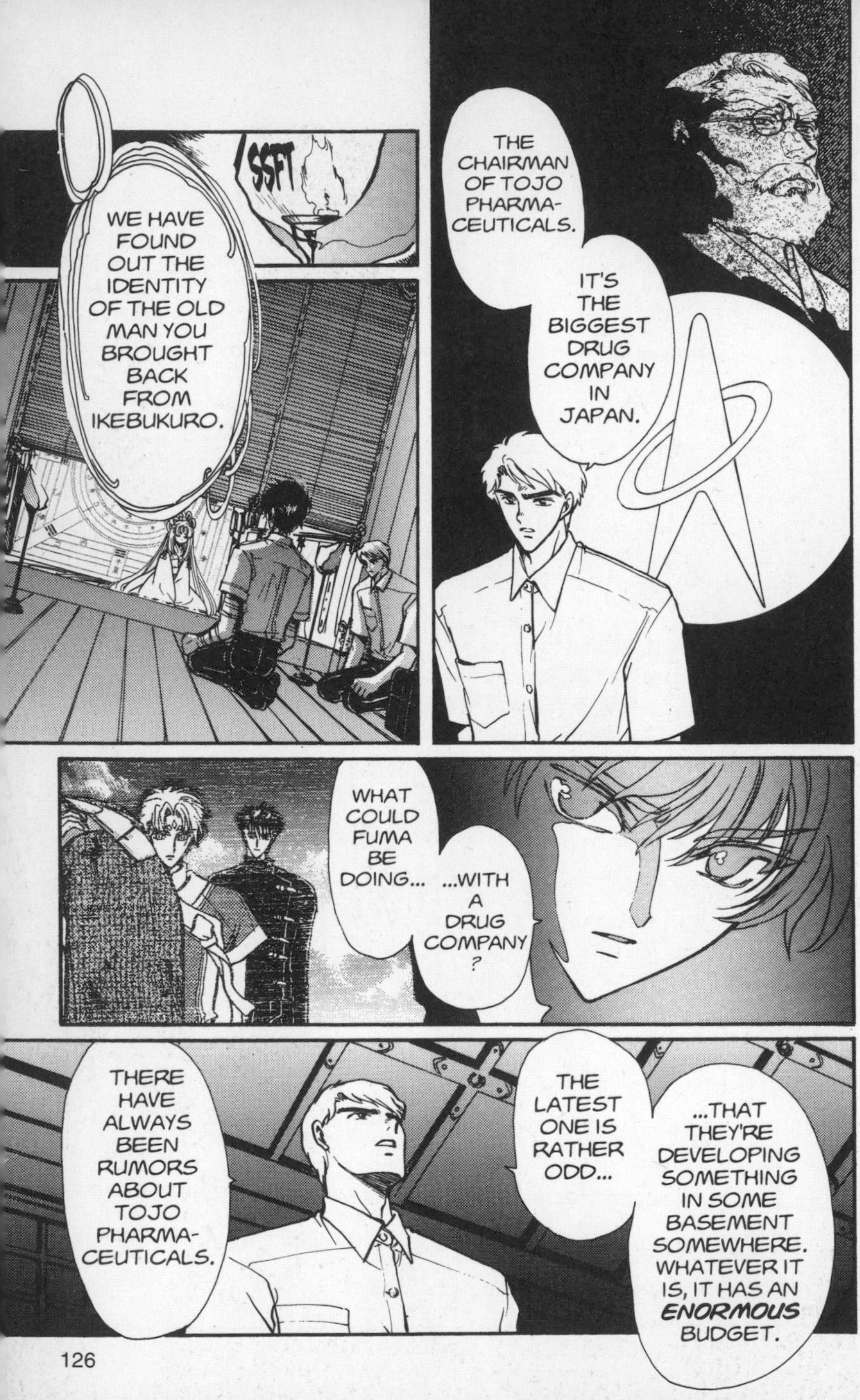
SSFT
WE HAVE FOUND OUT THE IDENTITY OF THE OLD MAN YOU BROUGHT BACK FROM IKEBUKURO.
THE CHAIRMAN OF TOJO PHARMACEUTICALS.
IT'S THE BIGGEST DRUG COMPANY IN JAPAN.
WHAT COULD FUMA BE DOING...
...WITH A DRUG COMPANY?
THERE HAVE ALWAYS BEEN RUMORS ABOUT TOJO PHARMACEUTICALS.
THE LATEST ONE IS RATHER ODD...
...THAT THEY'RE DEVELOPING SOMETHING IN SOME BASEMENT SOMEWHERE. WHATEVER IT IS, IT HAS AN ***ENORMOUS*** BUDGET.

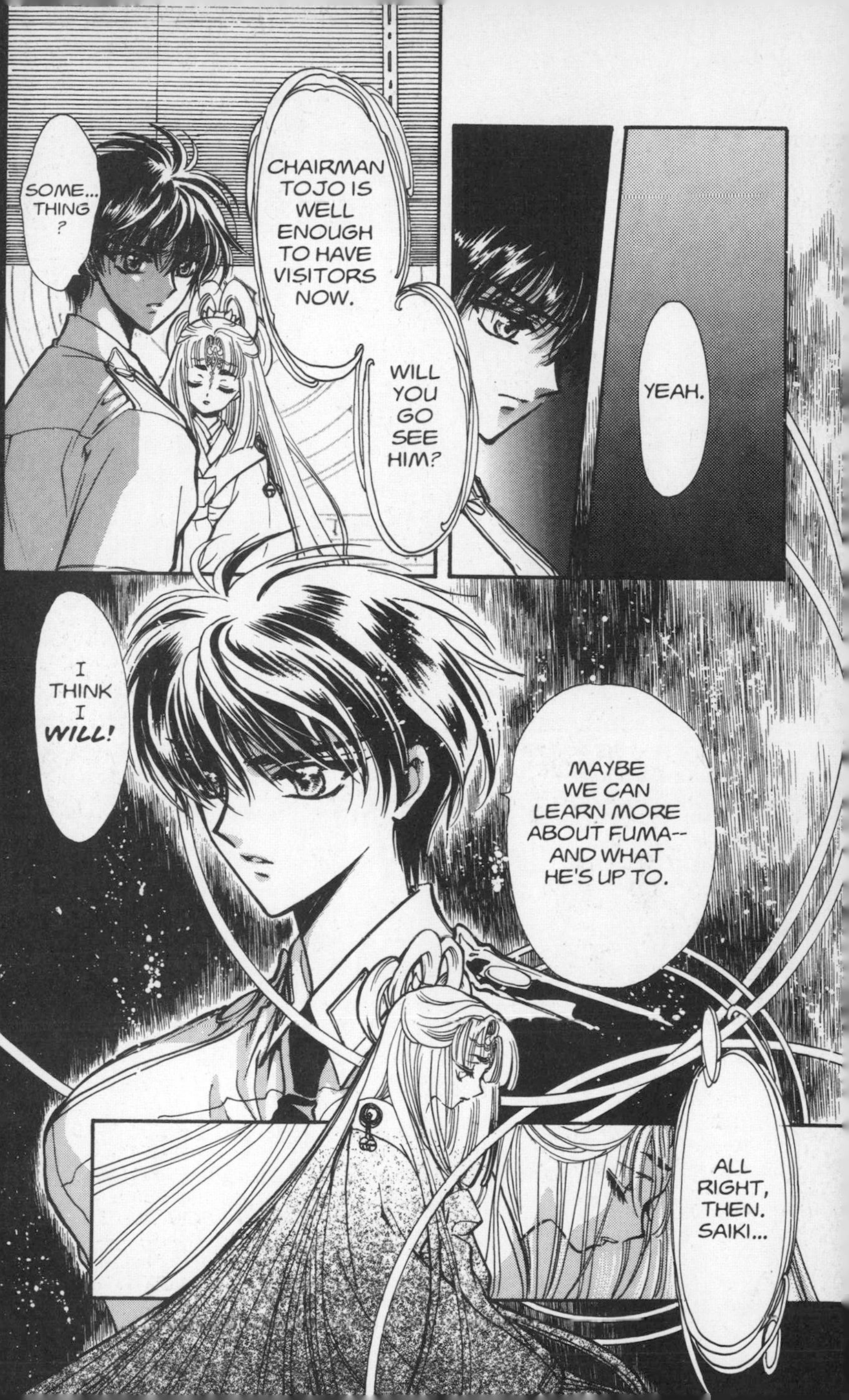
SOME... THING ?
CHAIRMAN TOJO IS WELL ENOUGH TO HAVE VISITORS NOW.
WILL YOU GO SEE HIM?
YEAH.
I THINK I WILL!
MAYBE WE CAN LEARN MORE ABOUT FUMA-- AND WHAT HE'S UP TO.
ALL RIGHT, THEN. SAIKI...

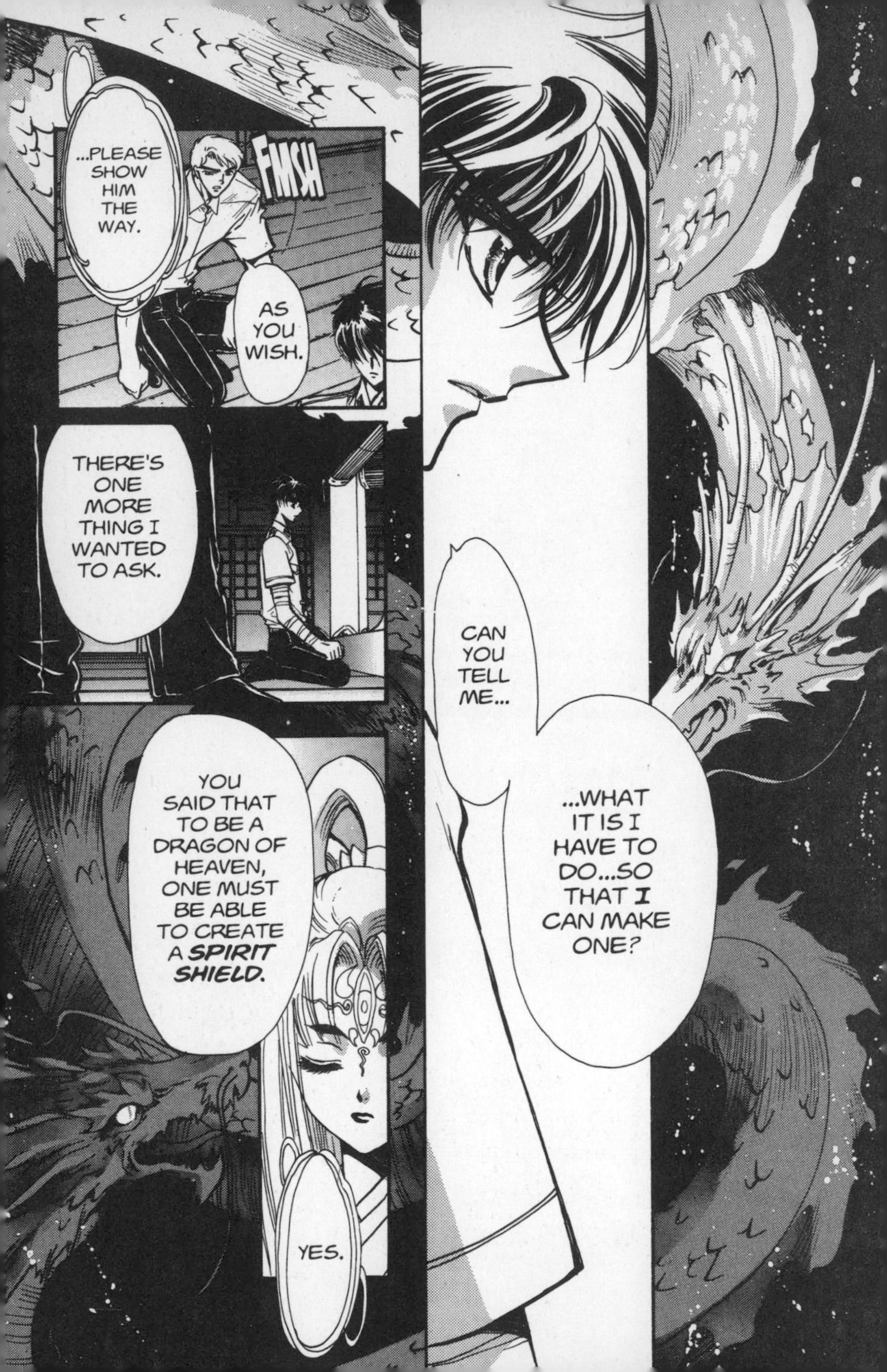
FMSH
...PLEASE SHOW HIM THE WAY.
AS YOU WISH.
THERE'S ONE MORE THING I WANTED TO ASK.
YOU SAID THAT TO BE A DRAGON OF HEAVEN, ONE MUST BE ABLE TO CREATE A SPIRIT SHIELD.
YES.
CAN YOU TELL ME...
...WHAT IT IS I HAVE TO DO...SO THAT I CAN MAKE ONE?

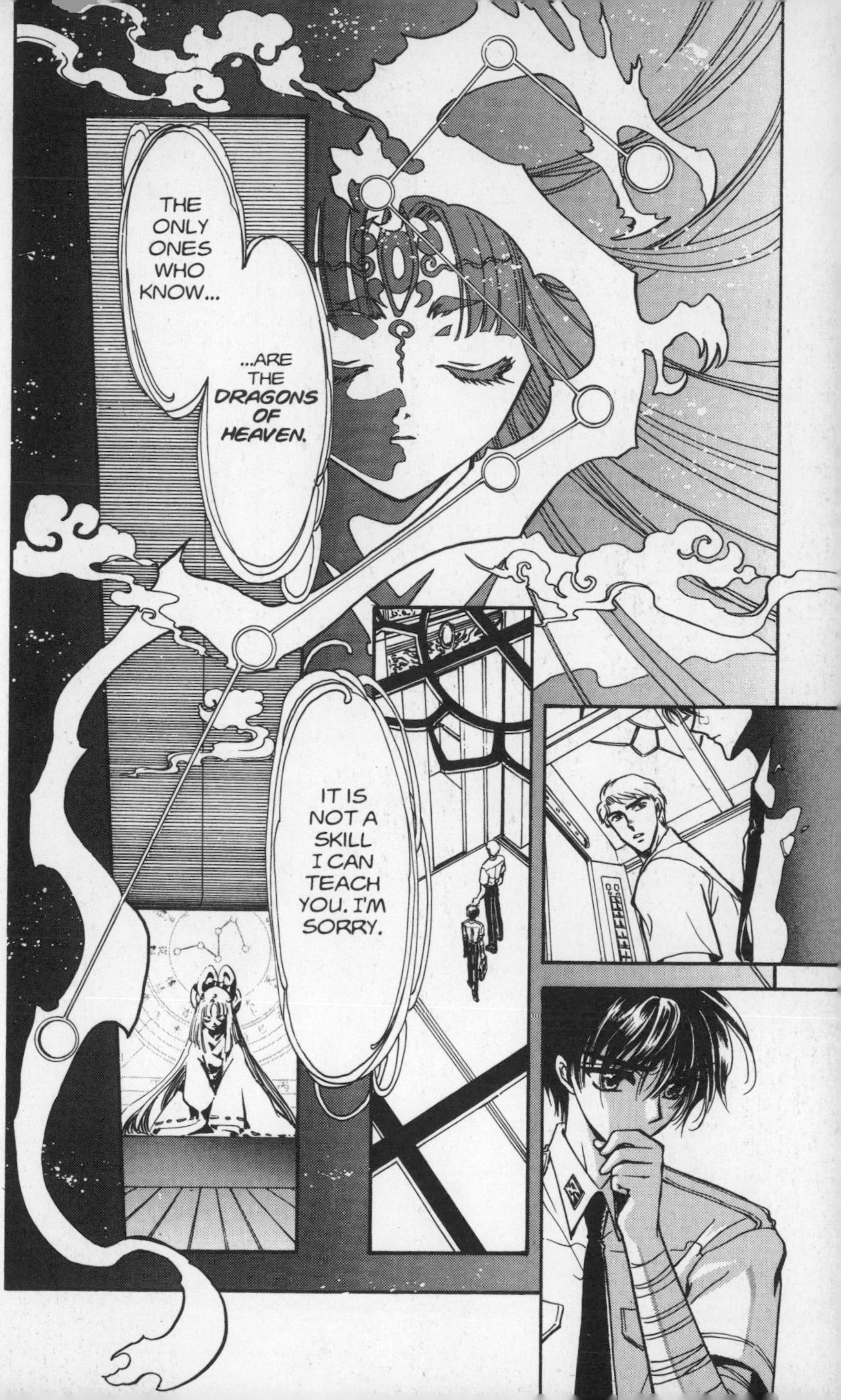
THE ONLY ONES WHO KNOW...
...ARE THE DRAGONS OF HEAVEN.
IT IS NOT A SKILL I CAN TEACH YOU. I'M SORRY.

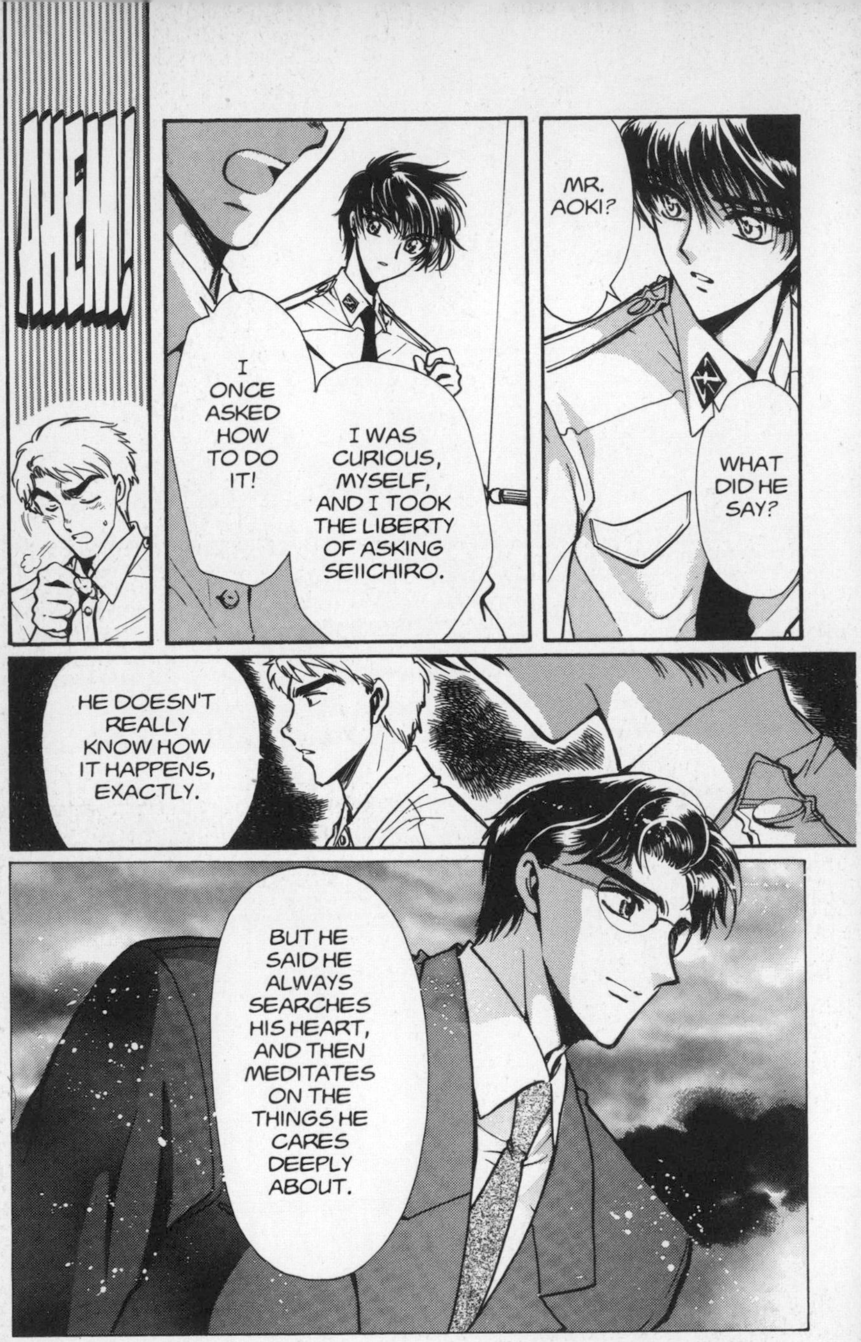
MR. AOKI?
WHAT DID HE SAY?
I WAS CURIOUS, MYSELF, AND I TOOK THE LIBERTY OF ASKING SEIICHIRO.
I ONCE ASKED HOW TO DO IT!
AHEM!
HE DOESN'T REALLY KNOW HOW IT HAPPENS, EXACTLY.
BUT HE SAID HE ALWAYS SEARCHES HIS HEART, AND THEN MEDITATES ON THE THINGS HE CARES DEEPLY ABOUT.

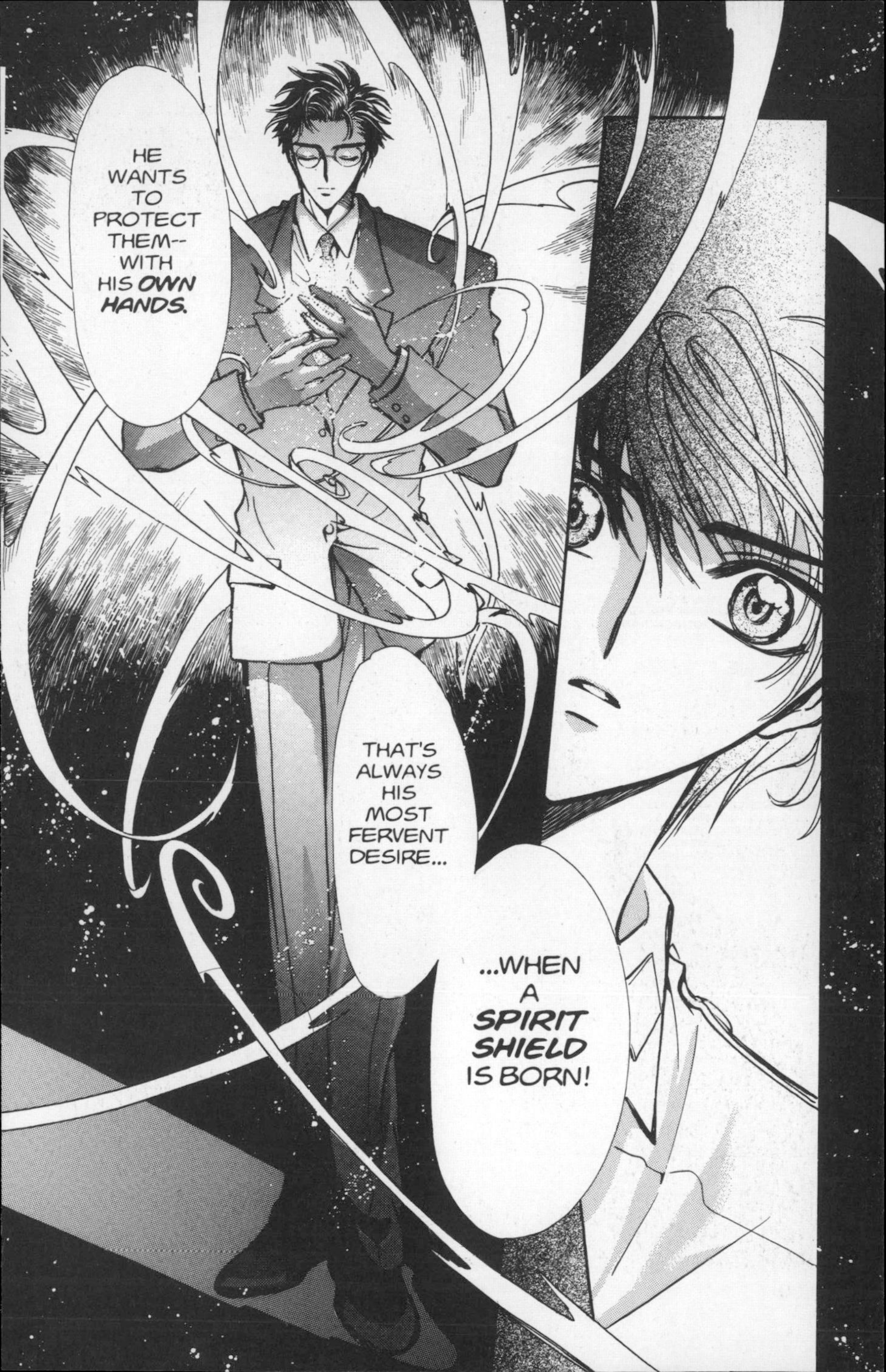
HE WANTS TO PROTECT THEM-- WITH HIS OWN HANDS.
THAT'S ALWAYS HIS MOST FERVENT DESIRE...
...WHEN A SPIRIT SHIELD IS BORN!

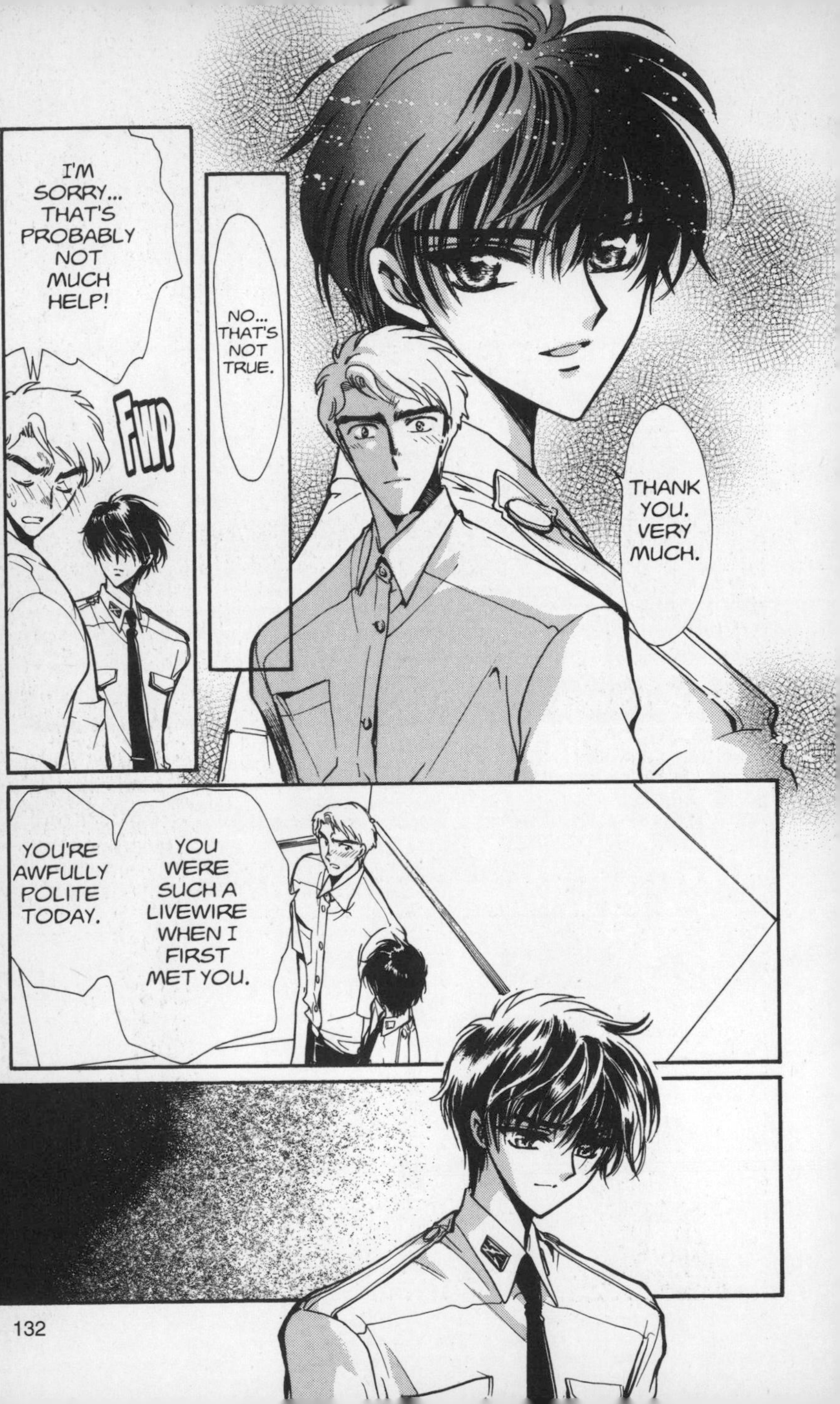
I'M SORRY... THAT'S PROBABLY NOT MUCH HELP!
FWP
NO... THAT'S NOT TRUE.
THANK YOU. VERY MUCH.
YOU'RE AWFULLY POLITE TODAY.
YOU WERE SUCH A LIVEWIRE WHEN I FIRST MET YOU.

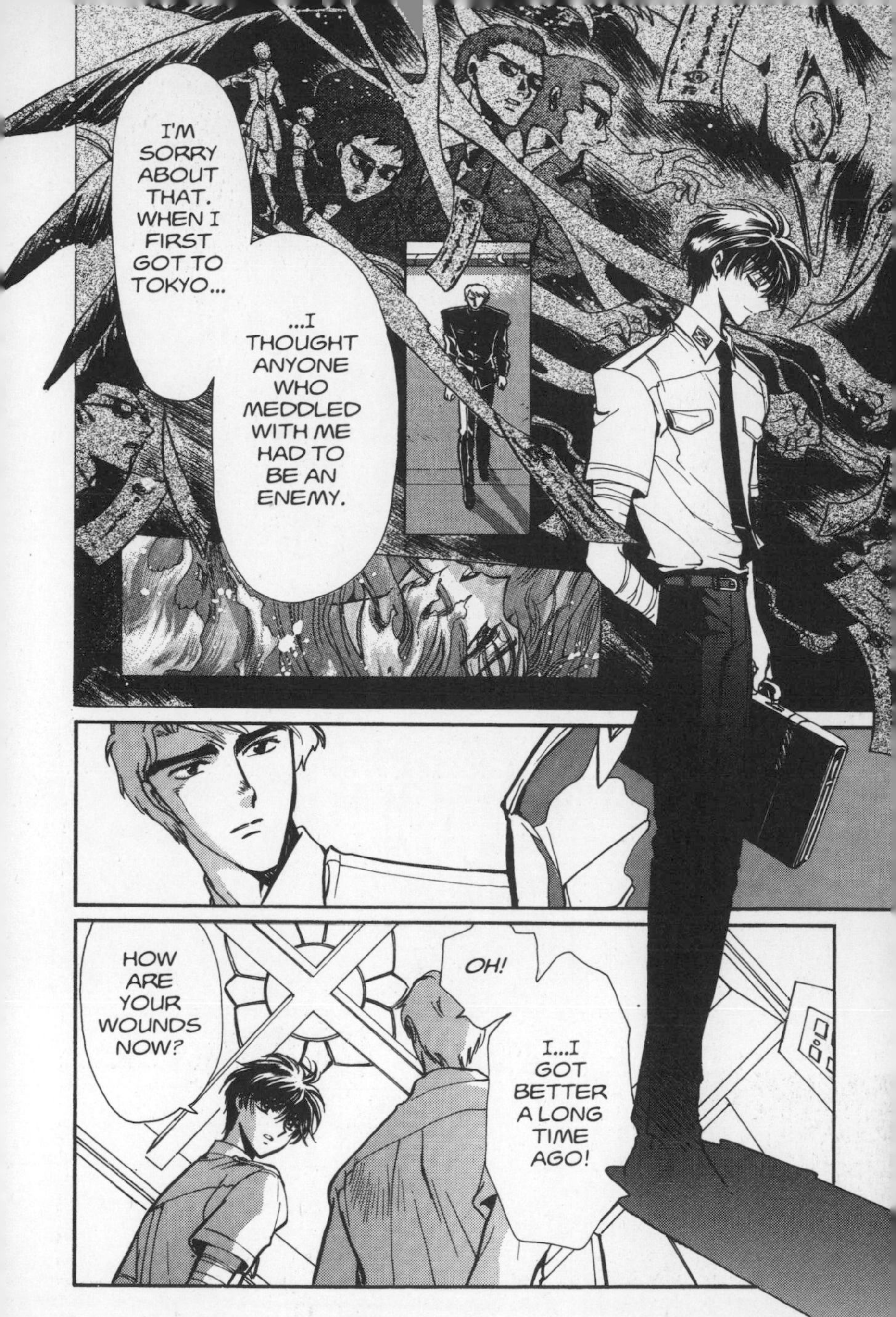
I'M SORRY ABOUT THAT. WHEN I FIRST GOT TO TOKYO...
...I THOUGHT ANYONE WHO MEDDLED WITH ME HAD TO BE AN ENEMY.
OH!
I...I GOT BETTER A LONG TIME AGO!
HOW ARE YOUR WOUNDS NOW?

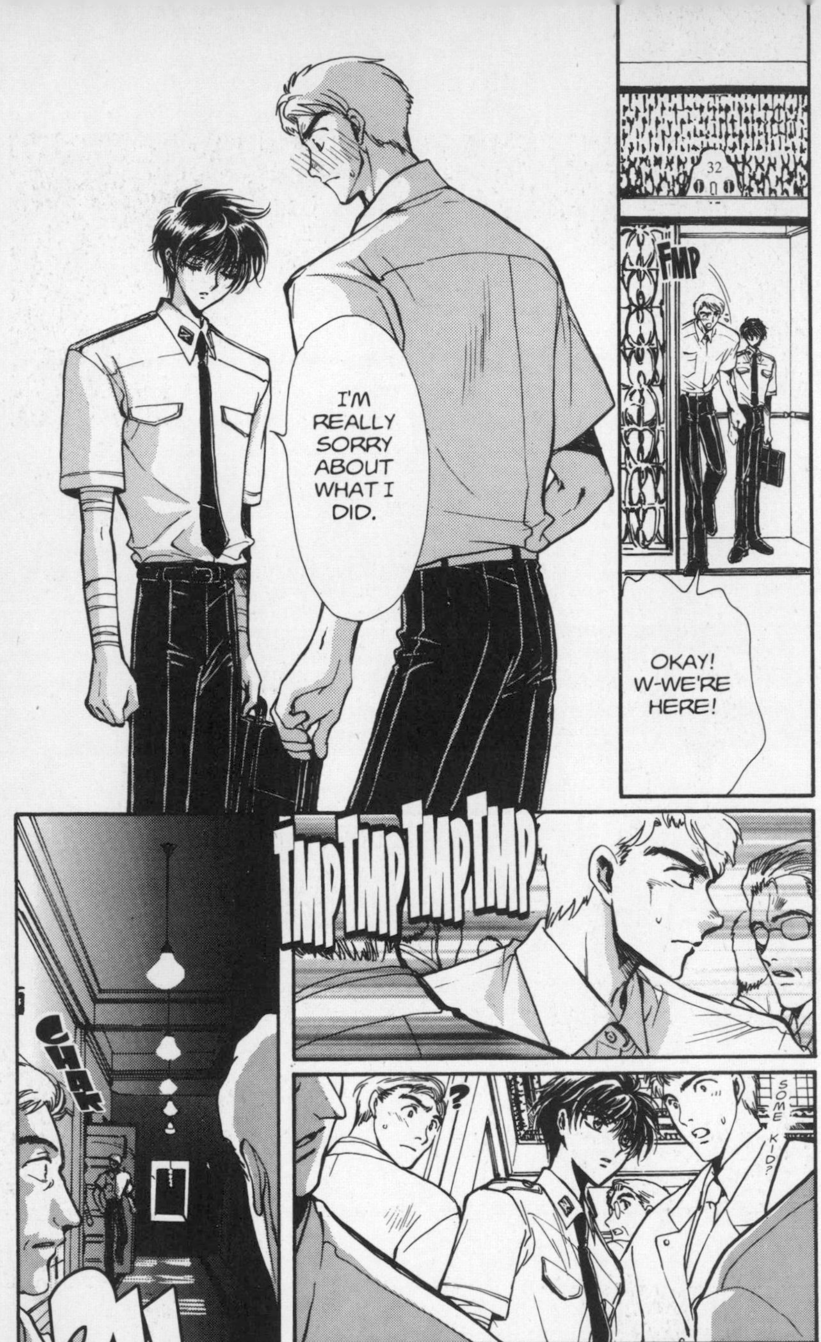
32
FMP
OKAY! W-WE'RE HERE!
I'M REALLY SORRY ABOUT WHAT I DID.
TMP TMP TMP TMP
?
SOME KID?
CHAK
?!..

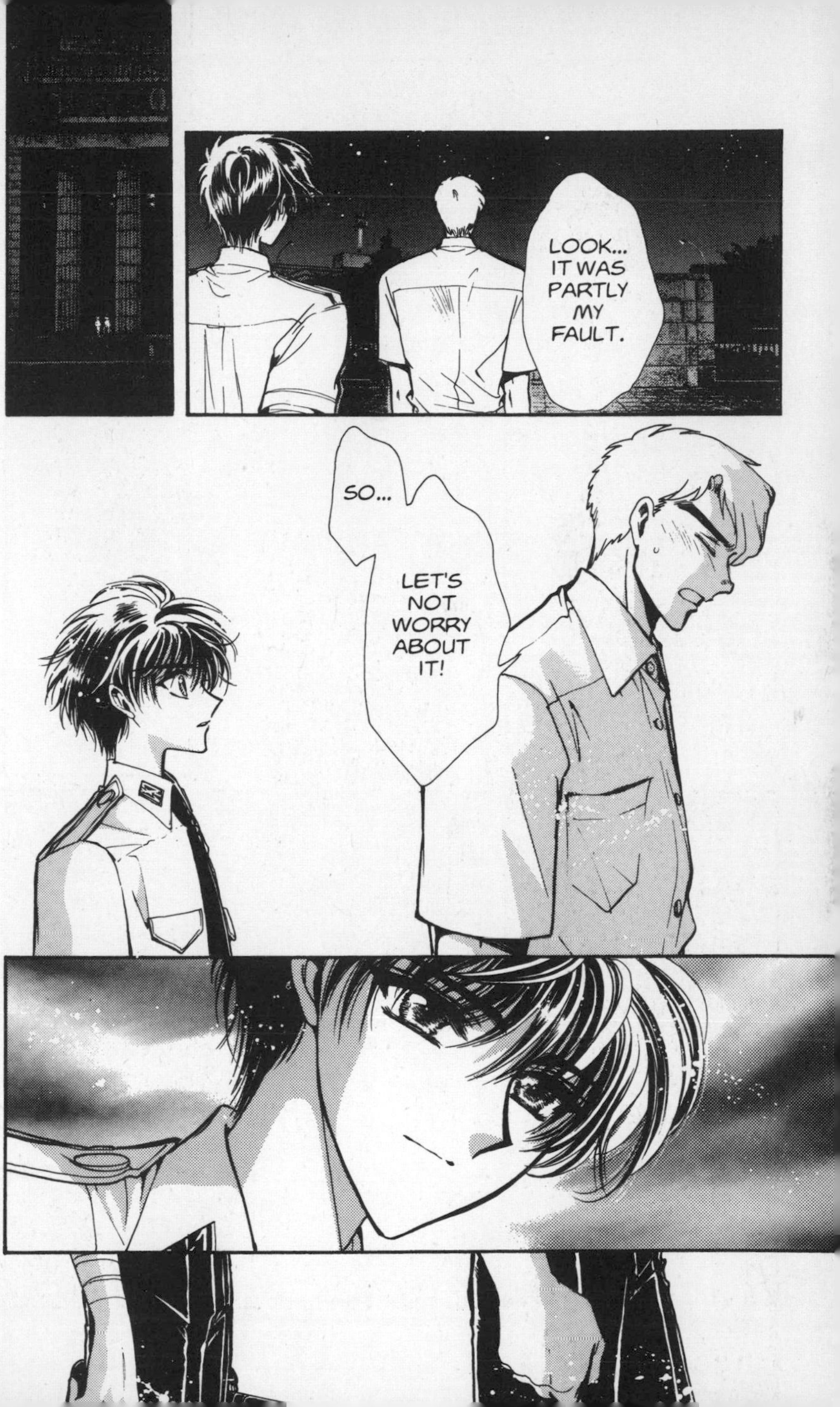
LOOK... IT WAS PARTLY MY FAULT.
SO...
LET'S NOT WORRY ABOUT IT!

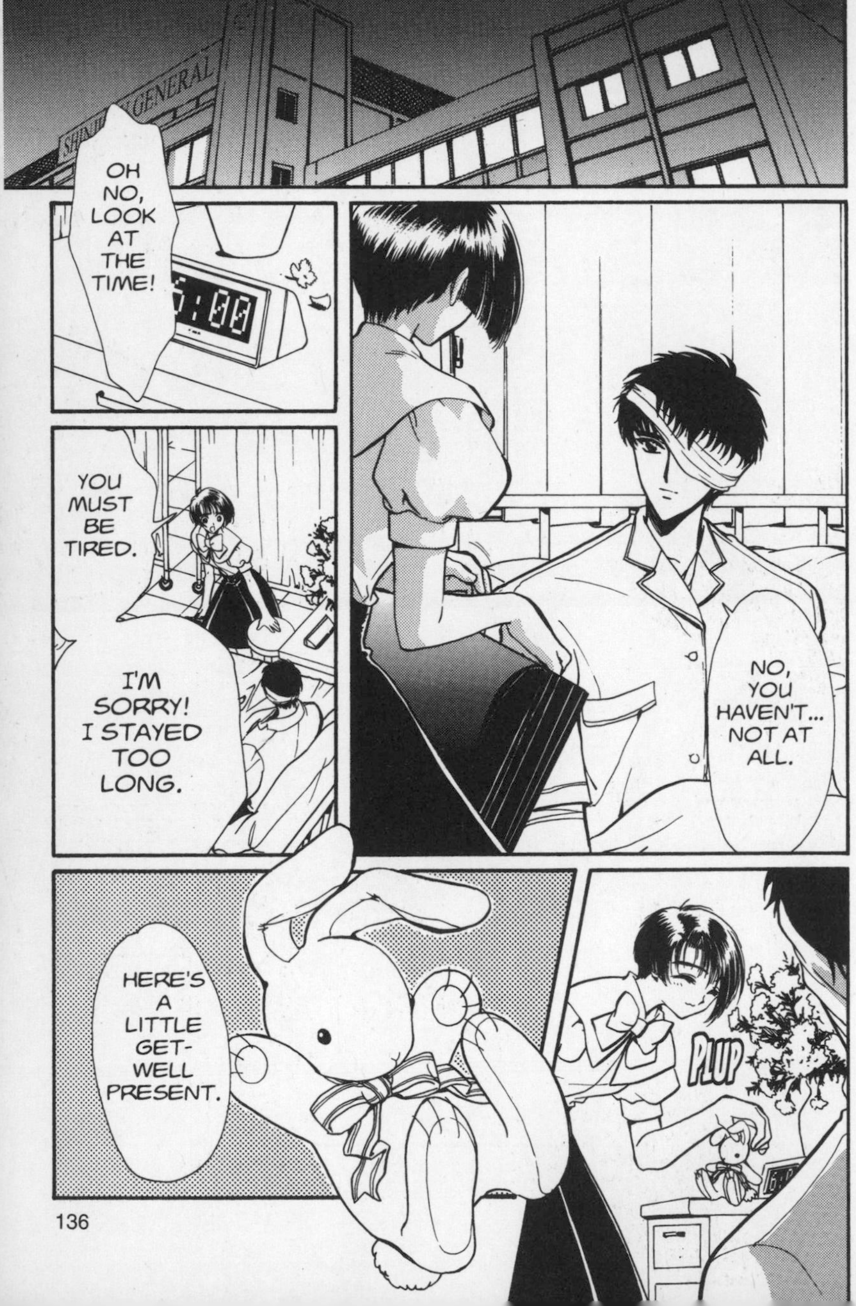
SHINJU GENERAL
OH NO, LOOK AT THE TIME!
5:00
YOU MUST BE TIRED.
I'M SORRY! I STAYED TOO LONG.
NO, YOU HAVEN'T... NOT AT ALL.
PLUP
HERE'S A LITTLE GET-WELL PRESENT.

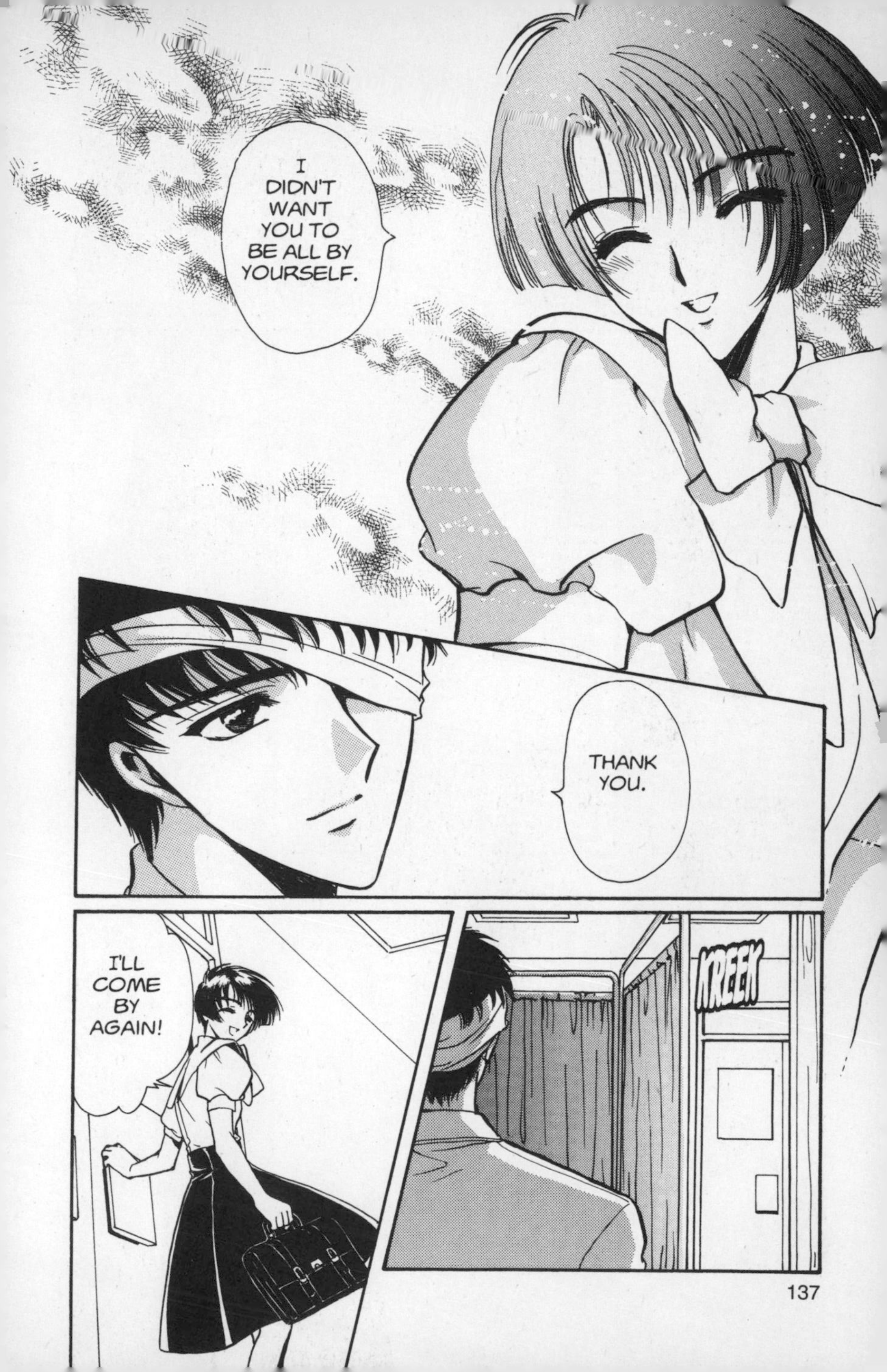
I DIDN'T WANT YOU TO BE ALL BY YOURSELF.
THANK YOU.
KREEK
I'LL COME BY AGAIN!

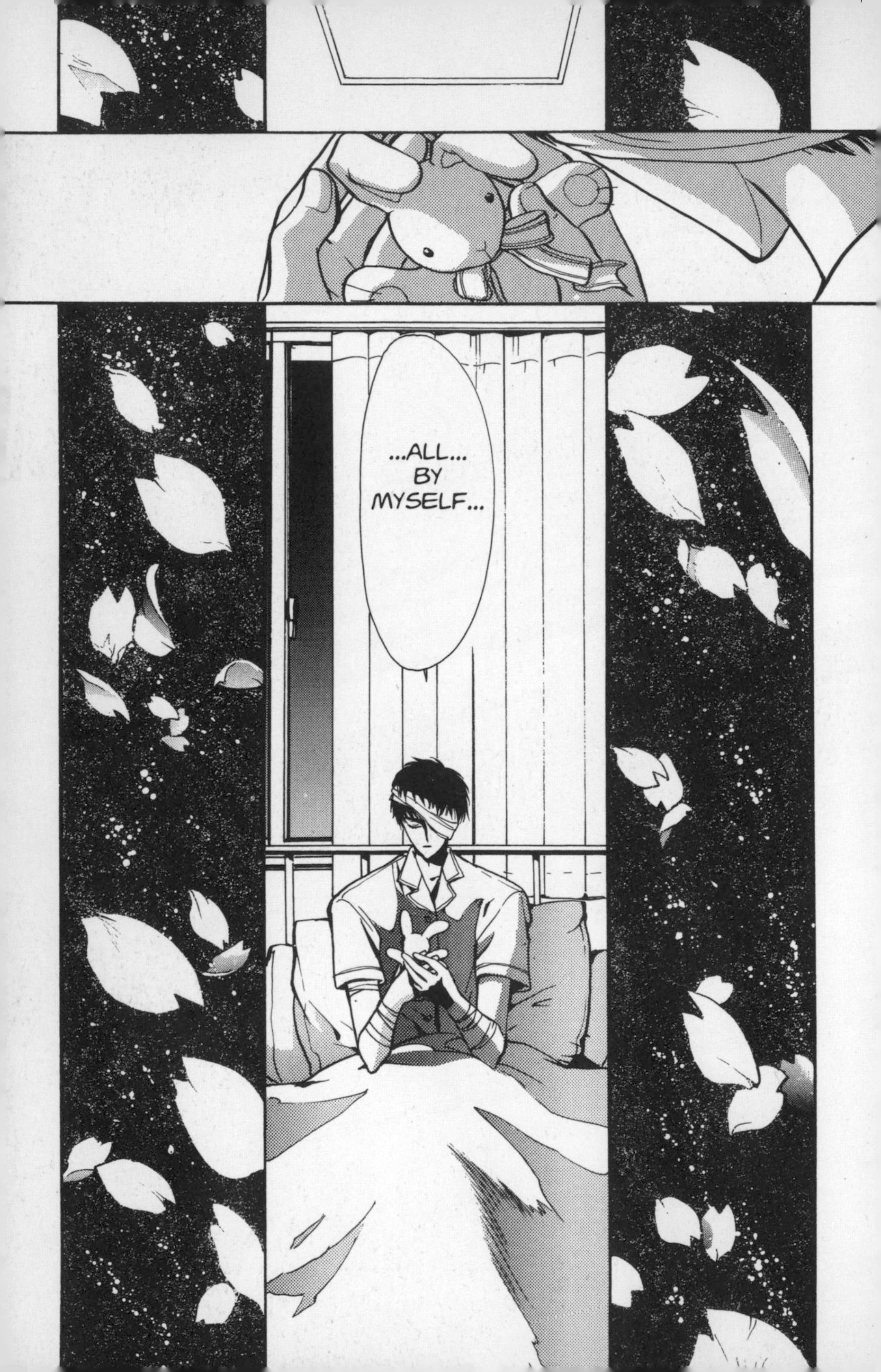
...ALL... BY MYSELF...

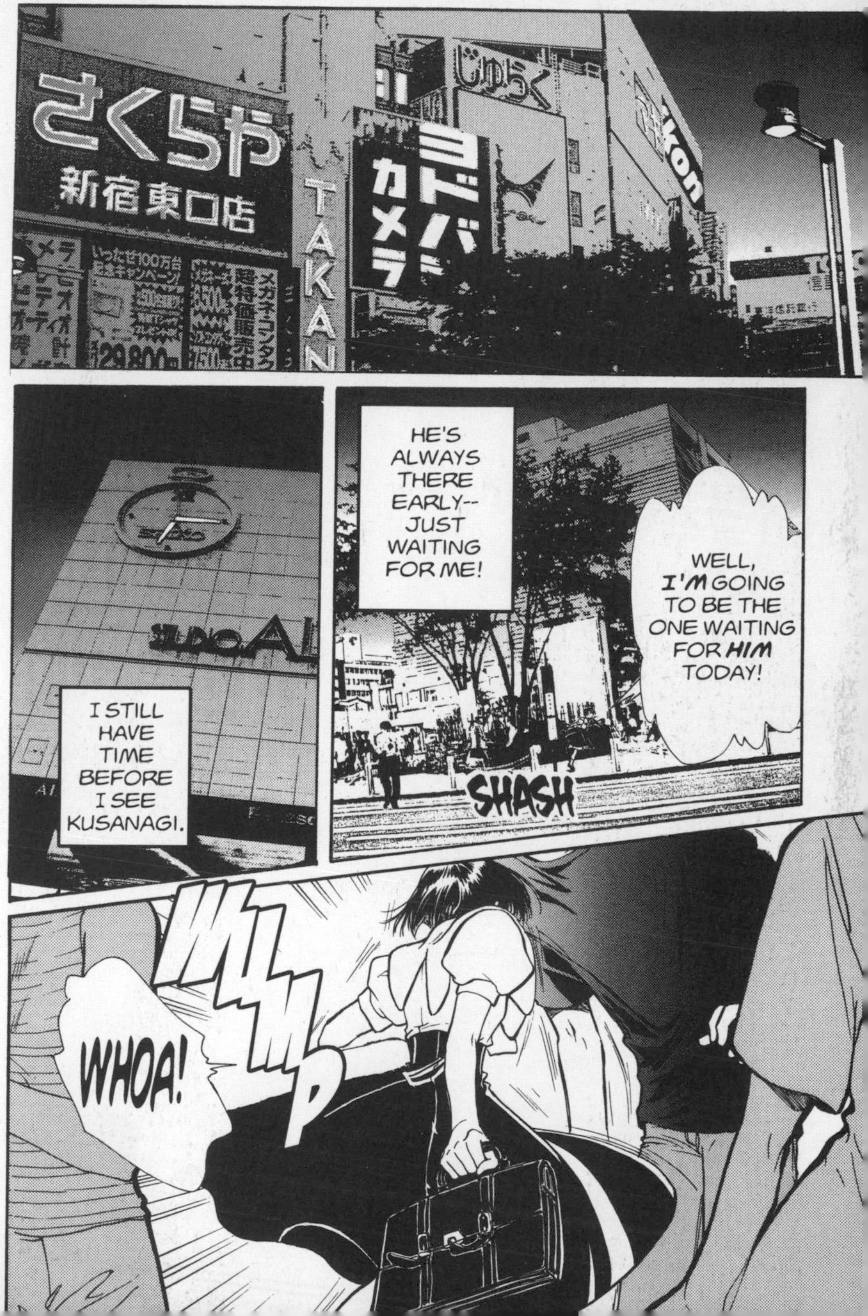
さくらや
新宿東口店
TAKAN
I STILL HAVE TIME BEFORE I SEE KUSANAGI.
HE'S ALWAYS THERE EARLY-- JUST WAITING FOR ME!
WELL, I'M GOING TO BE THE ONE WAITING FOR HIM TODAY!
SHASH
WHUMP
WHOA!

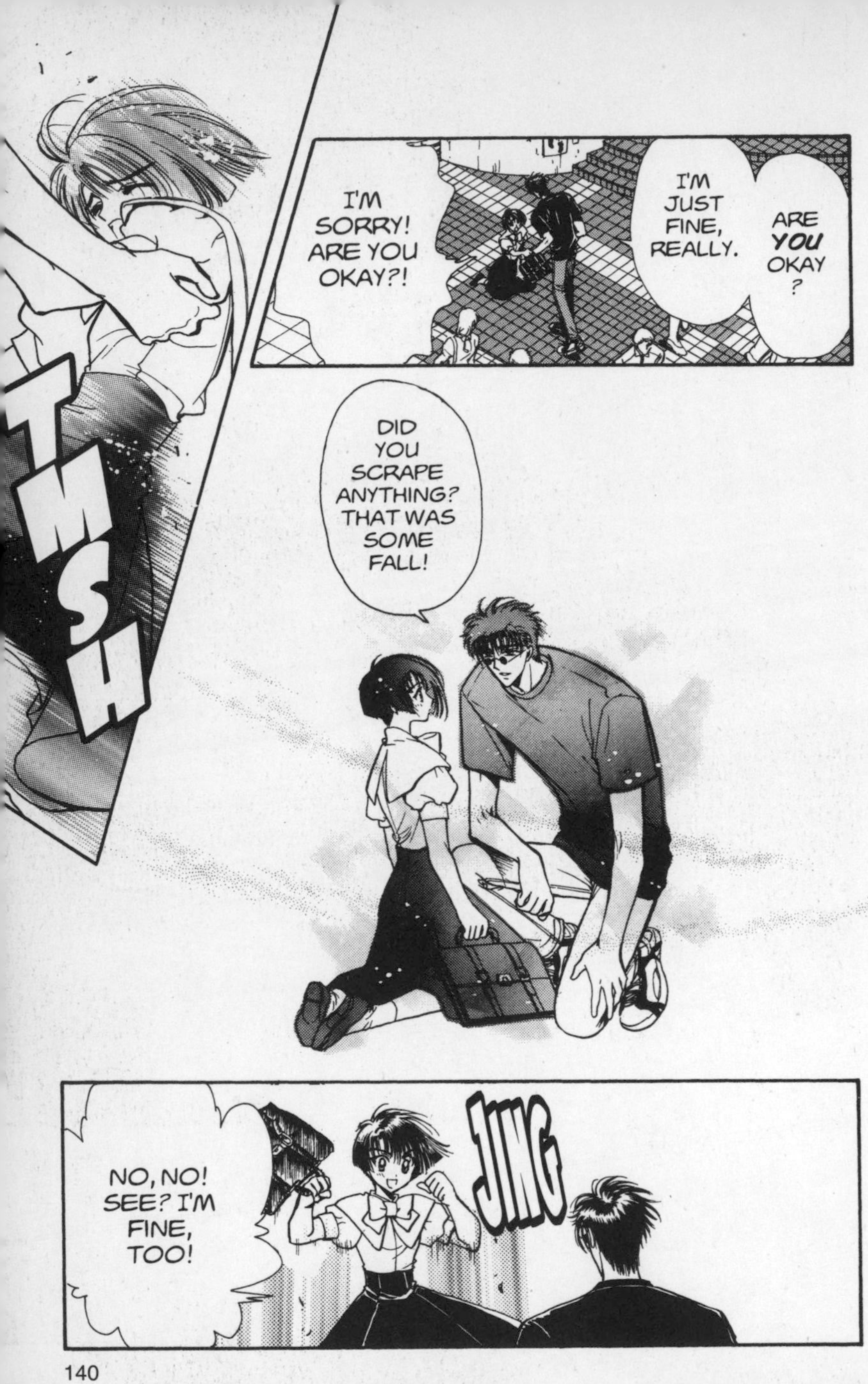
TMSH
I'M SORRY! ARE YOU OKAY?!
I'M JUST FINE, REALLY.
ARE **YOU** OKAY?
DID YOU SCRAPE ANYTHING? THAT WAS SOME FALL!
NO, NO! SEE? I'M FINE, TOO!
JING

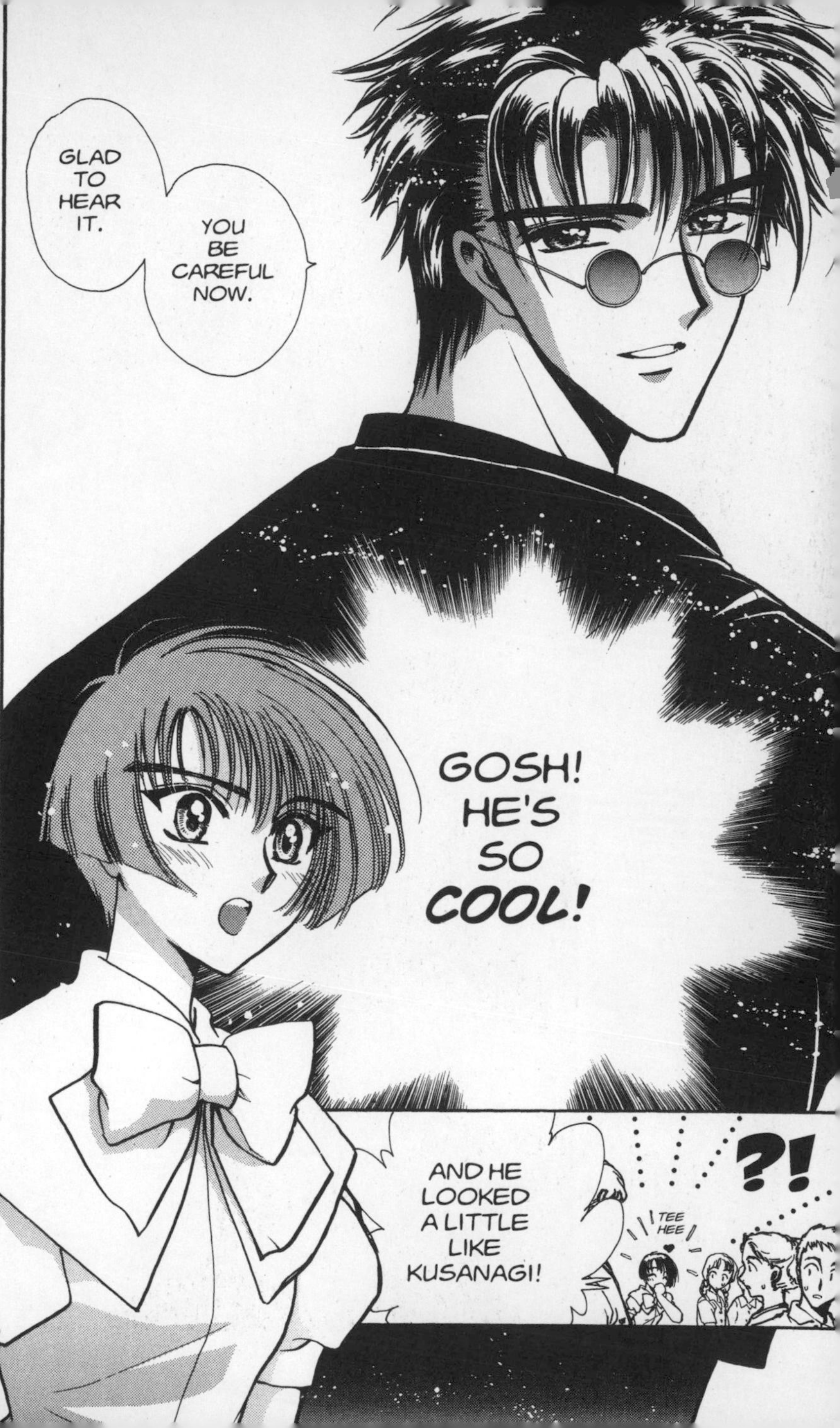
GLAD TO HEAR IT.
YOU BE CAREFUL NOW.
GOSH! HE'S SO COOL!
?!
AND HE LOOKED A LITTLE LIKE KUSANAGI!
TEE HEE

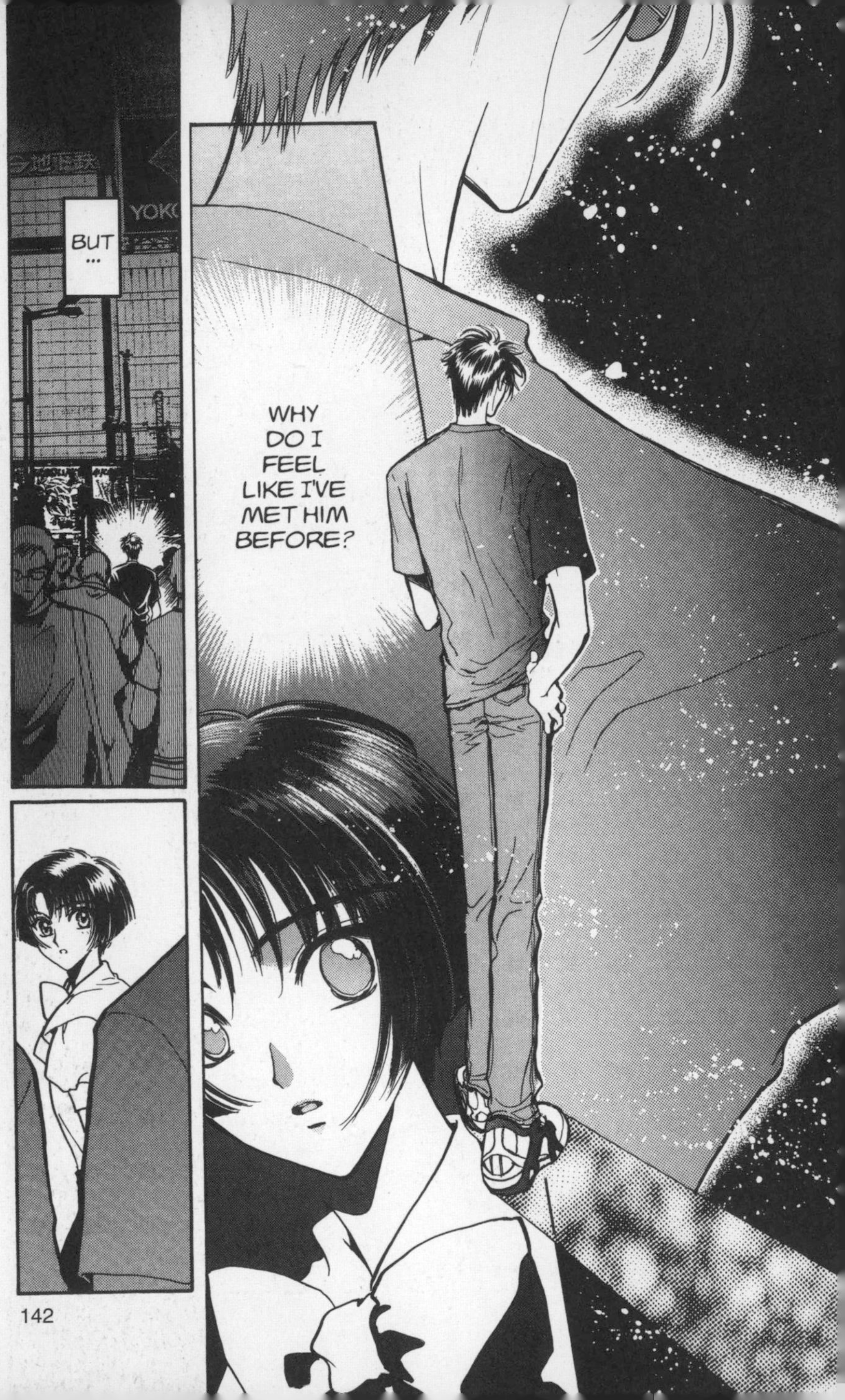
WHY DO I FEEL LIKE I'VE MET HIM BEFORE?
BUT ...

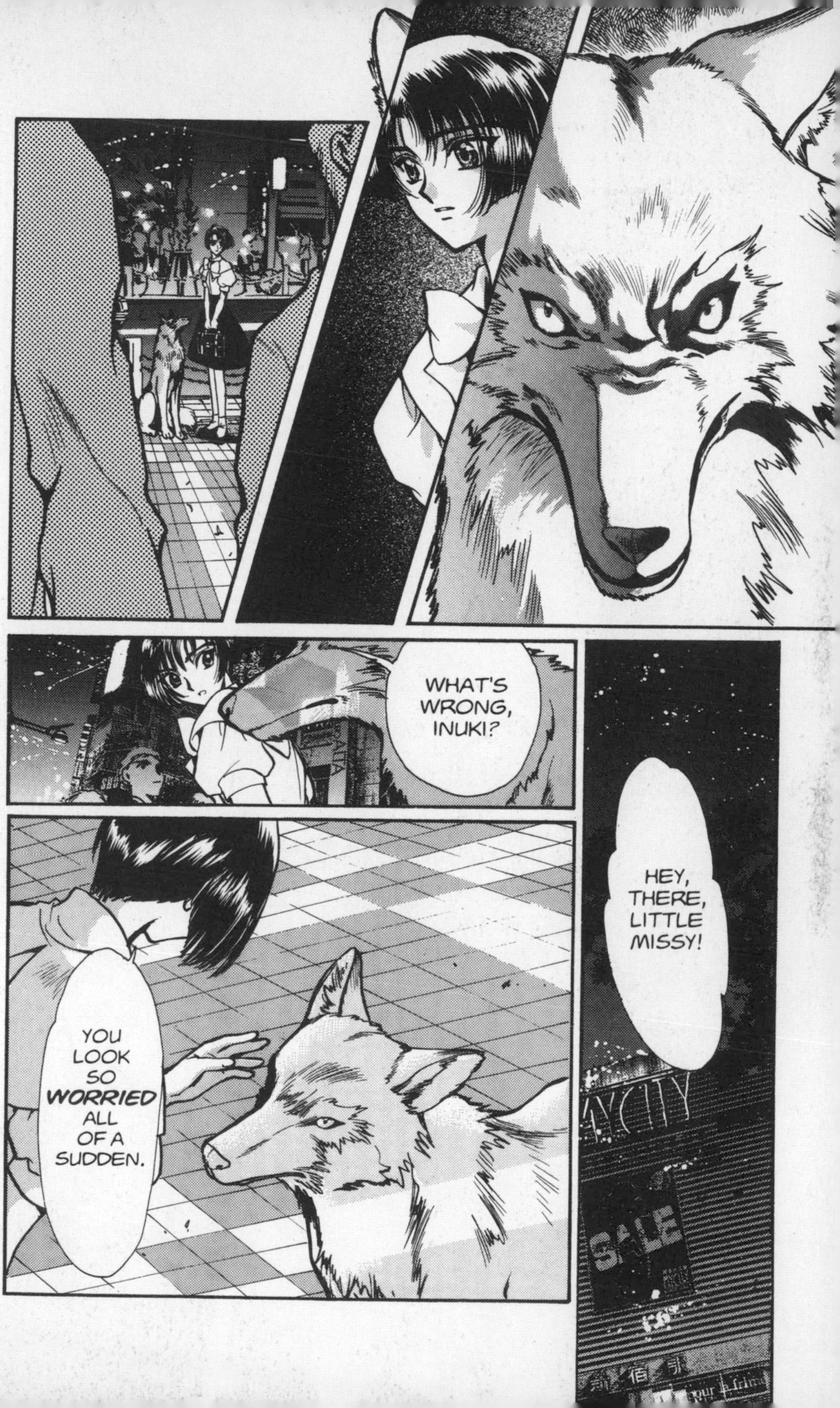
HEY, THERE, LITTLE MISSY!
WHAT'S WRONG, INUKI?
YOU LOOK SO **WORRIED** ALL OF A SUDDEN.
CITY
SALE

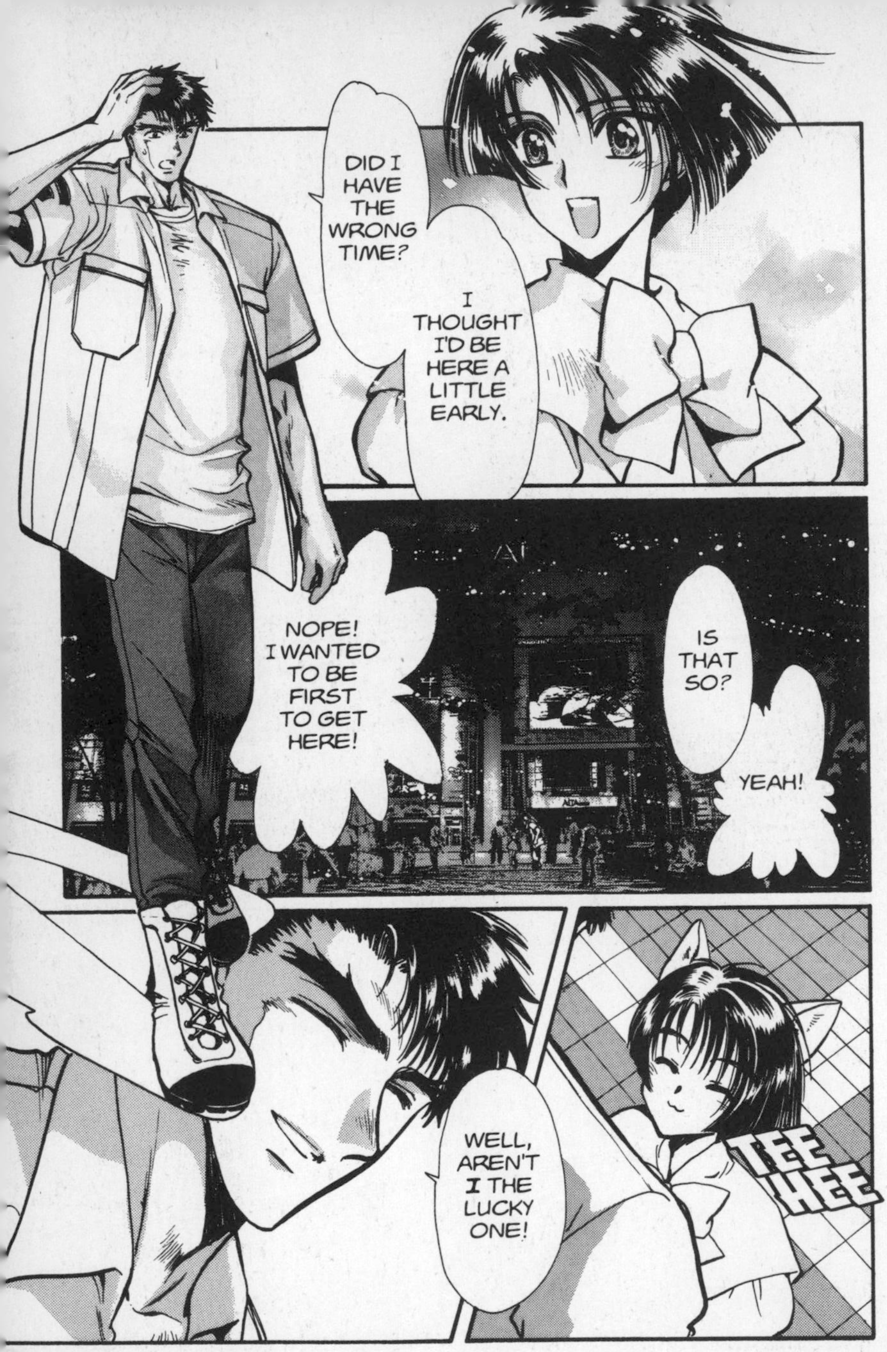

DID I HAVE THE WRONG TIME?
I THOUGHT I'D BE HERE A LITTLE EARLY.
NOPE! I WANTED TO BE FIRST TO GET HERE!
IS THAT SO?
YEAH!
TEE HEE
WELL, AREN'T I THE LUCKY ONE!

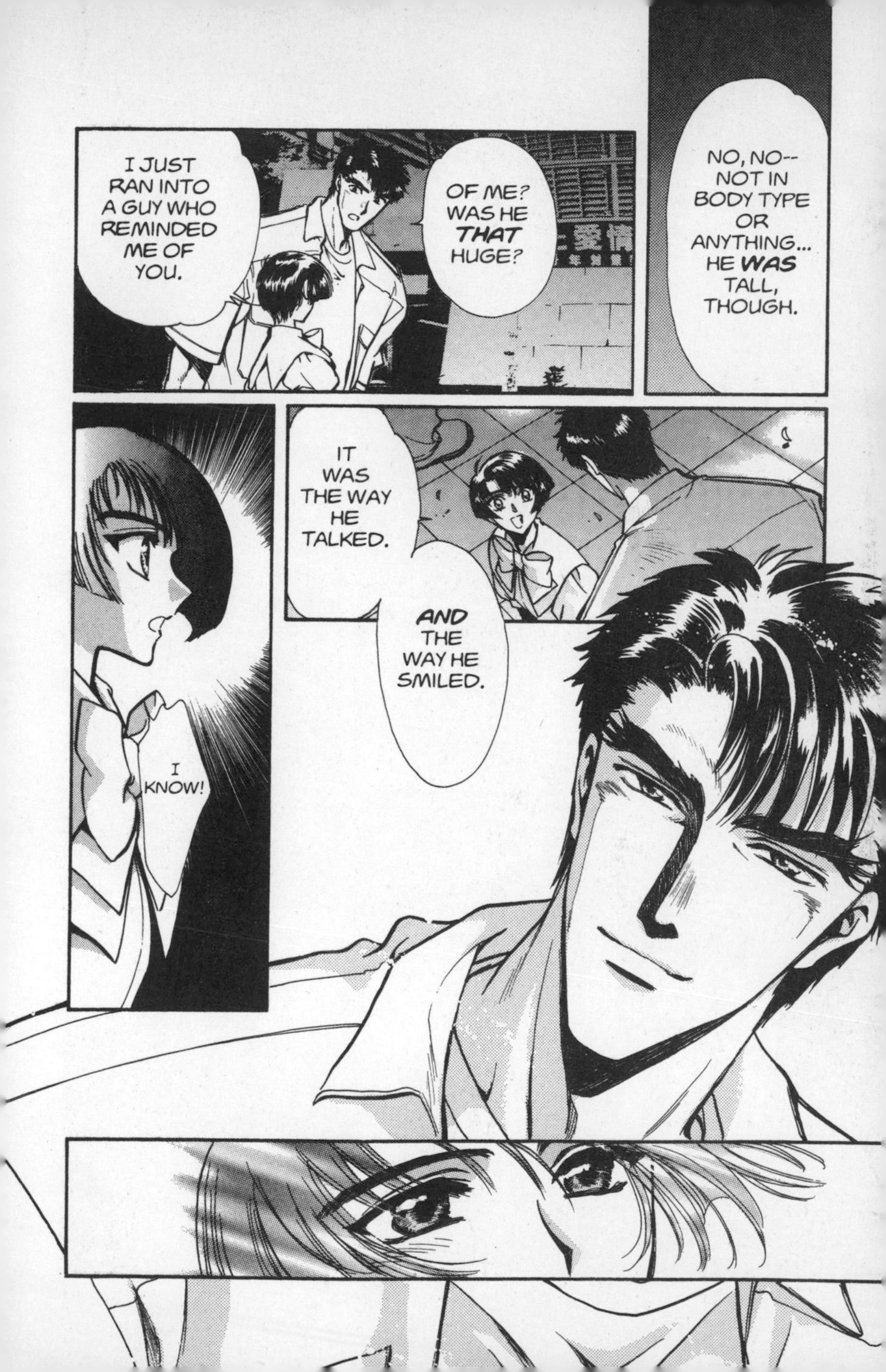
I JUST RAN INTO A GUY WHO REMINDED ME OF YOU.
OF ME? WAS HE *THAT* HUGE?
NO, NO--NOT IN BODY TYPE OR ANYTHING... HE *WAS* TALL, THOUGH.
IT WAS THE WAY HE TALKED.
AND THE WAY HE SMILED.
I KNOW!

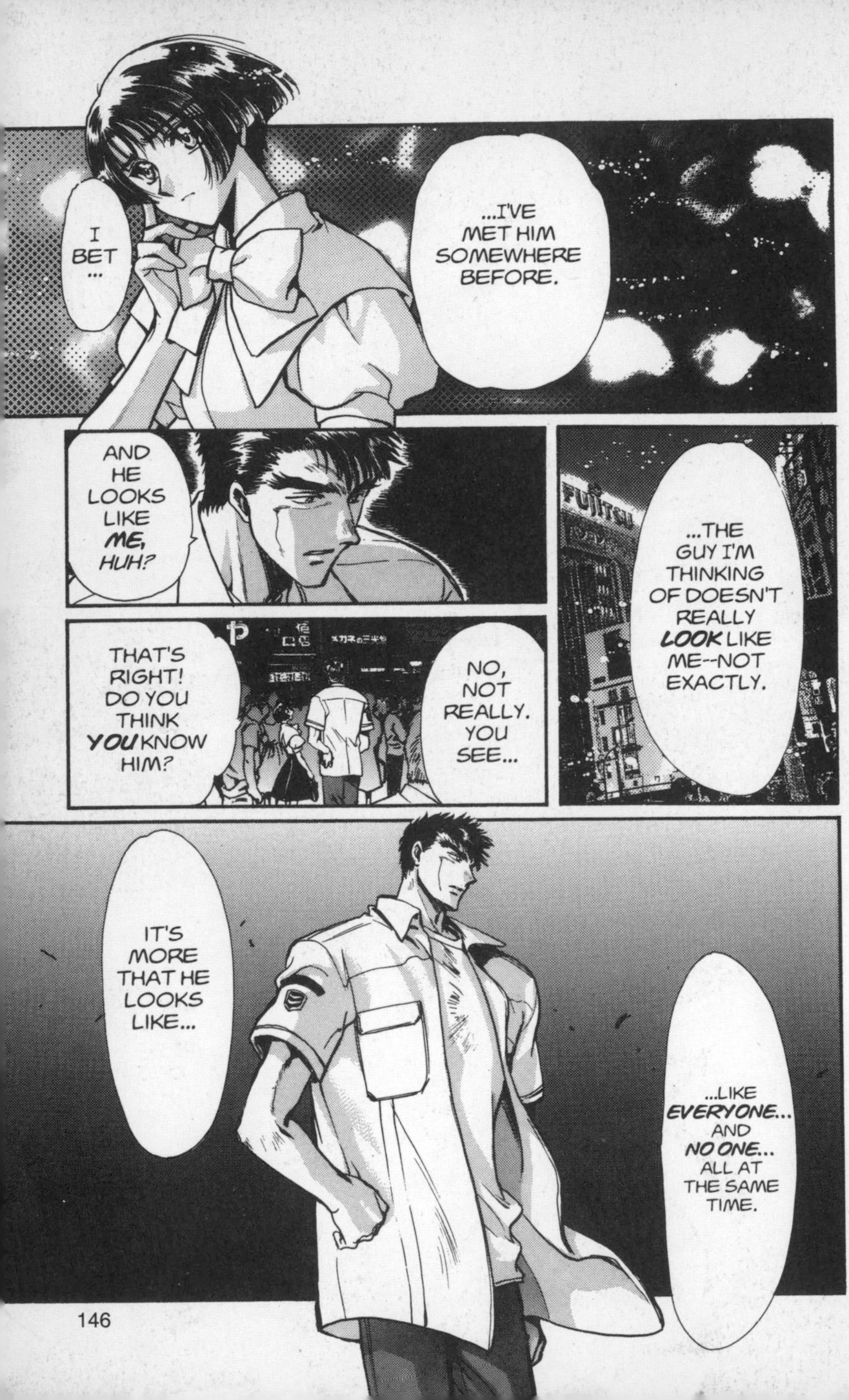
I BET ...
...I'VE MET HIM SOMEWHERE BEFORE.
AND HE LOOKS LIKE *ME,* HUH?
THAT'S RIGHT! DO YOU THINK *YOU* KNOW HIM?
NO, NOT REALLY. YOU SEE...
...THE GUY I'M THINKING OF DOESN'T REALLY *LOOK* LIKE ME--NOT EXACTLY.
IT'S MORE THAT HE LOOKS LIKE...
...LIKE *EVERYONE...* AND *NO ONE...* ALL AT THE SAME TIME.

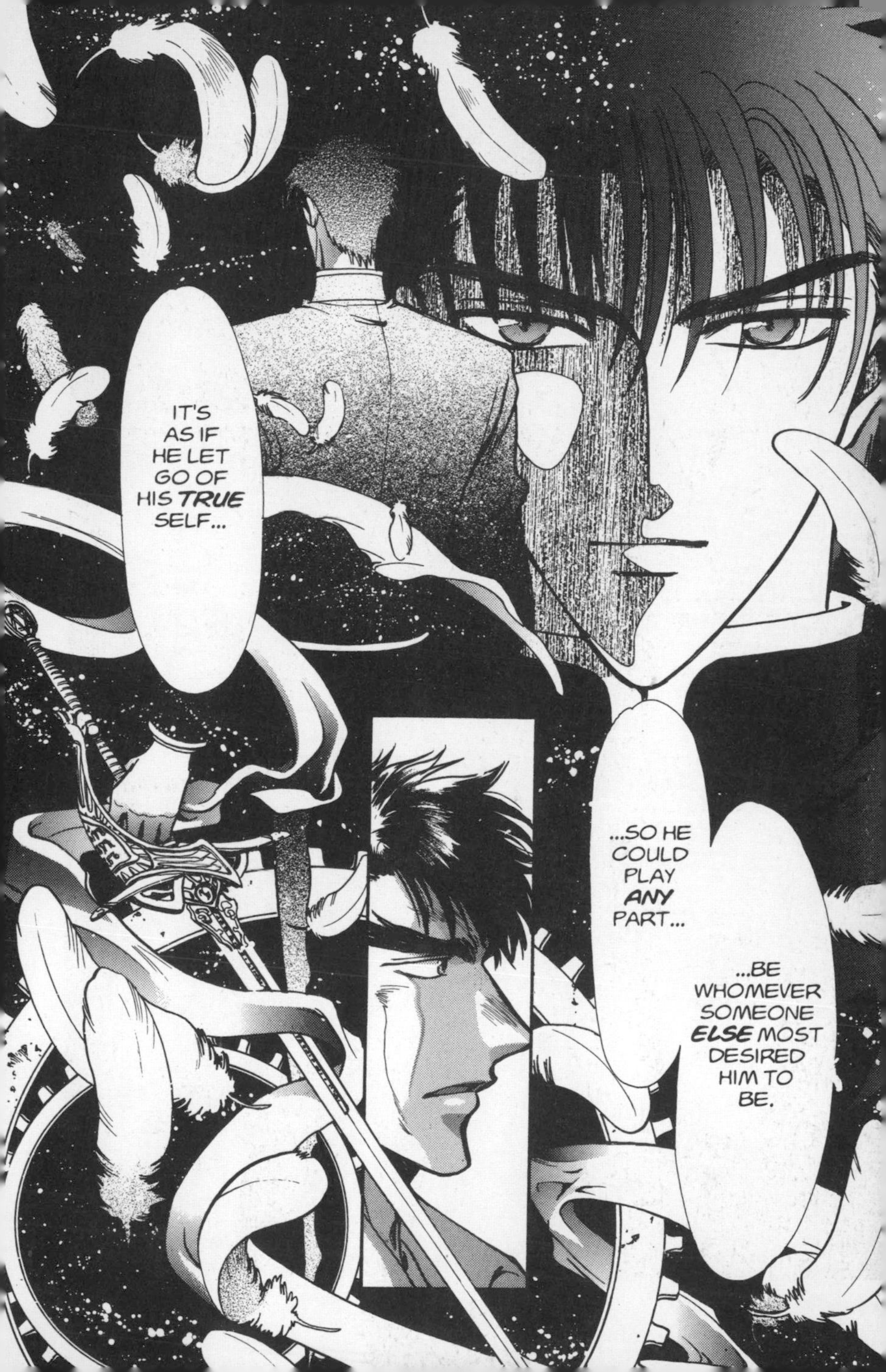
IT'S AS IF HE LET GO OF HIS TRUE SELF...
...SO HE COULD PLAY ANY PART...
...BE WHOMEVER SOMEONE ELSE MOST DESIRED HIM TO BE.

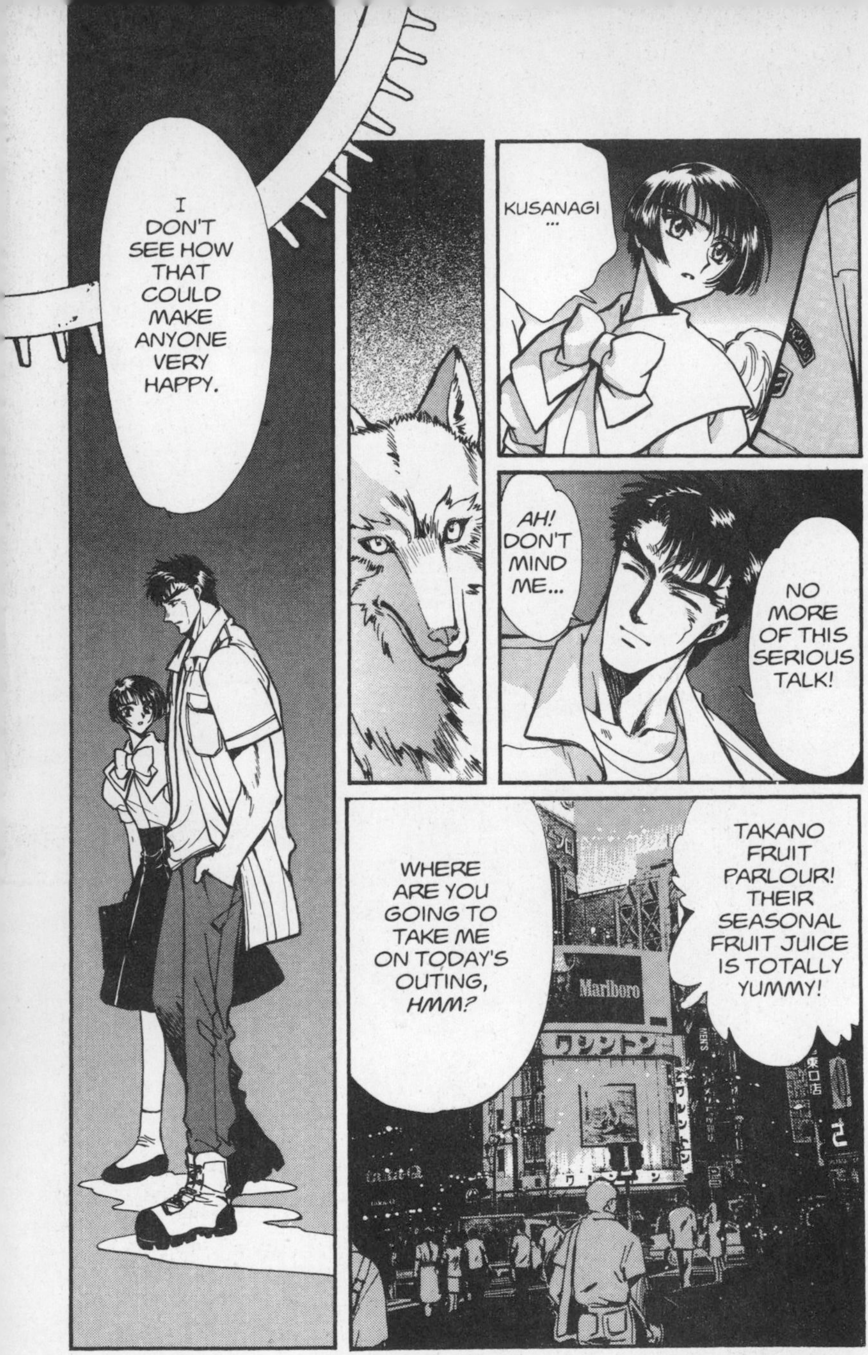
I DON'T SEE HOW THAT COULD MAKE ANYONE VERY HAPPY.
KUSANAGI ...
NO MORE OF THIS SERIOUS TALK!
AH! DON'T MIND ME...
WHERE ARE YOU GOING TO TAKE ME ON TODAY'S OUTING, HMM?
TAKANO FRUIT PARLOUR! THEIR SEASONAL FRUIT JUICE IS TOTALLY YUMMY!
Marlboro

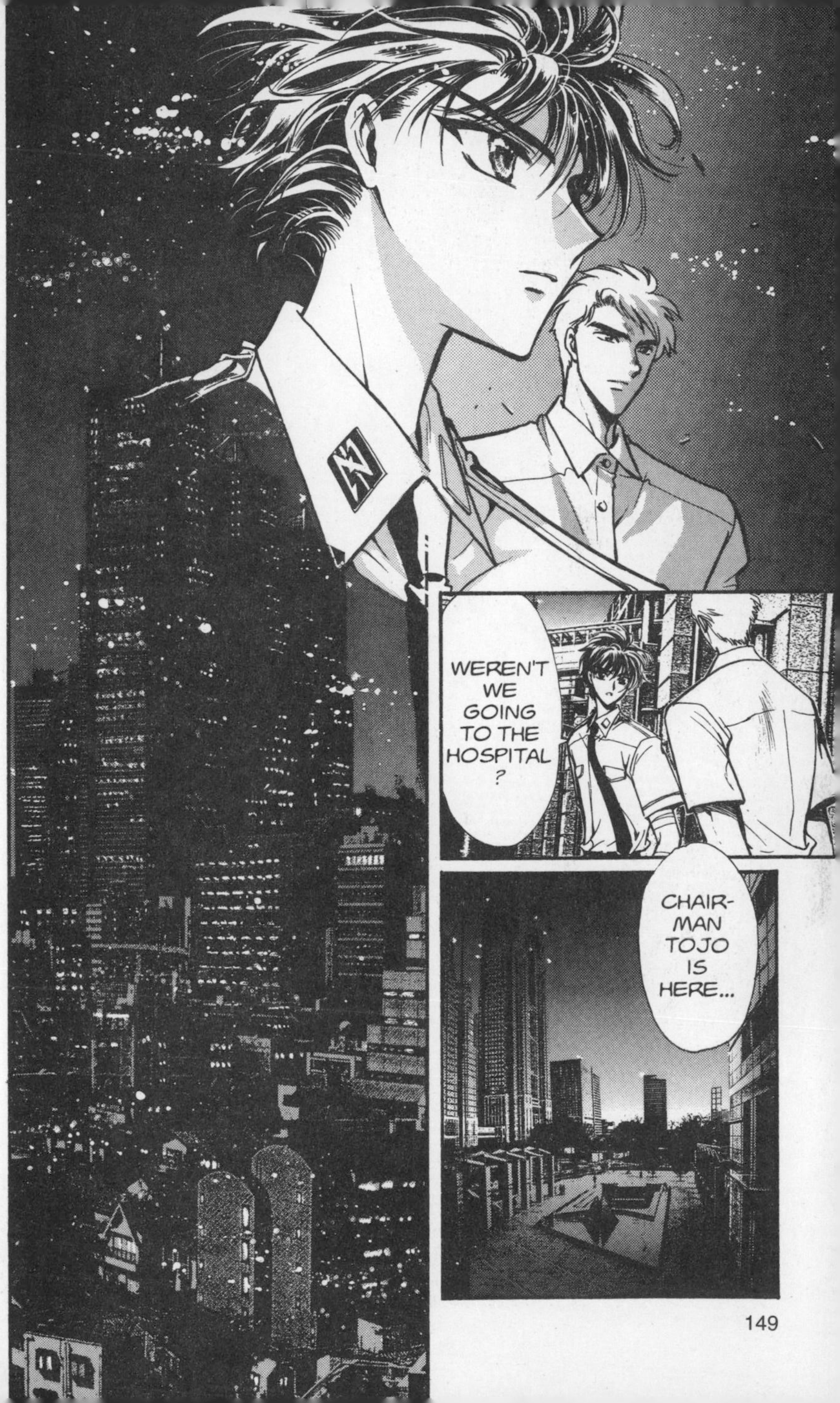
WEREN'T WE GOING TO THE HOSPITAL?
CHAIR-MAN TOJO IS HERE...

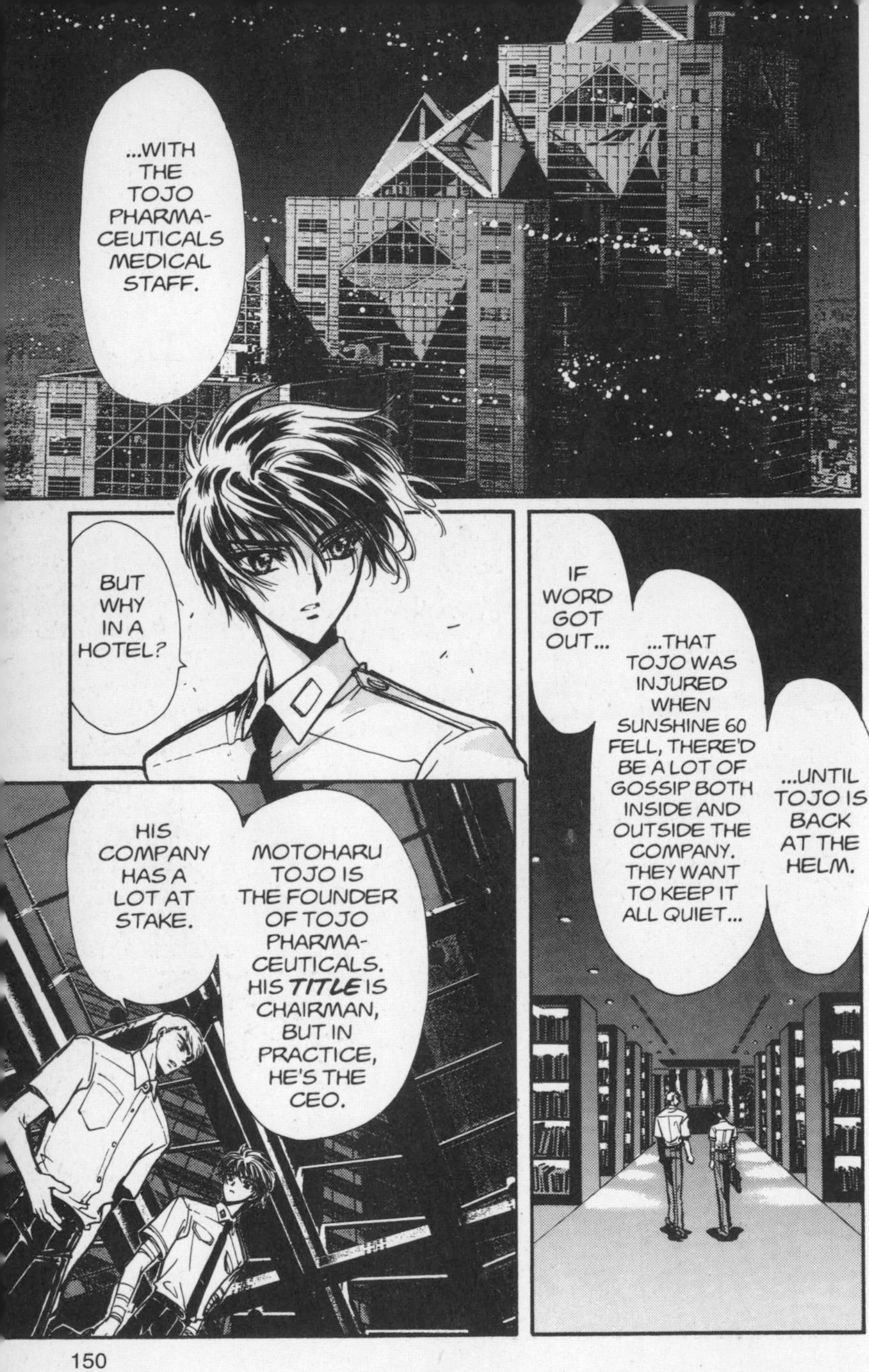
...WITH THE TOJO PHARMACEUTICALS MEDICAL STAFF.
BUT WHY IN A HOTEL?
HIS COMPANY HAS A LOT AT STAKE.
MOTOHARU TOJO IS THE FOUNDER OF TOJO PHARMACEUTICALS. HIS ***TITLE*** IS CHAIRMAN, BUT IN PRACTICE, HE'S THE CEO.
IF WORD GOT OUT...
...THAT TOJO WAS INJURED WHEN SUNSHINE 60 FELL, THERE'D BE A LOT OF GOSSIP BOTH INSIDE AND OUTSIDE THE COMPANY. THEY WANT TO KEEP IT ALL QUIET...
...UNTIL TOJO IS BACK AT THE HELM.

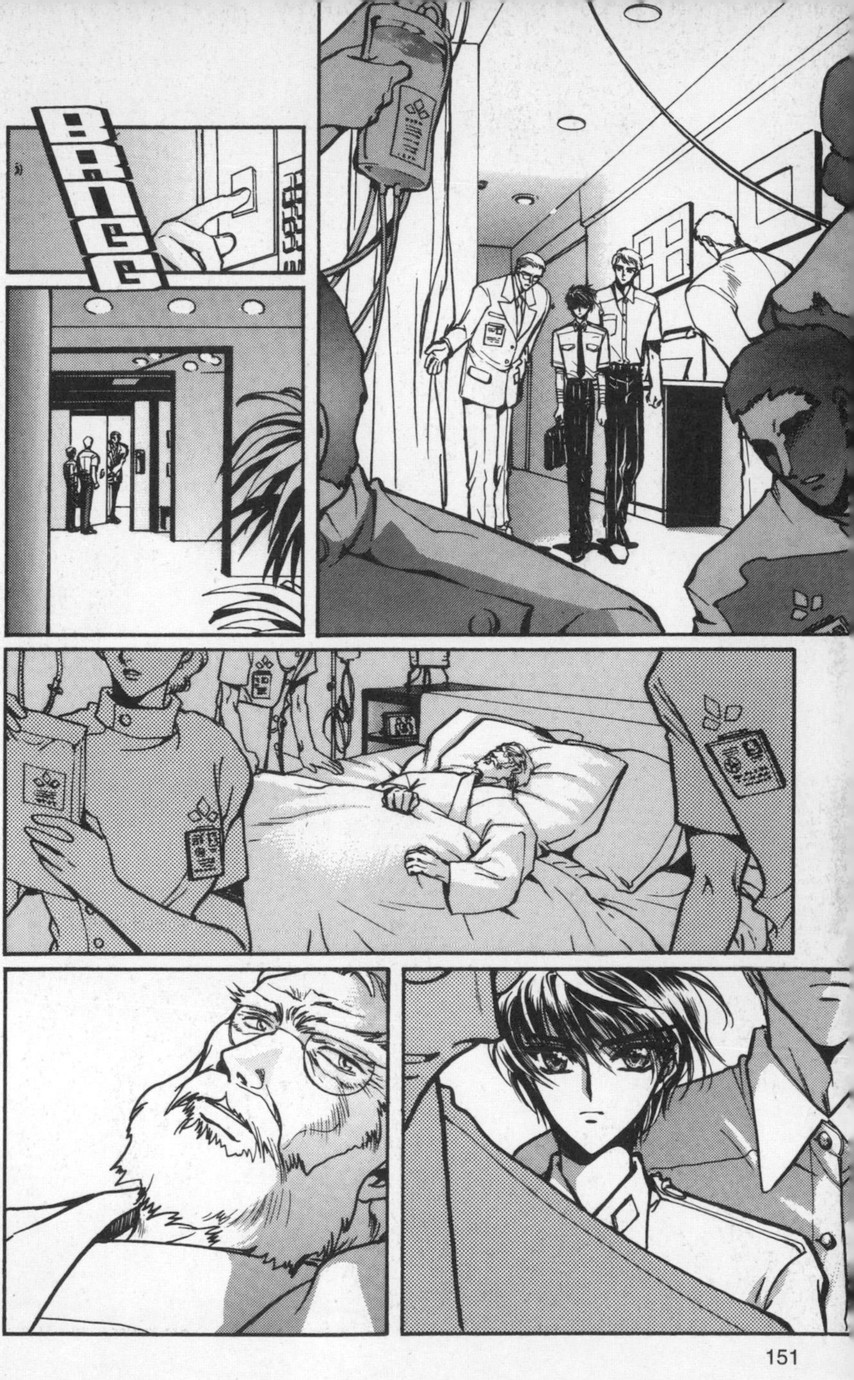
BRIGG

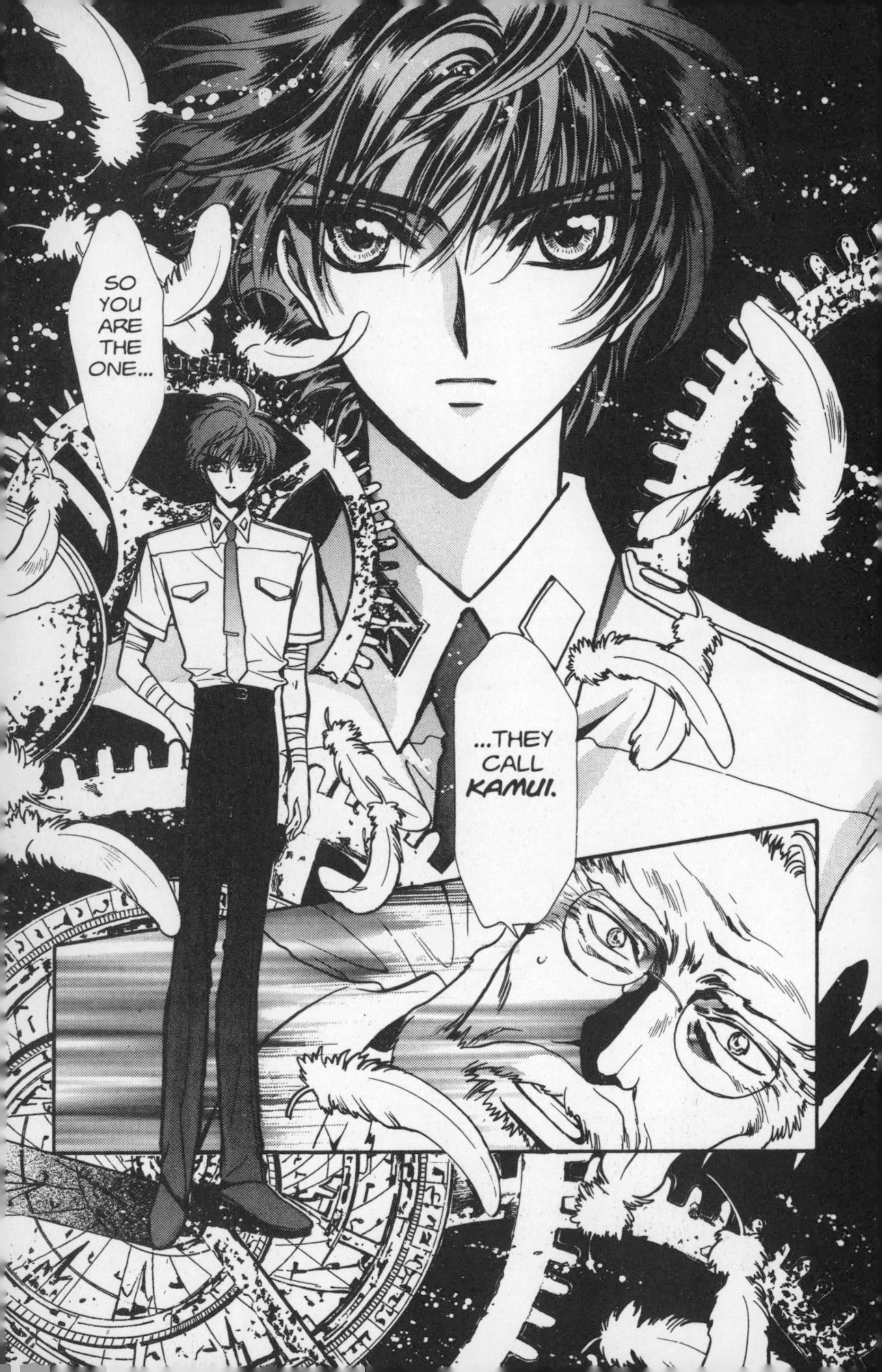
SO YOU ARE THE ONE...
...THEY CALL KAMUI.

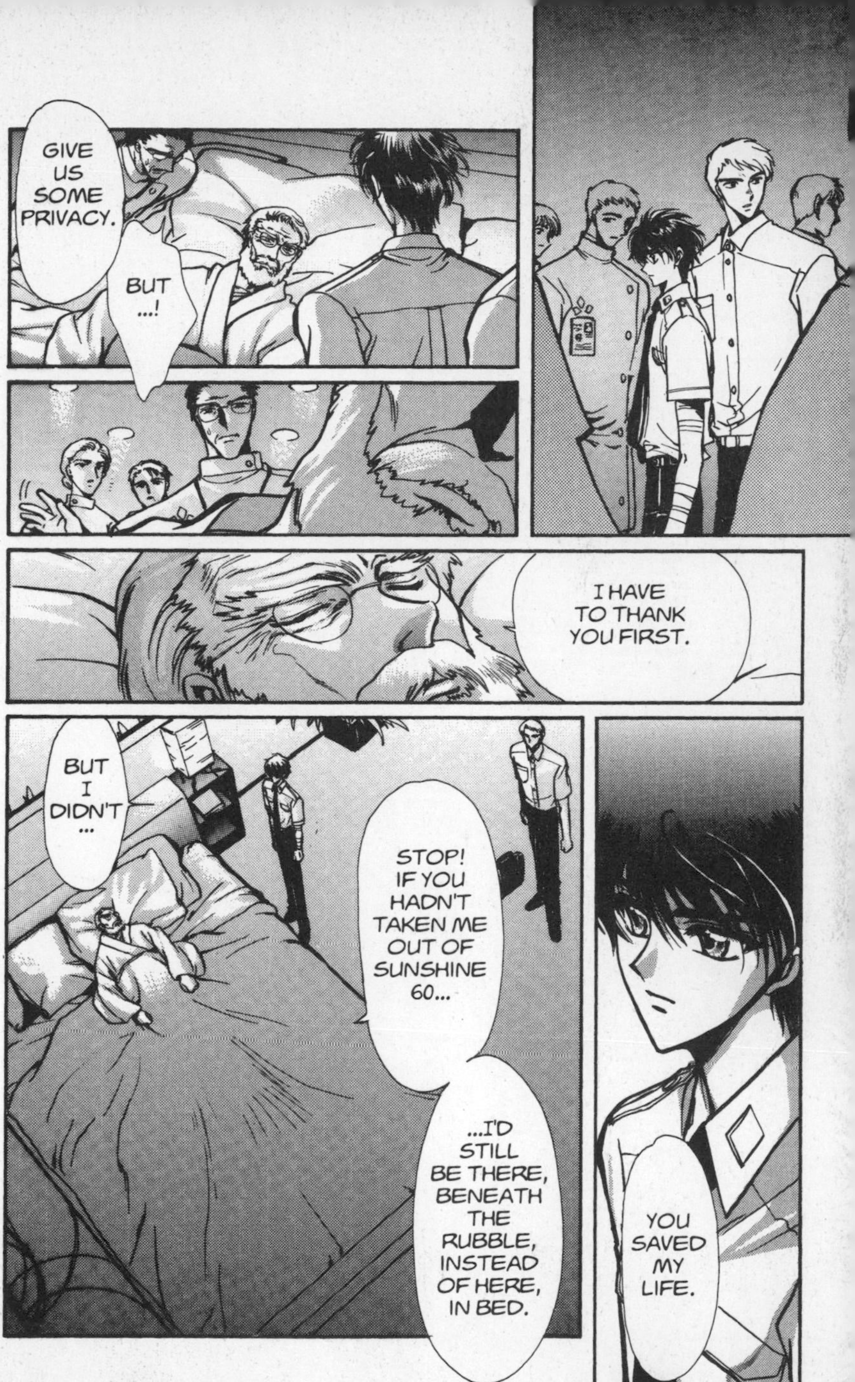
GIVE US SOME PRIVACY.
BUT ...!
I HAVE TO THANK YOU FIRST.
YOU SAVED MY LIFE.
BUT I DIDN'T ...
STOP! IF YOU HADN'T TAKEN ME OUT OF SUNSHINE 60...
...I'D STILL BE THERE, BENEATH THE RUBBLE, INSTEAD OF HERE, IN BED.

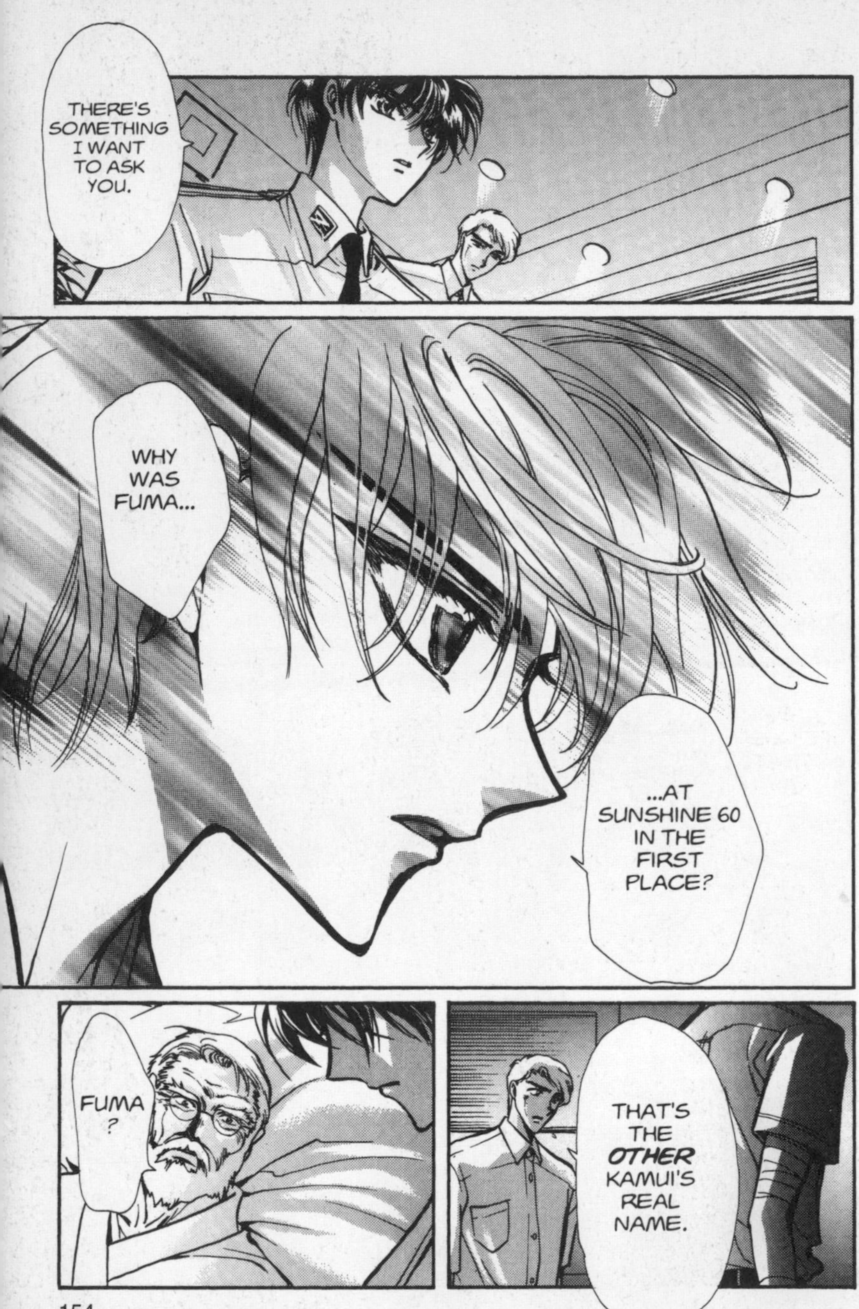
THERE'S SOMETHING I WANT TO ASK YOU.
WHY WAS FUMA...
...AT SUNSHINE 60 IN THE FIRST PLACE?
FUMA?
THAT'S THE ***OTHER*** KAMUI'S REAL NAME.

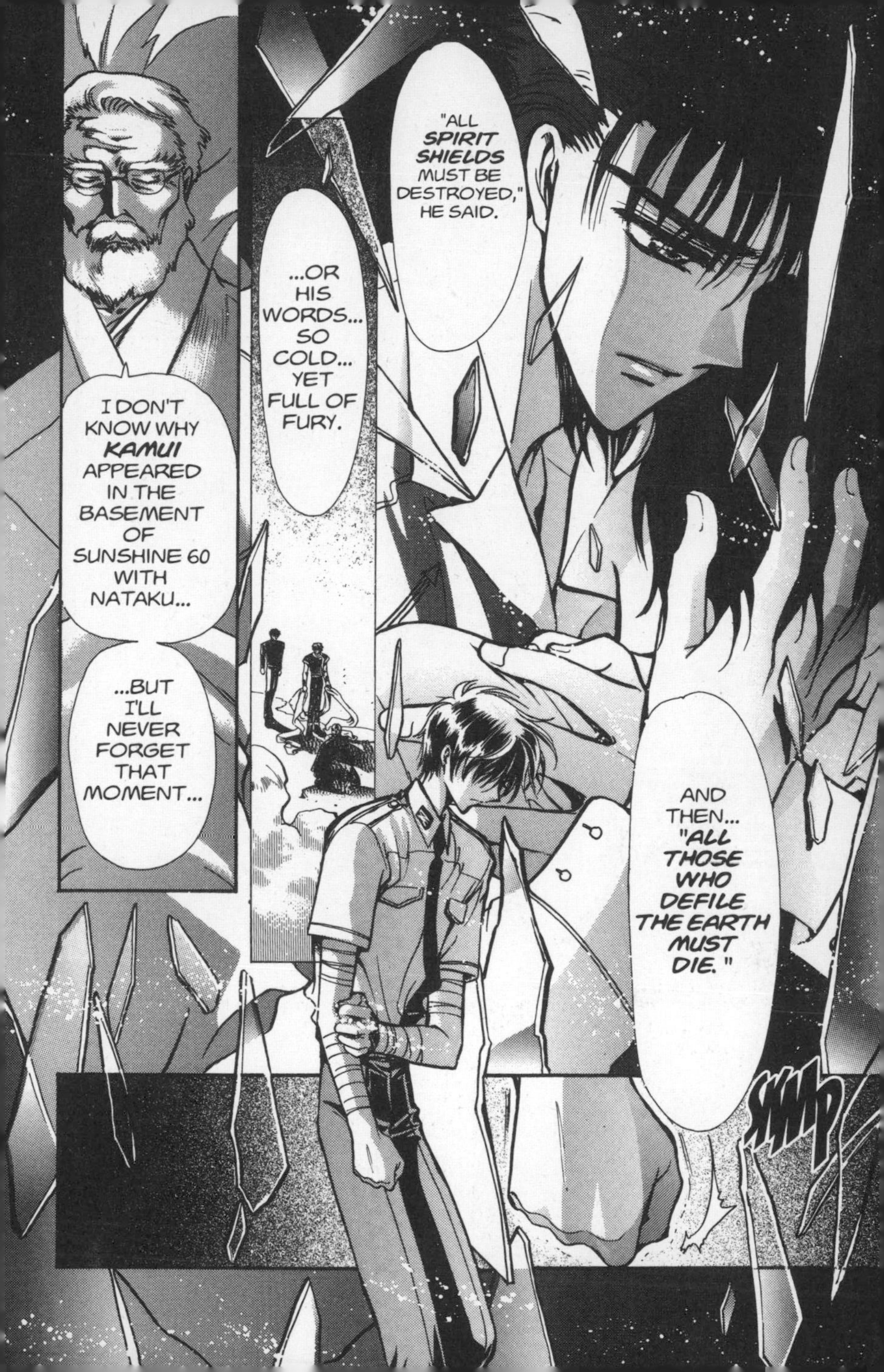
"ALL ***SPIRIT SHIELDS*** MUST BE DESTROYED," HE SAID.
...OR HIS WORDS... SO COLD... YET FULL OF FURY.
I DON'T KNOW WHY ***KAMUI*** APPEARED IN THE BASEMENT OF SUNSHINE 60 WITH NATAKU...
...BUT I'LL NEVER FORGET THAT MOMENT...
AND THEN... "***ALL THOSE WHO DEFILE THE EARTH MUST DIE.***"

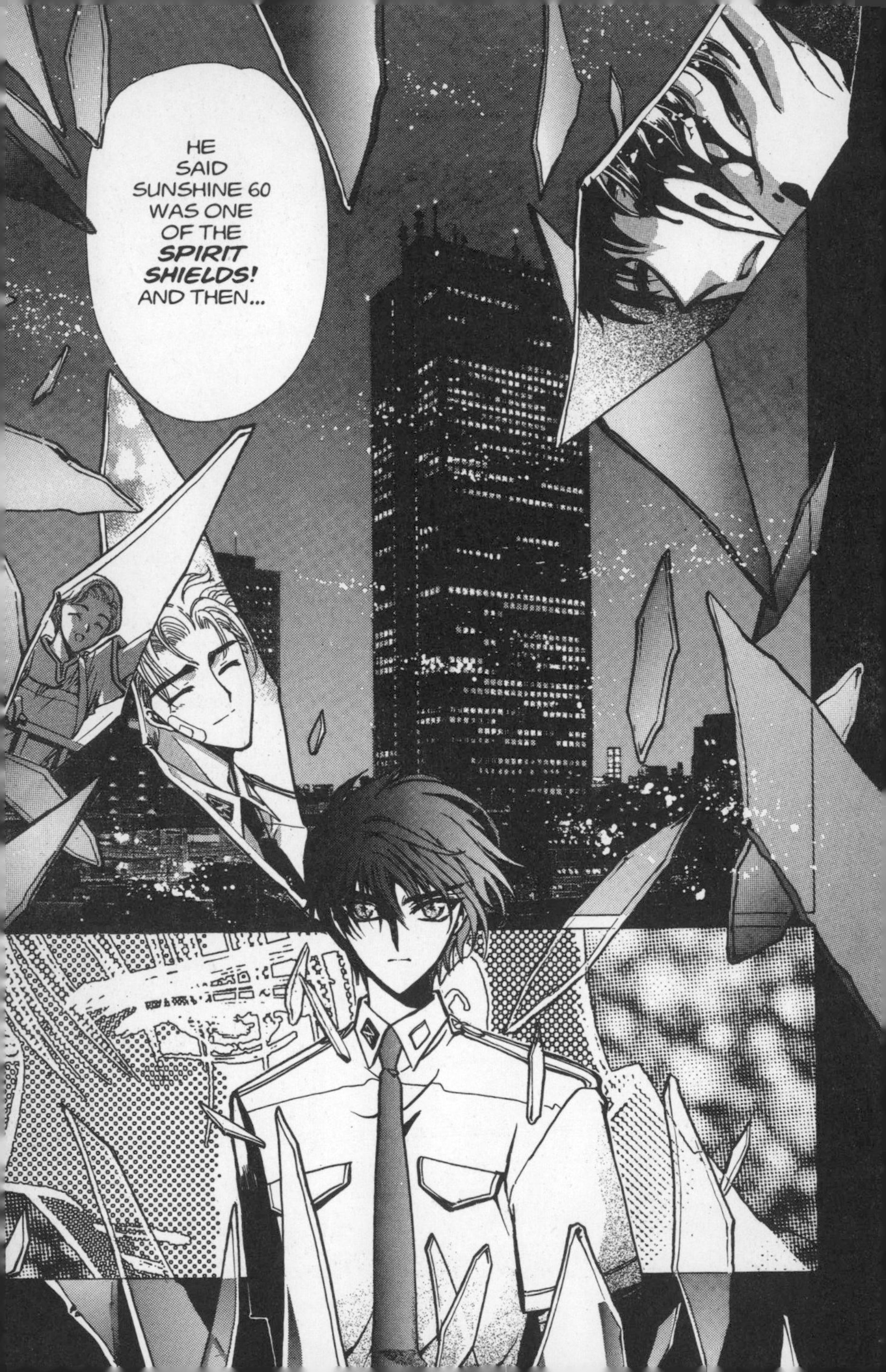
HE SAID SUNSHINE 60 WAS ONE OF THE SPIRIT SHIELDS! AND THEN...

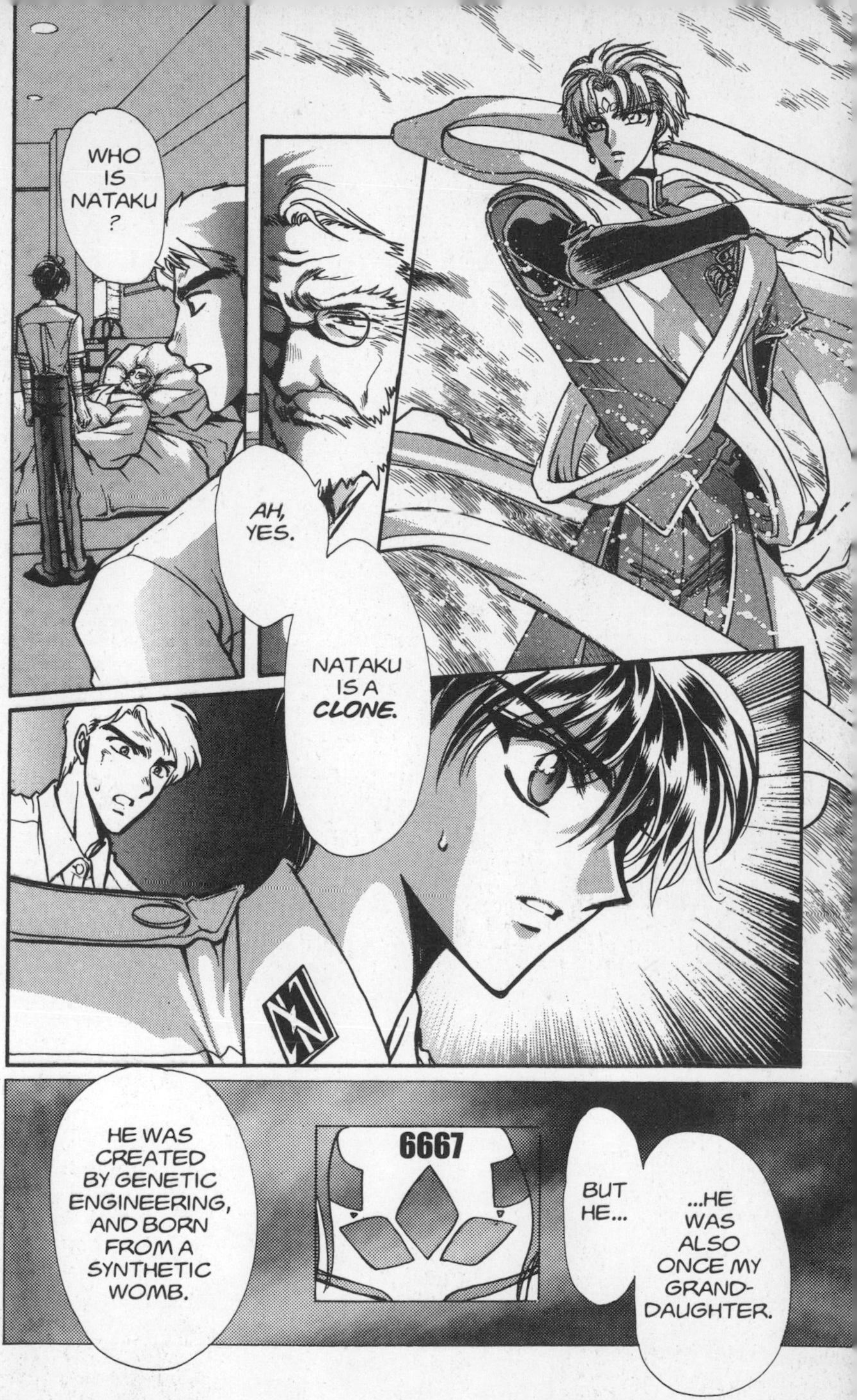
WHO IS NATAKU?
AH, YES.
NATAKU IS A CLONE.
HE WAS CREATED BY GENETIC ENGINEERING, AND BORN FROM A SYNTHETIC WOMB.
6667
BUT HE...
...HE WAS ALSO ONCE MY GRAND-DAUGHTER.

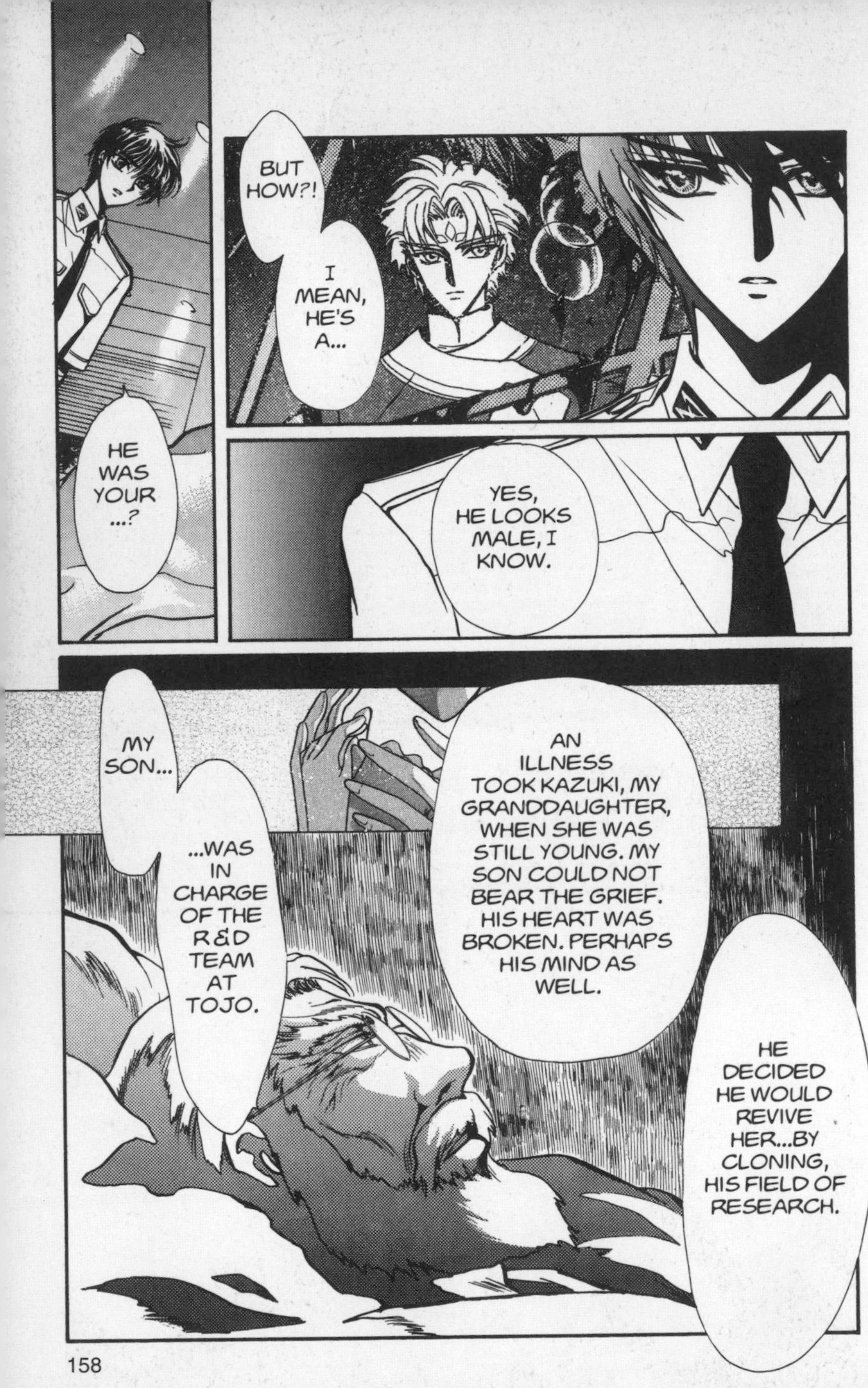
HE WAS YOUR ...?
BUT HOW?!
I MEAN, HE'S A...
YES, HE LOOKS MALE, I KNOW.
MY SON...
...WAS IN CHARGE OF THE R&D TEAM AT TOJO.
AN ILLNESS TOOK KAZUKI, MY GRANDDAUGHTER, WHEN SHE WAS STILL YOUNG. MY SON COULD NOT BEAR THE GRIEF. HIS HEART WAS BROKEN. PERHAPS HIS MIND AS WELL.
HE DECIDED HE WOULD REVIVE HER...BY CLONING, HIS FIELD OF RESEARCH.

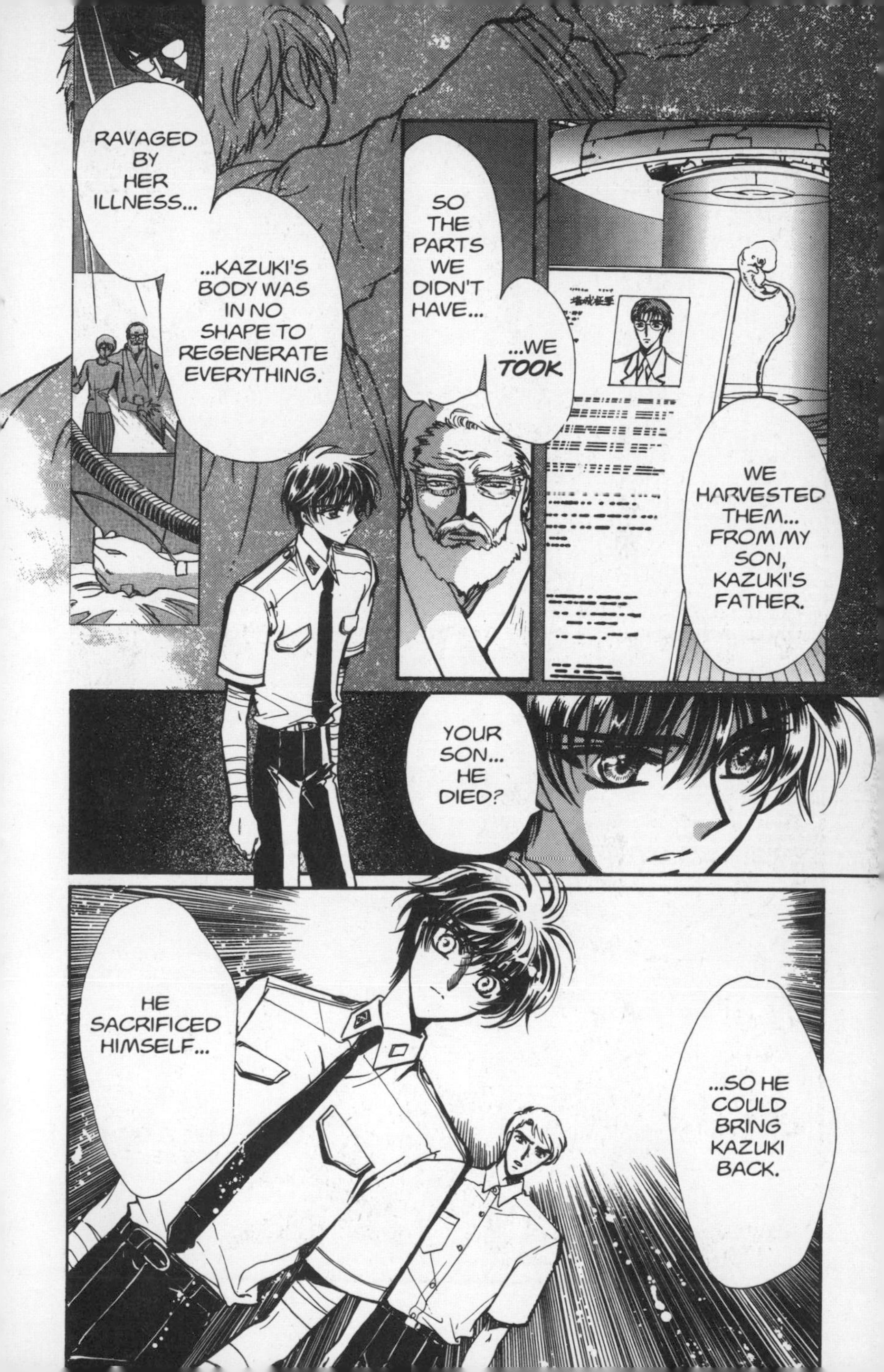
RAVAGED BY HER ILLNESS...
...KAZUKI'S BODY WAS IN NO SHAPE TO REGENERATE EVERYTHING.
SO THE PARTS WE DIDN'T HAVE...
...WE *TOOK.*
WE HARVESTED THEM... FROM MY SON, KAZUKI'S FATHER.
YOUR SON... HE DIED?
HE SACRIFICED HIMSELF...
...SO HE COULD BRING KAZUKI BACK.

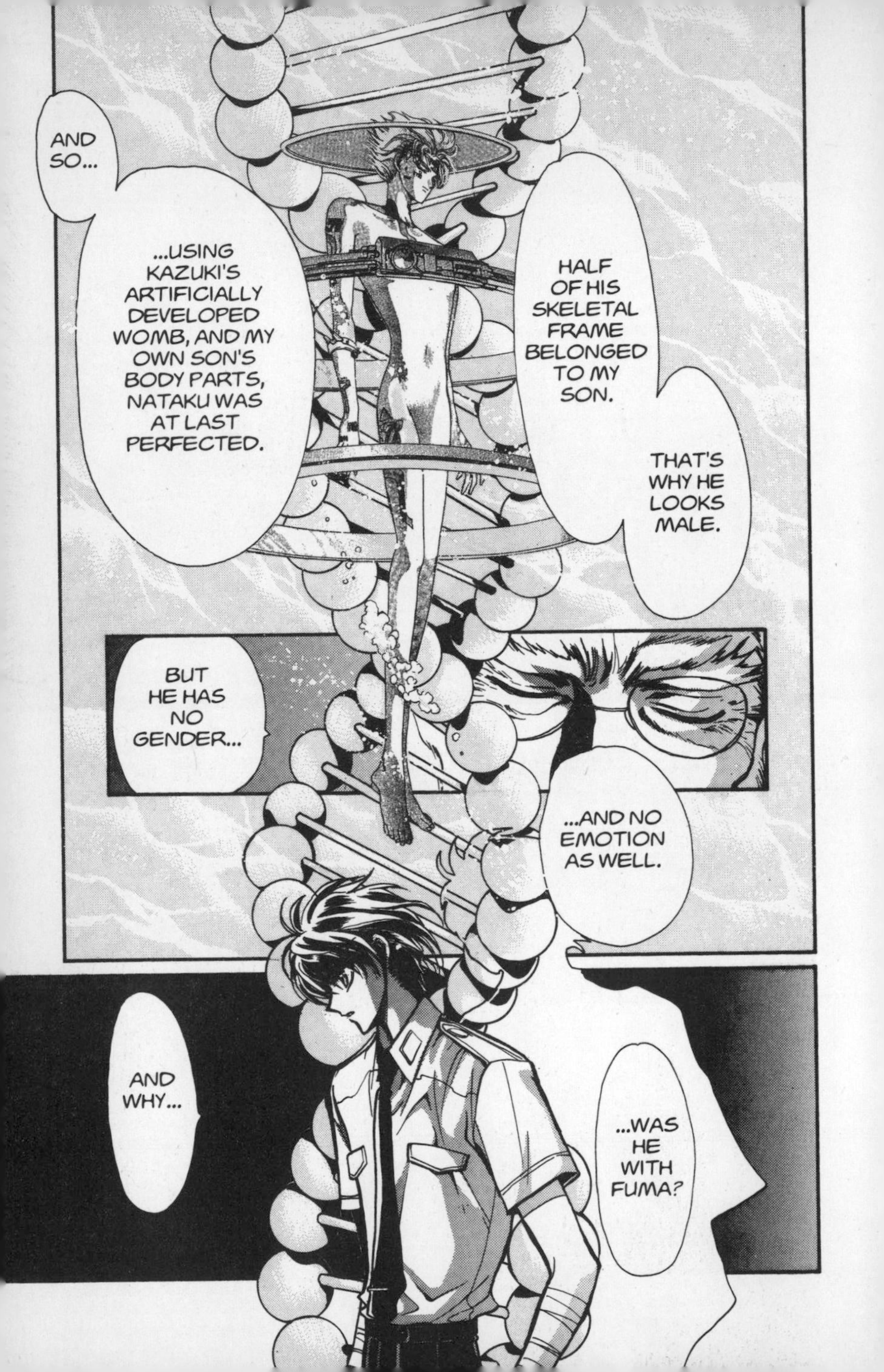
AND SO...
...USING KAZUKI'S ARTIFICIALLY DEVELOPED WOMB, AND MY OWN SON'S BODY PARTS, NATAKU WAS AT LAST PERFECTED.
HALF OF HIS SKELETAL FRAME BELONGED TO MY SON.
THAT'S WHY HE LOOKS MALE.
BUT HE HAS NO GENDER...
...AND NO EMOTION AS WELL.
AND WHY...
...WAS HE WITH FUMA?

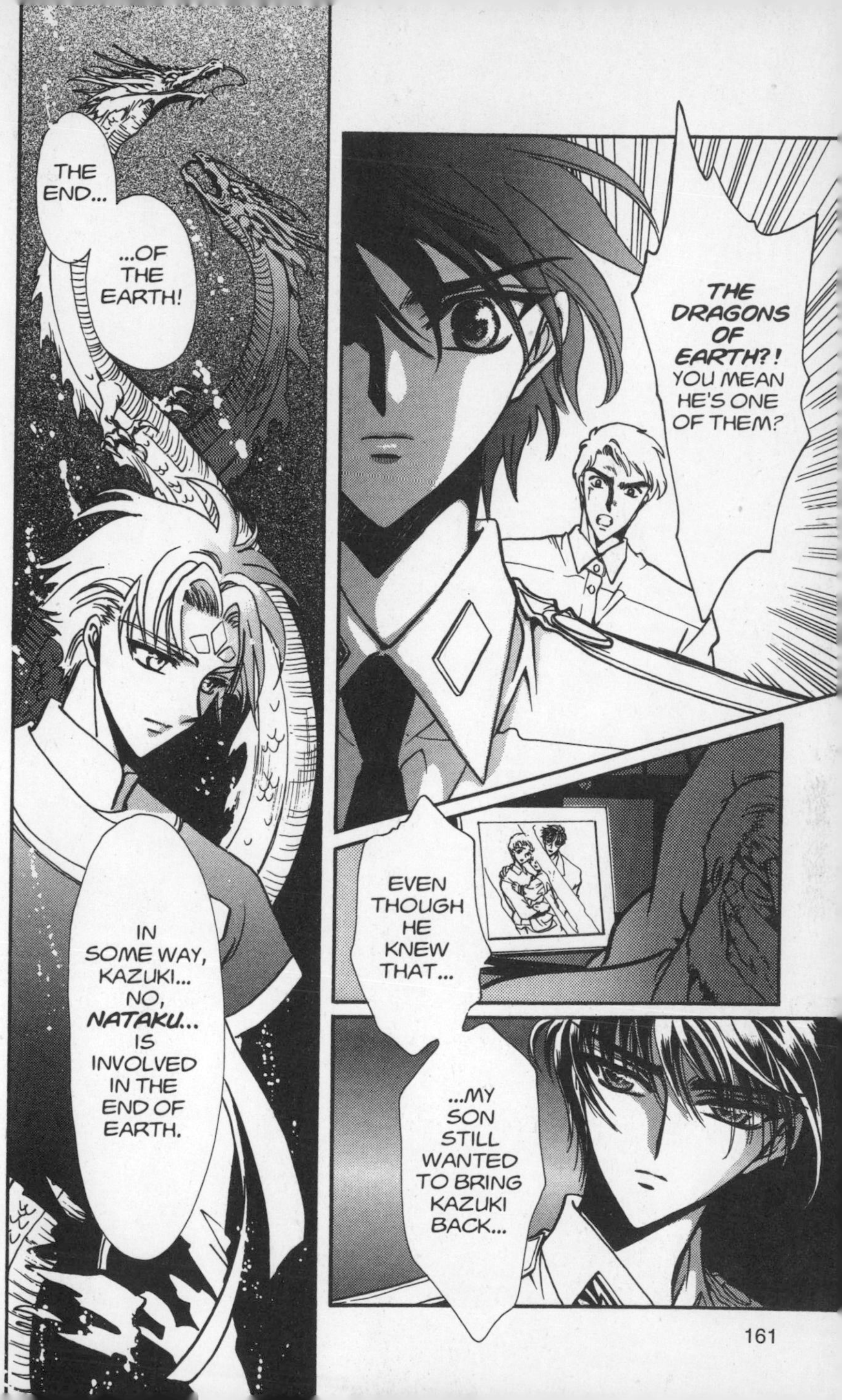
THE DRAGONS OF EARTH?! YOU MEAN HE'S ONE OF THEM?
EVEN THOUGH HE KNEW THAT...
...MY SON STILL WANTED TO BRING KAZUKI BACK...
THE END...
...OF THE EARTH!
IN SOME WAY, KAZUKI... NO, *NATAKU...* IS INVOLVED IN THE END OF EARTH.

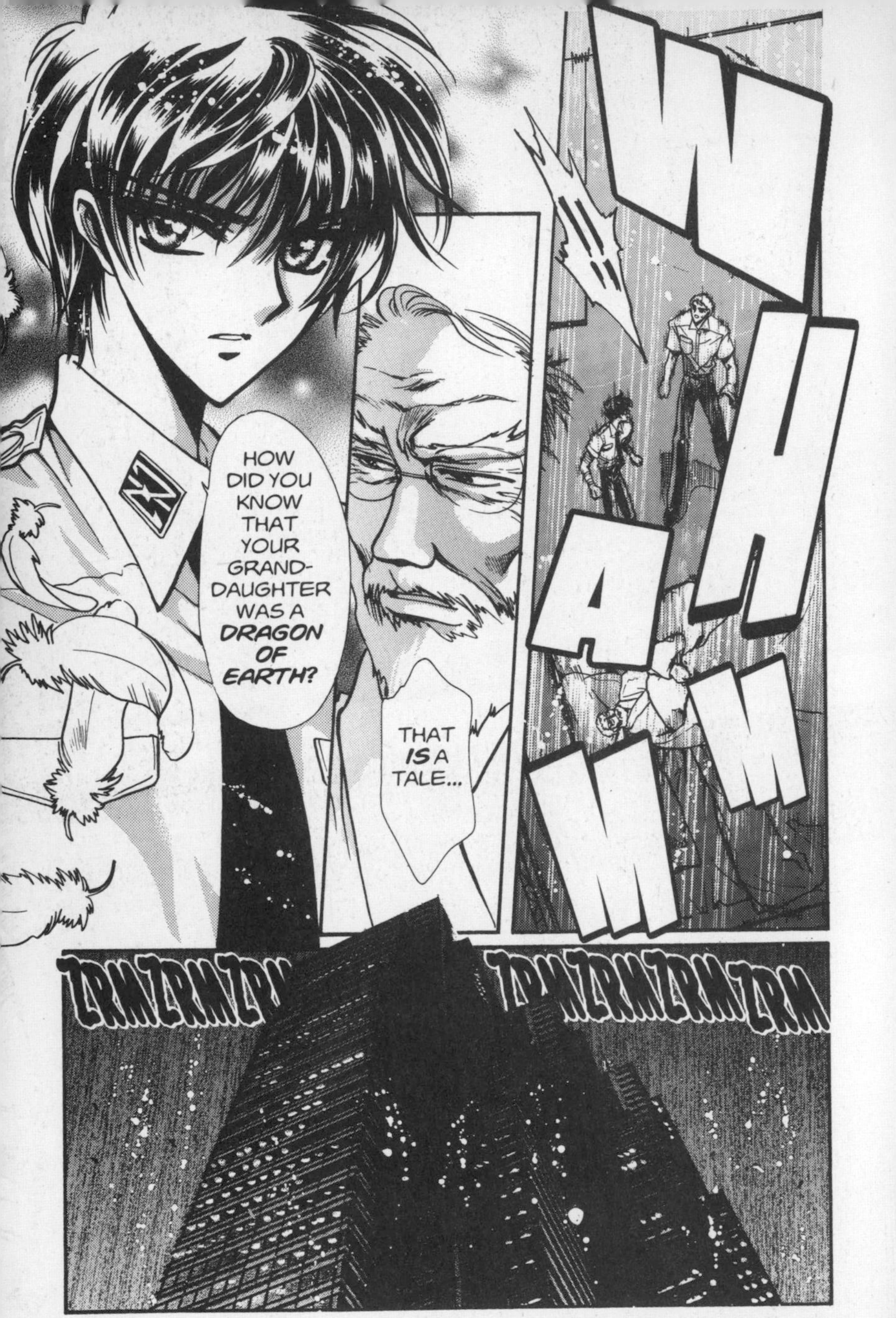
WHAMM
HOW DID YOU KNOW THAT YOUR GRAND-DAUGHTER WAS A DRAGON OF EARTH?
THAT IS A TALE...
ZRM ZRM ZRM ZRM ZRM ZRM ZRM ZRM

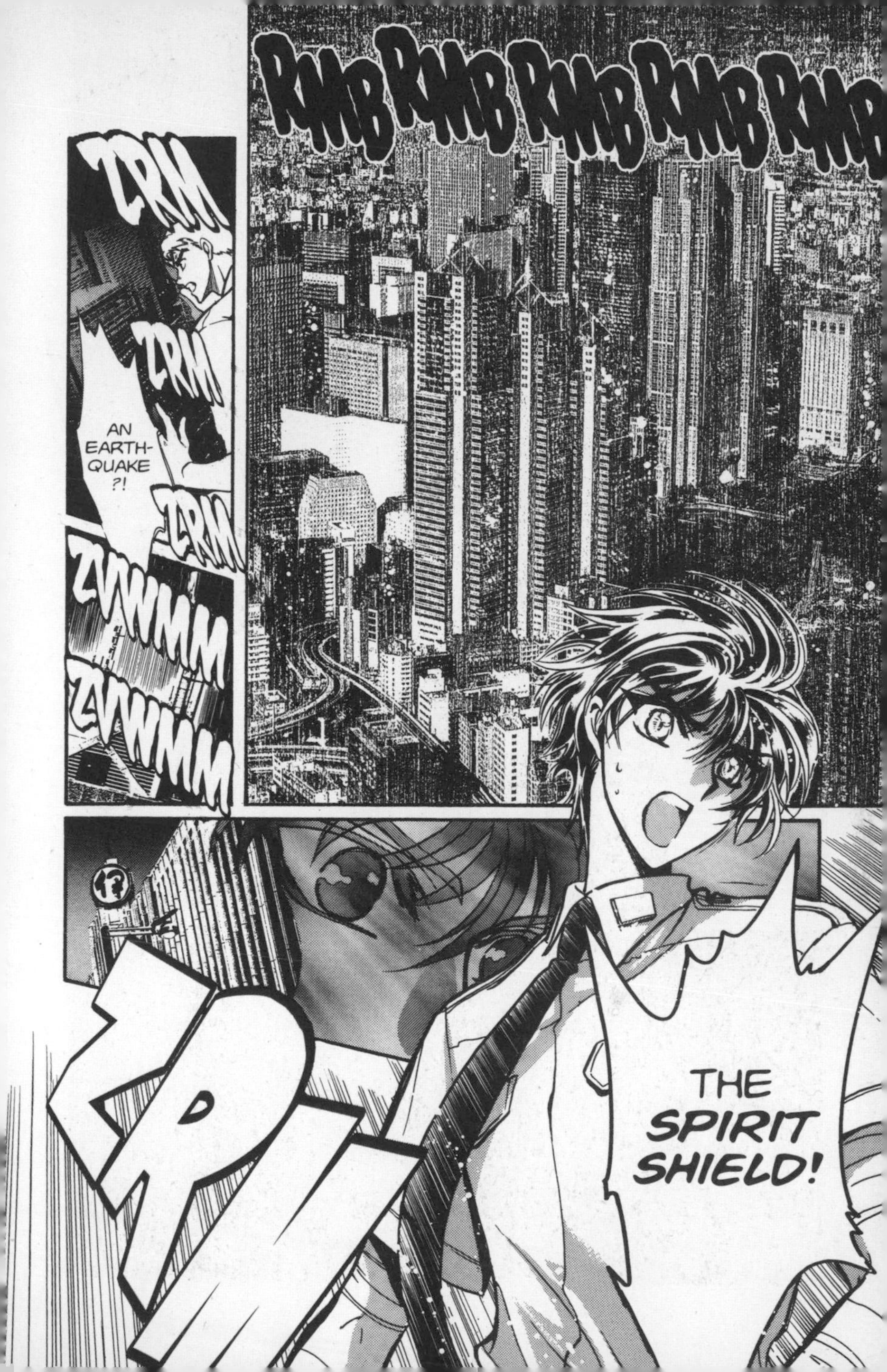
RMB RMB RMB RMB RMB RMB
ZRM
ZRM
AN EARTH-QUAKE ?!
ZRM
ZVWMM
ZVWMM
THE SPIRIT SHIELD!
ZAP

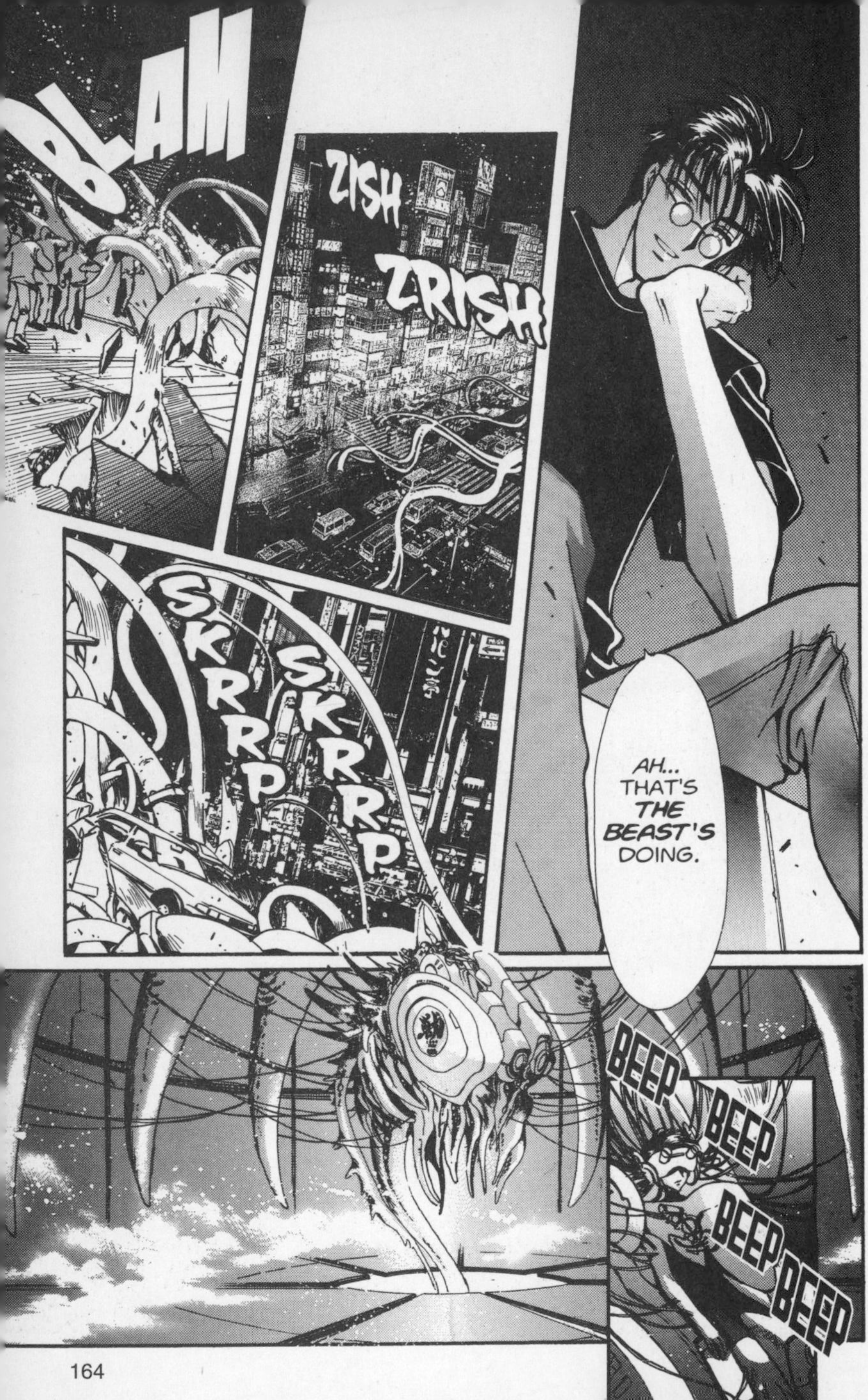
AH... THAT'S *THE BEAST'S* DOING.
ZISH
ZRISH
BLAM
SKRRP
SKRRP
BEEP
BEEP
BEEP
BEEP

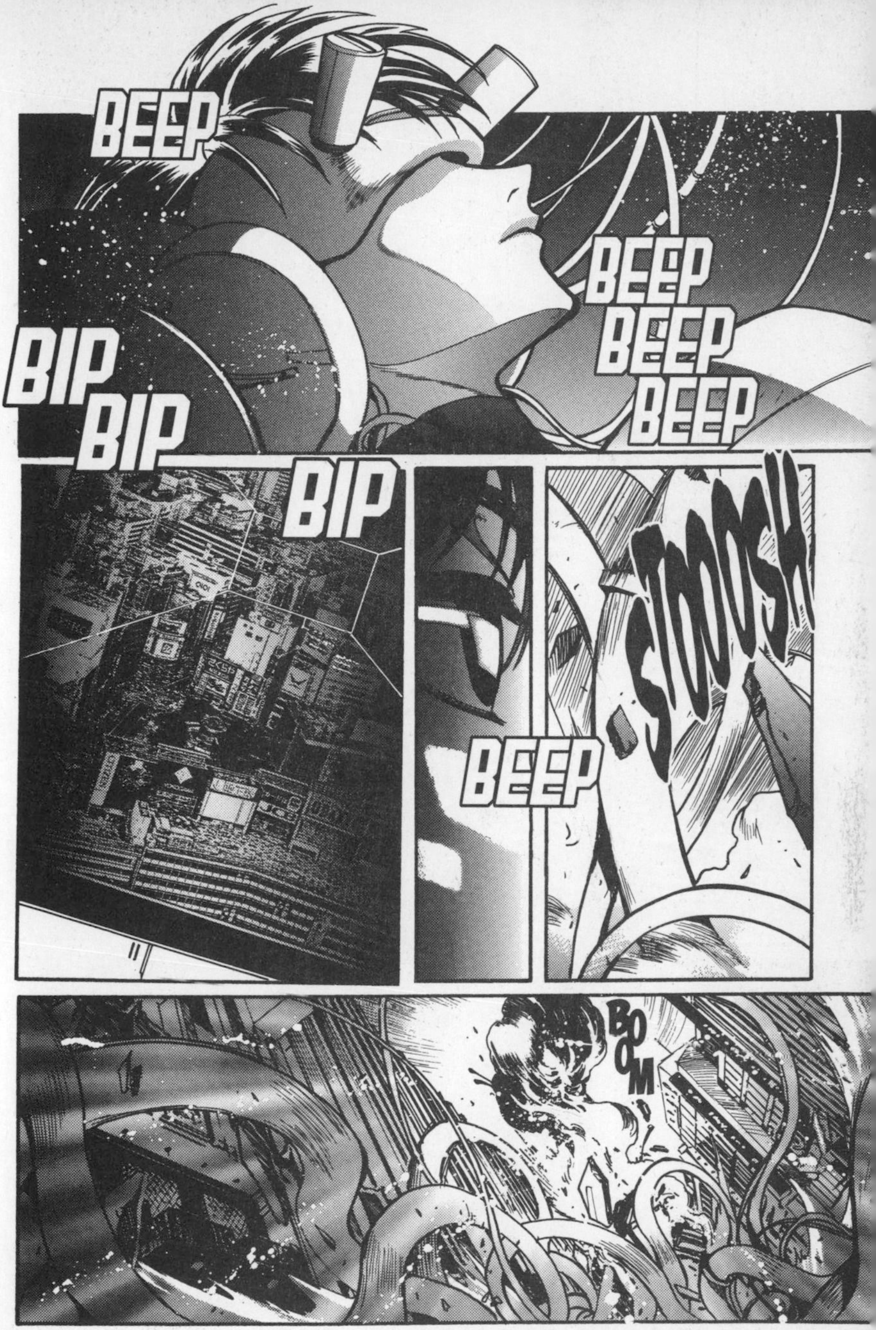
BEEP
BEEP
BEEP
BEEP
BIP
BIP
SWOOOSH
BEEP
BIP
BOOM

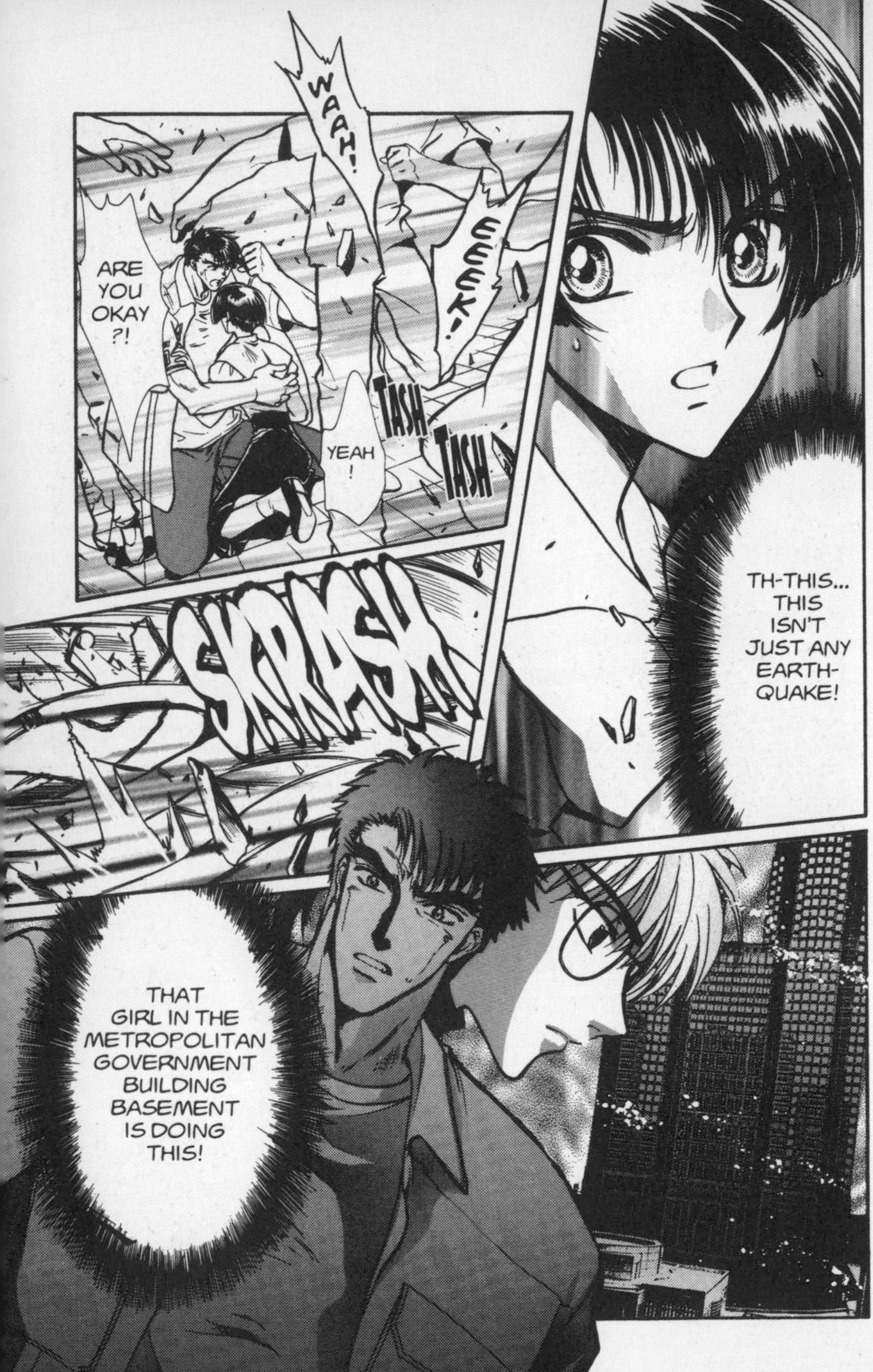
TH-THIS... THIS ISN'T JUST ANY EARTH-QUAKE!
WAAH!
EEEEK!
ARE YOU OKAY ?!
YEAH !
TASH TASH
SKRASH
THAT GIRL IN THE METROPOLITAN GOVERNMENT BUILDING BASEMENT IS DOING THIS!

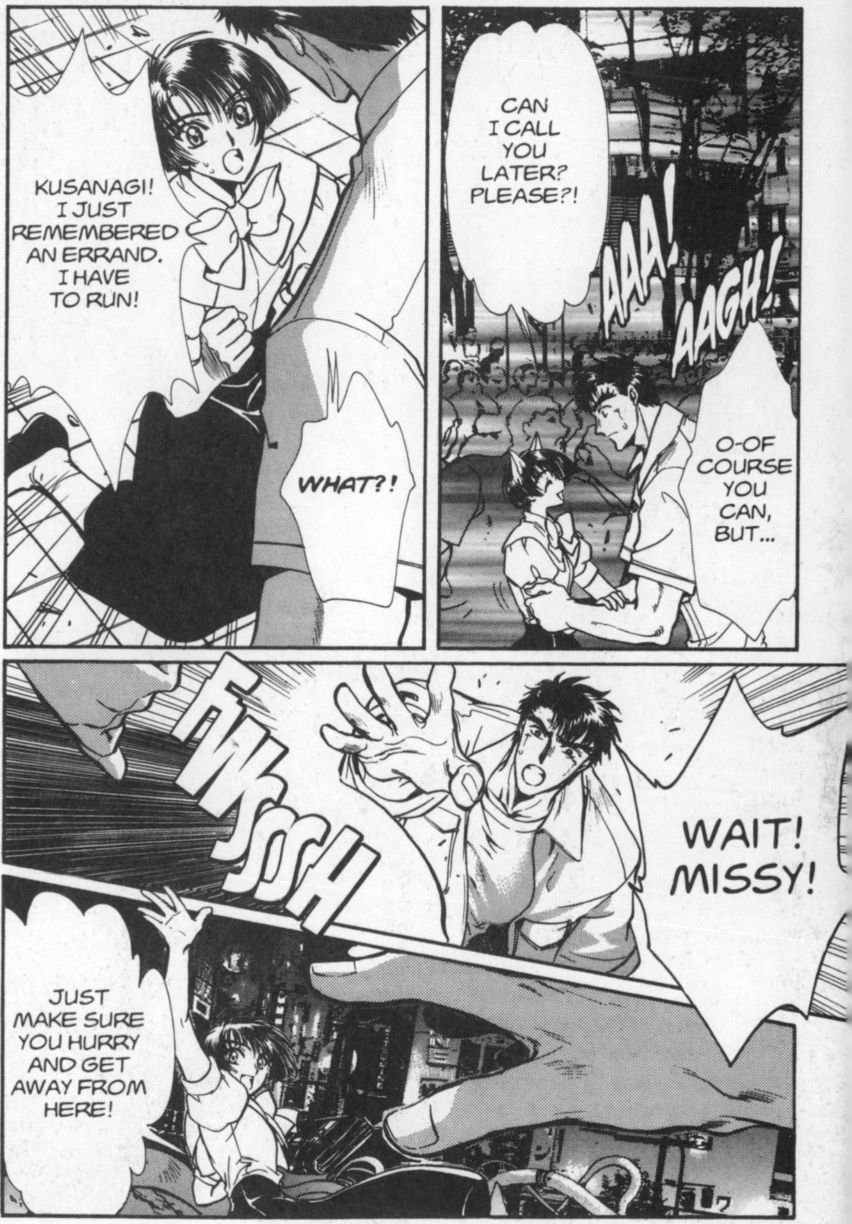
KUSANAGI! I JUST REMEMBERED AN ERRAND. I HAVE TO RUN!
WHAT?!
CAN I CALL YOU LATER? PLEASE?!
AAA! AAGH!
O-OF COURSE YOU CAN, BUT...
FWSSH
WAIT! MISSY!
JUST MAKE SURE YOU HURRY AND GET AWAY FROM HERE!

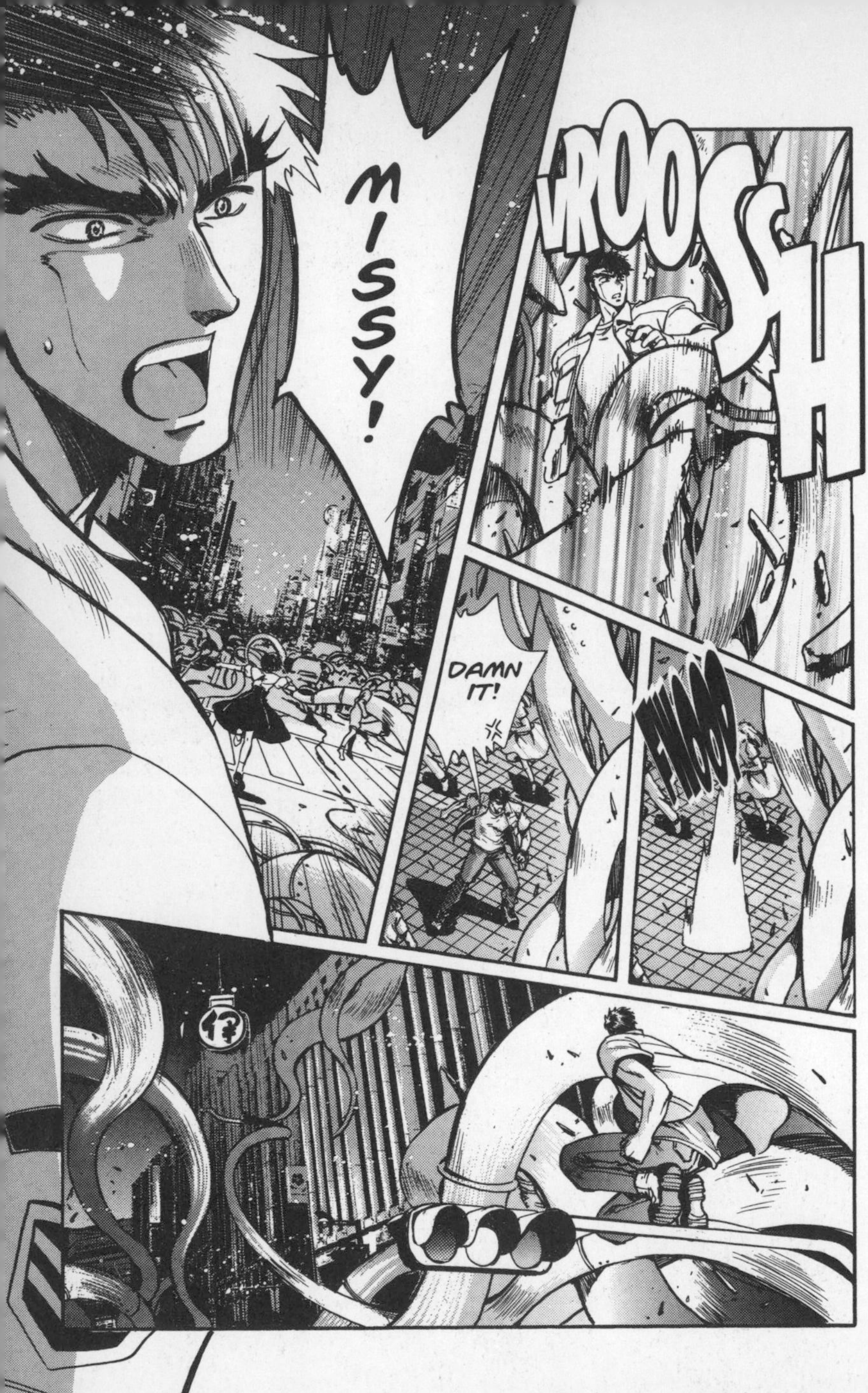
VROOOSH
WHOOP
DAMN IT!
MISSY!

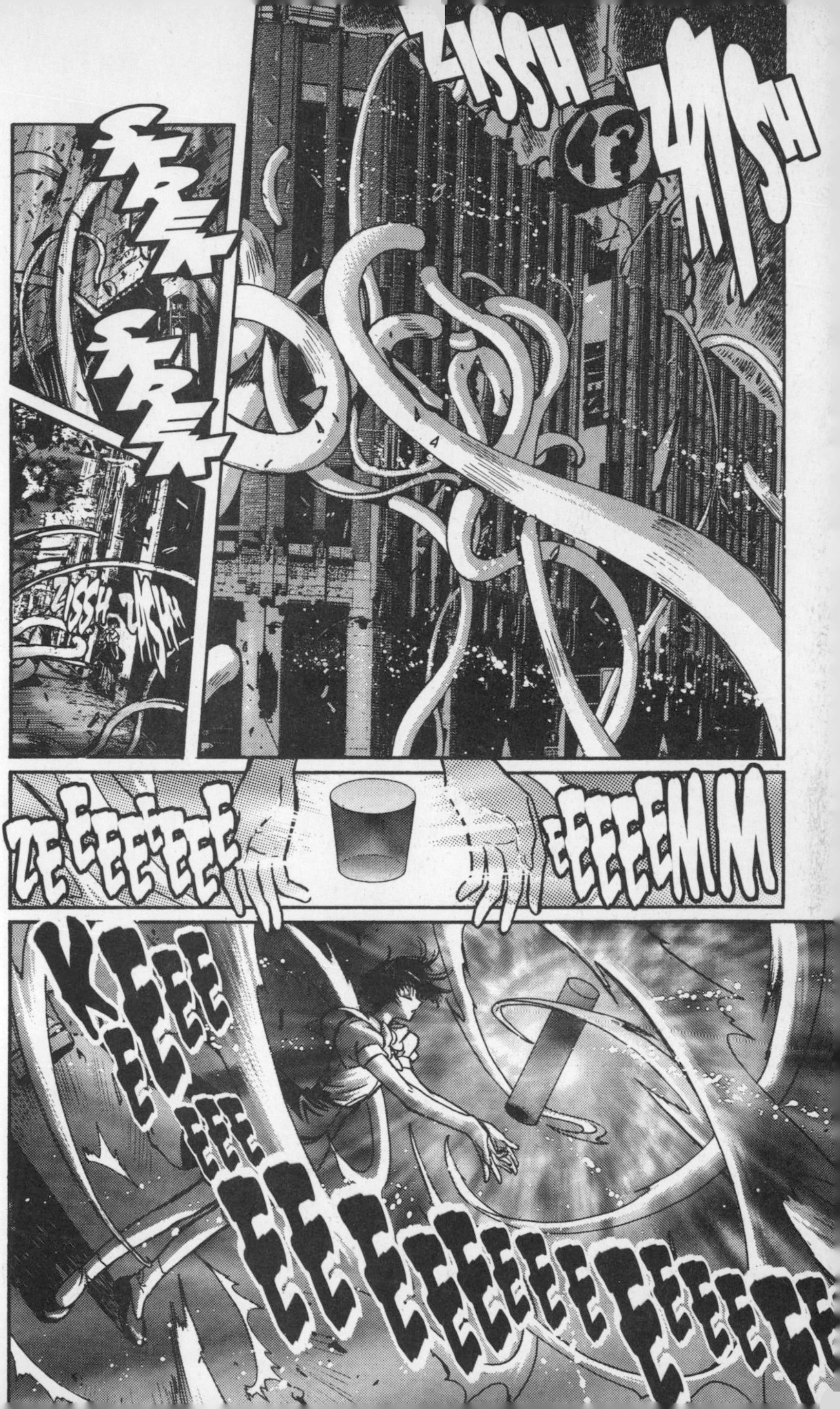
ZISSH
ZASH
ZISSH
ZASH
ZEEEEEEE
EEEEEMM
KEEEE

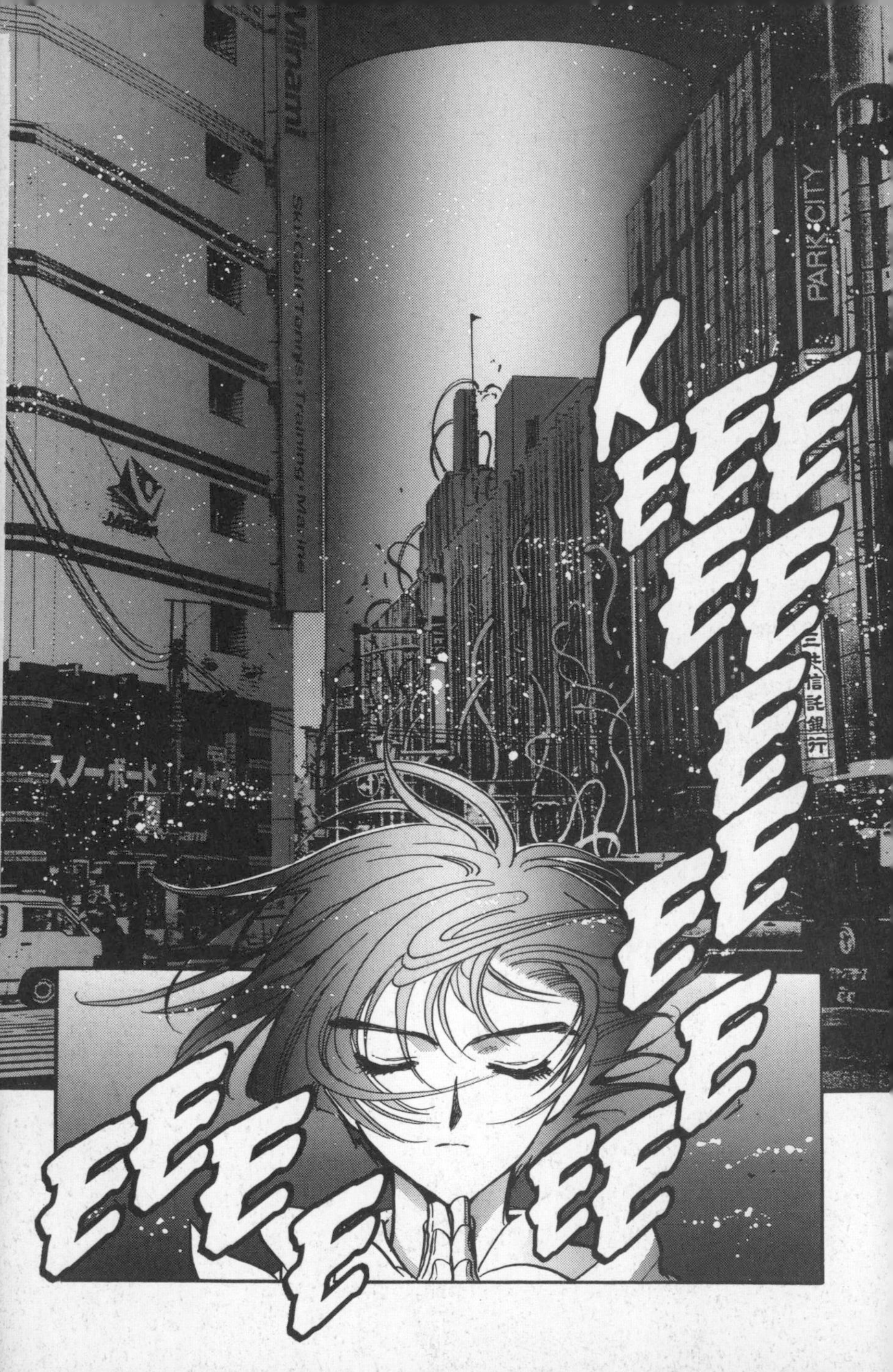
PARK CITY
三井信託銀行
スノーボード
KEEEEEEEEEEEEEEEEEEEE

X

SEIICHIRO AOKI

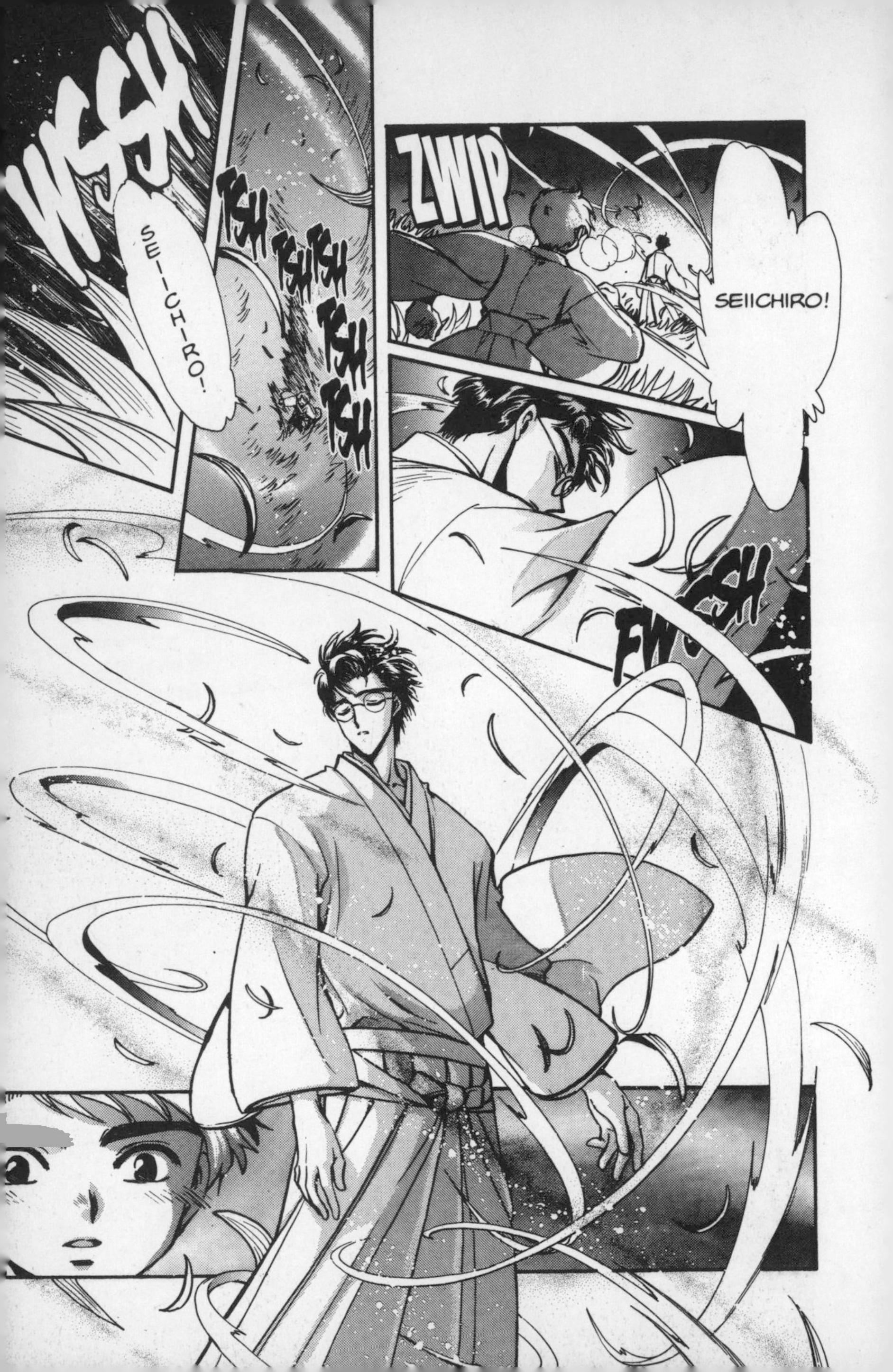
ZWIP
SEIICHIRO!
TSH TSH TSH TSH TSH TSH
SEIICHIRO!
WSSH

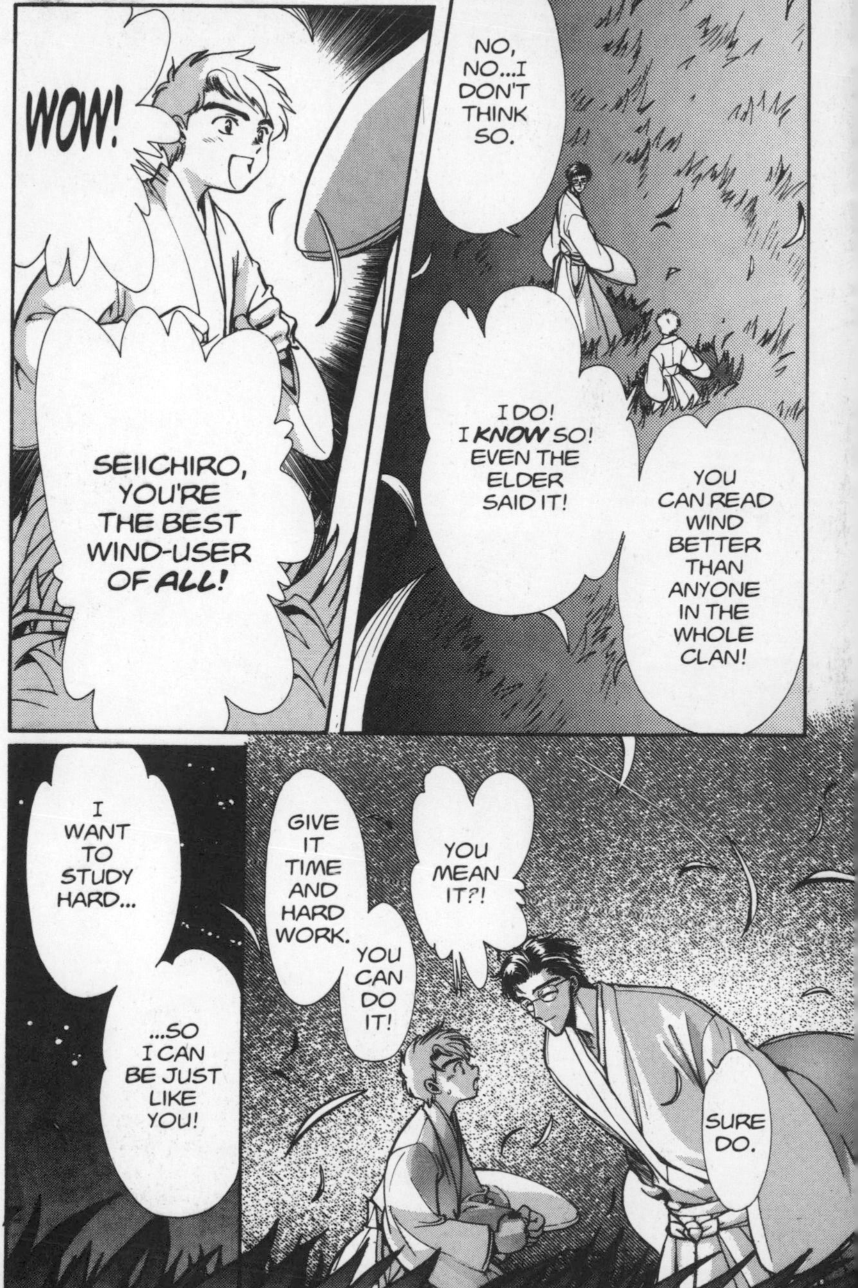
WOW!
SEIICHIRO, YOU'RE THE BEST WIND-USER OF ***ALL!***
NO, NO...I DON'T THINK SO.
I DO! I ***KNOW*** SO! EVEN THE ELDER SAID IT!
YOU CAN READ WIND BETTER THAN ANYONE IN THE WHOLE CLAN!
I WANT TO STUDY HARD...
...SO I CAN BE JUST LIKE YOU!
GIVE IT TIME AND HARD WORK.
YOU CAN DO IT!
YOU MEAN IT?!
SURE DO.

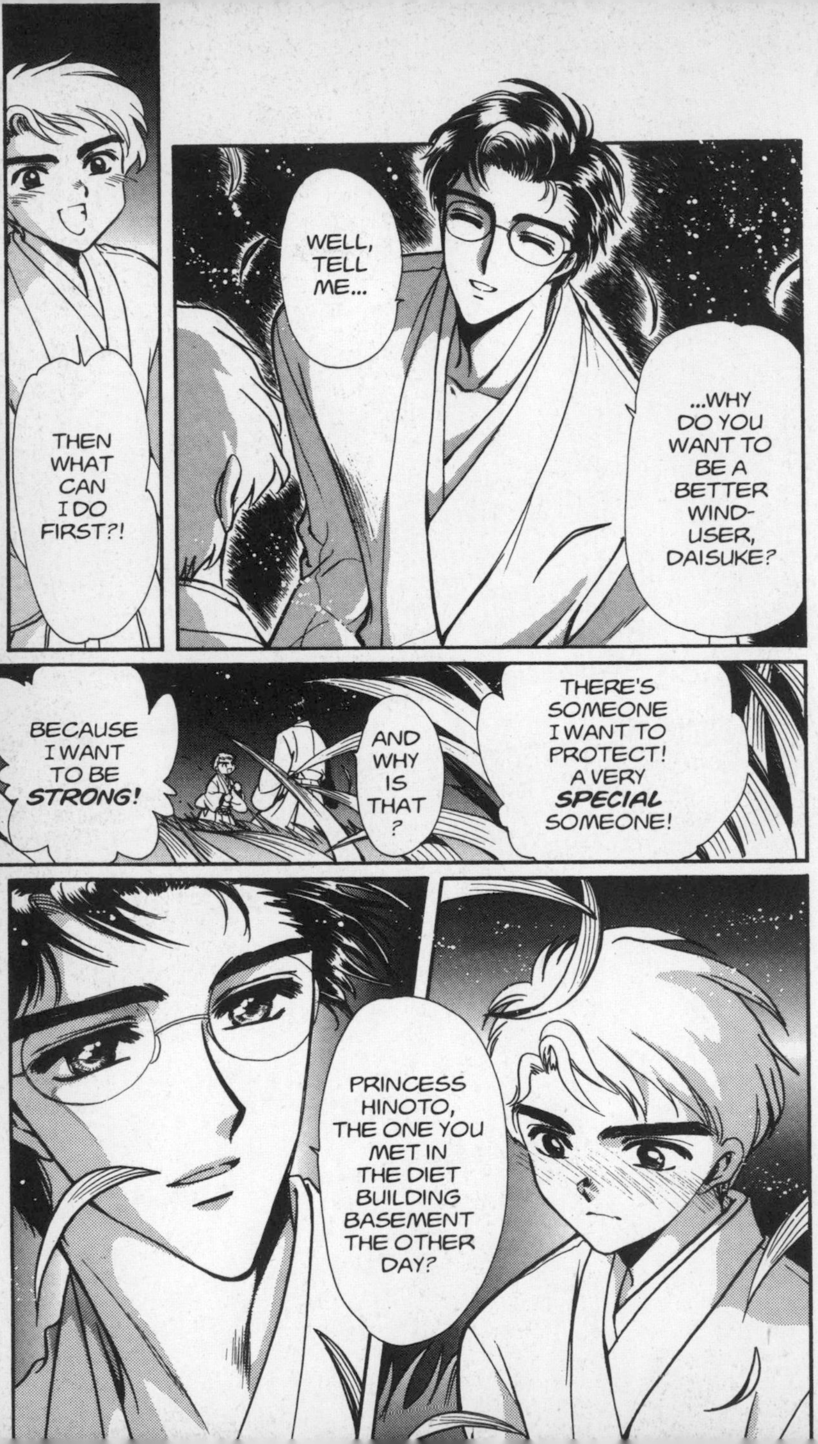
THEN WHAT CAN I DO FIRST?!
WELL, TELL ME...
...WHY DO YOU WANT TO BE A BETTER WIND-USER, DAISUKE?
BECAUSE I WANT TO BE **STRONG!**
AND WHY IS THAT ?
THERE'S SOMEONE I WANT TO PROTECT! A VERY **SPECIAL** SOMEONE!
PRINCESS HINOTO, THE ONE YOU MET IN THE DIET BUILDING BASEMENT THE OTHER DAY?

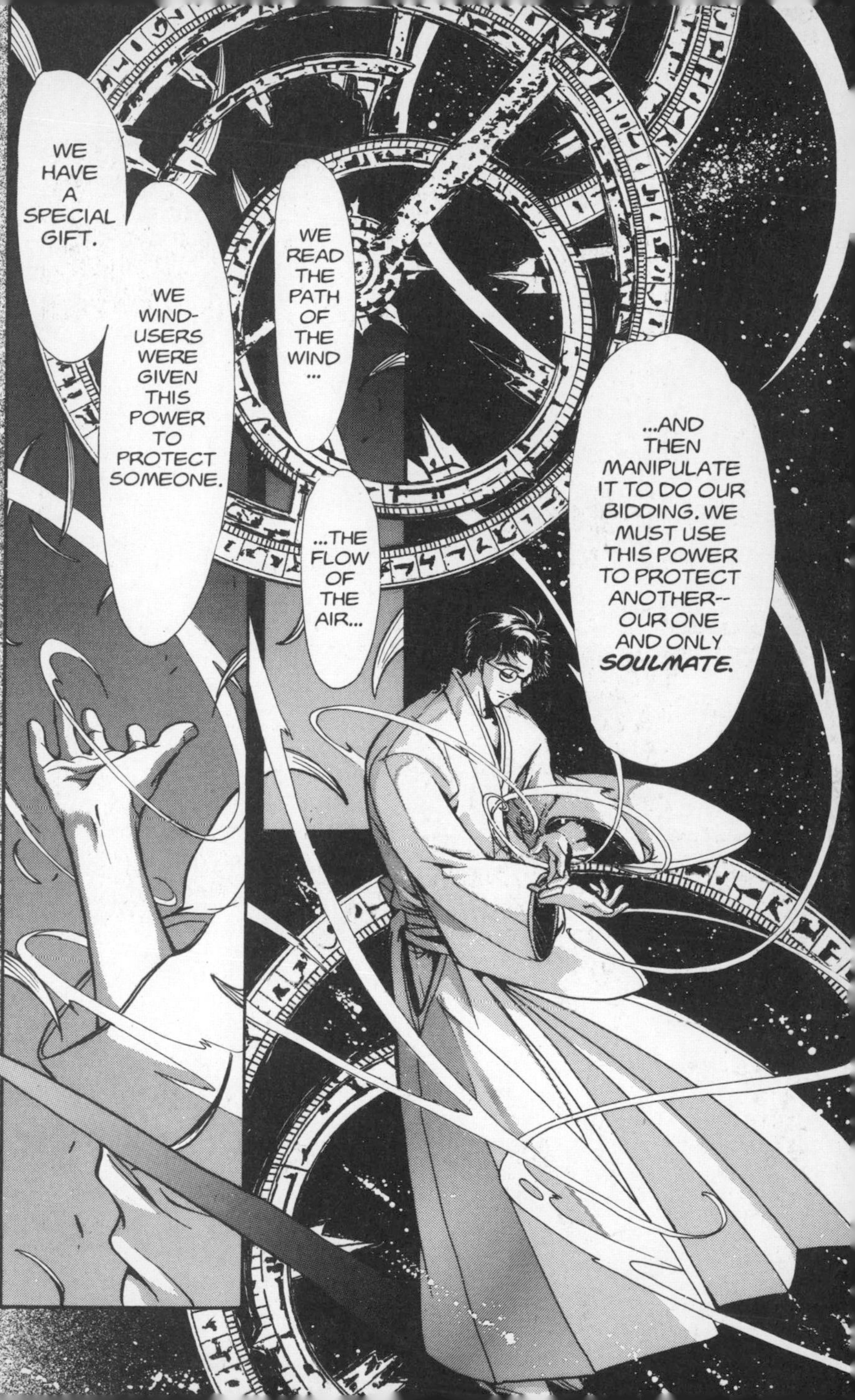
WE HAVE A SPECIAL GIFT.
WE WIND-USERS WERE GIVEN THIS POWER TO PROTECT SOMEONE.
WE READ THE PATH OF THE WIND...
...THE FLOW OF THE AIR...
...AND THEN MANIPULATE IT TO DO OUR BIDDING. WE MUST USE THIS POWER TO PROTECT ANOTHER-- OUR ONE AND ONLY SOULMATE.

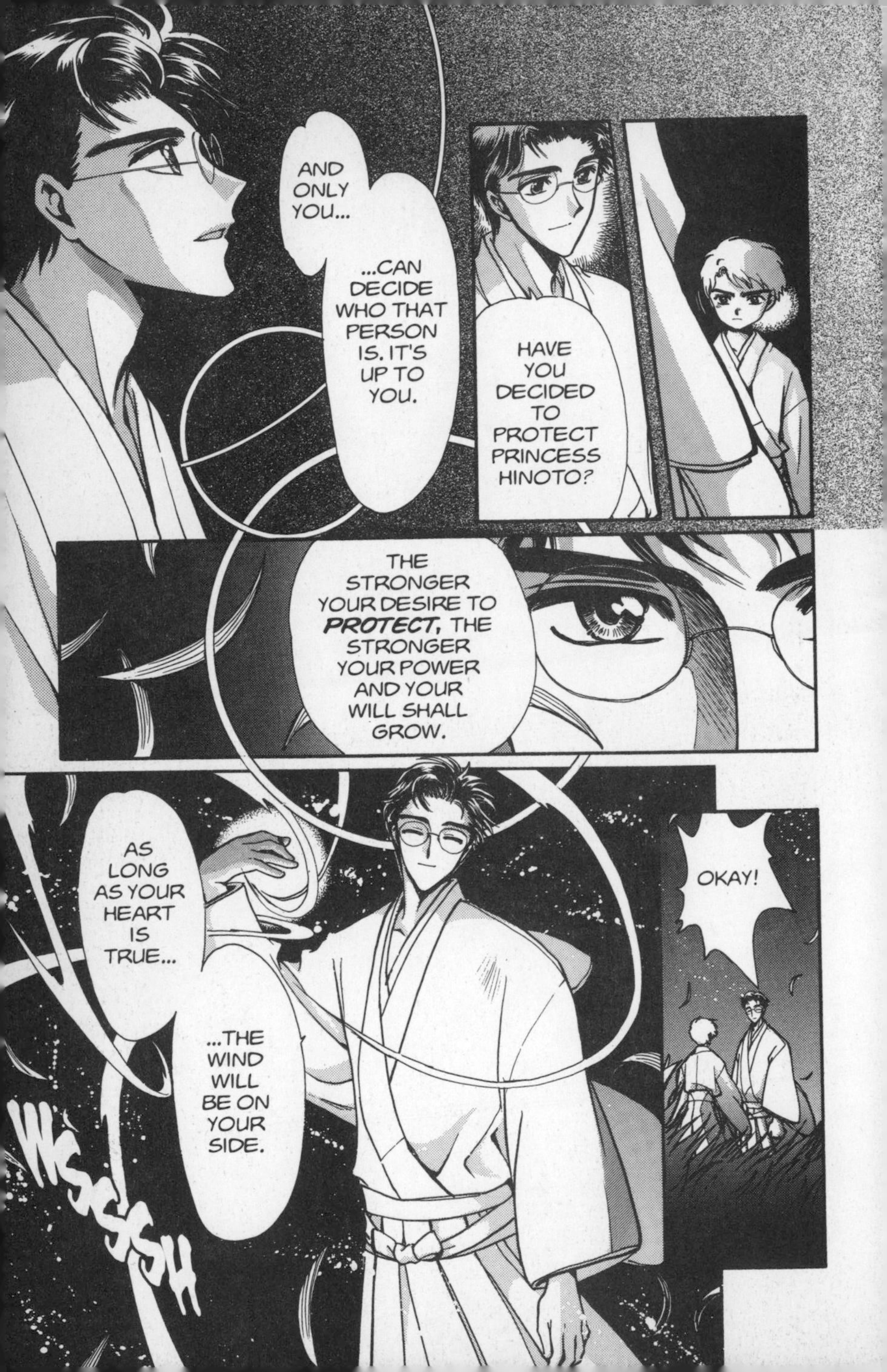
HAVE YOU DECIDED TO PROTECT PRINCESS HINOTO?
AND ONLY YOU...
...CAN DECIDE WHO THAT PERSON IS. IT'S UP TO YOU.
THE STRONGER YOUR DESIRE TO *PROTECT,* THE STRONGER YOUR POWER AND YOUR WILL SHALL GROW.
AS LONG AS YOUR HEART IS TRUE...
...THE WIND WILL BE ON YOUR SIDE.
WSSSSH
OKAY!

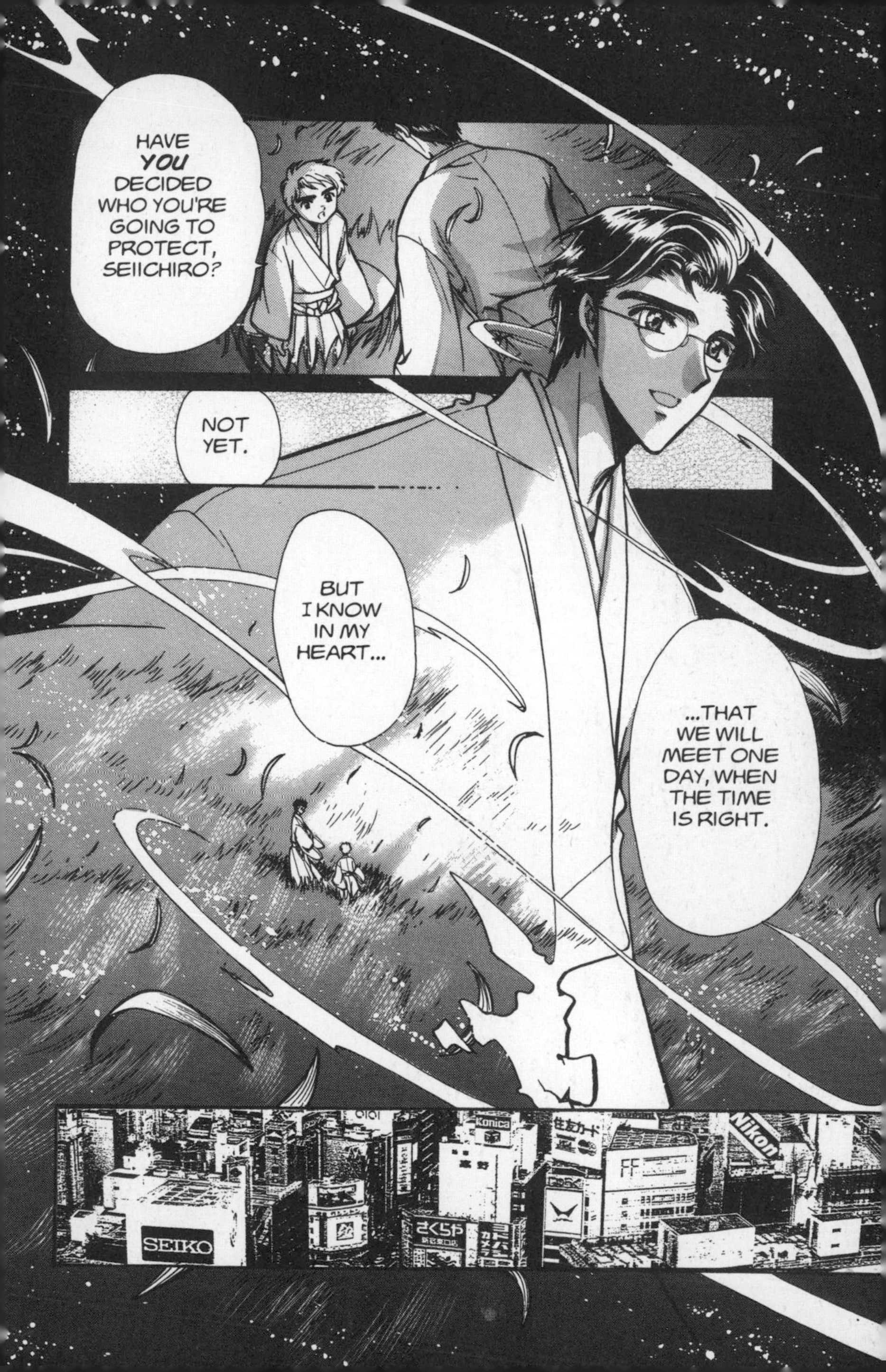
HAVE *YOU* DECIDED WHO YOU'RE GOING TO PROTECT, SEIICHIRO?
NOT YET.
BUT I KNOW IN MY HEART...
...THAT WE WILL MEET ONE DAY, WHEN THE TIME IS RIGHT.
Konica
Nikon
SEIKO
さくらや

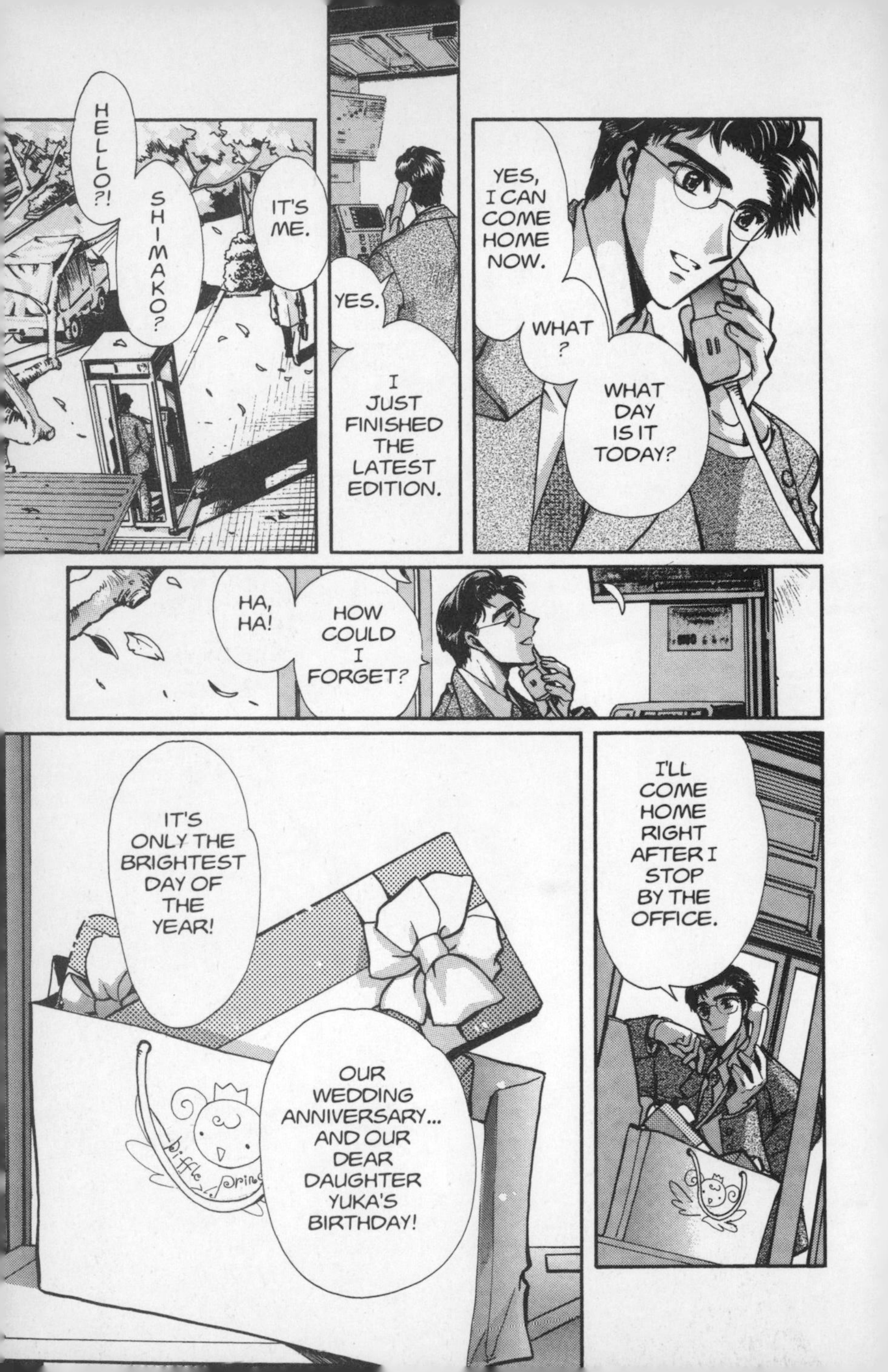
HELLO?!
SHIMAKO?
IT'S ME.
YES.
I JUST FINISHED THE LATEST EDITION.
YES, I CAN COME HOME NOW.
WHAT?
WHAT DAY IS IT TODAY?
HA, HA!
HOW COULD I FORGET?
IT'S ONLY THE BRIGHTEST DAY OF THE YEAR!
OUR WEDDING ANNIVERSARY... AND OUR DEAR DAUGHTER YUKA'S BIRTHDAY!
I'LL COME HOME RIGHT AFTER I STOP BY THE OFFICE.

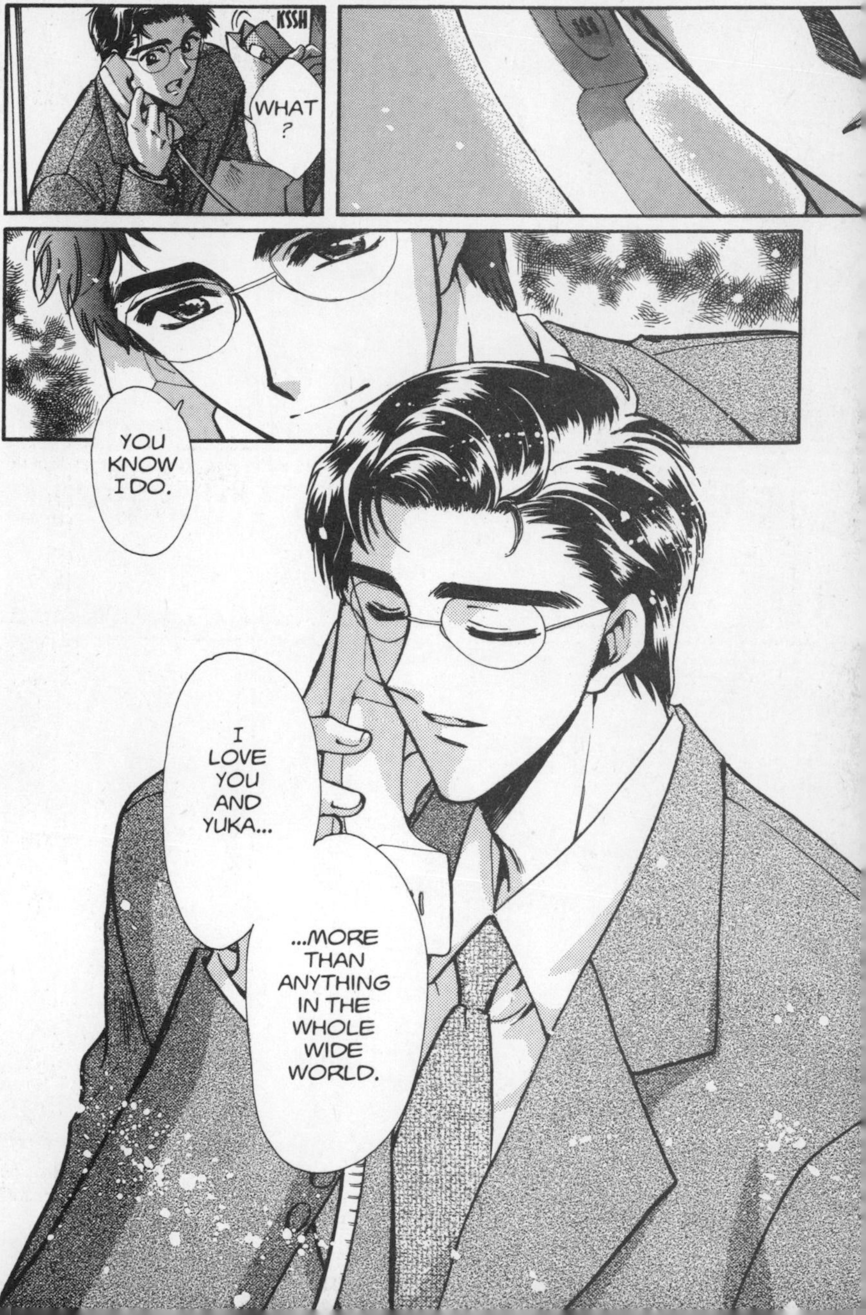
KSSH
WHAT?
YOU KNOW I DO.
I LOVE YOU AND YUKA...
...MORE THAN ANYTHING IN THE WHOLE WIDE WORLD.

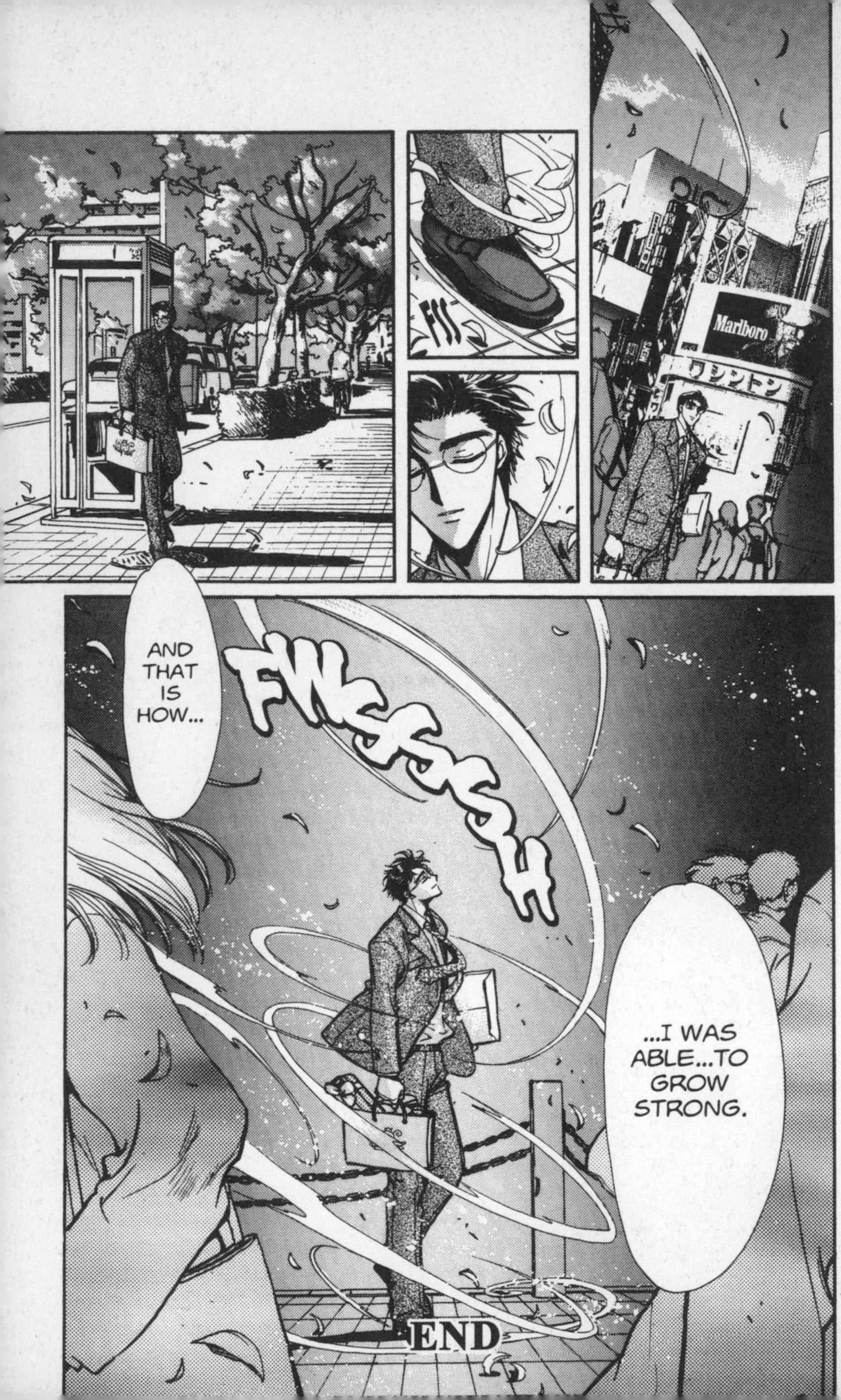

Marlboro
ワシントン
FSS
AND THAT IS HOW...
FWSSSH
...I WAS ABLE...TO GROW STRONG.
END

COMPLETE OUR SURVEY AND LET US KNOW WHAT YOU THINK!

☐ Please do NOT send me information about VIZ products, news and events, special offers, or other information.

☐ Please do NOT send me information from VIZ's trusted business partners.

Name: _____

Address: _____

City: _____ **State:** _____ **Zip:** _____

E-mail: _____

☐ Male ☐ Female **Date of Birth** (mm/dd/yyyy): ___/___/___ (Under 13? Parental consent required)

What race/ethnicity do you consider yourself? (please check one)

☐ Asian/Pacific Islander ☐ Black/African American ☐ Hispanic/Latino

☐ Native American/Alaskan Native ☐ White/Caucasian ☐ Other: _____

What VIZ product did you purchase? (check all that apply and indicate title purchased)

☐ DVD/VHS _____

☐ Graphic Novel _____

☐ Magazines _____

☐ Merchandise _____

Reason for purchase: (check all that apply)

☐ Special offer ☐ Favorite title ☐ Gift

☐ Recommendation ☐ Other _____

Where did you make your purchase? (please check one)

☐ Comic store ☐ Bookstore ☐ Mass/Grocery Store

☐ Newsstand ☐ Video/Video Game Store ☐ Other: _____

☐ Online (site: _____)

What other VIZ properties have you purchased/own? _____

How many anime and/or manga titles have you purchased in the last year? How many were VIZ titles? (please check one from each column)

ANIME	MANGA	VIZ
☐ None	☐ None	☐ None
☐ 1-4	☐ 1-4	☐ 1-4
☐ 5-10	☐ 5-10	☐ 5-10
☐ 11+	☐ 11+	☐ 11+

I find the pricing of VIZ products to be: (please check one)

☐ Cheap ☐ Reasonable ☐ Expensive

What genre of manga and anime would you like to see from VIZ? (please check two)

☐ Adventure ☐ Comic Strip ☐ Science Fiction ☐ Fighting

☐ Horror ☐ Romance ☐ Fantasy ☐ Sports

What do you think of VIZ's new look?

☐ Love It ☐ It's OK ☐ Hate It ☐ Didn't Notice ☐ No Opinion

Which do you prefer? (please check one)

☐ Reading right-to-left

☐ Reading left-to-right

Which do you prefer? (please check one)

☐ Sound effects in English

☐ Sound effects in Japanese with English captions

☐ Sound effects in Japanese only with a glossary at the back

THANK YOU! Please send the completed form to:

NJW Research
42 Catharine St.
Poughkeepsie, NY 12601

All information provided will be used for internal purposes only. We promise not to sell or otherwise divulge your information.

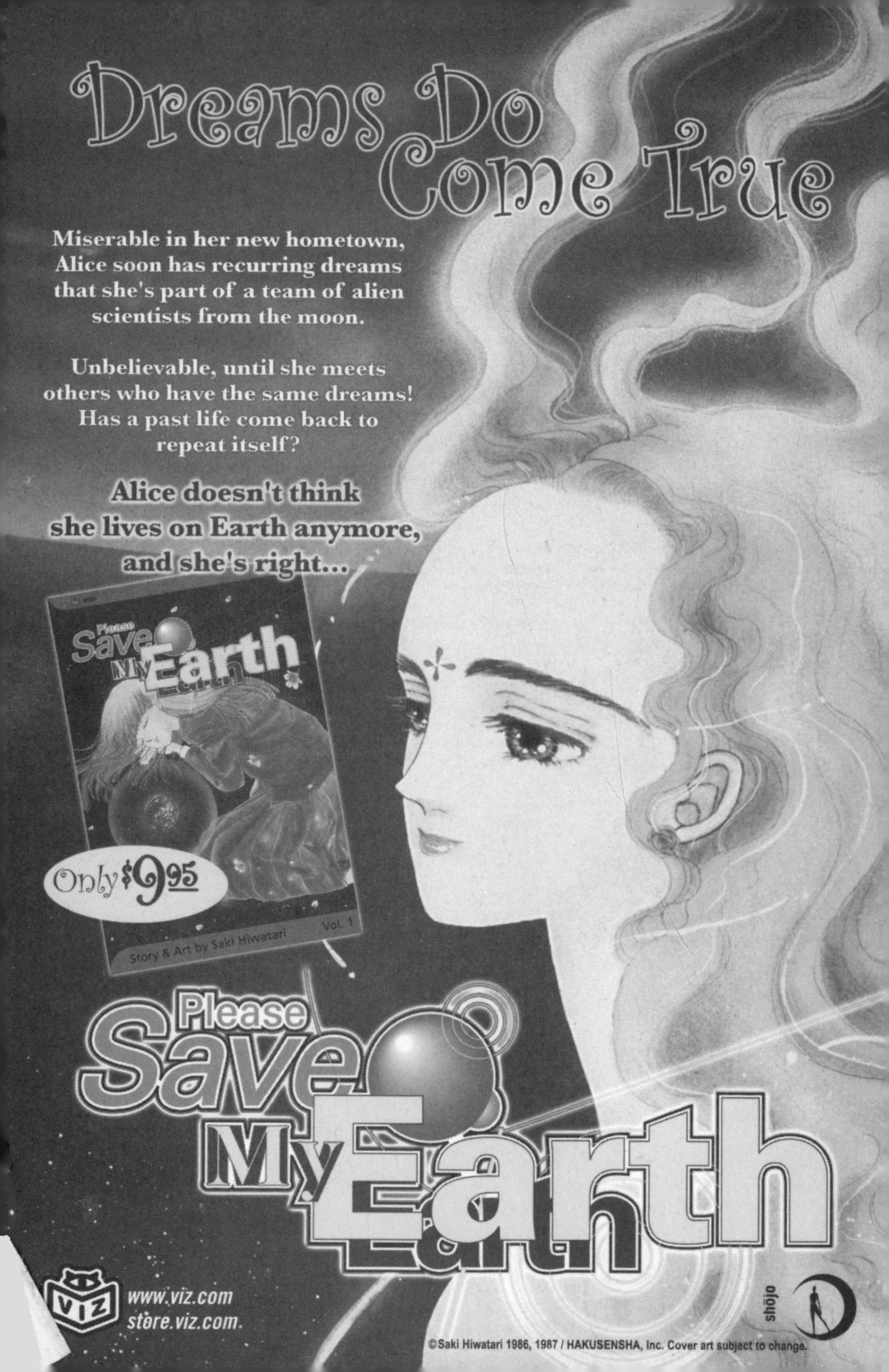
Dreams Do Come True
Miserable in her new hometown, Alice soon has recurring dreams that she's part of a team of alien scientists from the moon.
Unbelievable, until she meets others who have the same dreams! Has a past life come back to repeat itself?
Alice doesn't think she lives on Earth anymore, and she's right...
Please Save My Earth
Story & Art by Saki Hiwatari
Vol. 1
Only $9.95
Please Save My Earth
www.viz.com
store.viz.com
shōjo
©Saki Hiwatari 1986, 1987 / HAKUSENSHA, Inc. Cover art subject to change.